Rural Revolutions in Southern Ukraine

Cambridge, Massachusetts

Rural Revolutions in Southern Ukraine

Peasants, Nobles, and Colonists, 1774–1905

Leonard G. Friesen

Distributed by Harvard University Press
for the Harvard Ukrainian Research Institute

The Harvard Ukrainian Research Institute was established in 1973 as an integral part of Harvard University. It supports research associates and visiting scholars who are engaged in projects concerned with all aspects of Ukrainian studies. The Institute also works in close cooperation with the Committee on Ukrainian Studies, which supervises and coordinates the teaching of Ukrainian history, language, and literature at Harvard University.

Publication of this book has been made possible by the Ilarion and Donna Kalynewych Ukrainian Fund at the Ukrainian Research Institute.

Printed in the U.S. on acid-free paper

Library of Congress Cataloging-in-Publication Data

Friesen, Leonard G.
Rural revolutions in southern Ukraine : peasants, nobles, and colonists, 1774–1905 / Leonard G. Friesen.
p. cm. -- (Harvard series in Ukrainian studies)
Includes bibliographical references and index.
ISBN 1-932650-00-8 (alk. paper)
1. Ukraine, Southern--Rural conditions. 2. Agricultural colonies--Ukraine, Southern--History. 3. Ukraine, Southern--Colonization--History. 4. Social classes--Ukraine, Southern--History. I. Title.
HN530.9.S68F75 2008
307.209477'1--dc22
2006026142

Jacket design by Janis Owens Design
Jacket photograph: Walter Quiring and Helen Bartel, *In the Fullness of Time: 150 Years of Mennonite Sojourn in Russia* (Kitchener, Ont., 1974), 61, photograph 10. Used with permission.

Contents

Acknowledgments

In many ways, this project originated in Canada in the 1960s, where I grew up as the child of immigrants from southern Ukraine. The land of my forebears was barely ever talked about despite its impact on every day of my life. In time, I understood something about the experience of my own extended community, though the larger world remained hidden. In a very real sense, then, this book represents my own attempt to fill in the pieces, and thereby to make sense of the whole. In so doing, I want to acknowledge the vital, formative role that has long been played by my family, especially my parents, Jake and Anne Friesen, and my beloved "Grossma," Katharina Penner.

My own intellectual and academic journey took me from the Niagara Peninsula to Waterloo, and then Toronto; and eventually to the Soviet Union and its various successor states. I was enormously assisted in that journey by gifted academic mentors. They raised the questions that I needed to hear, and gave some sense of where I might look for answers. I am privileged to acknowledge with thanks the longstanding support of David Davies, Harvey Dyck, David G. Rempel, Richard Fuke, and Boris Mironov.

While completing this project, I have benefited from the productive environment found at a host of institutions around the world. I owe a special debt to those who made the libraries and archives of the former Soviet Union accessible to me, including the staffs of the Odesa Regional Archives, the Central Russian Historical Archive, and St. Petersburg's famed Saltykov-Shchedrin Library. In addition, the Inter-Library Loan Offices of the University of Toronto and Wilfrid Laurier University repeatedly brought materials to me when I could not travel to them.

A modest portion of this book survives from a dissertation that I completed at the University of Toronto. Thereafter I wrote several articles, some of which reappear here in a much altered form. I thank the *Russian Review*, the *Mennonite Quarterly Review*, and the *Journal of Mennonite Studies* for allowing me to include materials from their respective publications. I am also grateful for various research grants that I have received over the years from the Social Sciences and Humanities Research Council of Canada, and from Wilfrid Laurier University.

I was delighted when Harvard's Ukrainian Research Institute agreed to publish this study. Robert De Lossa, Pat Wright, Michael Flier, Marika Whaley, and Mary Ann Szporluk have been most helpful guides for me through this final process. They deserve much of the credit for this book's final form. Pam Schaus has significantly enhanced this study by creating the maps found within it, and I thank Aaron Klassen for permission to use the photographs included here.

Erma and Joseph D. M. Martin deserve special mention. They opened their home to Mary and me in 1978. Joseph gave me a firsthand opportunity to work with many of the technologies described in this study, while both of them modeled a life lived against the grain, similar to what I would later encounter in the Imperial peasant village. That year on their farm in rural Wallenstein profoundly enriched my life, as have the invaluable contributions made by Ruth and Enos Hunsberger, and Paul and Eva Burkholder.

My personal delight in the completion of this project pales in comparison to the joy of more than thirty years shared with Mary. Along the way, we've traveled to many lands, including those described in this book. We've also been wondrously blessed with the lives of Anna Ruth, Isaac Paul, and Laura Katarina. The story told in these pages is partly theirs. But the book is Mary's, in dedication.

Waterloo, Ontario

Map 1. Southern Ukraine, 1770.

Map 2. Rail lines and waterways in southern Ukraine, 1900.

Map 3. European provinces of the Russian Empire, 1900.

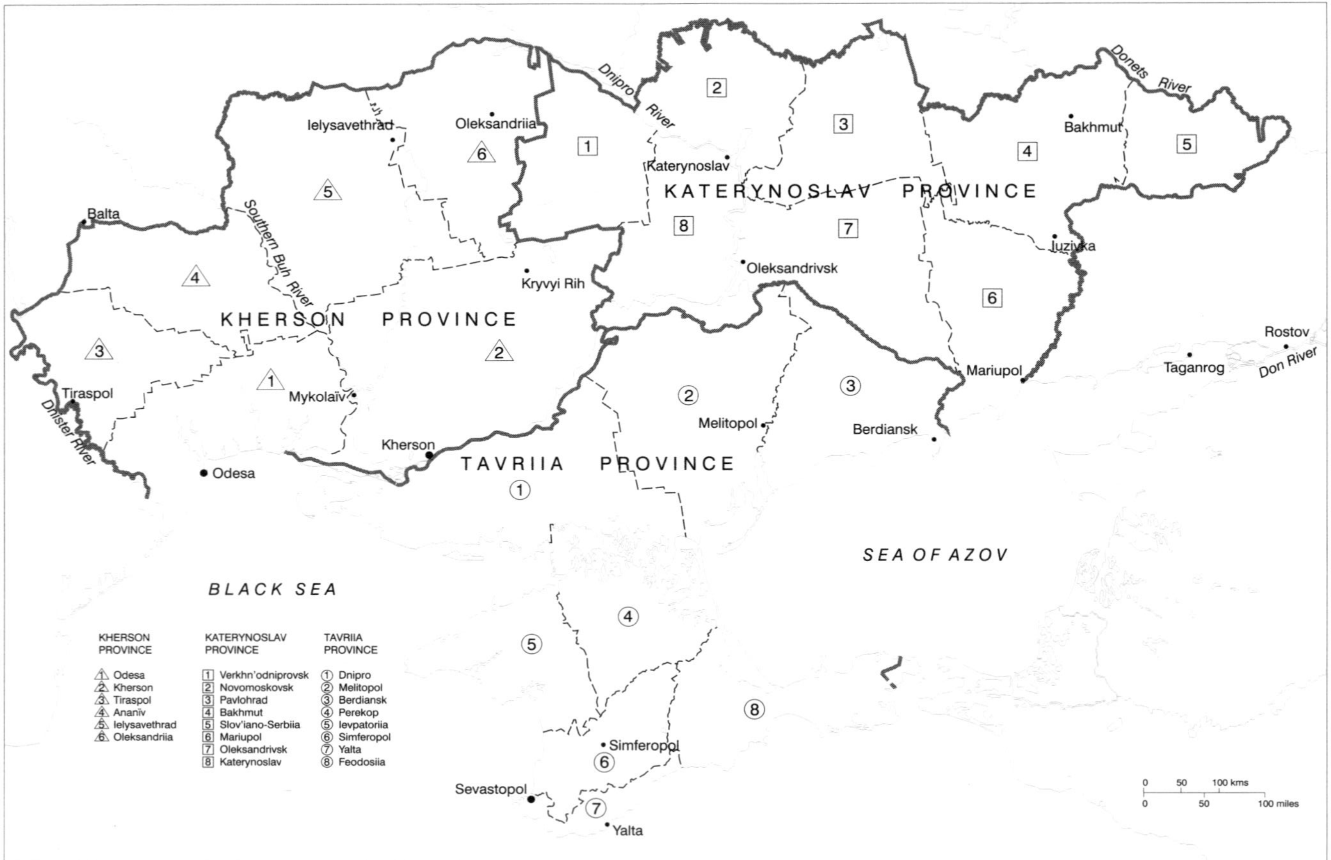

Map 4. Administrative boundaries of New Russia, 1900.

Introduction

THIS IS A STUDY OF CONVERGENT PATHS, and of the ambiguities and revolutionary transformations associated with agricultural change from the late eighteenth to the early twentieth century. It contributes to our understanding of Imperial Russia in four distinct ways. First, it describes and analyzes rural development patterns, giving special attention to the manner in which the previously parallel paths of several distinct rural populations converged over time. Second, this study deliberately avoids an empirewide approach in the hopes that a fuller understanding of a particular region might illuminate the shape of the whole. Third, it explores how, when, and why agriculturalists made adjustments to long-established agrarian practices; and fourth, it provides a fresh perspective on the link between the post-1900 revolutionary era and agricultural developments over the preceding century. The countryside under consideration here is the region north of the Black and Azov seas known as "New Russia."

"New Russia"—the southern Ukraine today—was the political term that officials gave to the wild steppe (*dikoe pole*) after it came under Russian control in the late eighteenth century. At that time, the region was home to scattered settlements of Cossacks and Tatars, frontier peoples who had previously made their home in this buffer zone between the Polish, Russian, and Ottoman empires. But this area did not stay sparsely settled for long. After a series of Russian victories on the battlefield in the late eighteenth century, St. Petersburg decided to populate the region as quickly as possible. To that end, European foreigners were encouraged to resettle there, along with Slavic peasants, nobles, and free settlers. A new set of social relations emerged as the newly settled agriculturalists began to utilize land in different ways. Markets were found, and access to them obtained. This earliest phase of settlement had come to an end by 1850, but the pace of change continued at a dramatic rate. In the second half of the nineteenth century New Russia was transformed from a frontier region capable of attracting agriculturalists to a settled hinterland characterized by out-migration and disputes over land. In no other part of the empire was transformation as rapid or pronounced.

From its very beginnings, New Russia did much more than simply mirror changes that had occurred over a longer period of time in the older centers of the empire. By 1900 New Russia clearly led the way in several nonagricultural areas. In that year port cities situated on the Black and Azov Seas rivaled St. Petersburg for dominance in the movement of goods entering and leaving the empire. Coal and iron ore deposits in the ridgelike formations crisscrossing New Russia were second to none within the empire in quantity and quality and stimulated the explosive growth of an industrial region that matched St. Petersburg and Moscow.

Given its reputation as the "breadbasket" of the empire, New Russia serves as an especially intriguing place in which to consider agricultural developments.[1] The region has been the subject of a number of important publications by Elena I. Druzhinina, whose last work dealt with the period from 1825–1860.[2] However, none of her works are free of the ideological constraints imposed on her as a Soviet scholar. More helpful for our purposes have been two dissertations by American scholars. The first, by Mose L. Harvey in 1938, focused on the movement of agricultural produce through Black Sea ports in an effort to gauge the growing importance of this region throughout the nineteenth century.[3] The second, by Patricia Herlihy in 1963, used consular records of several European states in an investigation whose focus was similar to Harvey's earlier study.[4] Herlihy subsequently moved beyond her earlier work when she depicted the emergence of Odesa in the context of its own dynamic hinterland.[5] Other recent investigations have broadened our understanding of urban and industrial developments within the region. Among these, Hiroaki Kuromiya has linked field and factory in the Donbas over the long haul, while Susan McCaffray, Charters Wynn and Theodore Friedgut have focused on the region's industrial sector from its origins in the late 1860s to the revolutionary explosions of the early twentieth century.[6] Finally, the history of Mennonites in southern Ukraine has developed into a thriving subfield of its own within colonist studies generally.[7]

Thus, some questions have been answered, while others have barely been asked. Regarding the latter, one of the questions that this particular work will not dwell on involves the differences that may have existed between New Russia's Ukrainian and Russian peasant communities. Were these distinct communities, or were they not? Such a consideration might seem vital in the present political climate, where the identification of southern Ukraine as "New Russia" may sit uneasily in some circles. Yet its absence here reflects not only the silence found in virtually all sources utilized but, more importantly, my own sense that Slavic nationalist identities did not play a major role in the New Russian countryside before 1900. Instead, all indications are that New Russia's peasants developed a strong regional identity during the course of the nineteenth century, though not a national one. Moreover, it was an identity that was determined in relation to other rural sectors within the region. This dynamic seemed most unlikely at the beginning, when the region's sheer vastness limited points of contact between the various communities. But paths converged in time. That said, the lack of importance attributed to ethnicity in understanding rural development in New Russia was explicitly addressed by Shcherbina, though I recall seeing no other source where the question was addressed in any detail.[8]

Instead, this study takes on another of these "blank spots" when it accounts for rural New Russia's transformation from a sparsely settled frontier with relatively discrete communities in the late eighteenth century to a region of dense settlement, multifaceted societal intercourse, and uneven prosperity in 1900. In this effort, and in keeping with other recent publications, this work favors a conceptual paradigm that errs on the side of flexibility.[9] Within that paradigm, I have been influenced most by Fernand Braudel, Immanuel Wallerstein, and Boris Mironov, who have stressed the importance of understanding, in Braudel's words: "long-term equilibriums and disequilibriums."[10] Braudel's depiction of preindustrial societies as ones where market-oriented economies coexisted alongside essentially autarchic peasants fits closely with my own reading of New Russia's pastoral economies in the first half of the nineteenth century. At the same time, the steady expansion of market-oriented economies within capitalism made it more difficult to maintain these parallel universes. By the late nineteenth century many New Russian agriculturalists realized that their various economies had become intertwined. As impossible as it had once seemed, the once-parallel paths of peasants, estate owners, and colonists did converge—in a manner that complements Eric Wolf's planetwide conclusions that the process of cultural transformation was always multifaceted. Thus, elite cultures from the colonial powers both shaped, and were shaped by, the diverse peoples they encountered in their explorations and conquests.[11]

Agricultural history provides a particularly effective way of identifying this revolutionary transformation over the long haul, as David Grigg has demonstrated.[12] In the end, the revolutionary transformation of the New Russian countryside was manifested less in the tumultuous events of 1905 than it had been in events that stretched over several generations. Similarly, 1905 itself was far less revolutionary than the process whereby a complex society of Cossacks, Tatars, and free peasants was overturned by the Russian conquest of the late eighteenth century and subsumed into a newly created "New Russia." To give a specific example, peasants became truly revolutionary not only when they burned down manor houses in 1905, but also when they responded to growing land shortages in the 1870s with the aggressive acquisition of recently manufactured steel-based agricultural implements.

The story of the region's profound transformation begins with the frontier conditions of New Russia in the late eighteenth and early nineteenth centuries, which had allowed peasants, estate owners, and colonists to settle and set out in essentially parallel paths. The process of conquest and settlement is discussed in chapter 2, and the rise and fall of extensive sheep breeding is examined in chapter 3. As will become clear, the various agricultural systems employed in the early nineteenth century depended on the sheer expansiveness of the New Russian frontier. The frontier's disappearance in the middle of the nineteenth century made it impossible for the various rural societies to follow paths that were anything but intertwined. A key stage in this process of convergence occurred in the revolution in landed relations during the middle decades of the nineteenth century, which will be considered in chapter 4. The fact that this process coincided with Imperial Russia's defeat in the Crimean War and the era of the Great Reforms in the 1860s meant that the changes experienced in New Russia (which contained the Crimea) may have been more pronounced than elsewhere. How did each rural sector respond to these altered circumstances? Perhaps surprisingly, winners and losers were not always easily identified, nor constant. Ironically, despite their initial hostility to the terms of emancipation, peasants proved to be the immediate beneficiaries of the reforms while the estate owners floundered. Only in the next decade did the tables start to turn.

In addition to internal dynamics, New Russian agriculturalists were also constantly influenced by events beyond their immediate fields. Chapter 5 considers some of these developments for the period after 1850, including urbanization, railroad construction, and the emergence of a thriving implement industry. Chapters 6 and 7 are part of a larger attempt to answer how the various rural sectors of New Russian society responded to the rapidly shifting landscape. Chapter 6 considers the rapid expansion in grain cultivation that characterized all sectors of rural society before 1900, focusing on the responses of the massive peasant population. In some cases, such as in the replacement of oxen with horses, the peasants got it right; in others, such as the almost catastrophic cultivation of wheat without periods of rest or adequate soil preparation, they did not. Chapter 7 considers how agricultural changes affected the social order within peasant villages; special attention will be given to the differences that persisted between communes of former state peasants and those of former serfs. In all instances, the translations found throughout this study are my own unless otherwise indicated.

Any student of the late imperial period finds it difficult to avoid the finality of the empire's end in the first two decades of the twentieth century. For the purposes of this study, we need to account for both the modest agricultural gains among peasants in the late nineteenth century and the revolutionary unrest that exploded after 1905. Was revolution the logical result of developments over the previous century, or are other explanations closer to the mark? Chapter 8 considers this question while examining the revolutionary tumult in 1905. Does that episode suggest that violent revolution was the inevitable result of the convergence within rural society? This study suggests that in some ways it was, but in most ways it was not. The fact that most of the New Russian countryside was remarkably stable in 1905—including most districts where points of contact between colonists and peasants were considerable—may provide one of the clearest indications that a rough equivalent to urban Russia's civil society was developing, one that appeared to be capable of extraordinary adjustments and advances.

On the whole, then, the New Russian countryside underwent considerable change during the period under investigation here. In the beginning, the very magnitude of the Black Sea steppe allowed for considerable space between the earliest settlements. Points of contact during the earliest settlement period were the clear exception to the rule. For the most part the region's agricultural communities traveled along separate and parallel paths. Yet in time these paths converged. Countless factors accounted for this revolutionary transformation, everything from population growth within New Russia itself to the volatility of international markets. As a result, the fate of the various rural societies had become remarkably intertwined well before 1900. During this process violence occasionally erupted between rural sectors, though more often than not tensions were greater within the various sectors than between them. In fact, there were numerous instances where the points of contact between sectors developed in mutually beneficial ways. When breakdowns did occur, as in 1905, they were overwhelmingly situated in those parts of New Russia where the changes had been too sudden and dramatic to allow adequately for peasant adaptation and adjustment. But these thoughts are for conclusions. We begin in chapter 1 with a description of the landscape that was, for a time, beyond the direct control of all external empires—a time before the formation of "New Russia."

1

ON THE EVE OF CONQUEST

THOSE WHO TRAVELED TO THE NORTHERN HINTERLAND of the Black Sea in the middle decades of the eighteenth century were often awestruck by the varied geography that they encountered. The physical landscape was marked by majestic rivers and modest streams; by vast arid plains and lush river valleys. It was a land graced by near-tropical breezes from the south, and assaulted by unforgiving Siberian winds from the east. Europeans were especially fascinated by the "exotic" peoples who inhabited the region—above all, the Tatars, who, in the words of a contemporary, "are continually ranging up and down those vast plains, and never go fewer than five or six thousand." The region's Cossacks were no less compelling, and were variously portrayed as trustworthy traders of various goods or as insolent rebels who moved about in warrior bands, terrorizing all who crossed their path. Those in search of markers to an even more distant past could find it along the Black Sea coast in the ruins of Greek cities dating back to the sixth century BC and earlier, or in the oblong granite monuments that marked the burying grounds for the Scythians and other ancient peoples of the steppe.[1]

More than the Tatars and Cossacks, however, or the extant signs of the Greek and Scythian civilizations, it was the land itself that first impressed travelers who set out from the city of Kyiv and headed in a southerly direction. Taken as a whole, the area soon to be known as New Russia comprised three distinct latitudinal zones. The most northerly section was hilly and the vegetation lush, in large part because of the many small rivers that flowed into it from the north.[2] Here verdant meadows were interspersed with stands of oak, birch, ash, and linden trees that extended for hundred of kilometers.[3] Its soils contained the richest "black earth" in the entire region, and were nourished by normally sufficient quantities of rain in summer and snow in winter. As such, this zone served as a natural transition point between the Ukrainian provinces to the north and the arid grasslands to the south, which comprised the second, and largest, zone.

Those who traveled southward from this hilly, partially forested zone immediately noticed distinct and dramatic changes in the physical landscape as the terrain became endlessly broad and flat. Some observers dreaded the prospect of prolonged periods in this zone, while others found it awe-inspiring.[4] Robert Lyall, an Englishman who traveled through the Black Sea hinterland in the 1820s, noted little of interest in the 130 kilometers between the start of this prairie zone and the Black Sea coast. Instead, he stressed the speed with which he managed to traverse it: "The whole tract...possesses little interest. The country is, for the most part, level, but in a few places hilly, and is enlivened with few villages." Another traveler, named T. B. Armstrong, echoed Lyall when he declared the steppe to be "wild and dreary." Some twenty years later, however, a German, Johann G. Kohl, was exhilarated by the same route:

> The mere consciousness of finding myself at last veritably on the genuine steppes, those immeasurable grassy fields, where, for hundreds of miles, no break occurs in the uniformity of the verdant ocean, where a calf that began to graze at the Carpathian mountains, might eat its way to the wall of China, and arrive there a full-grown ox—this mere consciousness, I say, occupied my imagination so much as to exclude all thought of ennui.[5]

The vegetation found in the steppe zone had to be extremely resilient, as the expansive nature of this zone—the future heartland of New Russian grain cultivation—offered little protection from the searingly dry, relentless winds of spring and midsummer. Dramatic climatic and seasonal shifts were the norm here. In general, winters were cold with minimal snowfall, summers long and also dry, and the short springs and autumns often suffered unpredictable frosts. The drawbacks to farming associated with these potentially harsh climatic conditions were partially offset by the zone's rich, black soils. In this setting, trees were rarely seen except in the great river valleys. Instead, the prairie was covered with more than a thousand different wild plants. The writer Nikolai Gogol described this steppe as "a wide expanse of land that looked like a green-gold ocean, upon which a million flowers were strewn."[6] Those who lived here could identify the subtle varieties of vegetation within this zone that depended on the particular soil composition, elevation, and exposure. Feather grasses provided the most common cover throughout, however. In spring, at the time of their flowering, they gave a silvery sheen to the prairie that seemed to move like waves on the sea. Some, including quack grass and mint, provided adequate fodder for livestock; others, including the deep-rooted goosefoot, and thistles, did not.[7] In almost all cases, the vegetation had to be hardy enough to survive long periods without any precipitation. Streams were few in number in this zone, and rarely flowed year-round. Ironically, water was otherwise plentiful in major rivers that cut through this zone. As a result, there were areas with an abundance of water available, and some with none at all. Soils were most fertile, and the vegetation lushest, in the northern reaches or near the major rivers. They became worse near the coastal area, where they were saline, lime-based, and less fertile.

This arid prairie zone continued on into the Crimean peninsula, which was joined to the mainland by the narrow isthmus of Perekop. The Crimean prairie was distinguished from its northern counterpart by its restrictive geographic setting within the larger peninsula, which made it a freshwater-starved island in a saltwater sea. This restricted physical space had worked against a nomadic lifestyle over the centuries, and accounts for why the Crimean Tatars had settled into permanent villages in the Crimea long before the Russian conquest. By contrast, the Tatars on the vast prairies just to the north had remained seminomadic. The soils of the Crimean steppe were the most saline in the entire Black Sea region, and made it difficult for agriculturalists to establish thriving enterprises in grain production and livestock breeding. At the same time, the multitude of salt lakes found here accounts for saltmaking, one of the region's oldest industries, and played a vital role in the region's early economic and social history.

The region's third and final zone began in the southern half of the Crimean peninsula, where hills rose up from the prairie and dramatically gave way to mountains that stretched almost to the sea itself. This was by far the smallest zone, even as it remained its most extraordinary.[8] Its Mediterranean climate and sandier soils resulted in vegetation that had more in common with Greece and Italy than the adjacent steppe.

Impressive growth spurts were possible in this climate and with these soils. One Russian noble of the early nineteenth century claimed that eighteen-year-old oak trees grown in the southern Crimea were the size of thirty-year oaks grown further north. Spring arrived earlier in this southerly zone, and the Crimean mountains to the immediate north almost entirely spared it from scorching winds in midsummer.[9] As Kohl observed:

> The southern coast of the [Crimea], both with respect to climate and population, is to be considered a separate country.... It is entirely protected from all the rough winds of the north, whilst it lies entirely open to the warm breezes that blow across the southern sea. It enjoys consequently an exceedingly mild climate, which allows the vine, the olive, the laurel, the pomegranate, and in short all the fruits of an Italian sky, to come to perfection.[10]

Although the area that would become New Russia naturally divided into these three distinct, horizontal zones, each of which eventually developed its own settlement pattern, the entire region was unified by four major rivers that began far in the north and ended in the Black and Azov seas. The Dnister, Buh, Dnipro, and northern Donets rivers had played a valuable role in the movement of people and goods since well before the ninth century AD, when the Eastern Slavs and the Varangians began to utilize the Dnipro in order to gain access to Byzantine markets. Even at that time, these majestic rivers had provided highly desirable settlement locations in an otherwise waterless steppe, assuring the earliest inhabitants of an important means of communication, protection, and a fresh water supply.[11] Wild fowl and beasts lived along the riverbanks, an abundance of fish swam in their waters, and the enormous river meadows, subject to spring and autumn flooding, contained the richest and darkest soils found in the region.

As valuable as these rivers were to New Russia's future development, they also posed a serious obstacle to its inhabitants. Water levels varied considerably throughout the year and hindered the movement of people or goods in midsummer, when water was at its lowest. Many smaller rivers and streams that served as tributaries dried up altogether in midsummer, and thereafter could only be utilized as pastures or hay meadows. The Dnister River, situated on the western boundary of New

Russia, was particularly winding and shallow, and had dozens of sandbars, which resulted in inadequate water levels for the shipment of goods. Though the Dnister flowed for more than seven hundred kilometers in this region, the actual distance covered was less than four hundred. Constantly shifting sand bars in the Donets River on the eastern end of the Black Sea steppe also hindered its value for navigation.[12] Such winding rivers were particularly susceptible to flooding, and affected future patterns of settlement and communications. The Dnister's width more than doubled in spring, when four-hundred-meter wide sections expanded to widths of more than a kilometer. At the other extreme, rivers more than ten meters deep in spring and early summer could be shallow enough to be forded by midsummer.[13]

River navigation was further impeded by rapids, islands, and a pronounced rocky ridge formation that made a long diagonal slash through the center of the entire region. During the nineteenth century industrialists would harness the mineral resources of this formation and initiate a vital regional industrial revolution. Before that, however, the earliest settlers were more inclined to view these outcroppings as detriments to the development of their household economies. The Buh River, for example, was only navigable in its southern reaches before a 75-kilometer stretch of rapids began that severely limited the transhipment of goods or people.[14] No less dramatic was the manner in which the mighty Dnipro River was divided in two by a 100-kilometer stretch in which 13 distinct rapids were hemmed in by banks that rose up abruptly to more than 60 meters in height. Such banks were common along the major rivers.[15] The great nineteenth-century Cossack historian, D. I. Iavornyts′kyi (Evarnitskii), identified 95 distinct ravines on the right (western) bank of the Dnipro alone, compared to 36 on the left (eastern) bank.[16] Their existence compelled the first settlers to establish their homes either close to their lands "on high" or "down below," near their source of water and transport. In the end, most settled close to the water despite the annual threat of flooding, and thus had to endure regular climbs up steep cliffs simply to reach their fields.

The Dnister, Buh, and Dnipro rivers also abounded in numerous islands in their lower reaches, where the actual channel could be more than 2 kilometers wide in places. Though the number of islands varied according to the time of year, with some completely submerged in spring, Iavornyts′kyi identified approximately 265 of them in the Dnipro alone.

Of these, Khortytsia island, situated at the southern edge of the river's rapids, was by far the largest—more than 25 kilometers in circumference. Its 27,000 hectares of rich and extensive meadows and forests made it a valued prize for centuries.[17]

The Black and Azov seas marked the southern extremity of this entire region, and served as its only natural border. Although the Azov Sea offered the greatest inland penetration, its usefulness was diminished by a shallow, sand-covered bottom which created constantly shifting sandbars and spits of land that clogged all river estuaries flowing into it. The Sea of Azov was also not a large body of water, with distances less than 275 kilometers in any one direction and an average depth of less than ten meters.[18] Its size, in combination with its full exposure to strong northern and eastern continental winds, contributed to sudden, powerful storms that further hampered navigation. Conditions went from treacherous in late fall to utterly impassable in winter, when ice often held the sea in its grasp for two months.

A dramatic change occurred when the waters from the Sea of Azov entered the Black Sea through the narrow and shallow straits of Kerch. The Black Sea, with an average depth of 1,300 meters and a volume more than ten times greater than the Sea of Azov, was highly conducive to sea travel.[19] In addition, there were good places for anchorage and refuge from sudden gales in the deep, natural harbors along the northern Black Sea shoreline. The very best harbors were those well removed from the shallow river deltas of either sea. Though the mouth of the Dnipro River froze over annually, the coastal regions to the west, as well as those on the southern banks of the Crimea, generally did not, a fact which dramatically increased their utility for settlement. It was of crucial importance to the subsequent development of this region that the Black and Azov seas, through the Bosporus and Dardanelles, provided New Russia with direct, year-round access to the Mediterranean Sea and European destinations.[20]

In many ways, the lands of the Black Sea littoral had long served as a meeting place for East and West, Asia and Europe, tropical and continental. Its history involved the interplay of a succession of major states, from the Greek, through the Polish and Ottoman, and on to the Russian. For centuries it had served as the principal link between Eastern Slavs and the world of Byzantium. Those daring enough to traverse the steppe southward along the Dnipro River to the Black Sea gained access to the cultural and trading center of Constantinople. Yet the very location of the steppe on the broad central Eurasian plain resulted in the periodic intrusion of various Asiatic peoples. Of these, the most notorious were the Mongols, who laid waste to Kyivan Rus′ in the thirteenth century, and in the process profoundly shaped the future of all Eastern Slavs. Both Poland, to the northwest, and the Ottoman Empire, to the south, had attempted to fill the vacuum left when the "Mongol yoke" collapsed in the fifteenth century. However, by that time, the Black Sea steppe had become home to a number of distinct and feared peoples. Of these, the Crimean Tatars, who formed a successor state to the Mongol "Golden Horde," enjoyed the reputation of being the most dreaded. Guillaume le Vasseur Sieur de Beauplan, a sixteenth-century traveler to the Black Sea region, wrote:

> Crim is a great peninsula in the Black-Sea, south of Muscovy. It is full of Tartars [*sic*] come out of the great Tartary, who have a king whom they call cham [*sic*], who holds the title of the great Turk; and these are the Tartars who so often make inroads into Poland and Muscovy, to the number of eighty thousand, who burn and ravage all they find in their way; and then return home with fifty or sixty thousand Russian slaves, and sell them aboard the galleys, for these people live only upon rapine.[21]

The Crimean Tatars were a nomadic, Turkic people who had entered the Black Sea region from Asia during the Mongol conquest of the thirteenth century. Thereafter they rapidly established hegemony over the Crimea as well as the prairie lands to the immediate north. Christian merchants and settlers who lived in the Crimean port cities and environs at the time of their arrival were easily accommodated, and continued to play an important commercial role. In fact, the historian A. A. Skal′kovs′kyi (Skal′kovskii) reported the existence of fifty-two Christian villages well into the eighteenth century, most of which had been settled by Italians and Greeks. At the same time, he noted the existence of almost fifteen hundred Tatar villages in the Crimea, a clear indication that their nomadic lifestyle had long since vanished. Though previously independent, the Crimean Tatar khanate had recognized the authority of the Ottoman Empire since at least the late fifteenth century. Tatar khans served as the first line of defense for the Ottoman Empire along its northern tier, and in exchange received large private estates, annual payments, and other perquisites.[22]

The Tatars in their long-established villages of the Crimean peninsula stood in sharp contrast to the nomadic Nogai Tatars immediately to their north. With a proud ancestry that dated back to their confederation with the Mongol horde, the Nogais had roamed the Transvolga region north of the Caucasus until the Russian conquest of the mid-sixteenth century compelled them to relocate westward. By the late eighteenth century the Nogais had shifted their center to the steppe region north of the Sea of Azov. Skal′kovs′kyi estimated that there were approximately 10,000 Nogais in the late eighteenth century, and almost 180,000 Tatars in the Crimea.[23]

The Nogai Tatars had earned their notoriety as slave traders. From the mid-fifteenth to the late seventeenth centuries, they had annually raided the southernmost settlements of Poland, Ukraine, and Muscovy, and hauled away thousands of settlers who were subsequently sold as slaves and distributed throughout the Ottoman Empire. Folk songs from this era still communicate the fear and dread caused by these annual raids, as well as the hostility engendered between the Tatars and their northern neighbors:

> On the holy day of Sunday, it wasn't the grey eagles screaming,
> But the poor captives weeping in bitter slavery,
> Raising their arms, shaking their chains,
> Begging and imploring the merciful Lord:
> "Send us, O Lord, a fine rain from the sky
> And wild wind from the Dnieper steppe!
> Maybe a swift wave will rise on the Black Sea,
> Maybe it will break the Turkish galley loose from its anchor!
> Oh, we have had enough of this accursed Turkish slavery;
> The iron chains have dug into our legs,
> They have cut our white young Cossack flesh to the yellow bone."[24]

Though it is difficult to determine the actual numbers involved, trade in slaves remained an integral part of the Tatar economy until the early eighteenth century, and during that time, most Slavs wisely chose to stay clear of the steppe region adjacent to the annual routes of the Nogai Tatars.[25] And yet, in spite of the threats imposed, Russian and Ukrainian peasants had already begun to stream into this region by the late fifteenth century. These settlers were soon identified as "Cossacks," a term that may have come from the Tatar word for "freebooting warrior." A Cossack settlement at the confluence of the Samara and Dnipro rivers, near modern-day Dnipropetrovsk, was noted in 1576.[26] Once in the Black Sea region, these Cossacks developed a seminomadic existence centered upon the Dnipro River and its tributaries. Cossacks made their principal homes in deep, wooded ravines, along river meadows, or on one of the several hundred islands located within the major river systems. Iavornyts′kyi described the multifaceted strategic and economic importance of these river-based locations: "Here [the Cossacks] hid from enemies, felled trees, pastured livestock, cut reeds for burning, fished for fish and crabs, hunted wild birds, goats and wild boars, managed apiaries, prepared medicines, and cultivated vegetables."[27]

From modest beginnings, Cossacks managed to penetrate southward into the Black Sea region by first gaining control of the waterways, which provided the best protection possible from the nomadic Nogais. Initially, and unwittingly, Cossacks served as an acceptable buffer for the northern states from their Turkic neighbors. In time the growing Cossack strength enabled them to mount their own successful campaigns against the Tatars and their Ottoman lords. Beauplan's account from the mid-seventeenth century described how Cossacks of the previous generation had attacked the Crimean Tatars and Ottoman Turks in spectacular raids along the Black Sea coast: "They are never more than between six and ten thousand men when they make their ravages, and cross the sea miraculously in pitiful boats they make themselves." By then, the Cossacks had come to control much of the Black Sea steppe, or most of what would later comprise Katerynoslav (Ekaterinoslav) and Kherson provinces.[28]

Cossack society of the Black Sea region developed unique institutions, beginning with a central headquarters (*sich*) that was initially situated below the Dnipro River rapids on the island of Khortytsia (hence the name, Zaporozhian—"beyond the rapids" [*za porogi*]). Beyond the Sich, however, by the mid-eighteenth century the Zaporozhian Cossacks were loosely divided into six "regiments," based upon their location within the region.[29] Further population increases resulted in the formation of two more regiments by 1768. Of the eight, the Samarskaia and Kodatskaia regiments had population concentrations sufficient for the establishment of towns and villages.

Despite hostile beginnings, relations between Cossacks and Tatars markedly improved in the course of the eighteenth century. Perhaps the most important reason for this was the dramatic decline of the Ottoman and the Polish empires and the rise of Russia. Almost all of the lands described here had previously been under the rule of the Ottoman Porte, and this Islamic, Turkic force had focused Cossack concerns southward. However, the Porte's failure to maintain its hegemony over its far-flung empire had resulted in a "process of decentralization and decline" by the mid-sixteenth century.[30] At that time, Istanbul's decision to focus its energies in the Balkans meant that the northern Black Sea littoral was effectively freed from external control until the early eighteenth century.[31]

Thereafter, the greatest threat to the region's autonomy did not come from Istanbul to the south, but from the north: the Ottoman Empire's decline coincided with Muscovy's abrupt emergence as an important regional power. Tsar Peter I's arrival on the Sea of Azov in 1696 with the recently created Russian-Cossack navy signified the transformation of Muscovy into a Russia that was imperial in orientation. However, Peter's initial success was short-lived, as the Ottoman Empire quickly drove Russian troops from the Azov shores. In time, Russia would again project its authority southward to the Black Sea coastline. Its emergence as the dominant regional power by the mid-eighteenth century dramatically altered relations with the Zaporozhian Cossacks. From the Russian perspective, as Bruce Menning has noted in other contexts, the extension of Cossack control southward seemed both to facilitate and force the need for Imperial Russian expansion in that same direction.[32] But the end goal for St. Petersburg was always to rule directly, without proxy.

For two generations after Peter's bold initiative, the Russian state followed a two-pronged policy toward the south. On the one hand, it engaged in periodic military ventures, as in 1735–37 when Russian troops briefly occupied the Crimea. On the other, in between periods of armed confrontation, the Russian state established a series of military posts and settlements along its frontier. Thus, each increase in the power and property of the Russian state was reflected in the establishment of another, more southerly, line of frontier settlement. Prior to the mid-eighteenth century, St. Petersburg had most commonly formed these new frontier settlements by forcibly relocating the empire's own peasants to the borderlands. Russian officials thereafter adopted pan-European practices of expanding the empire's population base by enticing foreign colonists with offers of special privileges and concessions.

The first state-sponsored settlement of "foreigners" in the Black Sea region occurred with the formation of New Serbia (Ukr. Nova Serbiia; Rus. Novaia Serbiia) and Slov'iano-Serbiia (Slavianoserbsk) in the early 1750s.[33] These settlements were located on both sides of the Dnipro River in the hillier, northern zone of the Black Sea region, and reflected the limits of Russian control at the time.[34] Despite the settlements' names, Serbs actually comprised a minority within both New Serbia and Slov'iano-Serbiia, since three-quarters of New Serbia's population in 1754 were said to have been comprised of Romanians. Less than 12 percent were Serbs, while Macedonians, Hungarians, Germans, and Bulgarians were also included. They were settled in six villages and organized into approximately twenty military regiments. The 1772 census recorded that more than 18,000 Romanians had immigrated to the Black Sea region, compared to 661 Serbs. By that time, Bulgarians and Moldavians had formed additional settlements in the same region.[35]

Yet neither New Serbia nor Slov'iano-Serbiia provided Russia with the military protection it had wanted. Indeed, their settlement actually had increased regionwide tensions, because it reinforced Zaporozhian suspicions of imperial designs on the entire Black Sea steppe.[36] To make matters worse, leadership within the colonies proved inept and untrustworthy during the 1760s, a time when frontier relations with Russia's southern neighbors were especially tense, culminating in the exile of Ivan Khorvat, the Serbian leader responsible for the Balkan influx. Meanwhile, neither settlement became as large or economically vibrant as St. Petersburg had anticipated, a fact that compelled imperial authorities to keep recruiting more colonists. Finally, in 1764, St. Petersburg decided to abandon this project. Thereafter both New Serbia and Slov'iano-Serbiia suffered a complete loss of autonomy within the transformed administrative units, and the colonists themselves gradually blended into the surrounding populace. This ill-fated experiment cost the Russian state more than seven hundred thousand rubles, with seemingly little in return.[37] Even so, the government would soon attempt again to lure foreigners to settle in these lands.

Fugitives from the Russian and Ukrainian provinces played an even greater role in the settlement of these northern reaches. They predated the Russian conquest by decades, even as they prepared the ground for it. Indeed, the frontier had long served as an important outlet for the empire's discontents. Runaway soldiers from the imperial Borisogleb and St. Petersburg regiments, for example, fled to the Black Sea region in

1757. Old Believers and other Orthodox sectarians settled in the recently formed administrative center of Ielysavethrad (Elisavetgrad) in the northern hilly zone between 1752 and 1760, and became the area's first merchants. In 1769, seventy-eight fugitive serfs formerly in the possession of the noble I. S. Gendrikov arrived in the frontier from the village of Ivanivka (Ivanovka) in the central Ukrainian provinces. None of these were isolated incidents, as is evident from the numerous surviving petitions from Russian nobles to imperial authorities before 1780 demanding the return of their fugitive serfs.[38] Few were returned, however, as St. Petersburg actually encouraged the settlement of fugitives, exiles, and Orthodox sectarians, and often ignored the petitions of the erstwhile masters. Nor would this spontaneous immigration cease with the incorporation of the entire region into the Russian Empire.[39]

In short, the lands north of the Black and Azov seas were in a unique position by the second half of the eighteenth century. The Ottoman and Polish decline had preceded Imperial Russia's ability to assert itself. This created a relatively stable and autonomous setting in which there lived Crimean Christians and Tatars, nomadic Nogai Tatars, Cossacks, fugitive serfs, and transplanted Balkan colonists.

What is known about the region's economic life on the eve of the Russian conquest? Although historians have correctly observed that the Black Sea region did not play a prominent role in Mediterranean trade at the time, there is little reason to endorse E. I. Druzhinina's conclusion that these lands were economically stagnant, paralyzed by inter- and intraregional conflict.[40] In fact, a vibrant land-based trading network existed at this time, one that linked Tatars and Cossacks together with Poles, Ukrainians, and Russians, and extended to Constantinople, Moscow, and beyond.

Trade links were multifaceted and dynamic. Cossacks, who regularly imported grain from Muscovy in the first half of the eighteenth century, had become net exporters by the second half, when their wheat, barley, rye, oats, buckwheat, and melons were regularly sold in Russian markets. There were forty-one flour mills operating in the Zaporozhian Sich in 1774, and the Russian army itself became a major consumer of Cossack grain during its various campaigns against the Ottoman Empire.[41] Cossacks herded sheep and cattle on the rich, natural grasses found throughout the steppe region. Their reputation with horses was especially noteworthy, and brought inquiries from several Russian provincial governors. Even the Prussian cavalry considered the purchase of Cossack horses in 1773, as did representatives from Poland and Armenia. Cossacks and Crimean Tatars actively bred sheep for both wool and meat, which were sold in Moscow markets as late as 1800. The number of livestock bred in the mid-eighteenth century clearly indicated their importance to Cossack economies. The Protovchanskii Regiment, with 943 families, owned 900 horses, over 5,000 cattle, and almost 14,000 sheep at midcentury. Nogai Tatars from the Orel river district alone had more than 100,000 sheep and 10,000 horses, despite the destruction wrought by the ongoing campaigns between the Russian and Ottoman empires.[42]

Finally, the plentiful fish stocks played a vital role in Cossack diets, and as a valuable export commodity to Russian markets. They also demonstrated the cooperation that was found between groups. The best locations for fishing were in the Buh and Dnipro deltas, areas under formal Tatar control. Yet permission was granted when the pursuits were peaceful and mutually beneficial, and fishing became one of the principal activities of Cossacks in peacetime. An account from the early nineteenth century listed the fish caught in the region as "the sturgeon, the beluga, the sudac, pike, carp, tench, thornback, bitchkie, perch, roach, dace, bream, whiting, plaice, and sometimes turbot." Foreigners enthusiastically declared that almost all fish were deemed to be larger, and of better flavor, than similar fish caught in and around the British Isles.[43]

In return for goods shipped to Russian markets, Cossacks received a wide range of manufactured goods, including linens, implements, and weapons. In March 1764, for example, the Cossack Leonin Pavlov brought the following goods into the Zaporozhian Sich from Muscovy: 6 "Pavlov" guns, 700 scythes, over 7,000 meters of Russian linen, and 285 meters of Suzdal cloth.[44] The modest trade in arms suggest that relations between Cossacks and the Russians was at least somewhat peaceful. Many of these goods were destined for Cossack markets. Others, including furs, hides, butter, fish, caviar, tobacco, wine, paper, and linen, passed through the Cossack lands en route to the Crimea and the Ottoman Empire.[45] At the same time, wine, figs, rice, raisins, brandy, and nuts entered the Black Sea region from the Ottoman Empire, Persia, and other distant points, though many of these products were also cultivated along the southern slopes of the Crimea for sale in the north. One account identified Cossack trades as including: "house and ship-carpenters, cartwrights, smiths, armourers, tanners, curriers, shoemakers, coopers, [and] tailors." All were said to be expert in soil cultivation and grain cultivation.[46]

Despite the diversity of goods shipped, salt was the single most important commodity in the region's economy on the eve of the Russian conquest. Salt was consumed directly by people and their livestock. Large quantities were also used to cure meat and fish, and even vegetables were often preserved in brine.[47] As noted above, this important mineral was readily available in the numerous salt lakes of the Crimean plain. P. S. Pallas has left a detailed description of these "lakes" in his account of the Black Sea region at the time of the Russian conquest. One lake, known as Chervone (Krasnoe) Ozero, deserved special attention, as it had a circumference of twenty-four kilometers, and a reported annual yield of eight hundred thousand poods of salt. Skal′kovs′kyi identified over one hundred salt lakes in the area of greatest concentration, which he considered to be more than adequate to foster an active interregional trade.[48]

It was primarily for the purpose of moving salt, fish, and other goods that the Cossack system of caravans of cart drivers, or *chumaks*, had developed. From the fifteenth century onward merchants and carters had established a series of dirt roads that traversed the prairie zone from the Russian heartland to the Black Sea coastal areas and on into the Crimea.[49] A letter written in 1755 by one such Cossack claimed that five thousand carts moved annually from the Black Sea region to the Ukrainian provinces of Muscovy along these roads, whereas other *chumak* caravans traveled to Moldavia, Wallachia, and Poland. A Cossack ataman identified as G. Fedorov claimed in that same year that fifteen hundred carts with fish and salt traveled annually to the left-bank Ukrainian provinces of Muscovy. The connection between the two products was a strong one, as a Cossack fishing enterprise might use up to 500 poods of salt in a season as a preservative. In addition, the annual carting provided an important income for not only the *chumaks*, but also for the Sich itself, which constructed tolls at key points en route. Under these conditions, formalized agreements were reached annually to guarantee safe transit and to permit bridge construction and the maintenance of ferries. These trade agreements, which gave visible expression to the high degree of cooperation among Cossacks, Nogais and Crimean Tatars in the eighteenth century, attracted international attention.[50] In that vein, in the 1750s, the French consul in Constantinople actively pursued an agreement with the Polish monarch, Stanisław Poniatowski, which would have allowed France to purchase Polish grain brought south to a Black Sea port by way of the Dnister River.[51]

In sum, the Black Sea region on the eve of the Russian conquest was anything but an economic backwater. Its inhabitants traded a wide range of manufactured goods and raw materials to the Ottoman and Russian empires and beyond. In certain respects, the Russian conquest would result in a revolutionary break with this past, as the diverse economic base gave way to an emphasis on wool and wheat production. But in other ways, patterns established in the Black Sea littoral by the mid-eighteenth century continued on after 1800. For one, the Russian influence was evident in the degree to which Poland had ceased to be the major trading partner for the Zaporozhian Cossacks and Crimea's Tatars. For another, the region was already ethnically diverse, with important roles played by Greeks, Tatars, Ukrainians, and Russians. The Balkan colonists, whose immigration had been the least welcome, had introduced corn cultivation to their Slavic neighbors. Settlers had come to live in this region by a variety of means, some of which were spontaneous, and others that had been planned. The most desired locations were those found along the region's major river valleys.

Many of these trends would continue into the new century. It was also clear by midcentury that the autonomy enjoyed by many societies and settlements in the Black Sea littoral was unlikely to continue. If the course of international events over the past century had made anything clear, it was that the Russian bear was growing rapidly, and that a final confrontation with the Ottoman Empire was all but inevitable. To the winner would go the spoils of the Black Sea steppe lands.

2

SOMETHING OLD, SOMETHING NEW

Settlement and Adaptation on the New Russian Frontier

IN THE EARLY 1840S, JOHANN CORNIES, the eminent Mennonite estate owner and "Imperial servitor," supervised a census of rural settlements in the contiguous districts (*uezdy*) of Dnipro, Melitopol, and Berdiansk in northern Tavriia province (*guberniia*).[1] Situated immediately to the north of the Crimean peninsula and bordered by the Dnipro and Donets rivers, these lands had been home to the nomadic Nogai Tatars and their pastoral sheep economies until Imperial Russia gained control of all of the lands north of the Black and Azov seas in the late eighteenth century. What happened to the lands in the half-century after their conquest? Had they been remade in the Russian image of estate owner and serf, or was something new unfolding in the frontier region formally known as "New Russia"?

Cornies's findings revealed an almost bewildering diversity in landholding, religious belief, and ethnicity. The Nogai Tatars of old were still found there, though they had apparently adopted a sedentary lifestyle. Almost a third of all villages in the three districts were theirs. Colonists, primarily from central Europe, were located in 17 percent of all villages, and a quarter of all villages comprised enserfed peasants on private landed estates. Finally, most peasants lived on lands owned by the state. Cornies further noted important distinctions within each of these groupings. For example, religious adherents among peasants ranged from Russian and Ukrainian Orthodox to sectarian Dukhobors, Molokans, and Old Believers (*Raskol'niki*). He also identified various colonists, of which the most prominent were Bulgarians, Mennonites, German Catholics, and Lutherans.

The investigation further identified enormous variation in village size and settlement pattern. Almost 60 percent of all peasants lived in massive villages constructed on state lands. The average village had almost 800 inhabitants, though many—especially Orthodox sectarian ones—had in excess of 1,000. The contrasts were often stark. For example, the Molokan villages of Novospaske (Novospasskaia), Astrakhanka, and Novovavylivka (Novovavilovka) in Berdiansk district had a combined population of 1,762 inhabitants. By contrast, Tatars, who comprised 22 percent of the total population, lived in villages that averaged 258 souls, followed by colonists with 120. Finally, the average serf village had barely more than 100 souls. Cornies also revealed important differences among the three mainland districts. Berdiansk was clearly a "colonist" district, with almost 6,000 colonists, compared to a mere 913 serfs on 3 noble estates. By sharp contrast, almost 4,000 serfs lived on 45 estates in Dnipro district, compared with a single colonist-owned estate.

The wild variations found by Cornies within Berdiansk, Melitopol, and Dnipro districts were replicated elsewhere in the region at this time. Taken as a whole, state-peasant settlements dominated the western portions of New Russia; private estate owners and their serfs dominated in the north; Greeks and Orthodox sectarians in the east; and Germans and Mennonites, together with estate owners, in the center.

How does one account for such diversity, especially at a time when the Russian state under Catherine II seemed committed to increased uniformity? Did it result from a settlement process that was predominantly spontaneous, or state-directed, or a mixture of both? What were the main characteristics of the region's settlements as they developed? What challenges or opportunities did the various groups face as they established their agricultural economies in this new environment? These questions form the heart of this chapter. It first considers the process of administrative integration and settlement that unfolded in the late eighteenth and early nineteenth centuries. Secondly, it provides a portrait of New Russian rural society in the mid-nineteenth century. Special attention will be given to case studies reflecting the diversity that characterized the New Russian frontier before 1860: the complex process by which free settlers became enserfed on private estates; the transition of the Nogai Tatars from a seminomadic to a more sedentary existence; and, finally, the challenges and advances made by the Mennonites, who were widely regarded as New Russia's most successful agriculturalists.

Conquest and Integration

The Russian Empire enjoyed many victories over the Ottoman Empire in the course of the eighteenth century, though none seemed bigger than the war that ended with the Treaty of Iași in 1792. The spoils of victory revolutionized Catherine's Russia, which secured a defensible southern border along the Black Sea coast and the rich and sparsely settled agricultural lands to the north of it. An unhindered southern passage to the Mediterranean promised expanded commercial success in European markets. The appointment in 1774 of Prince Grigorii Potemkin as "de facto viceroy of Southern Russia" signaled the importance that Catherine attached to this newly acquired region.[2] Almost immediately, however, officials had to confront two contradictory impulses. On the one hand, they wanted to settle New Russia as quickly as possible—and by almost any means possible—in the hope that strategic security and economic prosperity would follow. To that end, authorities were inclined to encourage the free settlement of fugitive serfs and rebellious sectarians. On the other hand, the government desired a methodical and complete integration of this borderland into the empire, for, as John LeDonne has shown, the empire's very ethos left little room for regional "diversity and dissent."[3] Catherine's fascination with the Enlightenment made her receptive to universalist principles of expansion, consolidation, and stability, and these were further underscored by the empire's dramatic expansion during her reign, under which Russia acquired an additional 320,000 square kilometers, including much of Poland. Finally, authorities who had been terrified by the ferocity and stunning success of the Pugachev peasant rebellion in the Transvolga region in 1773–74 concluded that systematic governance and social control were urgently required at both the empire's center and periphery.

These contradictory impulses were greatest in New Russia's southwest borderland, where Russian officials confronted the ongoing threat posed by the Ottoman Empire along the shared border. But that was not the only threat. The Russian annexation of the Crimean peninsula in 1783 made the empire vulnerable to any European naval power that might claim this strategic beachhead for an offensive thrust northward.[4]

In ideal circumstances, St. Petersburg might have hoped that the Russian landed nobility would lead an orderly settlement of the south. But the vulnerability of these newly acquired borderlands made them of little appeal to those with something to lose, especially the landed nobility, who did not commit to the prospect until Russian control was assured and large land grants were offered.[5]

In short, military conquest sparked the complex and contradictory process of New Russia's administrative and social incorporation into the empire. Over the next generation authorities were torn between a desire to support the expansion of serfdom as a means of obtaining social stability throughout the empire and an inclination to ignore those who refused to settle the new frontier. On the one hand, the government sought an end to special arrangements, as was evident in their treatment of the Zaporozhian Cossacks; on the other, they created new and more enticing ones. In February 1775, for example, St. Petersburg took actions to henceforth deny the Don Cossacks any special status. That decision did not bode well for their Zaporozhian counterparts, who had already incensed authorities in 1774 by claiming a portion of the Black Sea region in return for services rendered against the Ottoman Empire. The terms obtained by St. Petersburg from the Porte in that same year, which were enshrined in the Treaty of Küçük-Kaynarcı, freed authorities from their erstwhile reliance on Cossacks to safeguard the southern borderlands. In addition, the dreaded Pugachev rebellion of 1774 gave Catherine all the motivation she needed to assert her influence further. In June of 1775, Russian forces surrounded the once autonomous Zaporozhian Sich and forced its disbandment and dispersal.[6] The imperial decree of 3 August 1775 formally stripped these proud and fiercely independent Cossacks of all their lands—which henceforth were incorporated into the recently established province of New Russia—and placed them under Potemkin's direct control. Some Cossacks remained on the lands of their former hetmanate, others accepted an offer from the Ottoman Empire to resettle along the Danube.[7]

Such questions of jurisdiction were not easily adjudicated in the earliest years and occasionally prompted large-scale population shifts. Developments were especially uncertain in the Crimea, where Russia's formal acceptance of its independence in 1774 prompted many Greek inhabitants to quit the peninsula for lands north of the Sea of Azov.[8] However, this period of Crimean independence was short-lived, and abruptly ended with Russia's formal annexation of Crimea on 8 April 1783. Suddenly Crimea's Tatars were the ones who felt threatened and vulnerable. Almost half of them—200,000 in a total population of 450,000—chose to emigrate to the Ottoman Empire. Their abrupt departure alarmed Russian officials faced with the need to populate lands that were excessively underpopulated.[9] Catherine's response came quickly in a separate manifesto in 1783, in which she declared that the Crimea was to be administered as a distinct territory until its population base was sufficient to warrant provincial status. Its new name was to be Tauris, the ancient name for the peninsula.[10] Those Tatars who remained were promised full religious freedom in exchange for a simple declaration of loyalty to the Russian Empire.

Other bold initiatives characterized this early period. The viceroy, Prince Potemkin, further solidified Russia's hold on the south when he founded the Black Sea port of Kherson near the mouth of the Dnipro River in 1778. The rapid construction of the Black Sea naval fleet followed,[11] and other port cities were founded. Altogether, these developments assured that New Russia would have an urban feel from the outset. Other administrative modifications were undertaken in the last decades of the eighteenth century to bring the newly acquired Black Sea region in line with the rest of the empire. These measures included the division of the region into seventy discrete districts (*okruga*). At the same time, military settlements, heirs to the New Serbian and Slov'iano-Serbiia settlements of a previous generation, were not completely abandoned. Potemkin formed the Eleventh Military Region in the 1770s in a band of land that stretched from the Black Sea to Astrakhan, and provided a peacetime force of 32,000.[12]

The most enduring organizational decree was issued on 8 October 1802: New Russia was divided into the provinces of Katerynoslav, Tavriia, and Mykolaïv (Nikolaev). These were in turn subdivided into seventeen districts. Within that structure, the newly formed urban centers of Odesa (Odessa), Kherson, Taganrog, and Feodosiia were given special administrative and economic status in anticipation of the powerful commercial role they were expected to play. Mykolaïv's failure to meet these expectations, due largely to navigation difficulties on the silt-laden Buh River, prompted authorities to shift the provincial capital to the blossoming city of Kherson. The province was then renamed Kherson, after the city. Several new districts were formed in the succeeding decades in response to demographic increases, such as the formation of Yalta district in 1838.[13] Also, the region at the mouth of the Don River that included Taganrog and Rostov was eventually transferred from Katerynoslav province to the Don oblast.

New Russia's administrative integration into the empire coincided with the period of its most intensive settlement. Although the quick pace, and often—as we shall see—the illegal nature of this settlement made it difficult to document this rapid growth, an estimated 600,000 people lived in this region by the early 1780s. That number ballooned to approximately 900,000 by the dawn of the nineteenth century, and almost 2.4 million by 1851. The combined population of Katerynoslav and Kherson provinces escalated from 193,451 in 1783 to 1,016,126 in 1858, more than a fivefold increase. It was a pace unmatched by any other part of the empire.[14]

The legal, social, and ethnic diversity of New Russia's rural population further enhanced the region's unique status within the empire. The Tenth Revision of male souls, undertaken in 1858, revealed that serfs comprised 30 percent of the region's rural population. These were concentrated in northern Katerynoslav and northwestern Kherson provinces, where they lived on massive landed estates in villages averaging under fifty households.[15] In addition, approximately 60 percent of the populace comprised Russian and Ukrainian peasants who lived on state-owned lands concentrated in a band that stretched from the eastern half of Kherson province, through southwestern Katerynoslav, and into the mainland districts of Tavriia. Finally, one in ten inhabitants of the New Russian countryside in 1858 had roots outside of the empire. Known as "colonists," regardless of how many generations ago they had emigrated from their homelands, they were principally located in the southern districts along the Azov and Black seas from Odesa in the west to Mariupol in the east. Another important center for colonist settlement was found in the Dnipro River, beginning at the last set of rapids below the city of Katerynoslav.[16] At the same time, the legal delineation of New Russia's rural inhabitants as either "state peasants," "serfs," or "colonists" masked a considerable diversity found within each category.[17]

New Russian Estates and the Onset of Serfdom, 1774–1861

In the early 1790s imperial authorities conditionally awarded a massive estate of 8,175 hectares to the Russian noble and major-general identified only as Buzin. This parcel had recently been a part of the contested frontier between the Ottoman and Russian empires in the northwestern reaches of the Black Sea steppe lands. There was considerable uncertainty as to which state actually controlled these lands before 1790, but that factor had not slowed the pace of settlement, even though nobles hesitated to participate in it. In their place, a varied assortment of fugitive serfs, Orthodox sectarians, and former Cossacks were drawn to this region precisely because it was on the periphery of empire and thus barely within state control. This remained the case even when their hopes for a free buffer zone were threatened by Russia's victory over the Turks in 1792, which ended all the uncertainty about political control in St. Petersburg's favor. The disputed borderland was disputed no more, and soon thereafter Buzin was awarded his estate, which was included in the newly formed Tiraspol district of Kherson province. It remained to be seen how those who had freely chosen to settle on land now deeded to great lords such as Buzin would respond to the end of their independence and the loss of any legal claim to the land. Would they move elsewhere to new lands opening up within or beyond the region, or tough it out under their newly acquired lords?

Most chose to remain, especially given the generous terms that Buzin and his peers offered. St. Petersburg declared that the nobility's right to ongoing ownership of estate lands was tied directly to their ability to populate them. A ratio was set at a minimum of 13 peasant households for every 1,500 desiatinas awarded (a ratio of approximately 14.2 households per 1,635 hectares granted). Small numbers indeed, but authorities were faced with the fact that the abundance of land suddenly available for settlement in New Russia far exceeded the population base deemed necessary to settle it. For that reason, estate owners received generous terms to relocate to their newly granted domains. Yet even these terms were often difficult to meet. Buzin had an added incentive to be generous, because the location of his estate near the volatile Russo-Turkish front prompted many potential settlers to seek safer settings in the eastern portions of New Russia. Buzin realized that he needed the fugitive settlers more than they needed him, and this prompted him to grant the most generous terms possible.

In time, however, his circumstances changed. The empire became more confident in its relations with Istanbul, and the amount of prime land in New Russia available for settlement steadily declined as more immigrants arrived. Over the next twenty years Buzin successfully extended his control over those who lived on his estate. In fact, by the Seventh Revision of male souls in 1816, Buzin had managed to place new, more stringent obligations on those peasants now deemed to be "his." In a bold move, Buzin begin to restrict their right to move elsewhere. He further declared that, henceforth, all those settled on his estate had to purchase their freedom if they wanted it, at a cost of eighty thousand rubles, to be paid over eight years. The peasants reluctantly entered into such an agreement with him and began to make payments for a freedom they felt had always been theirs.

Everything proceeded smoothly until Buzin's death in 1820, at which time his heirs abruptly declared all previous agreements surrounding the purchase of freedom null and void. Those who had settled on the estate were no longer identified as free peasants but as serfs, and they were compelled to work indefinitely on the demesne. The estate's inhabitants were confronted with the prospect that their agreement with the late Buzin would not be honored and that their enserfment might be irreversible. Although defeat seemed certain, these newly minted serfs refused to acquiesce easily, and in the process revealed a spirit of independence that was not easily tamed. For three years they insisted that their right to purchase an unconditional freedom be honored, and to that end they even petitioned the governor-general for all of New Russia, Mikhail S. Vorontsov. Yet all their efforts were to no avail. The generation of their parents had settled in this region as free women and men. But those who lived on the Buzin estate in the 1820s were compelled to end their days as serfs.[18]

The situation on Buzin's estate was repeated on the majority of private estates in New Russia, reflecting the disparate challenges faced by imperial authorities, peasant settlers, and noble estate owners from the late eighteenth century to 1860. The stakes were indeed high in view of the fact that St. Petersburg valued the stabilizing role played by the provincial nobility at a time when the empire's provincial bureaucracy was almost nonexistent, especially in the newly acquired borderlands. Almost five million hectares were awarded to the imperial nobility in the fourteen years following the 1774 Treaty of Küçük-Kaynarcı. At the time, approximately 100,000 settlers already lived on these lands, for an average of 53 hectares per inhabitant. Land was clearly plentiful.[19] But as a result of the administrative sleight of hand that granted land ownership to the nobility, the share of estate peasants as a proportion of New Russia's overall population jumped from 1.32 percent in 1764 to 27.9 percent in 1781. The Zaporozhian Cossacks were among those whose legal status was dramatically altered following the liquidation of their Sich in 1775. The three large Cossack villages of Hryhor'ïvka (Grigorevka), Velyka Katerynivka (Bolshaia Katerinovka), and Mala Katerynivka (Malaia Katerinovka) were designated as state-peasant settlements in 1776, only to be redesignated again as private-estate "serf" villages in 1780 when their lands were awarded to a Russian noble.[20]

Newly awarded estates with large concentrations of former Cossack and free-settler villages already on them proved to be the exception, however, and were generally limited to the more densely settled Dnipro River region of central New Russia. In most cases, nobles shared Buzin's challenge of attracting settlers to overwhelmingly empty lands. In 1794 a noble named Kantakuzin was awarded 26,160 hectares, on which 29 male souls were found. Another noble, Ushakov, was awarded 11,990 hectares with only 22 souls on them.[21] In 1804 more than 872,000 hectares of land in the unsettled western borderlands of Kherson province, between the Buh and Dnister rivers, were awarded to estate owners on the condition that they settle these lands within twelve years. Yet fewer than 7,000 serfs had been resettled by the deadline, at which time they had an average allotment of 125 hectares. Not surprisingly, the dismally low numbers compelled the state to extend its deadline for minimal settlement quotas by an additional four years. Thereafter, in a further adjustment from the original terms of settlement, nobles who failed to settle sufficient numbers on their lands were fined, but still allowed to keep possession of their estates. Records from the early nineteenth century listed numerous holdings in the tens of thousands of hectares with only a handful of serfs on them.[22] Estates on the northern prairie zone of Tavriia province remained short of an adequate number of settlers well into the nineteenth century,[23] and as late as 1828 New Russia's Governor-General Vorontsov complained of millions of hectares in his jurisdiction that were still uninhabited.[24]

The inability of estate owners to secure minimum population densities, and the desire of the Russian state to do all that it could to settle and secure the region, opened the door for the otherwise illegal settlement of fugitive serfs. Much to the chagrin of nobles in the central Russian provinces, St. Petersburg repeatedly ignored the phenomenon of the fugitive serf well into the nineteenth century. In fact, legislation was introduced to restrict the movement of estate peasants within New Russia in 1796, years before movement to the region was forbidden. Estate owners regularly offered inducements, including very generous terms, to lure fugitives immigrating from the northern provinces. Over time, this resulted in a steady and illegal movement southward that included serfs and former Cossacks from the Ukrainian provinces, single homesteaders (*odnodvortsy*) from Kursk and Kharkiv provinces, and serfs from the central agricultural and central industrial regions of the Russian Empire.[25] Nor were local authorities keen to dissuade this movement. In one example, in 1827, a party of some 350 vagrants comprising a mixture of state settlers, serfs, and Ukrainian Cossacks was seen traveling out of Odesa toward Tavriia province. Most were officially identified as fugitives from estates in the central Russian and Ukrainian provinces. Even so, they were not turned back, or interfered with in any way, since their labor was required on the estates of the Crimea, including those owned by Governor-General Vorontsov.[26]

Fugitives who agreed to settle on estate lands initially had only minimal labor obligations imposed on them, and in return received boundless access to land for their own pursuits. All those found on the ninety-four estates awarded in 1776 were promised unlimited freedom on the condition that they not go elsewhere, a most reasonable concession given that an average of 4,360 hectares of land was available to every adult male. Overall, peasant subjects (*poddannye*) on most estates in the early 1780s were required to provide only two days a week in labor (*barshchina*) to the host estate, and often less. Tatars who lived on private estates in the Crimea, where labor shortages were especially acute, needed to return only a tenth of each year's harvest to the demesne, along with eight to ten days of unpaid labor annually.[27]

According to historian I. I. Ignatovich:

> The nobility of New Russia, having huge tracts of land at their disposal, did not hinder peasants from the use of it. On large landed estates peasant allotments were insignificant to the gentry's own income...[and the] gentry themselves declared that peasants should make use of limitless lands, looking to their own means, needs, and wishes.[28]

Although most nobles and provincial officials understood that conditions involving estate peasants had to be lenient as long as New Russia remained a strategically vulnerable, sparsely settled borderland, some disagreed. In a memorandum dated 22 June 1803, the military governor for the port city of Mykolaïv complained about the instruction that he had recently received from Tsar Alexander I, ordering him to be more lenient to the peasants in the recently acquired Buh River region. The governor feared that such treatment marked a dangerous precedent: "If the Buh-region peasants are to receive preeminence among all others, as instructed in the imperial edict [*ukaz*] given to me, will not peasants in other districts petition for the very same?" Yet his appeal for tougher measures went unheeded. Even the Russian Orthodox sectarians whom previous rulers had exiled beyond the empire's borders were now given legal protection and incentives to return. The edict of 20 November 1804 declared that all peasants in Tiraspol district (where Buzin had his estate) who had immigrated to estate lands from outside the empire were deemed free citizens regardless of their past history. Noble estate owners were not permitted to sell or otherwise register them as household serfs.[29]

The phenomenon of relatively free settlers living on estate lands situated in the borderlands gave rise to a category of peasant settlers that was unique to New Russia, and most especially to Kherson province: that of the *desiatinshchiks*, or legally free peasants living on private estates. A New Russian register for 1802 identified 193,000 such souls on private estates, of whom a mere 14 percent (28,000) were listed as serfs. The remaining 86 percent were judicially not bound, free to make arrangements to work other estate lands, relocate their movable property, or enter into marriage arrangements. Attempts by estate owners to impose their will on them were not legally supported, and met with stiff local resistance. For example, in 1818 bitter tensions (*ser′eznye vol′neniia*) erupted in the village of Razorinoe, Kherson district, after an estate owner sought to transfer peasants from his estate to another one. The category of free peasants, who were legally identified as petty bourgeoisie (*meshchane*), though more commonly known as *desiatinshchiks*, managed to attract even state peasants in the New Russian countryside until the ukase of 26 June 1821 blocked their ability to transfer to this designation.[30]

Surviving land contracts between *desiatinshchiks* and estate owners reveal how generous these arrangements were, as well as how the owners increased their demands over time. For instance, in 1819 a V. Shemiotov provided rural settlers on his estate in Tiraspol district with unlimited access to land. Peasants recorded: "Mr. Shemiotov has permitted each family to cultivate with the plow as much as is deemed necessary [by us], and as much as we are able to work in a given location." In return, Shemiotov received a tenth of all harvests. The estate owners increased their demands on the *desiatinshchiks* in the second quarter of the nineteenth century, however, just as they had done with the estate serfs. The *desiatinshchiks* were now expected to provide the noble with a sixth of all hay cuttings, to cut and cart the estate crops during the harvest season, and to assist in fall plowing and in general repairs to estate properties. By the 1840s the *desiatinshchiks* were also required to pay a fee of two to four rubles for each livestock animal pastured on the estate.[31]

Before 1860 the Crimea served as an important exception to the system of generous land and work terms, as it was the one part of New Russia characterized by aggressive increases in private landholding. Although Russians and Ukrainians had begun to settle the peninsula in the late eighteenth century, their numbers were small and relatively insignificant before 1820. Simferopol district, for example, had only seven Russian villages in 1816, with a total of 173 households. No more than 5 Russian nobles had established private estates on the Crimea's famed southern coastline. Their numbers swelled to 105 by 1823, and continued to increase until midcentury. This expansion was facilitated by the construction of a coastal road in the 1820s and the steady growth of viticulture along the warm, southern slopes. In addition to economic interests, the Mediterranean climate of the peninsula's southern slopes appealed to the empire's most distinguished families, including representatives of the Borozdin, Potemkin, Poniatowski, Safonov, and Bulgakov clans. Many had established lavish residences there by 1850. One observer who visited the Yalta area in 1827 commented on the transformation: "Whoever saw the Crimea three years ago would find it difficult to believe his own eyes, having found in such a short time, on such a small landmass, what for centuries had been described as infertile...and now is adorned with rich vineyards."[32]

Several factors account for the steady tightening of social control over estate peasants during the first half of the nineteenth century. For one, the terms awarded to the Russian Empire in the peace of Bucharest (1812) further distanced the Ottoman Empire from New Russia and weakened its ability to influence matters there. Also, the establishment of important administrative and port cities—especially Odesa, Kherson, and Mykolaïv, all of Kherson province—and the steady increase in New Russia's rural population, helped to transform the region from a frontier zone to an integral part of the empire. Over time, peasants in the region found themselves with fewer options.[33] As a sign of the change, 1827 marked the final year that fugitives from the central provinces were legally permitted to take up residence in New Russia. Thereafter they were either to be returned to their rightful owners, sent into the army in designated "criminal regiments" (*arestantskie roty*), or else forced into Siberian exile.[34]

New Russia provides a fascinating perspective on the emergence of serfdom, in view of the fact that events that transpired over centuries in the heartland of Russia and Ukraine were compressed into several decades here. The New Russian example also shows that the notion of a unified body of "peasant serfs" is as misleading as it is simplistic. Certainly, in New Russia, that category included former Cossacks, homesteaders, fugitive serfs, and Orthodox sectarians. Each grouping had its own identity; almost all valued their individual freedoms and balked at attempts to curtail them. All estate peasants were not the same, and this situation had created a peculiar dilemma for New Russia's estate owners by the mid-nineteenth century. For reasons of imperial demand and personal predilection, the estate owners were strongly oriented toward servile economies, yet such economies were not viable given the labor supply available to them. This unresolved contradiction explains why before 1860 estate owners favored extensive sheep-breeding operations run almost entirely by their serfs. It was, quite literally, the least that they could do.

As Peter Kolchin has demonstrated in his masterful study of American slavery and Russian serfdom, Russian estate owners in New Russia found it difficult to assert greater control.[35] They understood that the emancipation of their serfs would force them to rely on hired labor. Yet few were certain as to how to proceed.[36] It is also clear that New Russia's estate peasants did not regard themselves as a "servile race." Most had been drawn to this region in the mid-eighteenth and early nineteenth centuries precisely because it held the promise that they would be free to manage their own affairs. It is therefore difficult to measure their disappointment and anger when this very freedom was whittled away within their lifetime. Others found themselves enserfed after generations of free activity as Cossacks. All would understandably be frustrated by the slow speed and high costs involved in the emancipation process of the 1860s, and few would forget what they, or their forebears, had once been.

The Settlement of State Lands

The most populous category of New Russia's rural settlers in the first half of the nineteenth century were those who had settled on state lands. According to the Tenth Revision of male souls in 1858, this omnibus category accounted for 70 percent of the rural population (801,868 of 1,148,607 male souls), up from 65 percent in 1827.[37] The vast majority of these—over a half million males—were Russian and Ukrainian state peasants who had been attracted to New Russia with offers of larger land allotments, greater religious freedom, and civil autonomy. D. I. Bahalii (Bagalei), the late-nineteenth-century Russian historian of this settlement process, concluded that the majority of Ukrainians who had immigrated to New Russia came from lands that had been part of the Polish-Lithuanian Commonwealth before its dismemberment in the partitions of the late eighteenth century. The typical settlers originally lived in parts of Ukraine under Russia (on the left bank of the Dnipro), but during the protracted hostilities between the Russian and Ottoman Empires many escaped to areas on the right bank, which was part of the Commonwealth. After the wars, they tended to resettle in New Russia. Such was the case with Safron Zaporozhan, who was born in the village of Adzhamka (Adzhamskoe), in the northern reaches of southern Ukraine (Ielysavethrad district) at the beginning of the eighteenth century. Zaporozhan relocated to the Commonwealth during the Russo-Turkish war of 1768–74, where he lived for twelve years before returning to southern Ukraine. There, as a seventy-year-old, he chose to settle in the village of Malaieshty (Malaeshta), situated along the newly acquired western portion of Kherson province. At about the same time, Iu. Zhitnikov, originally from Voronezh province, also settled in Malaieshty. He had fled to the Commonwealth after having been wounded in 1778 while in the service of the Russian army.[38]

Like Zaporozhan, many who returned from abroad had previously been part of the former Zaporozhian Cossack Sich. As of 1785, these former Cossacks were officially said to number more than 60,000, and lived in 45 permanent villages and 1,601 temporary settlements (*zimovniki*). Approximately 5,000 of these former Cossacks opted to leave the Russian Empire in the late 1780s rather than forfeit their distinct status and freedoms. The majority of them settled in the Dunai (Danube) region, west of New Russia, where they again served as a buffer between the Russian and Ottoman spheres of influence. Those who remained within New Russia had to face the prospect of more limited circumstances than before. Thus, in the late 1770s the Cossack village of Pokrovske (Pokrovskoe), with some 350 males and 130 females, was awarded to a Russian noble. Other transfers followed, though not without some exceptions, since Cossacks aggressively petitioned St. Petersburg for the right to return to their former Zaporozhian homeland as independent settlers.[39] Their efforts proved partially successful. In May 1832 an imperial edict granted the Cossacks 80,000 hectares in Oleksandrivsk (Aleksandrovsk) district of Katerynoslav province. Taxation and land obligations were also waived in exchange for the same military obligations required of other Cossacks within the empire.[40]

An unusually high number of Russian peasants settled in the New Russian countryside at this time. Many immigrated to the region from the populous Russian center, especially Iaroslav, Kostroma, and Vladimir provinces. Those who wished to resettle to the south were first expected to clear themselves of any fiscal obligation to their home commune. Upon entry into New Russia, they were awarded land and temporarily freed from all obligations to the state. Though the average amount of awarded land decreased from 16 hectares per soul in the 1790s to less than 10 hectares by the 1840s, the actual amount awarded varied considerably in time and place. For example, the state's desire to secure the western border in the late eighteenth century resulted in relatively generous grants of more than 30 hectares per soul between the Buh and Dnipro rivers. Taken as a whole, the average state peasant in Katerynoslav province possessed 11 hectares of land in 1828, and more than 16 hectares in Tavriia and Kherson provinces. Even though allotment sizes ranged considerably within the three provinces, and between various state peasant villages, they remained well in excess of contemporary allotments found in the central Russian provinces. In time, the period for which peasants received a full exemption from all obligations fell from five years to three, and finally to eighteen months in June of 1812.[41]

Dukhobors, Molokans, Old Believers, and other Orthodox sectarians also quickly established themselves as discrete state peasant communities. The Dukhobors (in Russian: "spirit wrestlers") were members of an anti-Orthodox sect that had emerged during the religious upheavals of the late seventeenth century. Because of their unorthodox beliefs, since the reign of Peter I they had been driven into exile beyond the empire's secure borders—including to the lands north of the Black and Azov seas.[42] Many Dukhobors feared that after the Russians conquered the Black Sea region in the late eighteenth century, they would once again be forced to move to more distant realms. Yet, amazingly, the opposite occurred. The state's commitment to the rapid settlement of New Russia compelled officials to maintain a generous attitude to Orthodox sectarians. A manifesto issued by Tsar Alexander I on 25 January 1802 invited Dukhobors to settle in New Russia, and initially granted them more than 30,000 hectares in Berdiansk district, Tavriia province. Dukhobors were also granted a five-year exemption from the payment of taxes, as well as the right to lease the adjoining lands of the Nogai Tatars at the modest rate of seven kopecks a desiatina.[43]

The Dukhobors quickly surpassed imperial expectations with their stress on group solidarity, sobriety, and economic prowess. Their clean dress, communal landholding, and well-cultivated fields were all applauded, and deemed worthy of emulation. In 1832 Governor-General M. S. Vorontsov noted: "The large portion of Dukhobors are prosperous and even wealthy. They have extensive cattle breeding and improved sheep breeding. As regards their homesteads (*po domashnemu bytu*) and their economic activity, they belong to the best settlers of the state and may even serve as economic examples to be followed."[44] Dukhobors were also noted for their tendency to settle in villages that were among the largest in the region. By 1814, the eight Dukhobor villages in Melitopol district, Tavriia province, comprised a total of 1,155 souls. A decade later the number was closer to 2,500 souls, and by 1841 their villages numbered nine in total, with 4,505 souls; an average of almost 600 souls in each.[45]

Although their reputation as prosperous agriculturalists reduced the hostility that some officals directed against these sectarians in the early nineteenth century, others continued to regard them with suspicion. Already in 1816 the governor of Kherson province warned that Dukhobors had very poor relations with neighboring peasants. His counterpart in Tavriia province repeatedly complained that Dukhobors were actively attempting to proselytize neighboring peasants, and that they provided refuge for military deserters and fugitive peasants. In time, this negative campaign on the part of local officials proved effective and reinforced St. Petersburg's reluctance to permit religious diversity among peasants any longer than necessary. New legislation passed in 1839 allowed for the forced resettlement of Dukhobors to the Caucasus mountains and for their land to be turned over to state-peasant immigrants from the central Russian provinces. This measure considerably weakened, but did not completely mark the end of, Dukhobor influence in the region. Skal′kovs′kyi concluded that as many as nine thousand may have remained in New Russia after their supposedly forced expulsion.[46]

The Molokans and Old Believers largely shared the experience of New Russia's Dukhobors. Bahalii concluded that Old Believers may have been the single largest group of Russians to emigrate to New Russia before the late eighteenth century. They had also founded settlements in the northern hilly reaches of the Black Sea lands, just beyond the empire's grasp. Among their most prosperous settlements was the future district capital of Oleksandriia (Aleksandriia), where their active engagement in local markets attracted buyers and sellers from the Cossack, Turkic, Polish, and Russian realms.[47] Like the Dukhobors, from the 1750s on Old Believers living in Poland and Moldavia received special invitations from St. Petersburg to return and settle in the New Russian frontier. However, land disputes with the Zaporozhian Cossacks delayed the southward movement of Old Believers beyond New Russia's northern zone until the Sich was abolished in 1785. A large party of Old Believers settled in Dnipro district almost immediately thereafter, having been attracted by promises of religious freedom, financial assistance, and temporary tax exemptions. The Old Believer villages of Velyka Znam'ianka (Bolshaia Znamenka), Mala Znam'ianka (Malaia Znamenka), and Velyka Bilozerka (Bolshaia Belozerka) quickly established impressive reputations for their extensive market gardens and commercial prowess.[48]

Molokans were the last of the Russian Orthodox sectarians to enter New Russia, and many chose to settle alongside Dukhobor villages. Their eagerness to settle in New Russia merely confirmed the reality of sectarian interest in this open frontier, and in the process presented the state with a dilemma: How could the rapid settlement of the Black Sea region be undertaken without offending the state's fundamental commitment to Orthodoxy? A partial solution was realized under Alexander I when Molokans were settled in a separate block settlement along both sides of the Molochna River, which flowed into the Sea of Azov north of the recently established city of Melitopol. These lands, which had previously served as the meeting point for seminomadic Nogai Tatars and Zaporozhian Cossacks, were still largely unsettled in 1800. Within a short period of time, Molokans had resettled here in large villages. Even more settlements were formed in the 1820s following an immigration wave of Molokans from Astrakhan province.[49] There were approximately 4,500 Molokans in New Russia by midcentury, up from 1,500 in the 1830s. Like their Dukhobor counterparts, Molokans quickly established an enviable reputation as hardworking and frugal agriculturalists who maintained beautiful farms despite the increased pressures brought against them, such as restrictions against settling in towns, or traveling more than thirty-three kilometers beyond their villages to conduct business.[50] The reforms of the 1860s would usher in an era of increased mobility and economic opportunity for the Molokans—one that would benefit the entire region.

Peasants who lived on state lands were also differentiated by social function. For example, military peasants and free sailors had special arrangements. Peter I had first established five regiments of military settlements, with approximately nine thousand men in total, in order to protect the empire from southern attack. Their purpose, in John Keep's words, was to provide an "inner ring" of defense between the empire and the various Cossack hosts. Many of these were single homesteaders who had moved further south to escape a life of poverty in their former homelands. Here they readily accepted reduced fiscal demands and generous land allotments in exchange for the pledge to provide military assistance if called upon by St. Petersburg. It was the state's dissatisfaction with these settlements that had prompted the failed experiment with New Serbia and Slov'iano-Serbiia in the mid-eighteenth century. Thereafter, the state again returned to the military option and began to establish "soldier-farmer" settlements along its southern frontier.[51] An edict issued on 22 March 1764 offered all male state peasants perpetual control of up to 32.7 hectares (30 desiatinas) of land within the recently acquired northern, hilly reaches of New Russia in exchange for the promise of military service. Three-quarters of the seventy administrative units formed in this entire region, involving 1,549,000 hectares, were initially designated for military settlement. Yet despite the enormous allotments set aside for them, by 1800 military settlements were concentrated in a narrow band in northern Kherson province between the Buh and Dnipro Rivers. These settlements played a pivotal role in the war with the Ottoman Empire that ended with the Treaty of Eternal Peace in December 1791, whereby the so-called Ochakiv (Ochakov) oblast was brought into the empire. A period of extensive growth followed, and by the turn of the century

Kherson had surpassed Katerynoslav as the most populous province in New Russia.[52] At the same time, the proportion of enserfed peasants in Kherson dropped dramatically, since many of the new migrants were attracted to the military settlements.

By 1805, the fourteen thousand settlers who had settled in the newly formed Tiraspol district in western Kherson province comprised two-thirds of the district's entire population and represented the core of military settlement in New Russia. In the following years Tsar Alexander I sought to expand military settlements throughout the empire in the hope that state fiscal obligations would diminish. St. Petersburg moved aggressively to establish such settlements, which were even expected to conduct their domestic affairs by means of military order. The "soldier-farmers" were expected to wear clean uniforms at all times, even during field work, and were disciplined if they did not. The result was utterly incongruous, as Johann G. Kohl observed: "It is interesting and curious to see hussars and cuirassiers [cavalry soldiers] in full uniform, with their sabres at their sides, labouring behind the plough or driving their wild herds over the grassy steppes; - the sons of wild Mars engaged in the service of the gentle Ceres."[53]

Travelers to the region's military settlements in the first half of the nineteenth century commented favorably on their appearance. Simple and tidy huts were situated on regular streets lined with rows of trees. Robert Lyall observed in 1823 that Voznesensk's old buildings had been whitewashed after it was converted into a military colony in 1817. He observed that "the grand feature of this system is the organisation of an immense army from among the crown-peasants, who are to be employed in agriculture in time of peace, and to form nearly the whole of the land force of the empire in time of war."[54] Their numbers continued to increase until the 1850s as St. Peterburg encouraged the proliferation of military settlements on its southwestern frontier. By that time almost one in four rural inhabitants of Kherson province (and one in seven for New Russia) lived in military settlements. However, the failure of these settlements to play a supportive or a strategic role for the state in the Crimean War, and the state's subsequent decision to undertake drastic military reforms along Prussian lines, guaranteed the liquidation of military settlements as a distinct entity.[55]

Other subgroupings of state peasants reflected the unique challenges and opportunities posed by the region's physical geography. These included Dnipro pilots (*lotsmany*) and the "free sailors" (*vol´nye matrosi*). Dnipro pilots had long played a vital role in the economy of the southern region, though the Russian state formally recognized them only after Catherine II's tour of the newly acquired region in 1787. At that time the inhabitants of Kam'ianka (Kamenka) village skillfully guided the tsarina's flotilla through the Dnipro River's rapids, which prompted Catherine to found a special Society of Dnipro Pilots (*Obshchina dneprovskikh lotsmanov*). In return for their labor, these men were granted wide-ranging military and fiscal exemptions. By the mid-nineteenth century more than 2,600 such pilots were found in the villages of the Dnipro rapids, where they regularly guided boats and barges between the city of Katerynoslav to the north and the village of Oleksandrivsk to the south. The fact that Dnipro pilots were in greatest demand during the summer inhibited their own agricultural activity and prompted many to abandon their fields in order to oversee safe passage through the cataracts.[56]

The Society of Free Sailors was a more recent creation, although, like the Dnipro pilots, their very existence reflected the importance that was attached to early trade on the New Russian frontier. By the 1820s the products of over twenty Russian provinces were brought annually to the ports of the Black and Azov seas for international trade. Motivated by a desire to facilitate and expand that trade, in 1833 the state founded a Society of Free Sailors. It attracted those state peasants who had been raised on the water with the promise that they would be freed from all monetary and personal obligations in exchange for their expertise in navigation.[57] The state peasants who accepted this offer, including Kornei Ruban of the Nikopol Society of Free Sailors, were especially motivated by the desire to avoid the twenty-five-year term of military service that new recruits faced.[58]

The largest Society of Free Sailors was located along the Dnipro River in the village of Nikopol. It had approximately eight hundred male souls in service in 1835, its first year of existence, and membership mushroomed to eighteen hundred by 1847. Other important societies were located in Verkhn'odniprovsk (Verkhnedneprovsk), Slov'iano-Serbiia, Taganrog, and Rostov. Though additional obligations were few, males who were of "adequate height" were expected to serve for five years as members of the Black Sea Fleet (*Chernomorskii flot*), while all but the "decrepit" were to serve in times of war. Though the free sailors had access to lands adjoining their villages, Ruban recalled that few bothered to work, and instead relied on the low market prices in the region to purchase their produce. This changed in the late 1840s when grain prices rose in response to international demand. Reacting to this development, in 1849 the Nikopol Society conducted its first redivision of village lands among eligible households. Each peasant received an equal share of 3.6 hectares of land. Even so, the increased demand for assistance in navigation during the spring, summer, and fall seasons limited the agricultural engagement of the remaining family members.[59]

Like the Zaporozhian Cossacks, the Crimean and Nogai Tatars had reason to fear the rise of the Russian Empire in the prairies of the Black and Azov seas. Many had fought against the Russian state during its various eighteenth-century wars with the Ottoman Empire. Following its conquest, the Russian state was faced with the delicate problem of how to deal with the Tatars. How could St. Petersburg best assert its hegemony over the Nogai Tatars without driving them further into the Ottoman camp, thereby increasing the threat that they posed? One answer was to move them from the borderlands to the prairie region north of the Sea of Azov. Bounded by the Berda and Molochna rivers, the Azov steppe had long served as a disputed borderland between Cossack and Tatar spheres of influence. Russian and Ukrainian peasants had avoided it in favor of the lands along the Dnipro River valley. This left unsettled an enormous, arid prairie interspersed with numerous twisting ravines and small streams, an area containing 310,650 hectares of arable and another 74,120 hectares of nonworkable land. The settlement of this basin began in 1770 when a Russian count, Panin, persuaded the Edisanskii and Budzhakskii orders of the Nogai Tatars, with a total of almost twelve thousand souls, to establish permanent villages here.[60] Later Molokans were also directed to the region.

Potemkin's fears that the Nogais' support for the Ottoman Porte remained undiminished prompted him to order their relocation two more times. In 1777, many Nogai Tatars were forced eastward to the prairie between the Don and Kuban rivers, on the edge of the Caspian Sea. In 1790, Potemkin divided the Nogai in two: he sent a portion further east to the Kuma River; the rest were returned to the broad expanse of prairie north of the Sea of Azov. Anxiety over the loyalty of the Nogais was diminished only after Russian military victories in the 1790s made the point moot and at long last permitted the establishment of a secure homeland for them on the Azov steppe. By 1800 more than 4,000 Nogai families had relocated in this region, for an estimated total population of over 14,000. By one reckoning, the Nogais had demonstrated a surprising economic vitality by that time, with 12 fish factories, 400,000 cattle, 10,000 sheep, and up to 8,000 horses, even though they still largely rejected the more sedentary demands associated with grain cultivation.[61] They had also begun to adjust to new political realities: they sent numerous petitions to St. Petersburg for fiscal and military exemptions, and asked for land grants that would sustain their seminomadic ways, particularly their hunting and livestock breeding. Yet St. Petersburg repeatedly rejected these requests. Desiring a sedentary populace, the administration ordered the Nogai Tatars to resettle immediately into villages. Despite the imperial decrees, however, one contemporary observer noted that the Nogai Tatars still followed their traditional ways even though the state encouraged grain cultivation through the free distribution of seed grain:

> In summer, [the Nogai Tatars] with their sheep flocks, travel northward along the banks of the rivulets where they sow wheat and millet in remote places, and neglect all further cultivation till the time of harvest. At the return of winter, they again approach the Sea of Azov, near which they find grass preserved for forage, and, perhaps, a remaining supply of that hay which they had formerly made in the valleys. [Nogais] live in small huts constructed of felt, the largest of which are from about four to five and a half *arshins* [approximately 3–4 meters] in diameter.[62]

These huts were small and mobile enough to be placed on a cart and moved from place to place. A decade later, a Governor Mertvyi of Tavriia, the province where most of the New Russia's Tatars were located, gave an equally critical assessment of the Nogais' customs:

> In the course of August [1805] I was in the places occupied by the Nogai Tatars; I saw their abundant lands lying deserted, grain cultivation is minuscule in relation to the number of people and the land; and wells are not found on the waterless prairie. The nomadic Nogais, sticking to the places with water have trampled all the surrounding land [*utolochili krugom lezhashchuiu zemliu*]. They have few livestock, and in a word languish in poverty, though they have all the means to become wealthy.[63]

There were barely more than a hundred permanent homes among the Nogai Tatars of the Azov prairie in 1804, despite an overall population approaching twenty thousand. Obviously their conversion to a sedentary lifestyle had barely begun. V. P. Kochubei, the Minister of Internal Affairs, proposed to the tsar that Nogai Tatars be once again compelled to settle in villages, though this time with added incentives. The ukase of 4 May 1806, which followed, promised to those Nogais who wished to settle capital for the construction of homes as well as an immediate exemption from all fiscal obligations. As an added incentive, the state committed itself to construct mosques and minarets in the villages, and to that end set aside almost thirteen thousand rubles.[64]

This scheme appeared to work. There was a sudden and dramatic physical change in society. Indeed, the Nogais were reputed to have abandoned their nomadic ways within months. An official report of 15 December 1810 identified 67 villages, with more than 4,000 permanent homes and only 669 nomadic tents (*kibitki*). The latter were said to remain only among "old timers, orphans and widows...those without families, who are therefore unable to construct dwellings for themselves."[65]

The town of Nohaisk (Nogaisk) was formed in 1821 on the Obytochna River in the Azov steppe in order to encourage the development of Nogai trade and industry. Those who agreed to settle here were provided with compelling financial incentives. Yet despite imperial support, Nohaisk never developed into the important center that the authorities had envisioned for the Tatars. In 1824 Governor-General Vorontsov declared it to be the worst of all Tatar villages. It had made only modest gains by midcentury, by which time less than three hundred homes were recorded in and around Nohaisk, along with a stone mosque and two fairs (Ivanovskaia, held annually in late June, and Vozdvizhenskaia, in the fall).

By midcentury it was clear that the Nogai Tatars had not met imperial expectations. Some observers blamed the site of the Nogais' first villages, located on land several kilometers from the sea and on a river unable to sustain marine transport.[66] Others pointed to the persistence of seminomadic lifestyles, despite the construction of wood-framed homes. The "old ways" were most evident in the Tatars' continued reliance on carting. Though by no means exclusively a Tatar occupation, given the many Ukrainian peasants who annually engaged in it, carting nevertheless remained closely associated with the Tatars throughout the century.

Many records remain of the Tatar caravans, including some that Anatolii Demidov preserved from the mid-nineteenth century:

> Long caravans leave every year after the harvest, and convey the produce of these plains as far as Kaffa and Kertch [*sic*]. Scarcely can you distinguish this long train of waggons in the distance, before the frightful jarring sound of their creaking wheels reaches you, wafted on the wind. These rude waggons constructed entirely of wood, without a single particle of iron, are drawn by two powerful dromedaries of truly gigantic stature. The heavy load bearing upon the axle-trees rarely greased with a species of bitumen, produces a friction, the noise of which is perfectly deafening.[67]

As a measure of New Russia's vastness and relatively sparse settlement at this time, the oxen that were used to pull the carts (they were much more common than the dromedaries Demidov described) would graze at will during the night, while the carts were used to construct enormous pens on the broad grassy avenues. Kohl described the "imposing" width of these roads—the livestock could literally eat their way to the southern markets. "Towards evening we often saw on the road to Odesa the first of many of these caravans. They mostly consist of from 30 to 40 waggons drawn by oxen...but I have sometimes seen a line of from 300 to 400." Carters began their day in the early hours after midnight when they located and harnessed their beasts. Thereafter, the carts proceeded in a leisurely manner, unless forced to stop during the rains when the crude harnesses on the oxen seemed to irritate their hide even more.[68]

Despite their slow beginning as settled agriculturalists, Tatars did make modest agricultural gains as the nineteenth century unfolded, in part because of the influence of the Mennonite and German colonists who had settled on three sides of the Nogai villages. In 1834 the imperial authorities appointed Johann Cornies, the Mennonite estate owner, to instruct selected Tatars in sheep breeding and crop cultivation. As a measure of success, by 1850 more Tatars were breeding fine-fleeced merino sheep, and they had begun to expand their cultivation of potatoes as well.[69] Even so, it would be wrong to exaggerate such progress. According to the military-statistical survey completed for Tavriia province in 1849, the Nogai Tatars remained in an "infantile" state. They were consistently portrayed as lazy, careless, and meek. Even though racial bias undoubtedly played a role in the overall negative assessment of the Nogais, it is clear that their settlements never achieved the prosperity that had been hoped for. On at least one count, however, the Russian state had been successful, inasmuch as the Nogai Tatars did become a sedentary people by midcentury. Most now lived in homes constructed of earthen bricks, with straw or earthen roofs. Individual lots were up to six meters long and four meters wide.

Although religion and ethnicity divided the peasants who lived on state lands, there is little doubt that they were united in their predilection to settle in extremely large villages. State and individual initiatives, as well as the physical geography described in chapter 1, resulted in a distinctive pattern of settlement for New Russia. Settlers had first founded villages along the Buh and Dnipro rivers and their tributaries, where fish and fresh water were plentiful, and river transport directly accessible. Beyond the wide open expanses of the great steppe, Skal′kovs′kyi described how prior to the Russian conquest the river banks were already lined with "countless huts and earthen dwellings among the thorns, trees, willows, or simply under the open skies." Such places were well suited for gardens and the cultivation of vegetables, fruits, and hemp. In time, these separate farmsteads (*khutora*) were joined together with others to form gigantic villages that often numbered in the hundreds of households. This expansion was so sudden that the names adopted for settlements often suggested their origins as individual farms. Large state-peasant villages near Odesa included the "Burlatskii-farmsteads" (*Burlatskie-khutora*) and "Usatov-farmsteads" (*Usatovskie-khutora*).[70] Villages continued to expand as more migrants made their way into New Russia. In a typical instance from 1820, seventeen peasants from Poltava province stopped at the village of Velykyi Tokmak (Bolshoi Tokmak), in Melitopol district, with the intention of temporarily working in the fields. Yet they and their families never left.[71]

Some of the largest villages were located in the northern districts of Dnipro and Melitopol that Johann Cornies had surveyed. The largest of the villages were situated along the Dnipro River in the northern section of Dnipro district, an area where for more than 250 kilometers there were no rivers or streams flowing into the Dnipro, a feature that discouraged any settlement far from its banks. Also, the wells dug inland were rarely deep enough to assure a steady water supply and sustain village life. In a typical instance, in 1823, some four hundred male peasants and their families arrived in Dnipro district from one of the poorest regions of

Chernihiv province. Here they attempted to establish an inland settlement, but almost immediately they suffered a crop failure and locust infestation, which left them without grain for the winter. The lack of any cover on the steppe also left them without a source for heat, let alone with any material to use as roofing for the huts they desperately needed. Their only hope for water was in the construction of wells, and to that end they dug three of them at depths of five to eight meters. Without adequate timbers for a frame, however, the wells caved in and left them without a dependable source of water. The peasants would all have perished had the state not supplied them with credits for grain and money to purchase livestock and wood. Such difficulties reinforced the tendency to settle in large villages adjacent to adequate natural resources. By 1830 each of the Dnipro river villages of Velyka Bilozerka, Verkhnii Rohachyk (Rogachik), and Mykhailivka (Mikhailovka) had well over two thousand inhabitants. As they continued to expand, the problems of inefficient land use and poor communication became more acute.

Most state-peasant villages were constructed on the banks of rivers, or in ravines, which gave them a scattered, twisted appearance. Spurs commonly led off to smaller ravines. Others ended abruptly.[72] One account from Katerynoslav province explained that peasants would only build along a roadside if it was beside a river. Huts, the largest of which had three rooms, were in close proximity, making widespread fires a constant danger. Perhaps the only significant exception was found in the northern districts of Novomoskovsk, Pavlohrad (Pavlograd), and Oleksandrivsk, where homesteads were commonly separated by gardens and orchards in an orderly manner. Inside, the huts were often crude, as James Webster, the mid-nineteenth-century traveler, observed:

> We entered, and beheld, in a room heated and stenched by a stove, and swarming with fleas and filth, sundry persons of both sexes strewed about, sleeping on the benches. On the table was a half-devoured watermelon and a lump of black bread; from the centre of the room a child was suspended in a kind of cot, and in the corner stood the Virgin Mary, with a lamp and a bouquet of flowers.[73]

In addition to huts constructed out of mud and wood, peasants also made small grain sheds. Livestock shelters were rarely observed in the early nineteenth century, because animals were expected to winter outdoors.[74]

The Settlement of European Colonists

In his book aptly named *Human Capital*, Roger Bartlett has demonstrated how strongly Catherinian Russia promoted the settlement of foreign colonists within its steppe frontiers. Many factors played into this, including Catherine's commitment to the populationist views shared by many contemporaries and the commonly held belief that Western Europeans possessed a cultural sophistication and economic expertise that was largely absent in the empire. Aleksei S. Musin-Pushkin, of the Russian foreign office in Hamburg, declared that foreign colonists could

> by the skills they have acquired, by their handiwork, crafts, and various machines hitherto unknown in Russia, reveal to [Russian] subjects the best and quickest means of working the land, of increasing domestic livestock, of afforestation, of the useful application of all possible sorts of products, of setting up their own factories, of conducting the entire husbandry.[75]

In addition, officials remained concerned about New Russia's wide-open spaces and the opportunities they presented for peasant vagrancy and foreign invasion. Their concerns reinforced the call for increased social control within the region (which would be established through the gradual introduction of serfdom) and for the rapid settlement of foreigners.[76]

Following the failed experiment with New Serbia, the imperial manifestos of 1762 and 1763 signaled St. Petersburg's intent to reformulate its expectations and policies regarding foreign colonists. Abandoning the attempt to create military buffer zones in New Serbia, the 1763 manifesto sought colonists with agricultural and commercial skills rather than military prowess. Such various tasks were now separated, and to that end almost all appeals for colonists were accompanied by a promise of exemption from military service. The 1762 manifesto openly addressed "those Foreigners, who are desirous to settle themselves in Our Empire," and announced that prospective settlers were required to provide little more than an oath of loyalty to the Imperial Russian crown. In exchange they were promised complete religious freedom and a thirty-year exemption from the payment of taxes. Though obliged to quarter troops, they themselves were permanently exempted from military service. The state also committed itself to underwrite the costs of the immigration, and to assist in the construction of new homes, economies, and enterprises. Those who established agricultural communities were also permitted a measure of local self-government; indeed, no other government would be provided for them at that level. Communication between imperial authorities and foreign colonists was streamlined in 1773 with the establishment of a regional "Guardians' Committee."[77] Although these manifestos were intended first for the Transvolga region north of the Caspian Sea, they were applied to New Russia as early as the Treaty of Küçük-Kaynarcı in 1774.

Immigration to the Russian Empire virtually stopped during the short reign of Paul I, but was quickly revived following his abrupt removal in 1801 and the ascension of his son, Alexander. Thereafter, the introduction of new imperial regulations in 1804 sharply delineated yet another approach to immigration. The authorities declared that the open immigration policy of 1763 had been necessary because at the time Russia needed to settle the borderlands as rapidly as possible. This policy resulted in unforeseen difficulties, however. Contrary to imperial expectations, many who had immigrated were not productive in their new setting, and had failed to generate the anticipated wealth. Corrective measures were needed. A new strategy was also warranted because vast tracts of land were no longer available for the settlement of foreigners, given the state's decision to set aside unsettled lands for the future needs of its own subjects. St. Petersburg now declared that only the most desirable and successful colonists were welcome to immigrate.[78] Bartlett records how the manifesto of 1804 defined the ideal colonists as

> good farmers and people sufficiently skilled and experienced in wine-growing, the raising of mulberries and other useful cultures, also those expert in stock-breeding, and especially in the maintenance and increase of the best breeds of sheep, and having in general all necessary knowledge of the best agriculture.[79]

Bartlett also observed that the imperial emphasis on skilled agriculturalists after 1804 pointed to the "cultural and didactic" role that these colonists were henceforth expected to play. Also, and unlike previous manifestos, this one was deliberately directed at the settlement of New Russia, a region in which cultural interaction was to be encouraged.[80] It was immediately evident that with its provision for preferential status the new manifesto benefited some immigrant groups and hindered others. Chief among those now considered most desirable were Balkan settlers,

Germans, and Mennonites, all of whom had established their reputations after migrating to New Russia in the late eighteenth century.

Balkan Colonists

The Russian expansion under Catherine to the Black Sea and onward in the direction of the Aegean led many southern Slavs to hope that Islamic suzerainty would soon give way to a new era of Slavic rule. At the same time, St. Petersburg welcomed Balkan colonists in the belief that their immigration weakened the Ottoman Empire's commercial base and strengthened that of New Russia. Catherine first opened the door in 1778, when over thirty thousand settlers, including eighteen thousand Greeks, relocated to Katerynoslav province from the Crimea, where tensions with local Tatars had increased dramatically. Families that relocated northward were now awarded thirty desiatinas by St. Petersburg, along with a permanent exemption from military service and the obligation to quarter troops. They were also given a ten-year reprieve from the payment of taxes and assured that they would never be enserfed.

Additional thousands were lured by this prospect of a better life. They moved directly from the Balkans to the Bessarabia region west of the Dnister River between 1769 and 1791. Their hope that a Russian victory would benefit them directly seemed justified when the Nogai Tatars were moved to the Azov steppe during those same years, thereby opening the door for a large-scale Balkan settlement in the western Black Sea littoral. Though it is difficult to be precise, historians agree that Bulgarians comprised the vast majority of these new settlers. The rest consisted of a smattering of Moldavians, Serbs, Greeks, and even Russians and Ukrainians who had earlier fled the empire. By 1819 almost forty thousand Bulgarians had settled in Bessarabia—by then a province of the Russian Empire—and eighty-two colonies had been established by 1830.[81] These numbers were sufficient to warrant the establishment in March 1818 of a separate section of the Guardians' Committee to oversee relations between these colonists and the empire.[82]

Bulgarians soon founded settlements across the Dnister River from Bessarabia and into the western reaches of Kherson province. There were six new colonies by 1810. They established three more in the Crimea once it had been formally annexed. As of 1818, authorities incorporated a significant number of Kherson province's Bulgarian settlements into the newly formed military settlements, where they alone accounted for a quarter of all such regions (*okrugi*). In 1821 it was estimated that six thousand Bulgarians lived in Kherson's various settlements, double the number found in the Crimea. The final great Balkan immigration was prompted by yet another war between the Russian and Ottoman empires in the late 1820s, during which time another sixteen thousand Balkan colonists immigrated to New Russia, though mostly to Bessarabia.[83]

Such a simple tally of settlement and population increases among Balkan colonists conceals the considerable differences that existed among them. Most of the settlements in Tiraspol and Odesa districts had been almost exclusively settled by Bulgarians, with only an occasional sprinkling of Russians and Greeks. Settlement allotments also varied considerably, ranging from fifty-seven desiatinas per family in Kherson in 1837 to seventeen desiatinas in Tavriia. In addition, colonies differed in their proximity to markets, and to other Bulgarian settlements. For instance, the Bulgarian settlements of Feodosiia district, Tavriia province, were surrounded by a sea of relatively impoverished Tatar and Russian settlements, and were cut off from markets. By contrast, settlements in Tiraspol district were in close proximity to the Bessarabian Bulgarians, as well as the emerging markets of Odesa and beyond. Cultural differences were also pronounced. The Greeks who had lived in the Crimea for centuries before relocating to Katerynoslav had been influenced considerably by Tatar culture. For example, half of the twenty-three Greek villages in Katerynoslav were settled by Greeks who no longer spoke their native language, only Tatar.

The effects of cultural assimilation and economic progress were experienced unevenly within New Russia's Bulgarian settlements in the nineteenth century. As a rule, the colonists who were most isolated from other ethnic groups were able to maintain their ethnic distinctiveness, but at the cost of weaker ties with other agriculturalists and emerging urban markets. The inverse was also true. Bulgarian colonies established in Berdiansk district soon adopted technologies used by their Mennonite and German neighbors, and they profited from the expanding market opportunities there, but they were less successful at maintaining their cultural distinctiveness.[84] Often entirely unique patterns emerged. For example, the Ukrainian village of Parkany, situated in Tiraspol district at the confluence of the Komariv and Dnister rivers, was free of foreign colonists until New Russia's governor-general, the famed Duc de Richelieu, invited Bulgarians to settle among them in order to develop market gardening and sericulture. Greeks were invited to settle there in 1809, and the 1816 revision also recorded Moldavian settlers. A century later, Nikolai S. Derzhavin recorded that Bulgarian culture had been preserved in Parkany as the dominant language and special folk customs, though nothing of it remained in clothing, architecture, or much that was evident in domestic life.[85]

Although Bulgarians entered New Russia after 1801 with the highest ranking awarded foreign colonists in the legislation of 1804, their future path would be strongly influenced by the system of land tenure they adopted. Almost all Bulgarian settlements practiced communal forms of landownership and use (*obshchinnoe vladenie i pol'zovanie*). Individual families managed only their household plots. The remaining lands were communally maintained, as was the management of tree nurseries, communal storage facilities, schools, and churches. Under this system, similar to that of Ukrainian and Russian communes, all sons were eligible for a portion of the land and could turn to agriculture. The only exceptions were found in the Crimean colonies of Kishlau and Staryi Krym, where nonpartible and private landholding was practiced. As a result, successive generations in both of these settlements had to confront a problem virtually unheard-of elsewhere in the empire: rural landlessness. Both settings by the 1850s had almost twice as many households without land as with it.[86]

Bulgarians made their most important contributions to peasant agriculture by introducing artisanal trades and market-oriented agriculture. Greeks who relocated from Crimea to Katerynoslav province were most suited to an urban, commercial environment. They quickly created such a milieu after they founded the city of Mariupol in 1780. Within two years they had registered 144 merchants, over 200 petty bourgeois, and almost 1,200 artisans. Countless Bulgarian families maintained shops in their homes. Still others were skilled stone masons who constructed stone homes and churches, and bridges and dams throughout the region, often without any state involvement. Their development of a unique irrigation system known as the "Bulgarian wheel" was decisive in the spread of market gardening in New Russia. The connection between artisanal skills and specialized agriculture was obvious to all contemporaries, who regarded Bulgarians as the most successful agriculturalists. Though most became involved in livestock breeding and grain production, almost all were said to have brought with them a passion for sericulture, vegetable and fruit gardening, and viticulture. Richelieu's decision to settle them in Parkany in 1804 was prompted by the reputation Bulgarians had acquired in the development of mulberry plantations, one of which had been abandoned in Parkany by Tatars. Bulgarians were also said to have single-handedly introduced cucumbers, cabbages, and beans into New Russia, especially in the environs of Odesa. Even Ukrainian borshcht was said to have had a vinegar and apple base until the cultivation of cabbages became widespread.[87]

Mennonites and Germans

Whereas the majority of Balkan colonists who arrived in New Russia after 1789 were agriculturalists who easily adapted to life in the countryside, the same cannot be said for German and Mennonite colonists. Many of these immigrants were artisans and urban laborers hard hit by changes in their native lands. For example, the Germanic city of Danzig (now Gdansk) in the Kingdom of Poland had been a thriving international port in the mid-eighteenth century, spurred on by prosperous artisanal and agricultural sectors. Part of its success was attributed to the willingness of Polish authorities to attract the best settlers available with promises of religious and economic freedom. Dutch Mennonites had begun going there during the sixteenth century. The city offered them a safe haven from persecution in exchange for their expertise in artisanal work and the reclamation of land from the North Sea. It was during their sojourn in the Danzig area that these Mennonites began to assimilate German cultural forms, especially language.

Much had changed by 1800. After Poland was broken up in a series of three partitions involving the Prussian, Russian, and Habsburg empires, Danzig was incorporated into a far more militaristic and far less flexible Prussian state. Taxes for military exemption increased substantially, as did the restrictions on Mennonite land purchases.[88] At the same time, Danzig's relative position within northern Europe declined as a result of fierce competition with Elbing (now Pol. Elbląg) and other German cities that were better able to profit from an expanded Baltic trade. Meanwhile the Danzig merchants struggled with new tariff increases of up to 12 percent imposed by Prussia, which hoped to constrict Danzig's share of the lucrative North European grain market in favor of its competitors.

Semen Sokolovskii, a Russian diplomat in Danzig, graphically captured these larger commercial developments when he wrote in 1787:

> Many foreign ships that were accustomed to travel here for grain now prefer Elbing, having found that grains sold there are much cheaper. Many of the ships of the past summer arrived here not with goods, but only with ballast. They then retraced their path to Elbing, because *the merchants here, having paid such high tariffs to the Prussian crown, are unable to sell their goods, which they had already purchased at a high price from the Poles.*[89]

Though the increased taxation for military exemption affected only the pacifist Mennonites, the economic downturn affected many German laborers, artisans, and farmers. These groups were especially open to Russia's offer of military exemption, religious freedoms, and a six-year exemption from the payment of all taxes. Thus, many of the earliest Mennonite and German colonists to New Russia were of urban background, and they found it difficult to adjust at first to agricultural work. This was true beyond the Danzig region as well, most especially in Württemberg, home of many German emigrants to the Russian Empire. The fifty household heads of the New Russian village of Neihofnunh (Ger. Neuhoffnung), founded in 1822, included a baker, blacksmith, barber/hairdresser, stone mason, cobbler, two carpenters, two clothmakers, three tailors, twelve linen weavers, and twenty-four manual laborers. They also included one government official and one teacher. Less than half the households came with a background in agriculture, with one of these limited to previous experience in viticulture.[90]

The earliest Mennonite and German colonists were therefore unprepared for the circumstances that greeted them upon their arrival in New Russia. The urban markets that had long played a vital role in their economies were either nonexistent or rudimentary in their new homeland, despite lavish promises to the contrary made by Russian immigration agents. Even the agriculturalists in their midst would face a difficult transition. In 1789, the first party of Mennonites, made up of 228 families, settled in New Russia. They had been promised that their new setting would mirror Danzig and its environs. To that end, the two Mennonite delegates to New Russia in 1787, Jacob Hoeppner and Johann Bartsch, had selected a parcel of land located, in the words of historian David Rempel: "on the lower reaches of the Dnieper opposite the town

Berislavl [Ukr. Beryslav] on the right side of the Perekop road. Not only were there broad acres of fertile land and rich pastures, but the island of Tavan in the Dnieper would furnish a convenient means of transportation for the marketing of their farm products in the towns of Kherson, Nikopol and Berislavl."[91] Such a setting clearly appealed to the Mennonites, as it offered them the best chance for replicating their lives in the Danzig region. Upon their arrival, however, the first Mennonite immigrants were compelled to settle on Khortytsia, one of Potemkin's own estates. Khortytsia had relatively inferior soils. Its arable lands tended to be upon the vast steppe, and far away from the ideal settlement locations in the region's deep river valleys. Khortytsia was also well removed from local or international markets, and its continental climatic conditions were entirely alien to the first Mennonite colonists. Added to this, the colonists never received any of the building supplies that the immigration authorities in St. Petersburg had promised to float down the Dnipro River. Indeed, all communication was made more difficult by Khortytsia's location at the foot of the greatest string of rapids found on the Dnipro. Nor were most of the promised grants ever received. A report to the senate in 1798 noted that in the agreement reached with the late tsarina each Mennonite family had been promised 500 rubles to immigrate. Yet, as of January 1798, more than 80,000 of the promised 114,000 rubles remained unpaid.

The early German immigrants were no more suited to the conditions of the New Russian frontier than the Mennonites, and the state was no more successful in honoring its promise of cash and materials.[92] Of the 29 families that in 1786 founded the German settlement of Alt-Danzig (near the administrative center of Ielysavethrad in northern Kherson province), only 19 remained by the end of the century. The rest had been incapacitated and defeated by hunger, cold, and the consequent inability to adjust. Elsewhere colonists faced the loss of all their belongings when spring floods threatened the villages that were too close to the riverbanks. Other villages suffered from being too far away from water. In his investigations at the end of the eighteenth century, Samuel Contenius, the first head of the New Russian Guardianship Office, recorded his own dissatisfaction with the early results of colonist settlement. He could locate only 208 of the 910 Germans who had resettled from Danzig in recent years. Of 904 Germans and Swedes who had settled in Kherson district in 1787, only 148 remained a decade later. At that same time, Contenius proposed that Mennonites from Khortytsia be resettled within the region, since they had enjoyed very little success in their first attempt: "Not only do they not receive any advantage from agriculture, but only rarely are they able to supply themselves with enough grain for the entire year."[93]

How is it that settlements marred by such difficult beginnings were soon transformed into flourishing agricultural enclaves? Perhaps no debate in the historical literature of the German and Mennonite colonists has been livelier than this one. A careful analysis challenges easy explanations that stress either the generous privileges awarded at the point of settlement or a uniquely Germanic ethos combining a craving for order with an insatiable appetite for land.[94] There can be no doubt that the privileges awarded Mennonite colonists, including freedom from military service and generous land allotments of sixty-five desiatinas per household, permitted them to focus their resources on domestic concerns. Yet initially their economies did not exceed those found in the villages of Bulgarian colonists, who had settled on equally generous terms. Indeed, land was plentiful for all sectors of New Russian rural society in the early nineteenth century, including serfs and state peasants. This suggests that other factors must be considered, especially the system of land tenure employed, the average village size, and the background of the colonists themselves. Even a brief consideration suggests how intertwined these factors were.

The Mennonite and German colonists maintained land tenure practices in New Russia that were consistent with the ukase of 19 March 1764. By this decree St. Petersburg sought to impose hereditary household tenure on all future immigrants instead of the communal tenure practiced by most of the empire's peasants. The state granted land to the colony as a whole, and each family was to receive an equal and indivisible share. Upon the death of the household head, that share was expected to pass to a single heir in its entirety.[95] Consideration was given in instances when the heir to the property was too young to manage the homestead, and other provisions safeguarded the right of the widow and remaining children to obtain their portion of the movable property.

The elimination of communal tenure, which required repartitioning, and a refusal to divide existing landholdings made landlessness inevitable within the settlements. How could it be avoided when all immovable property was to be willed to a single heir? To prevent an immediate crisis, the state ordered that a sixth of each village's land be set aside so that future generations could establish farming households, even if they had not inherited the familial lands. The government further expected that many of the landless children would establish trades, thereby enhancing the agricultural life of the community. To that end, a portion of each village was to be set aside for future building sites for nonagricultural households.

Despite the care St. Petersburg showed in the establishment of these provisions, they were unevenly imposed upon the colonists. As noted above, the Balkan colonists quickly adopted the systems of repartitional landholdings that their neighboring peasant communities used. In contrast, the ukase of 1764 formed the foundation for landholding among the Mennonites and Germans in New Russia and played a major role in their prosperity. Mennonite colonies adopted a system whereby all lands were owned corporately by the village assembly, but divided into parcels of sixty-five desiatinas per household and worked accordingly. As shall be seen in chapter 3, the fact that these holdings were indivisible allowed for the rapid establishment of stable farming enterprises that were large enough to make efficient use of capital investment in a wide range of technologies. Such a system also appealed to many of the earliest German and Mennonite immigrants who had artisanal backgrounds and were therefore not inclined to concentrate their energies on agriculture.

Although Mennonites and Germans initially suffered because of their striking lack of agricultural expertise, in the long run they would benefit enormously. Future agricultural developments became possible precisely because so many of them preferred to work as blacksmiths, carpenters, tanners, harness and saddle makers, and millers.[96] Neighboring peasants profited from these developments as well. Still, it would be a mistake to conclude that Mennonites and Germans were equally satisfied with these developments. The fact that the number of the landless far outnumbered those with holdings by midcentury, led to an internal social revolt that was only resolved when the state was compelled to intervene. By then, Mennonites had clearly established their reputations not only as the region's leading agriculturalists, but also as prosperous artisans.

Village size also played an important role in the establishment of thriving Mennonite and German settlements. As Cornies noted in his survey of the 1840s, the average colonist village in mainland Tavriia province had 120 souls, less than a quarter the size of state-peasant villages. In his study of this region in the 1880s, Postnikov maintained that village size was an important factor in the relative success of Mennonite agriculturalists, because they were able to avoid the administrative confusion and logistical nightmare that confronted many state peasants. The combination of large village assemblies and the periodic redivision of lands among state peasant household heads consumed enormous energy and time. Often more disputes were created than solved. In smaller villages less time was spent in transit. German villagers were never situated more than ten kilometers from their fields, and most were only five kilometers away. By contrast, many state-peasant villagers lived up to twenty kilometers from their lands, and sometimes even further.[97]

A number of factors thus accounts for the prosperity of the Mennonite and German agriculturalists by midcentury: the privileges awarded to them at the outset, the adoption of inheritance practices which combined stable landholding with the development of a thriving artisanal trade, and the maintenance of relatively small villages. By 1848, more than 200 German and Mennonite colonies had been founded in southern Russia. The greatest concentration, comprising 45 Mennonite and 28 German villages, was found in the Molochna basin that bordered Berdiansk and Melitopol districts. Here settlers lived in close proximity to the settlements of Nogai Tatars and various Orthodox sectarians, including Dukhobors and Old Believers. Beyond the Molochna, there were also 18 Mennonite villages in the Khortytsia colony, along the Dnipro bend, and 31 German villages in Mariupol district, north of the Sea of Azov. All told, they farmed an astounding 600,000 desiatinas of land, and themselves numbered more than 100,000 inhabitants, double that of 1825. By midcentury, the wealthier among them had moved beyond their village settlement to purchase truly massive estates. Among the new estate owners was Johann Cornies himself, who purchased a 3,350-desiatina estate in 1832, to which he added another 1,600 desiatinas ten years later.[98]

New Russia in the Round: The Demographics of Change

New Russia remained an overwhelmingly unsettled and open frontier throughout the first half of the nineteenth century. A comparison with adjoining Ukrainian provinces in the early nineteenth century highlights the relatively sparse nature of its settlement (see table 2.1). In 1811, there were only 8.1 inhabitants per square kilometer in the region as a whole. The five provinces immediately to the north averaged 29.5. Within New Russia, Katerynoslav enjoyed the greatest density with 12.8 inhabitants per square kilometer, a reflection of the relatively long time that it had been under Russian control. Even though New Russia's population density almost doubled between 1811 and 1851, the regional average of 14.9 inhabitants per square kilometer still lagged far behind that of 37.3 found in the five provinces to the north. The table also points to a demographic levelling within New Russia itself, for while Katerynoslav remained the most densely settled province, the gap narrowed dramatically. Both Kherson and Tavriia provinces experienced increases of approximately 140 percent during this period, whereas Katerynoslav, after its early push, "only" increased by 35 percent. Although population densities in New Russia remained relatively low during the first half of the nineteenth century, observers were nevertheless struck by the rapid pace of its settlement, as table 2.2 suggests. Natural increases, the accelerated immigration of runaways and state peasants from more northern provinces, and Alexander I's successful initiatives to attract more foreign colonists to the region had made this growth possible.[99]

By any measurement, New Russia's population increased rapidly in

Table 2.1. Population densities in selected provinces of Imperial Russia, 1811–1851.

	Inhabitants (per sq. kilometer)	
Province	**1811**	**1851**
Katerynoslav	12.8	17.3
Kherson	6.4	15.2
Tavriia	5.1	12.2
New Russia	**8.1**	**14.9**
Podillia	37.5	45.6
Kyiv	25.3	38.9
Poltava	39.9	41.4
Kharkiv	22.9	30.4
Voronezh	21.7	30.0
Selected Ukrainian provinces	**29.5**	**37.3**

Source: Rashin 1956, 28–29; and Kabuzan 1976, 191.

the first half of the nineteenth century. An important component of this growth was the relatively large urban base of the population. A tenth of the empire lived in urban settings in 1860 and, as one might expect, the two most urbanized provinces were St. Petersburg and Moscow. More surprising, given that few New Russian towns had even been founded before 1770, was the fact that Kherson and Tavriia ranked third and fourth, and Katerynoslav province eleventh, in the empire's ranking of urban settlements.[100] New Russian cities served a wide range of overlapping economic, political, and military functions. For example, Odesa, the jewel of New Russia, was simultaneously a regional administrative center, commercial powerhouse, and thriving shipment point to Atlantic and Mediterranean ports. By the mid-nineteenth century it was more than double the size of any other New Russian city. In 1823, Mary Holderness captured the awe many felt about Odesa's extraordinary growth in face of past obstacles:

> The town of Odessa is a very flourishing seaport, and a most astonishing place. It is to be remembered that about twenty years ago a few fishing huts comprised the whole of its inhabitants, and that in 1812 a third of its population was destroyed by the plague.[101]

Table 2.2. Population figures (in thousands) for selected provinces of Imperial Russia, 1811–1851.

Province	1811	1838	1851	pct. increase 1811–1851
Katerynoslav	666	790	902	35
Kherson	370	766	889	140
Tavriia	255	520	609	139
Podillia	1,298	1,548	1,578	22
Poltava	1,625	1,622	1,689	4
Kharkiv	1,030	1,334	1,366	33
Voronezh	1,180	1,507	1,630	38

Source: Rashin 1956, 28–29.

Other centers, such as the northern cities of Ielysavethrad, Oleksandriia, and Katerynoslav, originated as military towns in the mid-eighteenth century, and had gradually grown into vibrant local trading centers. All served as important regional markets for locally produced agricultural goods. Urban settlement away from the coastal regions was still a rarity.[102]

One cannot conclude, however, that the development of urban centers on the Black and Azov coastlines immediately stimulated agricultural development in their hinterlands. As noted above, the soils decreased dramatically in quality as one went south in New Russia, a fact that discouraged rural settlement in the immediate hinterland of these emergent centers. Ironically the great cities of the south, like Odesa, were often separated from the region's agricultural hinterland by lands with extremely high saline levels. James Webster recorded the sense of desolation that he experienced as he departed from Odesa in the 1820s:

> Striped verst-posts marked out [our] direction over an immense plain. Nothing for miles interrupted its level appearance, excepting where, at intervals, it was dotted with the tumuli of the ancient Scythians, till it faded away in the blue distance.[103]

Almost two decades later, the traveler Demidov recorded that Odesa was "surrounded to a remote distance by immense steppes and endless deserts."[104] Indeed, Odesa's fast development came only in the late nineteenth century after an irrigation system was constructed to supply water to the arid lands beyond the city limits.

Conclusion

The process by which the Black Sea littoral was transformed into New Russia during the late eighteenth and first half of the nineteenth centuries produced revolutionary changes. A remarkable diversity was revealed at every stage and by every measurement; therefore, any attempt to identify unifying patterns or characteristics for this population must be undertaken with caution and skepticism. The majority of state peasants were of Ukrainian origin, and had settled in massive villages, but this category also included Nogai Tatars, former Cossacks, and fugitive peasants who had settled in the region prior to the Russian conquest. Settlers on private estates also included former Cossacks, Crimean Tatars, and others who had established roots on the open frontier only to find themselves suddenly deeded to a noble. So it went. By midcentury even a group as united as the Mennonites were sharply divided into landed and the landless.

Broadly speaking, however, as Cornies found in his survey, the main components of rural settlement consisted of large state-peasant villages, massive estates with relatively few serfs, and the colonists. Of the latter, the Balkan colonists gradually adopted many of the patterns of their Russian and Ukrainian counterparts, whereas Germans and Mennonites maintained a set of distinct differences. Regardless of everything that separated the state peasants from the serfs, they shared a common belief that the move to the Black Sea region would lead to unprecedented freedoms for them, including the freedom of religion, as with the Dukhobors and Molokans, and the free access to land, whether on state lands or as part of the demesne. How their diverse backgrounds on the open frontier would affect the settlers' agricultural initiatives remained to be seen.

3

LAND AND LIVELIHOOD

Sheep Husbandry and the New Russian Frontier

WOOL, WHEAT, AND BEEF catapulted New Russian agriculturalists onto the world stage in the first half of the nineteenth century, and nowhere was this more apparent than in Odesa, the principal port of the south. Only 7 ships weighed anchor in its sheltered harbor in 1794, the first year of Odesa's existence. The numbers increased exponentially thereafter, to 39 ships in 1795, over 500 in 1803, and approximately 1,500 in 1815. At the same time, Odesa's exports grew from 24,000 silver rubles in 1795 to 500,000 in 1802. By 1844, Odesa's share of the empire's export trade surpassed the ancient Baltic city of Riga and stood second only to St. Petersburg.[1] And beyond Odesa, merchants in other southern ports, from Berdiansk and Mariupol to Kherson and Mykolaïv, also claimed the largest possible share of the empire's expanding export market.

Such a robust commercial expansion within New Russia was facilitated by, and in turn helped to foster, the equally dramatic growth of the world economy. It was, after all, from the early eighteenth century onward that a number of western European states—beginning with Great Britain—first began to specialize in the production of foodstuffs and industrially manufactured goods. At the same time, burgeoning urban centers in England and France became more dependent on raw materials from around the world. In this way flax and hemp—and not wool or wheat as one might expect—were the most important Russian exports in the mid-eighteenth century, by which time Great Britain had become

Russia's largest trading partner. By signing the Anglo-Russian Commercial Treaty of 1766, Catherine assured that these fruitful relations would continue. Russian iron would become the main factor in this relationship by the end of the nineteenth century, and would remain so until British technological innovations made Russian products obsolete.[2] With seemingly unlimited opportunities in European markets, the only dark clouds on the New Russian horizon in the early nineteenth century appeared to come from the Ottoman Empire's threat to deny passage through the Bosporus and Dardanelles to European markets. However, the Treaty of Adrianople in 1829, which guaranteed full rights of passage in peacetime, gave the promise of long-term stability.

Following successive crop failures in western Europe from 1815–18, there was a demand for wheat from the Ukraine. After a slow beginning, wheat initially became the dominant product shipped out of Odesa and its neighboring ports. Meanwhile, commercial agents encouraged technological adjustments to the storage and treatment of wheat. These modifications dramatically reduced the spoilage that normally occurred during the overseas shipment of crops and helped spur Russian wheat exports. But was the rapid increase in wheat exports an indication of its importance to New Russian agriculturalists in the first half of the nineteenth century? Surprisingly, the answer is no, despite earlier suggestions by Mose Harvey and others to the contrary.[3] After an early flurry in grain production during the late eighteenth century, most New Russian agriculturalists would shy away from it until decades later.

Instead, it was agriculturalists from the central Ukrainian provinces who were the immediate beneficiaries of the opening of the Black Sea ports. They had long carted grain overland to Baltic destinations. Johann Kohl reported in the 1830s that Odesa's real granaries were to be found in "Bessarabia, Podolia, and Little Russia." Few New Russian farmers produced grains for export—only those who lived in scattered pockets in the immediate vicinity of Odesa and other major ports, or in a narrow strip along the main waterways. August von Haxthausen, a contemporary of Kohl's, eagerly anticipated a time when the Black Sea steppe—along with North America—would serve as the granary of "the greatest part of civilized Europe." However, that was but a fanciful hope at a time when New Russia resembled a frontier zone and enormous parts of it were still uncultivated. Haxthausen summarized the ambitious efforts at colonization in the following manner:

> We find along the banks of nearly all the rivers colonization completed, a thin strip along the margin being fully cultivated, and the population already tolerably dense. The large Steppe plains between the rivers on the other hand are almost wholly uncultivated, farms (*khutora*) being here and there pushed forward into them.

Similarly, Robert Bremner noted that:

> a traveller crossing the Steppes may occasionally be greeted by a cultivated spot, in some hollow where there is water; and in such a place a few shrubs may be found; but in general, there is nothing to be seen except a coarse rank grass, the sight of which becomes at last as wearisome to the eye as absolute barrenness.[4]

Contemporary investigations estimated that less than a tenth of all land in Kherson province had been plowed by the early nineteenth century. Decades later, cultivation was still limited to low-lying areas with adequate moisture where grains could serve as an important complement to livestock breeding.[5]

Although state peasants, colonists, and estate owners grew grains for household use in the first third of the nineteenth century, several factors blocked grains from becoming a leading branch of the New Russian economy before 1830. For one thing, both peasants and estate owners experienced chronic labor shortages that would only be overcome later in the century after significant population increases and technological innovation. Second, a near chronic shortage of oxen and horses further hindered all aspects of farming. Owing to the lack of teams, soils were worked less thoroughly, thus increasing the vulnerability of seedlings and the likelihood of drought. The feed available for livestock was reduced, which meant that fewer healthy and hardy beasts were available to haul grains to market, thereby increasing the losses of even harvested crops. Third, grains were vulnerable to the region's variable continental climate.[6] Cold, stormy winters often followed summers of unrelenting heat. However, many winters produced little snowfall and both winter and spring crops suffered. Early summer droughts also turned many a promising harvest into disaster. One agriculturalist, Demol′, observed that even with adequate spring rains, some years, such as 1838, could be harmful because of the frequency of late spring frosts. At the other extreme, a springtime drought of over sixty days in 1841 destroyed all grains except those sown early in the season in well-cultivated fields. But Demol′ generally regarded the summer rains to be insufficient: excessive sunshine often scorched vulnerable shoots. One observer from the dawn of the nineteenth century sardonically wondered if the attempt to colonize the steppe with agriculturalists might itself have been a mistake: "We find climates such as ours in wildest Arabia, where the lands remain uninhabited. But Russia, which is accustomed to doing the impossible, ordered the settlement of this same steppe."[7]

Those who did engage in crop cultivation had to adapt to the new challenges and opportunities facing them. The wooden sheared plows that Ukrainian peasants brought from the adjacent northern provinces easily shattered on the hard-baked virgin soils of the south and had to be replaced by more durable implements. Spring wheat, which was such a dependable staple in the north, withered under the relentless heat of the shelterless and saline southern prairie. Colonists faced similar challenges, although the historiographical legacy has emphasized their "Midas touch." Mennonites soon abandoned attempts to establish intensive market gardening operations in their Dnipro-bend villages when the local soils proved unsuitable, irrigation untenable, and local markets insignificant.[8] The most successful agriculturalists were those, whether from Ukraine or western Europe, who adapted previously acquired skills and expertise to the soils, climate, and marketing possibilities of their new home. No less important was their ability to learn from the successes and failures of their neighbors.

Finally, there were a host of difficulties associated with the transport of grains to market. The state was slow to provide central grain elevators and storage containers. It made no effort to improve the roads that linked the fields to the port cities of the south. The generally high tariffs that were passed throughout Europe after the Napoleonic wars discouraged the export trade in grains, and continued to do so until England abolished the Corn Laws in 1846 and a new era began. That change, along with the assurance of safe transit from the Ottoman Empire after 1829, finally prompted the beginning of extensive grain cultivation on the New Russian steppe. Until then, peasants and estate owners had sought to minimize expenditures of capital and labor in their economies.[9]

Cattle seemed far better suited to local conditions. They supplied food, milk, hide for clothing, and labor for fieldwork and seasonal carting.

Tallow served as a major export product used as a machine lubricant, lamp fuel, and as the basis for soap and candle production.[10] From modest beginnings, by the 1840s New Russian cattle numbered in the millions. They were sold at village and town fairs (*iarmarki*) and, on occasion, driven to major centers such as Kharkiv, St. Petersburg, and Moscow. The Black Sea fleet provided another important market for salted beef, as did local processing plants. Sixteen tallow-melting firms had been established in Katerynoslav province by 1816, and the number rose to over forty by 1860, at which time they employed almost a thousand workers.[11]

Although cattle breeding and grain production were important components of peasant and estate economies in the early nineteenth century, neither matched the importance of sheep breeding. The Cossacks and Tatars had considered sheep to be of "unequalled importance" well before the Russian conquest. Observers in the 1830s still considered sheep to be essential for the Tatars' survival. "Without them [the Tatars] would be cold, starving, and not even have the money to pay taxes." A report submitted to Tsar Nicholas I in 1837 by M. S. Vorontsov (governor-general of New Russia from 1823 to 1844), declared that sheep breeding was the cornerstone of the region's economy.[12] How could it be otherwise given the abundance of land that existed in the early nineteenth century, the dry climate, and the lure of national and foreign markets? By that time, the sheep in New Russia numbered in the millions.

Almost all of the region's agriculturalists had begun to breed sheep by the second quarter of the nineteenth century, and they did so in strikingly different ways and with different goals. Peasants, Tatars, and former Cossacks were interested primarily in supplementing their household economies with the hardiest, most versatile breeds available. Even so, the growing appeal of market production was evident in the shift to market-oriented sheep breeding during the second quarter of the nineteenth century. Bulgarian colonists adopted a similar strategy. Germans and Mennonites focused on fine-fleeced sheep breeding for European woolen markets, but their fascination with sheep had started to decline by the second quarter of the nineteenth century since their landholdings could no longer sustain large herds. In fact, by the middle of the century the great era of sheep breeding among Germans and Mennonites had ended for all but the few who were able to establish herds on large private estates. Finally, Russian estate owners also raised fine-fleeced sheep, as was required by the empire's conditions of settlement. However, despite their interest in the market, they rarely managed their herds with care or efficiency. In essence, Russian nobles combined the colonists' strong market orientation with the peasants' relative inattention to husbandry. The outcome was not a good one, and resulted in two crises in estate economies: the first in the 1830s, and the second in the tumultuous 1860s. Thereafter, fine-fleeced sheep breeding became the almost exclusive activity of only the largest of estate owners.

Sheep breeding in New Russia has long been neglected as an area of investigation. As late as the 1880s, provincial investigations of household economies did not bother to determine the number of sheep bred in peasant settlements. More recent studies have maintained a similar silence. With some effort, however, a study of peasant sheep breeding is possible. The prospect is somewhat easier in the case of estate owners and colonists, because they were the subject of numerous state and zemstvo examinations during the nineteenth century. In addition, colonists generally, and Mennonites especially, were meticulous record keepers.[13]

Peasants and "Safety First" Sheep Breeding

New Russian peasants quickly adopted sheep breeding on a grand scale in order to meet a wide range of needs, among which market values was only one. Although figures from the early period are rarely considered reliable, one gets a sense of the initial importance attached to sheep by considering the fact that approximately one million were thought to have perished during the severe winter of 1812. This staggering figure represented the loss of approximately half the sheep in the region, at a time when estate owners and colonists had barely begun their operations. Early peasant settlers acquired sheep from Cossacks and Tatars who had long pastured their herds on the region's succulent grasses and watered them along streams and rivers. The appeal of sheep breeding was powerful, especially at a time when markets were distant and capital limited.[14] Sheep hides and felt provided for winter and summer clothing, and wool from twice-yearly shearings could be sold to pay for taxes, leases on land, or manufactured goods. Though fine wool was required for the making of garments, coarser wools could be spun for household needs of clothing, bedding, and footwear. Thereafter, surplus wool could be sold to central Russian and European manufacturers of military clothing or for use as packing in mattresses and other furniture.[15] Sheep were also a dependable source of food and drink. Tatars preferred sheep's milk and meat over all others. Butter, curds, and even a special cheese called *brynza* were produced from sheep milk. Lambs could be sold in the spring, especially for the Easter feast days, to obtain income needed for seeding. Finally, sheep manure was commonly pressed into bricks (*kiziaki*) in order to heat homes, an important consideration in a region largely bereft of forests.[16] In short, peasants turned to sheep breeding in order to obtain everything from wool to meat, and from hides to cheese.

Peasants depended upon breeds that were resilient enough to endure the blistering heat of midsummer when water was scarce for weeks, and the fierce winds and blizzardlike conditions of winter, when fodder and shelter were often nonexistent. To maximize efficiency, peasant households normally combined their sheep into a common herd, especially when villages were small, although wealthier peasants occasionally pastured their sheep in separate flocks. The most typical collective within Odesa district after midcentury comprised from eight to ten households that paid shepherds' wages in proportion to the sheep from each unit. Given the average of approximately ten sheep per household, this resulted in herds of around a hundred sheep. In these cases, such by-products as milk and cheese were divided proportionally among the households.

Peasants usually pastured their flocks in an unregulated and inefficient manner. This was unfortunate, because sheep, in contrast to cattle, are fussy eaters who trample down as much good feed as they consume and damage grain fields and hay crops if left unattended. This problem was especially acute on clear sunny days, when sheep facing the sun are temporarily blinded. During the earliest decades of settlement, when peasant access to land seemed unlimited, sheep were often left to graze by day and night. However, the steady increase in settlement and grain production challenged peasants to alter their practices. S. P. Shchepkin noted that in areas with small land holdings, or in villages with pastures close to the buildings, coarse-fleeced sheep either spent nights at their owners' huts, or sheltered as a single flock near the edge of the village. Flocks in larger villages with distant pastures continued to spend nights either in the fields or near water.[17] In summer, peasants found temporary reprieve from the harsh steppe winds by moving their sheep into one of the deep river valleys that cut through the region. Peasants rarely constructed permanent shelters for sheep during periods of inclement weather, though temporary fences of earth, reeds, stone, or dried manure bricks were often built as partial hedges.[18]

The passage of time and the expansion of cultivated lands necessitated the introduction of more regulated herds. These were pastured in spring on virgin or long fallow fields, where the richest, most moisture-laden natural vegetation was found. Then, if land was available, the herd was transferred to year-round pastures (*toloka*) until it was moved once again to cultivated fields after the final hay-cutting and grain harvest. This last relocation was an important one. Peasants hoped that this would allow the pasture land a much needed respite for regeneration and that the resulting growth would sustain the herd over the winter months. By late fall, most peasants reverted to a less controlled form of grazing, while still protecting the lands under cultivation for winter crops and the hay meadows where the grass cover was insufficient to protect against the winter cold.[19]

The considerable fluctuation in winter weather made it difficult for peasants to determine the minimal levels of stored food and shelter required from the end of pasturing to the first sign of spring. New Russian winters were shorter but far less predictable than elsewhere in European Russia. Peasants in the central Ukrainian provinces, for example, could safely plan to pasture their herds for seven months of the year. Those along the Black Sea coast could count on ten or eleven months before snow cover made it impossible to continue. But, whereas there was only a 10 percent variation in the length of time herds could expect to pasture in central Ukraine, such variation was much greater in the heart of New Russia. Here some winters allowed continuous grazing, and others required five months of dried feed because of the heavy snowfall and consistently cold temperatures. The wet winters might be followed by heavy spring run-offs when pastures became too muddy to be used. Furthermore, dry-feed requirements in New Russia varied considerably from north to south, making the question of adequate winter feed of paramount importance for owners regardless of whether they had ten sheep, or several hundred. To make matters worse, the difficulty in finding and paying for an adequate labor force at peak times of the year reinforced a tendency to underestimate the amount of feed required. If labor costs in any given year were deemed too high to justify cutting and carting hay, or if the coming winter was expected to be a mild one, mature grasses were left in the fields at the risk of frost and locust damage.[20]

Preserved feed consisted of varying proportions and qualities of hay and straw, depending on what was available at a given time. Peasants commonly harvested grasses from natural pastures. Sown grasses were found among only a handful of colonists and estate owners. Hay for wintered livestock consisted of mixtures of various weeds and grasses, among them quack grass, nightshade, wild carrot, and various feather grasses, all of which were cycled through fallowed and virgin fields. The search for quality feed became especially important toward midcentury as virgin lands began to disappear and more extensive cultivation practices prohibited long periods of fallow. Many peasants responded by underestimating the quantity and quality of the fodder required. Consequently, although optimum fodder began with equal portions of hay and straw, the latter predominated over time. Even so, generalizations are difficult because the nutritional value of straw varied greatly. The grain threshed by machines was often very good, whereas that trampled (hence, threshed) by oxen was not. Not surprisingly, peasants were compelled to use oxen given the prohibitive cost of mechanized threshing during most of the century. An added difficulty occurred when hay that was gathered during the rainy fall season, or on summer mornings before the dew had evaporated, rotted and increased the chance of disease.

As peasants reduced the size of their pastures in favor of increased grain production, they were faced with a stark choice: daily rations for their herds could either be reduced to dangerously low levels, or else they could sell off their livestock at the very time that market values were at their lowest. Others might seek supplemental sources of winter feed, all too often with little concern for its nutritional value. For example, reeds were often found along the streams and river valleys of New Russia but, if cut green, they provided barely adequate nourishment. Other sources included the husks of oil products, especially hemp, branches (often cut in late autumn before the leaves had fallen), and a variety of root crops that included potatoes, large turnips, and sugar beets.[21]

Peasant breeders made the transition from pasturing to dry feed as gradually as possible in the late fall in order to preserve their fodder until the onset of spring grazing. To that end, herds were first given a diet of the best dry feed available. The poorest quality feeds were held back the longest in the hopes that an early spring or mild winter would render them unnecessary. With steadily diminishing pasture and hay lands, however, small landholders had to opt for mainly straw feed even though they realized that it would produce a poorer quality of wool. Part of the problem was the wasteful manner in which hay and straw were placed on the earth in small piles, which allowed sheep to trample it into the ground. Mangers reduced such waste, and although those with roofs curtailed moisture damage, they were rarely used. One study from the mid-nineteenth century claimed that mangers were almost unheard-of in all of Kherson province.[22]

Contemporary accounts suggest that peasants rarely gave salt to their sheep, despite the efforts of state representatives and the South Russian Agricultural Society to underscore its importance as a supplement to food and water, especially during harsh winter months. Estate owners attributed the improved health of their herds to its regular use.[23] But given the additional costs involved, peasants remained skeptical of the advantages despite the fact that the gradual decline in quality feed made salt application all the more critical. One midcentury report concluded that peasants provided salt only once a fortnight, and then only for their most prized livestock. A report to the agricultural conference of Ielysavethrad district in 1860 suggested that neither estate owners nor peasants provided salt to any significant degree, and another report went so far as to claim that salt was not essential to livestock diets. Because of the costs entailed, most peasants waited to provide salt rations until their herds had become diseased, at which time its application was of limited value.[24]

Sources of water for sheep varied widely in New Russia and included major rivers, seasonal water courses, natural and artificial ponds, and springs. Occasionally peasants were compelled to construct wells, as in Oboznivka (Oboznovsk) volost of Ielysavethrad district, which had no natural ponds, few streams, and no rivers of any substance. Here sheep breeders relied upon twenty-one wells that had been constructed by an estate owner and four peasant communes. Wells were a primary source of water in Berdiansk district, Tavriia province, where peasants followed the colonists' lead in digging them. Adequate sources of clean water were essential to prevent epidemics among the sheep, though shortcuts were possible during the spring and fall, when the availability of moist, succulent grasses made a direct water source almost unneccesary. During these seasons, peasants led their sheep to a pond or river only once or twice a week. With the onset of dry summer weather, sheep needed water at least once a day, usually in the morning, and close to where they had spent the night. For this reason, peasants preferred the hardier indigenous sheep as they required less water than the more delicate fine-fleeced sheep found on private estates.[25]

Breeding and shearing practices also influenced the well-being of sheep and the quality of their wool. Lambs born from a carefully monitored breeding program naturally produced a higher quality fleece. Unfortunately, the extensive peasant economies did not lend themselves to the continuous supervision required to produce quality fleece, nor was there much appreciation for its need. Peasants used two distinct types of sheep breeding: selective or free-range. The first involved the specific pairing of a ram and ewe, and was the most efficient since it normally assured a higher percentage of conceptions than that among free-range sheep. A monitored breeding program also provided some assurance that ewes would not be bred before their frames had achieved full maturity. Yet despite these advantages, peasant breeders resisted this labor-intensive method of selecting and isolating ewes, and usually opted for free-range breeding. Here rams were either kept with the ewes throughout the year or put with them in the fall months. The former method was the simplest, but the latter was preferable in order to prevent the rams from breeding ewes before they were physically mature, or too early in the season. Ewes did not develop a strong enough frame for effective breeding until three years of age, although, if left alone with a ram, they could be bred within a year's time. Rams were not suitable for breeding until they were two to three years old, and were then used for five years, the stronger ones lasting even longer. Peasants who lacked their own rams shared one between households or even with an entire village. Communal ownership of rams was rare, however. As late as 1884, only one peasant village commune in Slov'iano-Serbiia district of northern Katerynoslav province followed this practice.[26]

In many ways, peasant sheep breeding in 1850 still relied upon eighteenth-century practices similar to those used by the region's Tatars and Cossacks. There was a distinct shift, however, in the sheep breeds used. Unlike their estate or colonist counterparts, New Russian peasants favored the more versatile "short-haired," "coarse-fleeced" or "simple" (*prostaia ovtsa*) sheep, among which the Kurdiuch (*kurdiuchnaia*), Wallachian, Russian (*russkaia*), and Gypsy (*tsygaiskaia*) pedigrees dominated. Greek and Bulgarian colonists had actually brought these so-called "indigenous" sheep from the Mediterranean region into the Black Sea littoral in previous centuries, and it was here that local Cossacks and Tatars obtained them. Over time these coarse-fleeced sheep had spread from the Balkans to the Urals, all the while acquiring different names in different regions. Eventually their very origins were obscured. However, they all shared a robust physique and were relatively inexpensive to obtain, characteristics which more than compensated for their modest market value.[27]

Of the coarse-fleeced varieties, the Kurdiuch was the sheep of choice among peasants during the late eighteenth and early nineteenth centuries. The name refers to the sheep's fatty, bifurcated tail (*kurdiuk*), which peasants highly prized. Kurdiuch sheep were the hardiest of coarse-fleeced sheep and had been especially favored in the eighteenth century by the Cossacks and Nogai Tatars in the mainland prairie north of Crimea, and also by Greeks in the southeastern Kherson province—places with limited sources of fresh water and relentless summer heat. The long muscular legs of the Kurdiuch sheep were well suited to the semi-nomadic existence of Cossacks and Tatars, since they raised the animal's torso high enough to avoid lacerations from the prairie's sharp wild grasses and weeds. Depending upon the feed, Kurdiuch sheep could provide from 4.5 to more than 13 kilograms of dark-red (*ryzhaia*) or brown wool. They were generally considered the fattest of simple sheep, and in parts of the region were bred solely for their tallow. The Kurdiuch acquired many names in the larger region, a measure of the widespread, albeit highly localized role they played. For example the Kurdiuch sheep was variously known by the names "Ordynskaia," "simple," or "Kirkiznaia" in the Volga region, and as "Kalmytskaia" or "Gurtovshchitsnaia" along the Don. In Katerynoslav province they were known as Greek sheep, as well as "Chundukskie," "Chunduki," or "Chushki" sheep.[28] This suggests that the importance of Kurdiuch sheep was defined less by central markets than by household needs at a time when regional communication and transportation links were rudimentary.

By whatever name, by midcentury the Kurdiuch sheep had receded in popularity in New Russia, a fact which in large part reflected changing priorities in peasant economies. By the 1860s only the Nogai Tatars possessed large concentrations of Kurdiuch sheep, and although the sheep remained a popular breed in the Volga region and other areas of sparse settlement in the empire, their role in New Russia had ended. In their place, peasants turned to breeds of coarse-fleeced sheep that were less hardy—and therefore riskier, but also more profitable. The Wallachian sheep became the most popular coarse-fleeced sheep among the region's peasants at this time. It was the largest of the coarse-fleeced breeds, with ewes that weighed up to sixty kilograms, and rams up to eighty. The Wallachian sheep were still hardy enough to withstand shelterless winters on the open steppe. Their wool was long and lustrous, and almost always white, though black and gray hues were also found. Although the wool deteriorated rapidly if the sheep were neglected, proper care resulted in a marketable and profitable product. Poor quality Wallachian wool was sold for mattresses, and higher-quality wool was sold for the manufacture of coarse-woolen cloth. Almost all of the coarse wool exported in the early nineteenth century from the Black and Azov seaports came from these Wallachian sheep.[29]

By midcentury peasants were also eager to acquire medium-sized Russian sheep. As with Wallachian wool, the Russian sheep produced a desirable, pliable, rich product when the animal was provided with adequate shelter and fodder. In fact, the Russian and Wallachian sheep were commonly interbred. In his investigation of sheep breeding in the late 1860s, Shchepkin noted that distinctions between these two breeds were often blurred because peasants deliberately chose Wallachian rams for their Russian ewes. Interest in better wool production also led some peasants to acquire Gypsy sheep, which had been brought into New Russia by Bulgarian colonists. Their long, dense, gold-tinted wool was the finest and most delicate of all coarse-fleeced sheep and almost matched that of the European fine-fleeced merino sheep. The Gypsy's long tail was also an important source of tallow. Finally, Gypsy sheep were highly valued for their meat as well as for their milk, which allowed for a superior cheese (*brynza*).[30]

Despite these advantages and a high market value, peasants never developed a widespread interest in Gypsy sheep. Nor did they aggressively switch to fine-fleeced sheep, even after these imported breeds became more affordable. Instead, Gypsy sheep largely remained the property of the region's noble estate owners, as well as the German and Mennonite colonists.[31] Although peasants had begun to experiment with the interbreeding of higher quality "imported" rams with coarse-fleeced ewes, their reliance on a wide range of sheep products made them reluctant to experiment. Above all, the means by which peasants bred and maintained sheep required a minimum of effort and expense. Estate owners adopted many of the peasants' practices in caring for their own fine-fleeced sheep, a situation that would create a greater problem in their economies.

Peasant involvement in sheep breeding in the first half of the nineteenth century clearly demonstrated their desire to adapt to the new setting, though always in a cautious manner. They realized that coarse-fleeced sheep fulfilled a wide range of household needs while putting few demands on their breeders. Coarse-fleeced sheep were also ideally suited to a region with large unsettled tracts of natural grasslands, inadequate sources of labor, and access to attractive foreign markets. That said, peasants were not uninformed participants in the regional economy, and as the century progressed, they abandoned Kurdiuch sheep in favor of Wallachian and Gypsy sheep. The peasants' reluctance to adopt fine-fleeced sheep, however, reflected a reasoned interest in their herds that extended beyond the production of wool for the market. They needed to consider the added costs involved in the purchase and care of such sheep. Though important, the market was certainly not the peasants' only consideration. In pursuing sheep production, peasants followed the example established by the region's Cossacks and Tatars, as well as by the Bulgarian colonists, whose entry into New Russia had coincided with the introduction of Wallachian sheep there. The peasants' strategy was very different from the one adopted by the same region's nobles or the German and Mennonite colonists.

Colonists, Estate Owners, and Fine-Fleeced Sheep Breeding

In 1797, Prince V. P. Kochubei, a former minister of internal affairs, petitioned Tsar Paul I to provide free land grants to New Russian nobles and private citizens who were willing to introduce fine-fleeced Spanish and Saxon sheep breeds into their herds. The tsar's response, in the form of an imperial decree issued later that year, ordered the establishment of a station for the breeding of pure Spanish sheep in New Russia—one that could house six hundred rams and four hundred ewes. Such a setting would allow local breeders to observe the benefits of the more delicate European breeds against those of indigenous ones. At the same time, the Department of the State Economy (*Ekspeditsiia Gosudarstvennogo Khoziaistva*) proposed that the government also introduce sheepdogs and shepherds from Spain in order to provide guidance to New Russian estate owners. Little came of this initiative, however, because the ongoing hostilities between Russia and France greatly restricted commercial travel on the Mediterranean, and particularly with Spain.[32]

A second initiative was undertaken in 1804. The authorities purchased two hundred high-quality Spanish rams and ewes for distribution in New Russia, and agreed to an annual purchase of approximately two thousand ewes and fifteen hundred rams. In addition, the ukase of 12 January 1804 granted two desiatinas of land to estate owners for every European sheep that they imported within a period of ten years. Yet, despite these incentives, Katerynoslav's governor, K. S. Gladkii, reported in 1808 that foreign sheep breeds had received only minimal attention among estate owners in his province.

It was a French émigré and not a Russian noble who took the first significant step toward fine-fleeced sheep breeding in New Russia. Rouvier (Ruv′e) was a member of France's landed aristocracy when he lost his entire estate, along with its prized Spanish sheep herd, during the French revolutionary wars. Undaunted, he proposed that St. Petersburg provide him with a similar estate in the Crimea. After negotiations, Rouvier obtained a grant of 100,000 rubles along with 5,000 desiatinas of hilly land in the Crimea, and another 25,000 desiatinas of level prairie. In exchange Rouvier agreed to establish a herd of 100,000 fine-fleeced sheep in New Russia by 1817, and to instruct 100 student apprentices in the art of sheep breeding. In 1803 Rouvier and his son-in-law, Vassal, another French émigré, commandeered a Russian naval vessel, and loaded 100 Spanish rams on it. Rouvier's additional attempts to purchase Spanish sheep foundered on the uncertainties of the Napoleonic wars and led to increased purchases from German and Hungarian sources. Eventually he managed to acquire thousands of fine-fleeced sheep, some of which were crossbred with the finest available indigenous breeds. By 1808, Rouvier had an excellent flock of over 7,000 merino sheep. He gave their offspring to his children, whom he had provided with equally large estates. In 1810, Rouvier persuaded authorities to purchase even more fine-fleeced sheep in Bessarabia for relocation to private estates in Kherson and Tavriia provinces.[33]

A contemporary of Rouvier's from Silesia, Georg Müller, also established a sheep-breeding operation in New Russia after 1802, following the receipt of a 12,000 desiatina estate in Odesa district. Shortly thereafter, Müller departed for a tour of the German states. He returned in May of

1804 with 1,200 merinos and 25 skilled sheep breeders. After prolonged negotiations with the Duc de Richelieu, governor-general of New Russia, Müller received permission to pasture his sheep in the Odesa town pasture until his own buildings were constructed. In an important concession, the state also agreed to provide Müller with the former customs building in Odesa and a financial subsidy of 25,000 rubles, whereupon he constructed a wool-washing mill on site.[34] By 1808, Müller's sheep-breeding operation was flourishing with over 7,000 thousand merinos and another 25,000 sheep that had been crossbred with indigenous breeds. Such success was exceptional at this time, and the state decided to purchase 4,000 merino ewes and rams from Müller for distribution among New Russia's foreign colonists and state villages. In that same year, an inspection of Katerynoslav province revealed no fewer than 11 sheep-breeding operations run by nobles (*pomeshchiki*), while Rouvier's was the only one found in the Crimean peninsula of Tavriia province.[35]

Despite initial official encouragement and support, neither state peasants nor Balkan colonists ever established significant operations for breeding fine-fleeced sheep, and even Mennonite and German colonists were slow to develop them. The Mennonites and Germans had brought small numbers of sheep to the region, and they managed them in household economies along with hogs, cattle, and horses. Little else happened until after Richelieu presented ten pair of Spanish sheep to Mennonite colonists in 1804. By the following year the Molochna Mennonites had formed the Kura-Iushanlee Sheep Breeding Association, which purchased and distributed several hundred coarse-fleeced sheep.[36] Even so, the promise of massive holdings were slow to materialize. As of 1808, Mennonites from the entire Molochna settlement of 18 villages owned a mere 800 sheep. A third of these, 274, were concentrated in a single village, of which 157 belonged to a single farmer. Nevertheless, the state continued to encourage colonists' sheep breeding. Samuel Contenius, the first principal of the Guardians' Committee for the Settlers of New Russia, provided Mennonite villagers with 30 merinos. This herd formed the basis of a communal flock that was pastured on a 3,000-desiatina parcel of "reserve" land set aside for the development of future village sites. Both the sheep and pastures were supervised by the colony's civil authorities, who steadily improved herds by hiring skilled sheep breeders and by purchasing new stock from the state.[37]

German colonists followed a similar pattern. The village of Neihofnunh was formed in 1822 by German evangelical sectarians from Württemberg who had settled near the Azov city of Berdiansk. Each of the original fifty households received sixty-five desiatinas of household land, leaving a thousand desiatinas as communal pasture. However, unlike the Molochna Mennonites, most German settlers labored as blacksmiths, carpenters, and at other trades that left them unacquainted with any agricultural activity beyond market gardening. Furthermore, those Germans who settled close to Odesa, in the Crimea, or near the new administrative centers of Ielysavethrad and Katerynoslav quickly prospered from the sale of vegetables, grapes, fruit, and small fowl, and had little reason to engage in sheep breeding. The Germans who settled alongside the Molochna Mennonites were an exception: they followed the Mennonites' lead and established fine-fleeced sheep herds. Other Germans, such as the Josefstal colony along the Dnipro River, were only slowly able to develop profitable sheep-breeding operations. In the end, the transition from Württemberg artisans to New Russian farmers proved to be as difficult as it was slow.[38]

What is it that prompted imperial authorities, along with a modest number of estate owners and colonists, to take an active interest in fine-fleeced sheep breeding at this time, and against these odds? Of central importance was the British wool textile industry, which had expanded by 150 percent during the course of the eighteenth century. At the same time, modifications to the manufacturing process increased the demand for the long, silky wool of merino sheep. Unable to find sufficient wool domestically, British mills looked increasingly to foreign breeders of these sheep, and in the process sparked an international revolution in the supply of high-grade wool. Whereas merino sheep had been the exclusive domain of the Spanish lands before 1750, their breeding had spread to Saxony by 1770, and thereafter to Prussia, Austria, and North America. At the most distant point, breeders in Australia introduced merinos in 1797.[39]

The spread of merino sheep breeding to New Russia coincided with its worldwide expansion to other natural grassland frontiers. Like the broad steppe lands of Australia, Argentina, the United States, and British North America, New Russia also had an abundance of land relative to its population. New Russia was distinguished by its easy access to European markets, however. Most grasslands elsewhere were located at the outer fringe of urban markets, where market agriculture required improved transportation and efficient production in order to be competitive.[40] By contrast, agricultural development in New Russia was readily oriented to western Europe through its rapidly emerging Black and Azov sea ports. Kherson, Mykolaïv, Berdiansk, Sevastopol, and Mariupol were founded at this time, and Odesa shortly thereafter. Thus, with expanding and readily accessible local and international markets, along with an abundance of sparsely settled lands, New Russian estate owners seemed poised to exact large profits with minimal attention or effort. The perceived Russian advantage was furthered by the staggering difference in land values at the time between New Russia and western Europe. By one estimate, New Russian land as late as 1830 cost from ten to twenty rubles a desiatina, compared to the equivalent of three thousand rubles a desiatina in the German states.[41]

Despite such favorable circumstances, few gains were made before the end of the Napoleonic era. The governor of Katerynoslav province reported in 1808 that estate owners were concentrating their efforts on grain production, since the ongoing hostilities between France and the rest of Europe had decimated agriculture there and inflated world prices. After the Napoleonic wars, massive European crop failures in 1816 and 1817 led to a sharp increase in wheat prices in Odesa, suddenly making it profitable for producers from distances over six hundred kilometers to cart their grain to this burgeoning seaport.[42] The much-heralded explosion in New Russian fine-fleeced sheep breeding began only after this period of unusually high grain prices collapsed shortly thereafter. Skal′kovs′kyi estimated that the number of merino sheep in New Russia grew from nine thousand in 1808 to almost a half-million in 1823, and to two million by 1837. Two decades later, the number approached its peak of almost three million fine-fleeced sheep in the region. One enthusiastic observer proclaimed that merino sheep were increasing not daily, but hourly.[43]

Caution is required in the evaluation of any livestock numbers, given the haphazard manner in which the data were gathered and the inconsistencies that resulted from different reporting mechanisms. By one count, there were six hundred thousand merinos in Tavriia province in 1840; by another, almost a million. Nevertheless, it appears that a third of the empire's merino sheep at this time were found in New Russia.[44] They were concentrated on private estates of the Russian nobility, as well as in German and Mennonite settlements situated in the mainland counties of Tavriia province, the southern districts of Kherson province, and the

Dnipro River districts of Katerynoslav province. A completed study of 168 estate merino-breeding operations, which was undertaken by the Imperial Agricultural Society of South Russia, revealed that the average estate had 4,319 merino sheep. This figure is similar to one contained in a report on the wool market in Katerynoslav province in 1838, which stated that the average estate owner there had 3,381 sheep. Such province-wide averages concealed massive variations, however. For example, one estate owner in Ananïv (Ananev) district, Kherson province, had two-thirds of the 75,000 sheep found in the district, whereas the remaining estate owners had flocks of fewer than 2,500 merinos each.[45]

The central role played by Germans and Mennonites in sheep breeding within New Russia is shown in table 3.1. After modest beginnings, these breeders aggressively expanded their fine-fleeced herds in the 1820s and 1830s. New Russian German and Mennonite colonists together possessed almost 200,000 sheep in 1830, almost all of which were merinos. At that time, Mennonite families averaged almost 46 sheep, 10 more than

Table 3.1. Sheep breeding and the New Russian colonists, 1831.

	Colony (villages)	Families	Sheep	Sheep per family	Families per village
Mennonites	Khortytsia (17)	874	41,345	47.3	51.4
	Molochna (41)	1,698	75,783	44.6	41.4
	Total	**2,572**	**117,128**	**45.5**	**44.3**
Germans	Mariupol (20)	612	14,187	23.2	30.6
	Josefstal (1)	63	1,399	22.2	63.0
	Molochna (23)	963	51,748	53.8	41.9
	Crimea (5)	206	0	0	41.2
	Berdiansk (4)	118	6,648	56.3	29.5
	Novomoskovsk (3)	148	6,269	42.3	49.3
	Total	**2,258**	**80,251**	**35.5**	**40.3**
	Jews (14)	1,062	0	0	75.9

Source: RGIA (DGR), fond 383, op. 29, d. 630, fols. 1r–17r.

in the average German family. Mennonite involvement in sheep breeding in the Molochna settlement continued to expand, and peaked with approximately 170,000 sheep in 1838, an average of more than 125 sheep per family.[46]

Several factors allowed sheep breeders to expand their fine-fleeced sheep operations energetically after 1820. First of all, sheep breeding placed minimal labor demands on the estates in a region that had almost no servile labor. Second, collapsing wheat prices reinforced the belief that sheep breeding was less risky than other agricultural pursuits. The cost of a chetvert of wheat, sold from a southern port, went from 20 rubles in 1811–1820 to slightly more than 15 rubles in the following decade. In the 1830s it rose slightly to 17.12 rubles before plummeting to 5.43 rubles a chetvert in the 1840s. The concurrent inability of estate owners to obtain consistently adequate grain yields reinforced the belief that grain cultivation should be pursued only cautiously; the real profits were to be made in fine-fleeced sheep.[47] These factors all led to a dramatic increase in the export of Russian wool, as shown in table 3.2.

Table 3.2. Russian wool bound for foreign markets, 1800–1841.

Period	Poods exported
1800–1814	19,813
1814–1824	35,173
1824–1834	111,546
1834–1841	337,888

Source: Veselovskii 1846, 152.

This tremendous expansion in the wool trade coincided with increased accessibility to markets. Permanent clearing houses were established in Odesa, and seasonal ones at annual markets in Katerynoslav, Kharkiv, Ielysavethrad, Kremenchuk (Kremenchug), and a host of smaller centers. The city of Katerynoslav alone possessed four seasonal wool markets. To streamline marketing operations, authorities closed two of them in 1835, and in their place created the prodigious Petropavlovsk market, where by 1837 were selling 150,000 poods of wool annually. The largest sheepbreeders in the northern reaches of New Russia were able to sell their wool on site, since it attracted agents within and beyond the empire.[48] In fact, the demand was so great that estate owners could bring shorn wool to market without even having cleaned it in a rudimentary manner, thereby reducing their costs substantially. Not only were markets available, but by the 1820s estate owners also had the advantage of observing highly efficient merino sheep operations, many of which had been founded with state grants. The *Odesskii vestnik* in 1827 publicized several of these model operations. One enterprise, comprising 13,000 desiatinas, had been founded in the early 1820s on the sandy, windblown steppe lands of Dnipro district, Tavriia province. Within four years the owner, Salos, had built up a herd of 6,000 sheep, which produced an annual yield of almost 900 poods of wool. He had constructed four ponds on his sprawling estate, both for sheep to drink from, and for wool-cleaning operations, and had two large sheds erected for the herd's protection. Salos even operated a school on his estate for shepherds, where he trained twenty young men in the craft. Rouvier, one of the originators of fine-fleeced breeding in New Russia, was highlighted in a subsequent article. As of July 1826, his herd had grown to more than 70,000 sheep.

This first generation of estate owners played an important role in the spread of merino sheep throughout New Russia. Rouvier himself offered choice rams and ewes for sale at markets throughout New Russia, as well as in Moscow, Kharkiv, Poltava, and Tambov. Others purchased their own estates and began to develop large fine-fleeced herds. By the 1840s the most notable estate owners, such as Shval′bakh and Somov, had founded associations for their enterprises, including the Oleksandrivsk Association of Sheep Breeders in 1841. A similar initiative was undertaken by the Molochna Germans, who had previously established a sheep-breeding station in their colony in 1817.[49]

Nowhere was the link between state sponsorship and individual initiative more evident than in the establishment of regional and colonist agricultural societies. Tsar Alexander I and his successor, Nicholas I, endorsed these societies from the outset, and they also attracted state officials, nobles, and colonists. The societies were driven by the positivist belief that the Russian Empire would be improved through the creation of a more efficient administration that was managed by enlightened bureaucrats committed to the spread of knowledge.[50] To that end an

Imperial Russian Agricultural Society was founded in Moscow in 1818, followed in 1828 by the formation of the Imperial Agricultural Society of Southern Russia (hereafter, Agricultural Society). The Agricultural Society was, in part, concerned with "the maintenance and improvement of sheep," as well as "the means to manufacture products from cattle and sheep breeding, as in the preparation of tallow and hides, as well as the washing and sorting of wool." To accomplish this the Agricultural Society committed itself to ongoing experiments and observations in the New Russian countryside, as well as to the gathering of international data. Its findings were first distributed in printed form to its membership in 1833 and thereafter continued to be published several times annually until the end of the Russian Empire. From the outset, the Agricultural Society identified and encouraged a wide range of agricultural activity as well as sheep breeding, cattle and horse breeding, sericulture and the cultivation of mulberry trees, viticulture, and apiculture.[51]

In the same spirit, the Guardians' Committee for Foreign Settlers, located in Odesa and responsible for all colonists within the region, formed the Molochna District Agricultural Union in 1830. Like the Agricultural Society, it had a broad mandate to disseminate skills in afforestation, horticulture, sericulture, and viticulture. However, it differed from the Society in that it became the almost exclusive realm of one individual: Johann Cornies. Born in 1789, Cornies became, in Harvey Dyck's words: "unquestionably the most influential leader to have emerged from within these [Mennonite] settlements." In 1811 Cornies established a thriving operation that bred fine-fleeced sheep on a private estate within the Molochna Mennonite settlement. His reputation grew quickly, as did his personal wealth, and in 1824 he was appointed head of the Association for the Improvement of Sheep Breeding. Cornies responded by purchasing the best merino breeding stock available both from within and outside Russia. The improvement in Mennonite herds was rapid. In 1830, already a wealthy and influential figure, Cornies was honored for his work and appointed the lifelong chair of the Molochna District Agricultural Union. Two years later, a similar Agricultural Union was founded in the Khortytsia Mennonite Settlement, and from there it spread to other colonists in the region. With his unshakable belief in economic betterment and his almost unlimited power within the colonies, Cornies played a central role in the development of Mennonite sheep breeding, along with all other agricultural activities. By the time of his death in 1848, Mennonites had become widely recognized as model agriculturalists in not only New Russia, but the empire as a whole.[52]

The Crisis of Fine-Fleeced Sheep Breeding, and Responses

With few exceptions, breeders of fine-fleeced sheep in New Russia experienced a near-debilitating crisis in the late 1830s. Some emerged from this difficult period with modified practices and in a much stronger position. Most barely managed to survive it, even though they had not made any adjustments, but they were subsequently hurt by a second, related crisis in the 1860s. An understanding of the first crisis, and the various reactions to it, provides a fuller view of both colonists and nobles as agriculturalists.

In his important investigation of sheep breeding in the Russian Empire, S. P. Shchepkin blamed estate owners for the poor care given fine-fleeced sheep in New Russia. As the owners acquired more delicate breeds in order to take advantage of their higher market value, they refused to provide them with the necessary care. As if to justify the consequent crisis, sheep breeders from Katerynoslav claimed that the sheer numbers of sheep in their province made adequate maintenance of the herds impossible. Shchepkin thought the care of merino sheep was even worse in Kherson province where "estate owners until recently only wanted to improve the number of merinos without regard for the care of them, or for their breeding stock." Indeed, there was widespread evidence by the late 1830s that previously inflated market values for merino wool had encouraged estate owners to disregard the opinions of those who had long advocated improved husbandry.[53] Most herds lacked adequate fodder, since few nobles provided any grain feed or constructed adequate shelter during inclement weather. Instead, sheep breeders flooded their pastures with imported breeds in the hope that the quantity of wool produced would offset deficiencies in quality. At the same time, other agricultural pursuits, including horse breeding, were simply abandoned.[54]

Beginning in the 1830s a dramatic increase in disease among fine-fleeced sheep led almost annually to significant losses and a steady decline in overseas markets. Natural pastures and hay meadows disappeared because agriculturalists began to cultivate more land in response to a steady rise in grain prices, and breeders had little alternative but to keep grazing their herds on existing pastures. Steadily increasing land values further strained the willingness of breeders to set aside adequate pastures for their sheep. As a result, the quality of feed became poorer on all but the largest estates. Under these conditions, livestock were even more susceptible to disease. Other factors now came into play, especially the New Russian climate, which had long made the region vulnerable to disease. Sudden shifts from intense heat to coolness, especially in the spring and fall, were particularly hard on sheep without a good wool cover or constructed shelter. Sheep that had wintered on low-quality feed also lacked sufficient body fat to protect their hides from cuts and damage from field grasses. Snowless winters and arid, hot summers reduced the supply of natural food sources available and increased vulnerability to disease.[55] Fewer sources of water were available during periods of heavy demand, especially during the warm summer months. Entire herds could become infected, since common watering holes were often the final destination for sick and dying cattle and sheep. Their bodies were then left to decompose on the open steppe, along shorelines, or in the watering holes themselves. Even when they were buried, carcasses were placed in shallow graves, often with their legs protruding. High levels of contamination were spread quickly by the dogs that roamed freely from village to village, or by livestock from other villages that used the same watering holes. With such little attention to the overall health of the herds, old sheep and young lambs were particularly susceptible to disease, and they exposed the others. In addition, villagers and estate owners often consumed water from the same source, a practice that made them vulnerable to disease.[56]

Owners regularly shipped diseased livestock to markets. Few owners quarantined sick and dying animals from healthy ones. Little was done to counteract illness and epidemics when they struck, as it was then considered too late to provide the sheep with salt or high-quality fodder. Vaccinations existed, but their use was hampered by cost, a shortage of qualified veterinarians, and superstition. As one sheep owner suggested, peasants who resisted having their children vaccinated against smallpox were unlikely to provide such preventative care for their own livestock or for the demesne herds under their supervision. The fact that serf and demesne herds often were pastured together increased the likelihood that disease would spread from one herd to another.[57]

The most common diseases afflicting New Russian sheep were diarrhea, worms (*glisty*), scab (*korosta*), mange (*sheluda* or *chesotka*), smallpox (*ospa*), and a variety of hoof diseases.[58] Diarrhea was commonly found in lambs soon after birth, and, if not contained, could spread through the stages of golden, mucous, and finally bloody discharges, and would almost certainly result in death. Disagreements about the cause of the illness hampered effective treatment. Given the popular belief that diarrhea came from spoiled ewe's milk, most breeders exacerbated the problem by removing lambs from their mothers as soon as possible after the onset of the disease. Worms generally appeared during the damp, rainy season of late fall. The most infectious of all sheep diseases in New Russia was scab, which could strike entire herds. Caused by a parasitic mite that was almost invisible to the eye, scab made the skin dry, brittle, and scaly. The fleece of an infected animal either fell off on its own, or was bitten off, or the irritated skin was rubbed off against a tree or fence post. The resulting cuts and infections led to further economic losses, since the remaining fleece of diseased sheep was of decidedly low quality. Scab was initially a problem only in the southern, saline sections of New Russia, but by midcentury the disease had begun to spread into the northern districts as well. As with diarrhea, there was little knowledge about treatment, and few efforts were made to cure the disease. Smallpox was only curable if a vaccination was administered, preferably in the fall. Without it, half a herd might die within a short period of time. Increases in smallpox were noted in the second half of the nineteenth century.[59]

Although aggregate figures for the region do not exist, the losses from disease and death were substantial. A correspondent to the *Odesskii Vestnik* in 1828 lamented that during the previous year he had lost ten to twelve sheep weekly from disease. A 1862 survey of Katerynoslav province suggested that 10 percent of all sheep in Oleksandrivsk and Verkhn'odniprovsk districts had died from illness that year, with losses on estates only marginally less than on peasant allotments. Another source indicated that scab alone accounted for annual losses of up to 10 percent of breeders' flocks each year. A stunning 16 percent of livestock in Kherson province was said to have perished in 1873 alone. Yet in many instances, breeders remained entirely ignorant of the disease, and especially of how it could be avoided or eliminated.[60] By the 1840s official reports were sounding the alarm about the decrease in the quality of wool production. The Department of Agriculture, attached to the Ministry of State Domains, notified the Agricultural Society in November 1848 that foreign factories were extremely dissatisfied with the quality of Russian wool. The report concluded that estate owners needed to provide better care for their herds if the situation was to be improved. Current practices in the washing and sorting of wool also came under criticism.[61]

In fact, a gradual and prolonged depression in regional wool prices was underway. Wool that had sold in the 1820s for up to sixty rubles a pood had fallen to no more than twenty rubles a decade later. Thereafter, and with the noted exception of the early 1860s, the decline was relentless, and Russian wool producers contributed to this collapse by their lax attention to the preparation of woolen export products. Prices paid for wool were determined by its cleanliness. There were three gradations: "muddy" (*griaznaia*), which was the normal state of the animal; "half-clean" (*peregonnaia*), by which sheep were driven through a small river or pond prior to shearing; and "washed" (*mytaia*), which involved a careful process using tubs with hot water.[62] Despite the obvious advantages of some form of wool cleaning, estate owners habitually sold wool in its unwashed state. "Muddy" wool was, by far, the most common category of wool brought to foreign markets, in part because the water shortage throughout much of the New Russian steppe made it difficult to establish more progressive washing operations. Nor was there much incentive to do so, since decades of high demand for Russian wool had minimized the cost differential between "muddy" and "half-clean" wool. Why incur added expenses in a cleaning operation when it barely altered the market price?[63]

In time, of course, quality did matter. When it did, these selling practices would come back to haunt New Russian breeders in the 1830s, as would the state's decision not to hire enough state inspectors to maintain exact standards, a factor that further lowered the market value of Russian wool throughout the century. Unscrupulous owners added to the problem when they disguised sacks of wool by putting a thin cover of washed wool over heavier, unwashed wool. In order to combat these practices, the Agricultural Society, as early as 1830, had proposed the appointment of wool inspectors who would establish uniform quality standards for wool throughout the region. Even definitions of "washed" and "unwashed" were woefully inadequate for European markets. Yet twenty years later the Agricultural Society was still having difficulty establishing uniform definitions and standards, despite the fact that every year thousands of laborers were entering New Russia to prepare wool for export.[64]

International factors played an equally important role in the transformation of New Russian sheep breeding. Of utmost importance were the rise of Australian exports and the simultaneous revolution in the British wool industry. As noted earlier, the genesis of Australian sheep breeding coincided with similar developments in the Russian Empire, and signaled the worldwide integration of enormous and far-flung regions into a Europe-centered economy.[65] For starters, it was soon apparent that sheep breeding and wool production were ideally suited to Australia, with its vast grasslands and arid climate. Unlike New Russia, grain cultivation was not viable in the South Pacific given the "tyranny of distance" separating producers of perishable goods from British markets. But wool, at ten times the value of wheat in the early nineteenth century, proved highly cost efficient and profitable for Australians, and they turned to it in staggering numbers. The sheep population in Australia skyrocketed from fifty thousand in 1813 to twenty-three million in 1860.

From the outset, Australians realized that their products could only compete in European markets if they were of high quality and supported by an efficient communications network. By midcentury, Australian sheep breeders had begun to dig dams for water, fence in pastures for greater efficiency, and inoculate their herds against disease.[66] At the same time, improvements in maritime travel and the subsequent introduction of inland rail transport further enhanced the marketability of their wool. No less important was Australian attentiveness to the changing needs of the British wool industry, where significant technological advances allowed the mechanization of combing between 1835 and 1870, which in turn made possible a sharp increase in steam-powered loom weaving. Corresponding changes in British fashion reduced the previously strong demand for pressed woolen cloth that came from the coarse-fleeced sheep breeds. The new market reality supported breeders who developed finer breeds and were able to produce a finer, high-quality wool. They were able to capitalize; the others would be left far behind.[67]

New Russian sheep breeders had numerous opportunities to respond positively to the daunting challenge and exciting opportunities before them. An article in *Odesskii Vestnik* in 1843 commented on the increasing number of complaints about Russian breeders from German and English industrialists, and on the ever attentive posture of Australian wool producers. The Agricultural Society published a report warning that English and Belgian factories generally regarded the quality of Russian wool to be well below that produced in Australia and the German states and of equal or lesser value than that of Bohemian and Hungarian imports.[68]

Initially, New Russian breeders and officials were confident that they could respond effectively to the declining market value of their woolen exports and surmount the Australian threat. They made efforts to improve the quality of estate fine-fleeced sheep breeding and to coordinate the efforts of the Ministry of State Domains, provincial governors (themselves responsible to the Ministry of Internal Affairs), and the Agricultural Society. In 1827 readers of the *Odesskii Vestnik* were invited to submit suggestions on how best to protect sheep from the spread of disease. Yet a decade later the Agricultural Society published an article, translated from the French, on the growing number of French breeders who vaccinated their sheep. The editor suggested that although such practices were found here and there in the environs of Odesa, they were almost entirely absent elsewhere in New Russia. The article was clearly intended to serve as a call to arms for the region's fine-fleeced sheep breeders.[69] In 1840 the same Agricultural Society published a "Manual for Sheep Breeders and Owners of Merino Sheep" in its journal, and was otherwise active in promoting improvements. Finally, in a letter sent in December 1849, the governor-general of New Russia recommended that the Agricultural Society establish regional standards to be followed in wool production. He further urged that more vigilance be shown in monitoring the wool export trade from Odesa and other port cities.[70]

Despite these efforts, the overall state of estate fine-fleeced sheep breeding continued to decline in view of the fact that estate owners refused to innovate. Most owners continued to define themselves as helpless victims of larger climatic and international marketing forces well beyond their control. One of New Russia's most progressive breeders lamented:

> We want to go forward, but often move backwards. We do not learn anything from anybody. We do not utilize the experience of others. We do not read anything related to agriculture, and if something appears before us in print, then it will not be seen to relate to the soil in this region, nor to the conditions in this country.[71]

An article translated from the *Bradford Chronicle*, written as late as 1861, was presented to members of the Agricultural Society in order to inform them of ongoing British concerns. Though the article acknowledged that some improvements had been made to the quality of New Russian wool, it stated that New Russian wool continued to lag well behind Australian wool in the ranking of European importers. The price to be paid for inferior quality can be seen in export figures. By 1865 Russia exported five million poods of wool to England, a small amount compared with the equivalent of over one hundred million poods from Australia—and this at a time when the American Civil War had made European markets receptive to wool imports from all parts of the world. By midcentury New Russian breeders had realized that they were even unable to compete with Australia at woolen markets in Moscow. Yet their only response was to demand that all imports be hit with a 20 percent tariff. With the internal markets collapsing, the president of the Agricultural Society, Prince Kolubev, warned of the complete collapse of New Russian wool production as it entered the second half of the nineteenth century.[72] Even so, on the eve of serfdom's abolition few of the large estate owners had completely abandoned sheep breeding. Although its fortunes had clearly fallen, sheep breeding continued to be a less risky endeavor than extensive grain cultivation, since the owners of these massive estates lacked an adequate labor force to care for the grain crop and the grain market was even more fluid than the wool market.[73] The peasants, who had long maintained more modest investments in simple sheep breeding, continued to rely on it as a supplement to their household economies.

Sheep breeding among the Mennonites ran a different course. The biggest change in the second quarter of the nineteenth century clearly occurred within Mennonite sheep-breeding operations. Unlike the region's noble estate owners, the Mennonites reached their high point in sheep breeding in the mid-1830s. Thereafter, it declined rapidly. For example, Molochna Mennonites had 170,000 sheep in 1838, but the number fell to 150,000 in 1840, and barely 100,000 in 1843.[74] Ironically, Russian nobles were expanding their fine-fleeced sheep breeding at the same time most Mennonites had decided to decrease herd sizes on their "model" operations. What accounted for this decision? The answer lies in the unique position that these agriculturalists occupied between the peasantry and the estate owners. Compared to the latter, the Mennonites' operations were modest. Their holdings of sixty-five desiatinas or less could not compete with the vast expanses of estates that had thousands of desiatinas. By the late 1830s the Mennonite villagers had discovered that with relatively intensive breeding operations their herd sizes had expanded beyond what was viable. Johann Cornies sent a clear warning note:

> Sheep are extremely important, they give a fine profit for little work, but other activities cannot be ignored. For example, the natural grasses which sheep eat into the very ground are disappearing from the fields. Already one can see that wool from sheep on these fields is of less value, and there is not as much of it. Also, the ewes are producing less milk, butter, and cheese.[75]

Mennonites knew that they had to make some hard decisions. They could maintain large merino sheep herds, but only by giving their horses less pasture. That would leave the horses with less energy, and they would not be able to plow so deeply. A decline in grain cultivation was sure to follow. Such a trade-off was unacceptable given the steady decline in wool prices and the increase in wheat prices at the time. Mennonites had already responded to the expanding grain markets. Grain sales within the Molochna settlement alone rose from 150,000 rubles in 1839 to over 200,000 rubles in 1846, whereas wool sales dropped in that same period from 131,250 to 54,566 rubles.[76]

By midcentury, then, the era of expansive sheep breeding and wool production had clearly passed, and those colonists who chose to remain engaged in it pursued a threefold approach. First, they steadily improved the quality of sheep in their colonies, while decreasing the quantity. To that end, and under Cornies's firm control, each Mennonite colony in 1843 formed a common herd of the finest ewes to serve as the core herd for the settlement (*po odnomu korennomu stadu*). Secondly, Mennonites who were still interested in large-scale sheep breeding sought ways to maintain their herds beyond their settlements in lands deemed largely unoccupied. In 1826, Cornies himself initiated this process by distributing sheep to the Nogai Tatars whose lands bordered the Molochna colony. The following terms were applied: the household head was to receive fifty ewes for a six-year period, after which they were to be returned, along with half of the offspring. The Tatars promised to maintain Cornies's sheep in the best condition and gave him the option of visiting his herds at any time in order for him to reward those who were following his program. Cornies placed almost eleven thousand sheep among the Nogais by the end of 1832.[77] Others soon followed his example, though none approached the scale of Cornies's involvement. On 1 November 1838 Dietrich Neufeld of the village of Altona in the Molochna settlement signed an agreement with Murman Mulmaliev, a Tatar from the village of Akkerman. Neufeld agreed to lend Mulmaliev forty-two ewes and two rams for a four-year period, after which both the offspring and the proceeds from the sale of wool were to be divided between them. More than 250 similar contracts between Mennonites and Tatars had been agreed upon by the 1840s, and the arrangement had become an important source of income for all parties. Even so, there was a tendency for Mennonites to shift away from undue reliance on sheep grazing, as seen in an 1848 agreement to pasture forty-six cattle—and not sheep—on Nogai lands.[78] Nevertheless, by midcentury, the Mennonite skill in fine-fleeced sheep breeding had spread to neighboring Molokans, Dukhobors, and Nogais, all of whom had begun to develop their own herds.[79]

The third alternative, practiced by both Mennonites and Germans, involved the purchase of large private estates for their own use. This radical departure was made possible by the enormous profits that many had acquired from grain and wool markets in the early nineteenth century. The most prosperous agriculturalists now sought far larger domains away from the constraints of village life, and it was here that they continued to engage in fine-fleeced sheep breeding on a massive scale. Initially, they concentrated on the mainland districts of Tavriia province, where land was plentiful, estate purchasing possibilities many, and prices low. By 1841, Mennonites from the Molochna settlement had purchased eight estates with over fifty thousand desiatinas, and Germans from the same district had purchased an additional ten thousand desiatinas. Some of these holdings had reached the size of the great Russian and Ukrainian estates in the south. The estates of the Mennonites Johann Cornies and Wilhelm Martens, and the German, Fein, quickly became three of the top four sheep-breeding operations in all of Tavriia province. Together, they maintained 220,000 merinos, more than a fifth of the provincial total.[80]

Conclusion

There were at least three distinct approaches to sheep breeding during the first half of the nineteenth century. Peasants were primarily motivated by the variety of needs that coarse-fleeced sheep met. Although reluctant to adopt fine-fleeced herds, their shift from the Kurdiuch to the Wallachian breed demonstrated their desire to take advantage of market opportunities after household interests were secured. Balkan colonists followed a similar path; indeed, they had played a vital role in the introduction of Wallachian sheep into peasant economies. By contrast, Germans, and especially Mennonites, were motivated by international market interests from the start. After Johann Cornies set things in place, their involvement in fine-fleeced sheep breeding developed quickly. But they just as quickly shifted away from sheep breeding when the markets so dictated, and when their landholdings could not sustain both pastoral and grain economies. Finally, the estate owners took an approach to agriculture that lay somewhere between the peasant and Mennonite approaches. The nobles wanted to gain the profits of the Mennonites without instituting any system of care for the more delicate sheep breeds. As a result, their animal husbandry did not differ markedly from that of the peasants, especially given the important role played by serfs in their operations. Though informed about international trends, the nobility were not attentive to them.

Like other frontier regions, New Russia at this time was blessed with considerable land holdings relative to the population and an abundance of natural resources.[81] Under such circumstances, several societies were able to exist almost independently of each other, as we have seen in this chapter. Even so, it is important to note that places of contact and overlap did exist; for instance, when peasants acquired new breeds of sheep from colonist immigrants, or when Mennonites relocated their herds onto Nogai lands. Such points of contact were more the exception than the rule; however, the situation was about to change with the forthcoming revolution in imperial land policies.

4

A REVOLUTION IN LANDED RELATIONS AND LAND USE 1840–1880

SERFS ON THE ESTATE OF A PRINCE BOBRINSKII, immediately north of the Crimean peninsula in Melitopol district, responded defiantly to the publication of the Emancipation Manifesto on 19 February 1861. They claimed that freedom was finally theirs and let it be known that they would immediately and henceforth conduct their affairs as free men and women. Estate officials were alarmed by this show of independence. They declared that serf labor obligations were still required by law, even though the situation would change in the not-so-distant future. Yet these official declarations were uniformly dismissed by Bobrinskii's serfs, many of whom had been brought to the estate from Kharkiv and Tula provinces in the 1830s. They clung to the belief that they were free now. Finally, and in desperation, the estate bailiff successfully petitioned provincial authorities to dispatch a regiment of the imperial army that was stationed some sixty kilometers away. The regiment quickly restored order, jailed seven peasants and administered corporal punishment to four others deemed to be ringleaders in this willful act of disobedience.

Unrest on the Bobrinskii estate was no small matter: more than 500 serfs were listed in the 1858 Revision. Soon, similar protests spread to peasants on adjoining estates, including estates in the villages of Obytochna and Denisovka. Situated less than six versts away in Berdiansk district, peasants in these two villages declared in April 1861 that the Emancipation Manifesto had immediately freed them from all future labor obligations to the lord of their estate, Count Tolstoi. Sensing that the former serfs were highly agitated and on the verge of civil disobedience, provincial officials attempted to correct the "misinformation" that had spread among these villagers. The peasants vociferously insisted that the decision to work on estate lands now depended solely upon the "free will of every peasant." Even local police, who were summoned after one of Tolstoi's own agents had been assaulted, were initially unable to restore order when they arrived on 19 June. Although the peasants appeared to give in to police pressure and agreed to make good on their labor commitments, on an estate of 1400 serfs only 6 showed up in the demesne fields the following day. Meanwhile the overripe grain on Tolstoi's own fields was flattened down and ruined. On 24 July 1861 the local police were joined by a detachment of 100 Cossacks who ordered peasants to appear for work on the morning of 27 July. Only 30 appeared on that day, and despite the Cossacks' efforts to bring in the remainder, only 130 former serfs had been rounded up by the end of the day. Now the authorities took a new approach: they identified and apprehended 16 individuals who "seemed to be the leaders in the *bunt* and in other disturbances." The tactic succeeded, and thereafter serfs returned to the estate fields and order seemed to be restored.

Both protests disturbed provincial officials, given the overall prosperity of the serf villages involved and the history of decades of social peace there. In the end, most officials blamed the local authorities, who had failed to enforce estate labor demands when the issues were still relatively minor.[1] Of even greater concern was the realization that these incidents were not isolated exceptions or just reactions to the Emancipation Manifesto. In the 1850s and early 1860s there had been numerous other incidents on the great landed estates of New Russia. The vast array of peasant protests ranged from collective lethargy at home to individual flight abroad. All these examples suggest that the era of relative social harmony on the New Russian frontier had come to a dramatic halt. A new world was beginning to emerge during the second half of the nineteenth century, and the overall change was dramatic.

As late as the 1840s, New Russia still looked much as it had in the first quarter of the nineteenth century: a region where nobles presided over relatively tranquil serf villages on massive estates in the north, along both sides of the Dnipro River, and in the Crimea. Elsewhere there were much larger settlements of state peasants, primarily in a band of districts to the north of the Black and Azov coastlines and along the Dnister River. Finally, foreign colonists were concentrated along a sharply delineated east-west axis, from the German and Mennonite colonies in mainland districts of Tavriia in the east to the Greek settlements along both banks of the Dnister River in the west. New Russia was a world of several seemingly parallel universes, where contact between diverse agricultural communities was generally benign, minimal, and localized.

By the 1880s, however, a revolution in landed relations and land use had utterly transformed New Russia. Nowhere was this change more evident than on the private estates, where one generation of estate owners had anticipated the end of serfdom, a second barely managed to survive it, and a third thrived as a result of it. At the other end of the spectrum, the change was equally great. Those who labored on the great estates of New Russia had become increasingly disenchanted with their serf status in the years before the 1861 Emancipation Manifesto. Thereafter, despite the complexity with which serfdom was abolished and their initial protests to the Manifesto's terms, former serfs experienced a period of modest gains in the 1860s. Not surprisingly, for much of the decade former serfs and lords appeared to compete in a "zero-sum" game, whereby one gained at the other's expense.

New Russia consisted of more than the worlds of lord and peasant, however. The revolution in landed relations within certain colonist settlements at this time also had a far-reaching impact. Although the changes within the Bulgarian and Greek settlements were minimal, the same cannot be said with regard to Germans and Mennonites. From their earliest discrete settlements both groups expanded their holdings exponentially during the second half of the nineteenth century through large-scale land purchases all over New Russia and beyond. They established either new villages or massive private estates on these newly acquired lands. Such developments had a profound social and economic impact on New Russia's peasants, who went from years of relative prosperity and social peace to a decade of sharply increased tension and conflict. In short, the "in-between" lands of New Russia disappeared in midcentury, and as a result previously separate universes now intersected in a host of ways. Time would tell how well each sector would weather these changes.

What was the nature of this great transformation in landed relations and land use, and how can we account for the speed with which it transpired? What clues do these events give about the stability of the

New Russian countryside during the period of the Great Reforms? How successfully were New Russia's rural inhabitants able to adjust to their new circumstances? The events of this period have garnered renewed attention among historians interested in the changing relations between the Russian state and society.[2] That is not surprising given the significance attached to the emancipation of serfs in 1861, the reform of state peasants in 1866, and the end of a separate designation for colonists, which culminated in the military reform of 1874. In the larger historiographical picture, views on the social stability of the late Russian Empire and its potential for transformation into a parliamentary state are often linked to the events described above. Far less attention has been directed to the agricultural context and significance of the emancipation of the serfs—its long-term impact on rural society beyond the narrow confines of former serf villages. And almost no attention has been directed toward the New Russian countryside.

Land and Labor: The Background to the Emancipation Manifesto of 1861

By the mid-nineteenth century wheat had clearly become the new darling of European agriculture. After Great Britain abolished all taxes on imported grains, estate owners from France to Sweden were quick to sing its virtues. Suddenly the doors to international trade and commerce were thrown wide open, and by the end of the century British consumers alone would rely on foreign producers for more than 80 percent of their food requirements. Russian and Ukrainian producers enthusiastically responded to the new opportunities, just as they had done when the Napoleonic wars briefly and significantly improved market opportunities for continental grain producers. Subsequently, a period of stable relations with the Ottoman Empire in the 1830s and 1840s, the introduction of telegraph communications, and rapid advances in steam-powered vessels, all helped to strengthen the link between New Russia's producers and European consumers. Moreover, the concurrent drop in prices for exports of Russian wool further motivated New Russian agriculturalists to diversify their economies by cultivating more grains. As a result, Odesa's wheat exports expanded from an average of slightly more than 600,000 chetverts in 1830–34 to more than 950,000 chetverts in the following decade. By the late 1840s average exports topped 2 million chetverts, and they reached more than 3 million in 1853.[3]

New Russian grain producers contributed to these trends—especially those in close proximity to market cities or to an efficient means of communication and transport. The first areas brought under extensive, market-oriented cultivation in Katerynoslav province, for example, were in the south, close to the Sea of Azov. Taken as a whole, Katerynoslav province was the first to make the transition to large-scale grain cultivation. But after 1840 it was the private estate owners from Kherson province who made the greatest gains. Grains sown on private estates there increased from 127,000 chetverts in 1843 to almost 300,000 chetverts a decade later.

During the second quarter of the nineteenth century estate owners in both of these provinces seemed ideally placed for burgeoning international markets.[4] There were more than 2,400 estates in Kherson province at midcentury, and although the average estate only had approximately 1,800 desiatinas, many were truly enormous. For example, the Skarzhinskii estate had 70,000 desiatinas, and three other lords had holdings in access of 40,000 desiatinas. Yet all of these paled in comparison with the holdings of Baron Shtiglits, which spilled into three estates and comprised 126,000 desiatinas. With such land-rich neighbors, it is hardly surprising that estates in the region with fewer than 500 desiatinas were deemed to be "small holdings."[5]

Although detailed statistical investigations are lacking for this period, the best guess is that the average noble grew grains on 20 percent of his estate lands and set aside another 30 percent for pasture. That left half of most estate properties for hay meadows. In his study of Katerynoslav province at midcentury, V. Pavlovich concluded that the typical noble maintained a thousand fine-fleeced sheep for every thousand desiatinas on his estate. In addition, he set aside approximately one hundred desiatinas for the cultivation of wheat intended for regional and international markets. Finally, he grew rye and other grains on approximately fifty desiatinas. Under such conditions, most nobles had invested only modestly in grain production before midcentury, and they had done so with an eye to improving market values. By contrast, their serfs were far less active in cultivating grain, and did so almost exclusively to satisfy household needs.[6]

Overviews such as Pavlovich's provide a sense of regionwide dynamics, though they also conceal the dramatic advances that certain grain cultivators made during the second quarter of the century. Of these, Mennonite and German agriculturalists were the most active in the shift to grain cultivation, though few of them would have anticipated the market trends even as late as the early 1850s, when the cultivation of more than ten desiatinas on any given farm was still deemed excessive. For example, on 28 April 1852, the Mennonite preacher and agriculturalist Jacob D. Epp recorded in his diary:

> I finished the sowing today: wheat, 1 chetvert on 2 destinas [*sic*]; barley, 7 chetverts on 1 desiatina; oats, 7 chetverts on 1 desiatina; and millet, 1/2 chetvert on 1/3 of a desiatina. I borrowed the grain for seed and for our own use.

Epp cultivated only 7 of his 40 desiatinas (smaller than the norm of 65 desiatinas) in 1852, and these tended to be the fields most distant from the village, since he reserved the prime lands for livestock pasture. Yet less than two decades later the portion Epp devoted to grain cultivation had ballooned to more than 30 desiatinas.[7] Similarly, individual villagers in the German colony of Firstenau, in Berdiansk district, sowed only a few desiatinas in the 1820s and 1830s, barely enough for household consumption. Their cultivated land expanded to 10 to 15 desiatinas by the 1840s, however, and around 20 desiatinas a decade later. Subsequently, the growth of wheat cultivation increased exponentially, occupying more than 40 desiatinas of a 65-desiatina holding—an illustration of how Mennonite and German colonists were leading the way in New Russian grain cultivation. They also started to use a rational "four-field" system under which a quarter of all arable land was routinely rested from use as a grain field, hay meadow, or pasture—a practice that seemed to increase soil fertility and the likelihood of prosperous harvests.[8]

Owing to the initial terms of their settlement, the Germans and Mennonites were both enabled and compelled to reduce sheep breeding and experiment with grains. Almost all who settled in New Russia had received generous indivisible allotments ranging from fifty to sixty-five desiatinas per household in hereditary and perpetual tenure (see chapter 2). In addition, the imperial authorities ordered a sixth of all lands in each village colony to be set aside for future distribution among landless descendants.[9] Thus, Mennonites and Germans were able to adjust to the new circumstances of the steppe and prosper, in large part because these inheritance practices brought stability to landed relations. They avoided the splintering of holdings that adversely affected peasant farmers. In addition, the villagers who did not inherit a homestead contributed to the prosperity of the colony by settling on smaller household plots in the villages. Here they engaged in a range of agriculturally related crafts and trades. The descendants of Mennonite and German farm holders thrived in flour milling and the agricultural implement industry. Though a host of other factors, including initial privileges and cultural and educational background, were also important, the combination of a ready labor supply, artisanal support, and non-divisible landholding was decisive and proved to be the basis for the agricultural success of the Germans and Mennonites in Russia.[10]

Despite, or, ironically, because of their massive holdings, New Russian estate owners found themselves in a totally different situation—one that was not conducive to labor-intensive grain cultivation. The critical problem was their inability to provide an adequate labor supply for the vast amounts of land at their disposal. The average estate owner in Katerynoslav province had fewer than 67 male serfs, and the numbers fell to 60 and 52 serfs in Kherson and Tavriia provinces respectively, well below the empirewide provincial average of 100 serfs.[11] More than a tenth of these, in Tavriia province at least, were household serfs who were rarely available for field work. Ninety-seven estates in that province had no serfs at all. With less than a single male serf for every 500 desiatinas, estate owners would likely have viewed any reference to their economies as "serf-based" as largely ironic.[12]

The nobility's decision to begin developing extensive grain economies following the 1830s crisis in sheep breeding only exacerbated the labor shortages on their estates. How could they make ends meet? With few options available, many simply chose to increase their serfs' labor obligations. By the 1850s, New Russian estate owners regularly extracted no fewer than three days of obligatory labor (*barshchina*) a week from their male and female serfs in Kherson and Katerynoslav provinces, and often more. During peak seasons of haymaking, harvest, and carting these obligations increased to five, and even six days a week, but over winter they would drop just as dramatically. Under normal conditions, one day of labor consisted of the work of a given husband and wife and a pair of oxen. Peasants without oxen had to rent them from wealthier peasants or else suffer a significant increase of their labor obligations on the demesne. Estate owners occasionally acquired their own inventories in order to compensate for the peasants' meager resources. The peasants who used the owners' possessions were then forced to do more work. By 1850 a Prince Kochubei had acquired an inventory of over 100 oxen, 40 plows, 55 harrows, and 2 threshing machines for his estate in Dnipro district with its 126 male serfs. Other estates in the mainland districts of Tavriia province, where the machine-intensive operations of the colonists were most developed, began to follow suit. This practice gave the landowners a decisive advantage in dealings with their serfs.[13]

Increased *barshchina* demands forced peasants to spend less time managing their own economies during peak seasons in the agricultural cycle. When they were first settled, for example, peasants from the village of Vasylivka (Vasilievka), Melitopol district, were only required to set aside every third week to labor for their lord, identified only as Popov. Two decades later the requirement had grown to every other week, and by the 1850s even more was demanded. Those owners with fewer serfs increasingly compelled them to do more work. The Sokologorsk estate in Melitopol district consisted of 15,000 desiatinas, and possessed fewer than 20 serf families. By the early 1850s all of these families were denied any land other than their household plots, which forced them to labor regularly on the demesne lands. In Feodosiia district, 36 estate owners, who owned a total of 282 serfs, also required their serfs to fulfill daily labor obligations by the early 1850s. These increases were not limited to field work, since the expansion in grain cultivation meant that more laborers were required to haul goods to market. In a typical case in the 1850s, it took serfs from Vasylivka forty days to cart estate-produced vodka to the Crimea in the winter.

By midcentury, in response to rumors that the government would soon proclaim emancipation, estate owners began to alter the legal status of their serfs in a bid to maintain their dependency and vulnerability. The simplest way was for nobles to execute a paper transfer that gave their full serfs the status of household (*dvor'*) serfs, an act that dramatically reduced the serfs' legal right to land allotments. By 1859, the census count of almost 17,000 household serfs had ballooned to over 62,000, as many estate owners routinely identified more than half of their serfs as household serfs. Yet many of these "non-agricultural" serfs remained active in field work regardless of their designation. An example can be observed on Baron Shtiglits's 35,000-desiatina estate in Rogachitskii in Tavriia province. In 1858 Shtiglits identified 178 of his 1,922 serfs as household serfs. Yet an examination of their occupations reveals that 78 of the 178 were in fact shepherds, 28 were involved with the breeding and maintenance of oxen, 7 looked after beef cattle, and 11 were in charge of the horses. In total, more than half of those identified as household serfs were actually employed in the livestock economy, and in many cases their labor duties were so demanding that they were not able to maintain their own gardens. This pattern was repeated throughout the province. Thus, the recent scholarly assertion that a growing number of Russian nobles felt morally unable to justify the institution of serfdom on the eve of its abolition seems to be entirely inconsistent with developments in New Russia.[14]

Even with their more aggressive approach, nobles found that increased *barshchina* demands were insufficient to sustain their economies, and many of them were forced to rely on hired laborers during times of peak demand, such as seed-time and harvest. S. A. Sekirinskii's study of 99 estates in Tavriia province for 1858 identified 18 nobles who relied at least partially on hired labor. For example, one noble, Skodov, annually hired up to 300 laborers for his estate in Dnipro district. Otherwise he had to rely on 90 male serfs to maintain almost 11,000 desiatinas of land. General Mal′tsev hired hundreds of peasants annually to supplement the labor provided by his 222 male serfs, who were scattered across almost 24,000 desiatinas on three separate estates in the same district.[15]

Potential hired laborers for these estates seemed plentiful by midcentury. They arrived annually in the thousands from the central Ukrainian and Russian provinces to the north. In 1859 the historian Skal′kovs′kyi noted that 100,000 laborers entered New Russia legally, though the actual number may have been two-thirds higher. By his estimate, almost one-third of all estate labor in New Russia was completed with hired labor at that time.[16] Even so, it would be incorrect to assume that the region's estate owners had grown accustomed to non-serf labor by 1860. Only in such limited areas as the heavily grain-producing Taganrog region had hired labor actually come to define the overall system of agriculture.[17] In fact, their experience in the free-labor market before 1860 had actually convinced most New Russian nobles that hired labor threatened the viability of their economies. Leading the charge was the otherwise progressive Agricultural Society, whose members overwhelmingly favored economies based upon serf labor. By comparison, hired labor was deemed unreliable and expensive. A published account from 1848 estimated that a noble with 1,500 desiatinas could produce an annual income of 2,400 rubles from *barshchina*, but barely more than 400 rubles with hired labor. Another estate owner claimed that he hired 600 laborers a year during the summer months with a partial advance payment, only to find that many departed for other estates before completing the tasks they had agreed to do.

The problems associated with hired labor prompted New Russian estate owners to meet with each other to discuss common concerns. The first Congress of Estate Owners, held in 1859 in Pavlohrad district of Katerynoslav province,[18] concluded that nobles with the largest holdings were most vulnerable to the vagaries of the hiring market because of their dependency on it. By contrast, smaller estates required fewer laborers and were better able to squeeze optimum use out of their serfs. Smaller estate owners also had the luxury of being able to wait until the last moment before determining the number of laborers required, since for them the available supply far exceeded their demands. Nobles believed that it was essential to negotiate from a position of strength, because potential laborers could sense when a request for their services was desperate and they negotiated accordingly. To avoid this situation, nobles dependent on a large workforce would often visit several bazaars and hire small work parties at each.

All estate owners complained about the capriciousness of their hired laborers, and of how the custom of paying peasants by the day, rather than the season, left owners with little control and jeopardized each year's harvest. Similarly, most of the nobles who sat on the provincial committees that had been established by St. Petersburg to oversee the abolition of serfdom maintained that estate economies in New Russia would be ruined if forced to depend solely upon hired labor.[19]

There were, however, important exceptions to the attack on hired labor within the region. Although they were more dependent on hired workers because of their lack of serf labor, the Germans and Mennonites fared relatively well in the labor market. Indeed, there is evidence to suggest that peasants preferred to work on colonist farms because of the conditions under which they were hired. Unlike the estate owners, the colonists worked side by side with their hired laborers. Either men or women led teams of hired peasants to cut grain during the harvest, and in the words of one observer: "[the Germans] make no distinctions between themselves and their laborers; they eat all together, and from the very same table. However many times the owner drinks vodka, coffee, or wine, so will it be offered to the laborers. However many times he stops for breakfast or lunch, so do his laborers."[20] Under such close supervision, hired peasants clearly were compelled to work harder on colonist farms, but they seemed ready to do so. Many chose to return annually to the same colonist farms in a pattern that occasionally spanned generations.

The fact that nobles were generally land rich but cash poor was an obstacle for those who wanted to modernize their estates. Earlier, estate owners had been able to obtain credit by mortgaging their lands or their serfs,[21] but the closure of the state loan bank in 1859 dealt their economies a crippling blow. Although other credit institutions were opened in the following decades—most notably the Kherson Land Bank in 1864—their resources were meager at first. Cash-strapped estate owners remained vulnerable because of their constant need for loans. Also, the lack of competition allowed the existing financial institutions to increase interest rates.[22] In 1860 the first Congress of Estate Agriculturalists reported that the majority of estates had been mortgaged to government financial institutions. That was an exaggeration in New Russia's case, considering that the number of mortgaged estates there was relatively low when compared to other parts of the empire; however, the report helps to explain the high state of anxiety experienced by the region's nobility on the eve of emancipation. In fact, only one-quarter of all noble estates in Katerynoslav province (499 of 2,021) were mortgaged in 1860, although their holdings included at least half of the province's serfs. Under the circumstances, the estates in greatest financial need were also the largest and the ones with the most serfs. Whereas the average estate in all of New Russia had 55 serfs, the average mortgaged estate had more than 120.[23]

The Crimean War and Its Aftermath

The Crimean war of 1853–56 exacerbated the challenges that estate owners on the peninsula faced. The mortality rates of livestock and serfs skyrocketed as a result of war. Agricultural activity suffered as peasants and their animals were commandeered to haul troops and provisions to the front or to cart wounded soldiers back to cities and hospitals. The roads used to haul goods to market became badly worn from the movement of troops and supplies and were not quickly repaired. Energy went instead into the construction of military installations. Throughout the peninsula agriculture fell into ruins as fields were left unsown, sheep were commandeered to feed the troops, and vineyards were destroyed by neglect and vandalism.[24]

The region's hardships did not end with the cessation of hostilities in 1856. Shortly thereafter the Crimean Tatars began to emigrate from the empire, thereby draining labor resources from an already shallow pool. Such an outcome was hardly surprising. During the war, many Russians had treated the Tatars as little more than agents of the Ottoman Empire. Immediately after the war, there were rumors in Crimea that St. Petersburg intended to rid the peninsula of all undesirable elements, especially Tatars. In response, beginning in 1858, entire Tatar villages started to emigrate. By 1860 crowds of a thousand families or more appeared before the authorities to request permission to move to the Ottoman Empire. More than 165,000 Tatars had left the peninsula by the end of 1860, a figure that included 278 entire villages in Perekop district alone. Their departure was often spontaneous: they planted crops in the spring, but did not stay to harvest them in the summer. The sudden loss of the Tatar labor force hit Crimea's nobles hard, since they already suffered from an acute shortage of labor. Many petitioned the authorities to bring in peasants from the more populous lands to the north, and although the state supported their request, the resettlement was too slow and meager to fill the void. To the chagrin of local nobles, only 153 peasant families had been relocated from the central Ukrainian provinces to the Crimea by 1861.[25]

Serf Responses to the Late Period of Serfdom

Recent literature has emphasized the diverse means by which peasants voiced their opposition to the Soviet state under Stalin. By contrast, with the exception of pathbreaking works by Daniel Field and David Moon, studies of the imperial era have followed the lead of Soviet historians in stressing overtly aggressive serf outbursts on the eve of the emancipation.[26] There is no doubt that New Russia's serfs increased the frequency of their opposition in the 1840s, and especially in the following decade, even though it rarely amounted to a direct challenge to their lords' authority. Those who did confront their lords directly were quickly punished, as the serfs on the Fedorov estate of Ievpatoriia (Evpatoriia) district learned. In 1849, Fedorov transferred all estate peasants in the village of Kenehez (Kenigez) from *barshchina*, or occasional labor, to full-time work requirements. All except the aged and those under ten years of age were now expected "to work every day, not excluding high feast days." Despite higher labor demands, Fedorov's peasants still received no compensation for footwear or clothing, and only a minimal food allowance. Some years later, these same peasants requested that Fedorov reconsider this arrangement, and that they be permitted to revert to *barshchina* arrangements at the rate of three days per week. An incensed Fedorov refused their request and declared that their very demand was tantamount to engaging in an uprising (*bunt*) against the established order. Police were summoned and order restored, if indeed it had ever been lost. After an investigation, four peasants received fifty lashes each for their alleged role as ringleaders. One of these was also imprisoned and another placed in a military regiment for convicts (*arestantskaia rota*).[27]

Peasants in the prereform era quickly realized that any direct challenge or confrontation with their lords was foolhardy and opted instead for more indirect ways to exercise control over their lives. Contemporaries observed, for example, that the increase in *barshchina* demands did not necessarily result in greater productivity. In fact, serfs seemed to work less when more was required of them, in part because the increased work load for the estate made it harder for the New Russian serfs to feed themselves adequately. The added labor demands often limited the time available for serfs to work their own lands. Occasionally estate owners, captivated by the idea of large profits from grain production, even denied their serfs the lands necessary to sustain themselves, and thereby unwittingly contributed to the periodic famines. One-third of the sixteen thousand peasants who died of hunger in Tavriia province in 1844 were serfs, even though serfs comprised less than 7 percent of the province's rural population. Circumstances were so harsh that serfs from the Kankrin estate—where up to five hundred died from a lack of nourishment in the late 1840s—actually pleaded with the Marshal of the Nobility for Melitopol district for permission to join the army. When the serfs were asked to account for this request, they responded, "It can't be worse in the army than at our lord's!"

Although few volunteered for the army, a vast and growing number did seek to quit their surroundings. By one estimate, close to a thousand serfs fled eastward from estates in Tavriia province annually, enough to prompt authorities in the late 1830s to place an army unit at Perekop on the northern bottleneck of the Crimean peninsula. The unit was charged with the capture and return of fugitives. A report from 1841 identified serf vagrancy as a crisis that involved hundreds of serfs in each province of New Russia and that was spreading into adjoining regions.

Peasants also spread rumors to justify their acts of civil disobedience. Many claimed to have fled in response to promises from the tsar. One such rumor from Slov'iano-Serbiia district in the mid-1840s maintained that the tsar had promised that "those who manage to arrive in the Caucasus will immediately receive a pair of oxen, two cows, up to 100 rubles, and free land."[28] The linkage between rumors of this sort and the strong memory of the Cossack Sich was not merely coincidental. Settlers in New Russia still cherished freedoms that had only recently been taken from them.

The steady movement of peasants from the north in search of their own freedom also played a role in disrupting the supply of labor in New Russia, especially during and immediately after the Crimean War. David Moon has identified this "volunteer phenomenon" as being prompted by the government's efforts to undergird its armed forces immediately after the outbreak of hostilities in October 1853. Hundreds of serfs quickly made their way to the south, motivated by rumors that full civil freedom would be granted to all who arrived in the south and volunteered for a brief period of military service.[29] Serfs from the most northerly districts of Katerynoslav and Kherson provinces responded positively to these rumors: "The tsar sits in a gold palace and to all who come he grants their freedom, but to those who do not appear, or are late, they will remain as before in bondage."[30]

At first, peasants fled south at night, and as scattered individuals, though the situation soon changed. The war's end in 1856 actually fueled more peasant unrest: rumors circulated that freedom would be given to all serfs who voluntarily relocated to the Crimea and helped rebuild its shattered economy. Entire villages, comprised of large and intact extended families, brazenly left the lands of their lord and headed south. Parties of up to seven hundred individuals were seen departing from Verkhn'odniprovsk district, often leaving in broad daylight. Ten nobles from that district suddenly found themselves entirely bereft of serfs. The fugitive serfs refused to turn around when confronted. Armed with scythes, pitchforks, and stakes, they challenged a state already undermined by defeat in the Crimean War. Documents from Ananïv district, in northern Kherson province, linked the spread of rumors to soldiers on leave who had returned to their own villages and reported that "the mighty emperor had already long ago ordered that peasants be freed from the power of the noble, but that these same nobles have concealed this decree from their serfs."[31] Is there any wonder that acts of disobedience against estate owners followed? As serfs from the village of Pokrovske succinctly put it: "We do not want to be serfs. Instead we want to serve God and the government."[32]

By all accounts, peasants in New Russia whose land was made part of private estates after the conquests of the late eighteenth century had consistently resisted the attempts of estate owners to enserf them. After the Crimean War, even though the estate owners and local authorities warned the serfs to disregard the rumors of personal freedom, peasants from Voronezh, Poltava, Kharkiv, Chernihiv, and Kursk provinces in the Ukrainian north were resettling as essentially free settlers in the recently vacated lands of the Nogai Tatars in the Molochna basin.[33] In short, by the late 1850s the New Russian serfs had good reason to believe that better times lay ahead, even as estate owners feared the dawn of that new age.

The Emancipation and Immediate Reaction

Given the frustrations and failures associated with the hired-labor market, to say nothing of the challenges of capital-intensive agriculture, it is not surprising that New Russia's noble landowners joined the majority of their peers throughout the empire in resisting the emancipation of the serfs. Yet, when confronted with the seemingly irreversible will of Tsar Alexander II and his "enlightened" bureaucracy, the empire's nobility acquiesced. Rather than mount a direct challenge, they instead sought the best terms available in the new era, and if first impressions are anything, they succeeded handsomely.[34]

The Emancipation Manifesto of 1861 consisted of twenty-two separate enactments contained within 361 pages and was as complex and confusing as it was long. In essence, the Manifesto required that serfs remain in the custody of their lords for two more years, during which time land charters for the eventual emancipation were expected to be drawn up. The charters could either determine the final arrangement between nobles and serf villages or else serve as an interim arrangement for a seven-year period. In addition, the final size of the peasant allotments and the so-called redemption payments were determined both by regionally defined norms (changing population densities within the empire altered allotment sizes as well as the payment schedule per desiatina) and the legal status of the peasants (household serfs were only entitled to a maximum of a half-sized allotment, and often less). The redemption payments were also at least partly determined by the amount that serfs had owed to their lords before 1861 and by the amount of demesne lands that the serfs had previously worked. Thereafter it became the peasant commune's corporate obligation to pay the full cost of these allotments—known as redemption payments—over the next forty-nine years. Those payments were to be made to the state, which had agreed to compensate the nobles immediately.

Despite, or perhaps because of its complicated format, the final terms of the Manifesto clearly left estate owners with considerable latitude. For starters, there were no adequate records of land values or of the financial arrears owed by serfs, let alone the amount and location of the land worked by serf and lord respectively before 1861. Such distinctions were all the more difficult to determine in regions such as New Russia, where the principal obligation had been in labor, and where there was little distinction between peasant and demesne lands.[35] Under these circumstances, New Russian nobles capitalized on the options available to them. Land charters arranged in 1861 provided serfs with allotments that ranged, according to government decree, from 3 to 6.5 desiatinas per male soul,[36] well below the size of lands previously available to them. Overall, serf holdings in Katerynoslav province decreased from 533,452 to 344,614 desiatinas, and serfs in Tavriia ended up with almost 30 percent less allotment land than they had worked before 1861. Not only did serfs now have less land available to them, the distance from village to field often increased when estate owners deliberately intermingled their own holdings with those of their peasants.[37]

Allotments were not only smaller, they were also often of decidedly poorer quality, and included ravines, swamps, roads, and infertile sandhills. Examples abound of the harsh settlements that estate owners imposed on their serfs. In one instance, Strukov, an estate owner in the Dnipro lands of Katerynoslav province, ordered four entire villages to be moved to waterless stony lands on his property. In another, peasants in the villages of Ustynivka (Ustinovka) and Vasylivka in Dnipro district were given land in a sandy region that appeared unsuitable for grain production. Undaunted, these former serfs attempted to sow one desiatina per household in 1862, only to experience a complete crop failure. Thereafter, they left the village allotment lands as pasture and leased additional land for grain production from their former lord.[38] Former serfs on the Hromokliia River in Kherson district were denied lands immediately adjoining the river. Fishing and berry picking on estate lands were also prohibited. Even swimming required the estate owner's consent.[39]

A phenomenon unique to New Russia, which involved a special category of landless peasant known as the *desiatinshchik*, made the situation of some ex-serfs even worse. As mentioned above, many estate owners, beginning in the 1850s, converted a significant portion of their serfs to the status of *desiatinshchik*s by altering their legal status from fully-landed to household serfs, thereby depriving them of any right to full allotments after their emancipation. This administrative sleight-of-hand seemed to pay off handsomely for the owners. This practice affected almost 20 percent of all former serfs in New Russia (24,809 male revision souls), the highest proportion of which were located in the northern districts of Kherson province. More than half of the households in some villages received little more than their household plots after 1861.[40] Many did not even obtain that and were compelled to remain entirely dependent on sharecropping or the leasing of lands. As a result, the *desiatinshchik*s came to be some of New Russia's most vulnerable inhabitants.[41]

The imposition of greatly inflated redemption payments added an additional burden to post-emancipation peasants. In one instance, terms from the land charter awarded three villages in northern Katerynoslav province a total of 646 desiatinas at 47 rubles, 16 kopecks per desiatina, whereas the market value had been 13 rubles, 49 kopecks.[42] In addition to these inflated land values various taxes were imposed in order to meet the needs of the state and the newly formed provincial landed assemblies (*zemstvo*s), as well as local communal obligations, including the supply of materials and labor for local road and bridge repairs.[43]

Serf responses to this entire process serve as an indicator of social discontent in New Russia and as a benchmark for comparison with peasant unrest in 1905. Together, they help us determine if conditions among New Russian peasants improved between 1861 and 1905. Available information suggests that former serfs were vociferous in voicing their disillusionment with the reform process of the early 1860s, and repeatedly forced the state to restore civil order in the New Russian countryside with armed force. Up to 15,000 peasants from Tavriia province were involved in disturbances between 1861 and 1863. Official reports from Katerynoslav province declared that, at its peak, entire volosts of peasants were united in an opposition movement that took shape in three distinct phases.[44]

In the first phase, from the end of March to the beginning of October 1861, estate peasants first heard, and then rejected, the conditions set forth in the Emancipation Manifesto. The historian Mikhail Maksimenko describes a typical case from Melitopol district:

> The village of Ekaterinovka [Ukr. Katerynivka] belonged to the noble, Buturlin, and had 540 male souls as of the tenth revision [1858]. Most of these were peasants who had been relocated by the noble [to Katerynivka] in the 1830s from Tula and Kharkiv provinces. There were also a significant number of fugitive serfs here who were subsequently enserfed. The lord, having experienced an acute shortage in labor, endeavored to have his needs met by the increased exploitation of his serfs. In the years before the reform all of the work was completed by the peasants according to excessively onerous conditions. They were barely able to secure basic provisions for their families. Hence they were exceedingly disappointed when, on the 25th of March they were informed of the manifesto and its statutes, in which they did not find what they had hoped for. It was then suggested that this was not the real manifesto, but a fake, and that it was incorrect to say that three days [a week] of labor obligations were still required of them. Doubt in the authenticity of this manifesto was strengthened when the colonist, Jakob Manberger, appeared in the village intent on hiring labor. He proposed [*vnyshil*] that they were now free men, and that the manifesto, which had been read to them, was not authentic. On the 25th of March the peasants did not fulfill their labor obligations. The efforts of the district police officer [*ispravnik*], Tolstonogonov, to have the peasants honor the demands of the lord were unsuccessful. The peasants of Ekaterinovka then sent villagers to neighboring settlements to persuade them to follow their example. The appeal was picked up, and on the following day peasants from the neighboring village of Annovka [Ukr. Annivka] joined them, as well as from Mikhailovka [Ukr. Mikhailivka] and Elizavetovka [Ukr. Ielyzavetivka]. In sum 1,300 people were soon involved in these disturbances.[45]

Representatives of the governor were quickly dispatched to Katerynivka. They gathered the peasants together in the village square, but were unable to persuade them to fulfill their labor dues. Order was restored only after three regiments were dispatched to the village on 6 April, followed by public floggings and arrests. At the same time serfs in Odesa district refused to honor their labor obligations in February and March of 1861, believing that the Manifesto that had been read to them was fraudulent and contrary to the tsar's wishes. Others maintained that the tsar was about to seize all land from the nobles and give it to peasants. Similar disturbances were reported in Tiraspol and Ananïv districts of Kherson, and the entire northern rim of Katerynoslav province. However, serfs in the Dnipro districts of Novomoskovsk and Verkhn'odniprovsk were reported to be quiet and entirely accepting of the stated terms.[46]

A common ploy used by authorities throughout the empire, as seen in Katerynivka, was to blame the unrest on outsiders. Reports from Katerynoslav described the hunt for a transient, Lugov, who was said to have entered the province from St. Petersburg in order to stir up unrest among serfs. Even as authorities sought to arrest him, they feared that his incarceration would set off explosions throughout Slov'iano-Serbiia district, where he was rumored to be. In other instances, such as the one discussed in the introduction to this chapter, serf unrest in New Russia was linked to the relatively recent relocation there of serfs from the Ukrainian heartland: those serfs may have had unrealistic expectations about the future awaiting them in their new homeland.[47]

In addition, the very terms of emancipation added to the confusion, especially the institution of a two-year period of continued servitude during which the old arrangements were to fade away and new ones to emerge. Peasants who were initially confused by these terms eventually concluded that the watershed point would come in February 1863—the anniversary of the initial Manifesto—when complete and immediate freedom would be awarded. Official reports suggested that order could be assured only when the terms of the 1861 Manifesto had been "explained" to peasants, often with the assistance of regiments called to the site. Real dangers arose when peasants sought out others to interpret the Manifesto for them. For example, reports spoke of a "misunderstanding" among serfs from the village of Novosilka (Novoselka) in Bakhmut district who did not want their lord's representative to present the Emancipation Manifesto to them. Instead, the serfs chose one of their own, Sergei Khar'kovets, who read it and explained its essence to them. Almost immediately, the Novosilka serfs declined to fulfill any further requests for *barshchina*. At the same time, they sent four of their villagers to the neighboring village of Druzhkovka with the message that all labor dues should cease there as well. Once again, it took the arrival of the army, and the subsequent arrest of Khar′kovets, to restore some order to the villages.[48]

The second phase in peasant discontent began in the fall of 1861 when, with order restored, New Russian nobles began to introduce and implement the land charters. They faced the critical problem of determining exactly how much land had been worked by the peasants there prior to their emancipation. Faced with perennial labor shortages on enormous estates, the region's nobility had previously made large tracts of land available to their serfs so as to deter them from relocating elsewhere. As a result, serf land use had often been defined by the interests and requirements of individual households rather than by a noble's edict. Though much of this had been radically altered with the advent of extensive demesne grain cultivation from the 1840s onward, the issue of who had access to which land remained unresolved, and left most nobles uncertain as to how much land their serfs had actually worked.[49] Serfs and lords had often maintained separate sheep-breeding economies, yet pastured them together, and this further confused the issue. Could anyone expect that estate lords would record these ratios fairly?

Many serfs were disturbed by the twofold obligation of having to pay for their allotments at inflated prices and having to serve their lords for a transition period of two years.[50] Some refused to sign the new land charters composed by their lords or again attempted to withhold labor obligations as well as the payment of land taxes. A representative observer from Katerynoslav province noted that on 14 March 1862:

> ...[serfs] from the villages of Fedorovka [Ukr. Fedorivka] and Avgustinovka were gathered at a village council (*sel′skii skhod*) in order to verify the land charter they had received from the estate owner, Count Koskul. They refused to accept and fulfil the separate obligations, and pledged in addition that from the seventeenth onward of the present month they would neither fulfil their labor obligations nor those required in the land charter.[51]

In Kherson province, the refusal to sign land charters occurred most often in Ananïv and Tiraspol districts, where only 20 percent of all land charters had been signed by the summer of 1862.[52] Rumors continued to abound that the Manifesto of 1861 had not been issued by the tsar, but by the circle of "enemies of the people" (meaning estate owners and bureaucrats) who surrounded him. Hence many serfs continued to await the authentic Manifesto. Others claimed that they were not serfs at all, but state peasants, and should not be included in the land charters.[53] Unrest in Tavriia province centered in the mainland district of Melitopol, where serfs refused to honor labor obligations to their landlords and instead plowed up demesne hay fields for their own use.[54] It was during this period of negotiating land charters that serfs first realized their long-held and essential right of access to ponds, wells, and rivers had come to an abrupt end. Serfs from Kushkivka (Kushkovka) village, Odesa district, were informed that the right to fish in the adjoining river, or hunt along its banks, was henceforth the sole right of the estate owner.[55] The fifty-nine households of Kovalivka (Kovalevka) village were denied swimming rights in the Buh River, and serfs from Sofiïvka (Sofievka) village in the same district were not permitted to start trading establishments within the village.[56]

Unlike the disturbances of 1861, most of those recorded in 1862 remained localized and rarely invited outside intervention. The provincial authorities were still not satisfied, however. The governor of Katerynoslav province reported in August 1862 that the greatest impediment to progress at the time was the estate owners' refusal to gain the trust of their serfs: "With such unpleasant terms the peasants question the validity of these land charters, and naturally decline to sign them."[57] Regional administrators made personal forays into the countryside in order "to persuade peasants to trust the new law" and to abide by it.[58] Troops were made available to restore order in the most troubled areas, as on the estate of Prince Grigorevskii, where peasants burned down the sheep sheds on 30 April 1862, killing more than a hundred merino ewes.[59]

That same month witnessed the beginning of the third phase of the serf reaction to the terms of the Emancipation Manifesto. It came at a time of growing disillusionment with the entire process. Rumors spread that the "real" Emancipation Manifesto would be issued on the second anniversary of the first one (19 February 1861). Maksimenko estimates that more than ten thousand serfs were involved in disturbances during the course of 1863. In almost all cases peasants were demanding greater access to land and the liquidation of their obligations to the lords. A police report to Governor Zhukovskii of Tavriia province in April 1863 declared that "the peasants of Nasypkoe village continue to seize and make use of all of the lord's land and hay meadows." Order was restored only in May 1863, when these peasants, newly designated as household serfs, were compelled to accept quarter-allotments of land. At the same time serfs on the estates of Count Tolstoi refused to honor their labor obligations, and thereby threatened the harvest of hundreds of desiatinas.

The largest disturbances in Tavriia province occurred in Dnipro and Melitopol districts, where estate owners were the most vulnerable. In January 1863 more than twelve hundred serfs belonging to Prince Grigoriev and Count Kochubei announced that they only intended to work for their lords until 19 February 1863. They insisted on the final receipt of their land on that day at no cost. If their request was denied, "the authorities could do with them what they wanted, but they would no longer work on the demesne for their allotments, or for a wage (*obrok*)." This disturbance dragged on for two months, and included the personal intervention of the governor himself before arrests were finally made and the peasants conceded defeat.[60]

Estates in Slov'iano-Serbiia district, Katerynoslav province, reported nighttime attacks on their estates beginning in late December 1862. However, the peasants, armed with wooden sticks and farm tools, were no match for the Cossack regiments that were quickly dispatched to the site. Similar outbursts were reported in the serf-rich districts of the northern portion of the province, where large crowds of serfs would gather at bazaars and markets to exchange news and opinions.[61]

In almost all cases, order was restored under the visible threat of physical force and with the arrest of those deemed to be instigators. By 1864 provincial governors were reporting that disturbances were negligible and the former serfs—now labeled "temporarily-obligated" peasants—had adjusted to their new circumstances. An abundant harvest in that year was clearly beneficial, as were the opportunities available for peasants to lease additional land when needed. Reports of tension now focused on the peasant communes, where some peasant villagers turned against the leaders who had negotiated the land charters on their behalf.[62]

In general, New Russian serfs in the early 1860s exhibited the same hostility to the Emancipation Manifesto as was found elsewhere in the empire, though perhaps to a lesser degree, given the relative ease with which troops maintained order. In addition, the presence within the region of large numbers of state peasants and colonists, whose experience of emancipation was less harsh, had a stabilizing effect on the region, as did the ready availability of supplemental forms of income for most peasants. Nevertheless, serf discontent in the 1860s did result in numerous disturbances that briefly and significantly threatened the peace of the region. It remained unclear as to how former serfs and estate owners would adjust to the new circumstances in the coming decades. The region was rapidly losing its frontier character. Would they be able to make the necessary adjustments by transforming their extensive economies into intensive ones?

Life after Emancipation

At first glance, the Emancipation Manifesto appears to have placed estate owners in a commanding position within the countryside and made their former serfs even more vulnerable. And yet, despite the famed "cut-offs"—by which Lenin later referred to lands denied to peasants after their emancipation—inflated redemption payments, and shifting land allotments for most serf households, the initial results clearly favored the peasants, and the estate owners seemed to be disoriented. Many nobles neglected agriculture on their estates and hurried to divest themselves of their properties. In 1868 the governor of Kherson province expressed his dismay at the turn that estate agriculture had taken in the new era: "land is worked by the least expensive means. Root grasses are not sown in the hope that natural hay meadows will do. The wasteful allocation of pasture for livestock, especially sheep, often gives so little fodder that, in spite of the breadth of the prairie, livestock often die from insufficient food."[63] In the immediate reform era nobles generally worked only a small portion of their land with hired labor. The rest was left in pasture or else leased back to their former serfs. At the same time, most of the estates in the province were still faced with crippling debts and fewer resources to alleviate them.[64]

Four years later, the governor's annual report declared that estate agriculture had steadily declined after 1861, and again the problem was blamed directly on the shift to hired laborers: "of one hundred peasants hired as laborers, forty will not honor their agreement."[65] A paper presented to the Agricultural Society in 1864 declared that estate owners could not decide whether land should be leased out or worked with hired labor. The situation of noble estate owners was perhaps best described two years earlier by the vice president of the Agricultural Society: "the destruction of serf labor…has arrested, and will continue to delay, the development of our agriculture. It has resulted in a decrease in the amount sown at present, if not by half, then at least a third, and it will continue to decrease." If trends continued, he predicted regional paralysis, with the devolution of all southern cities, including Odesa, into simple peasant villages.[66]

A particularly poignant account from this period was left by an anonymous estate owner who wrote: "At present, the economies of the majority of our nobles are similar to ships after a storm, with ragged rigging, and without sails or a rudder." Suddenly New Russian nobles were haunted by their neglect of agriculture before 1861. They simply did not know how to manage their estates, and they could not be expected to introduce new techniques when they had not bothered to master the old ones. "We have often heard discussions," the author continued, "between several gentry estate owners, who declared in extreme naivete that it did not take any brains to engage in agriculture, and that scientific knowledge was utterly useless for it."[67] Those most concerned about agricultural progress in the region recognized that few nobles in New Russia had bothered to educate themselves, or their children, in agriculturally related skills; nor had they paid any attention to prudent accounting and cost-saving measures. This proved to be a heavy legacy for them after 1861.[68] With only noted exceptions, estate owners did not know how to proceed.[69] It was with dismay that Skal′kovs′kyi referred to a landowning friend who had more books in his home (none relevant to estate management) than wheat on his farm.[70]

Part of this void was soon filled by agricultural journals, which burst forth with articles from successful estate owners and agricultural societies and provided important clues on how the region's nobility might best proceed.[71] In response, New Russian nobles developed several different strategies in this era of revolutionary change, among which was a renewed interest in large-scale sheep breeding. In many respects sheep breeding was a natural involvement, given the enduring assumption that fine-fleeced sheep produced a healthy profit with only minimal input. Having weathered the wool-marketing crisis of the late 1830s, it now seemed as if New Russia in the early 1860s was ideally suited to large-scale investments in fine-fleeced sheep breeding. Through it the estate agriculturalists might yet be saved.

Both regional and international factors prompted New Russian estate owners to expand their investment in sheep breeding in the decade following the Crimean War.[72] Of special importance was England's steadily growing urbanization coupled with the temporary blockade of American products during their Civil War, which increased demand and drove the prices offered by Odesa exporters well above previous levels (see table 4.1).

Table 4.1. Export prices (rubles per pood) at Odesa for uncleaned merino wool, 1847–1876.

Years	Price
1847–1851	4.97
1852–1854	6.41
1857–1861	8.33
1862–1866	7.92
1867–1871	5.09
1872–1876	6.43

Source: Grotto-Slepikovskii 1897, 44.
Note: No figures are available for 1855–1856.

Regional wool prices in the ten-year period after 1847 almost doubled and remained high until the mid-1860s. New Russian estate owners now sought to take advantage of these rising prices, especially in the southern districts where massive estates were situated, and where serf labor had suddenly evaporated.[73] While statistical information for this period must be used with caution,[74] one source estimates that the number of fine-fleeced sheep in New Russia increased by 60 percent from 1856 to 1864 (from 4,417,000 to 7,186,000), and that wool exports reached almost twenty million poods by the latter date.[75] These rapid increases allowed sheep to play a far greater role in New Russian estate economies than in other regions of the empire. In 1864 there were an estimated 239.7 sheep for every hundred people in South Russia,[76] a ratio that left it second only to the vast Siberian steppe regions of the empire. By contrast, the central Ukrainian provinces of Voronezh, Kharkiv, and Poltava counted 94.8 sheep per hundred people. Within the southern steppe provinces themselves, sheep accounted for 40 percent of all large livestock (including cattle and horses), whereas that number slipped to 28 percent of the total in the above-mentioned provinces of central Ukraine. There is no doubt that at this time New Russian nobles dominated the empire's fine-fleeced sheep market.[77]

Yet another measure of the burgeoning wool trade was found in the export figures (see table 4.2). These figures clearly indicate that favorable market conditions during the reform era encouraged estate agriculturalists to increase herd size, since wool exports were greatest (1862–66) immediately following the period of highest prices (1857–61) (see table 4.1). Had this trend continued, it could have spelled trouble for the former serfs who had also come to depend on estate lands. However, the period of expansion of the wool trade came to an abrupt end in the late 1860s, when changing market demands combined with an unprecedented pressure to use land for grain production. Fine-fleeced sheep breeding ceased to be a viable pastoral economy for all but the largest of New Russia's estate owners. As table 4.1 shows, prices for wool in Odesa from 1867 to 1871 were the lowest they had been since the late 1840s, and marked

Table 4.2. Wool exports from the Black and Azov seas, 1847–1881.

Years	Weight (in thousands of poods)	Value (in thousands of rubles)
1847–1851	292	3,382
1852–1856	330	2,248
1857–1861	455	7,621
1862–1866	591	6,227
1867–1871	538	5,602
1872–1876	518	4,561
1877–1881	516	3,686

Source: Grotto-Slepikovskii 1897, 52.

a dramatic decline from the previous decade. Declining foreign wool prices immediately resulted in a decline in wool exports: they fell from an average of 590,800 poods during 1862–1866 to 537,600 poods and 518,000 poods during the next two five-year periods.[78]

During these years Russian wool producers were still confronted with the bad reputation that their exports had gained, itself a reflection of the lax attention they had paid to all aspects of sheep breeding. They had become aware of the problem during the crisis of the 1830s, but they still had not adequately addressed it. At the same time, by the late 1860s many estate owners realized that they had exhausted their pastures. Their herds had expanded without regard for available land, and virtually no attention had been directed to the provision of essential food sources. Often they were left with little more than weeds to feed their herds, and rates of disease and death began to skyrocket. A survey of Katerynoslav province suggested that 10 percent of all sheep in Oleksandrivsk and Verkhn'odniprovsk districts died from illness in 1862. Another source indicated that scab alone accounted for annual losses of up to a tenth of the herds.[79] The years 1867 and 1868 were particularly difficult: a combination of various diseases prevented many of New Russia's sheep breeders from marketing any fleece then. Losses reached an estimated three out of eight million animals and prompted countless estate owners to sell off entire herds.[80]

New Russian sheep breeding might have disappeared completely had several factors not intervened. For one, the price of wool, which had dropped precipitously at the end of the 1860s, rebounded slightly thereafter, and then stabilized for much of the following decade. This was partly due to the sudden dearth of wool available for sale at southern ports after frustrated owners rapidly sold off their herds.[81] Secondly, estate owners continued to believe that sheep breeding, for all its difficulties, remained well suited to their large land base and vulnerable labor supply. Nevertheless, the relative importance of sheep breeding in New Russia had permanently declined. Once again, as they had done decades earlier, New Russian sheep breeders called for increased tariffs on imported wool from Australia, though this time from the current twenty kopecks a pood to three rubles. The state took no action, however, nor did the newly formed zemstvos support them, in large part because the latter's interests had shifted from sheep breeding to grain production.[82] The sudden decline in sheep breeding was clearly reflected in regional reports to the Valuev

Commission in 1872–73: only one submission mentioned an absolute increase in numbers. Agricultural reports from Kherson province did not even consider sheep breeding, focusing on grain production instead.[83]

The expansion of sheep breeding on the New Russian steppe had been undertaken with a minimum of attention and supervision on many estates, as if neglect were a virtue. While some estate owners adapted to changing market conditions, others continued to rely on previously successful practices. To give but one example, only twenty-six of the eighty-two large private sheep breeders questioned in an agricultural survey of the region in 1880 had bothered to introduce even a partial selective-breeding program for their herds.[84] Their reluctance to invest in improved sheep breeding was a source of considerable frustration to S. P. Shchepkin, a longtime proponent of agricultural development in New Russia. In 1869 he enviously observed the efforts being put into grain cultivation:

> While land [in New Russia] was inexpensive, agriculturalists were mainly concerned about increasing numbers of merinos, and this increase can mainly be attributed to *metis*, i.e., the cross-breeding with coarse-fleeced sheep. But before sheep breeders could reach their goals, agriculture took on a broader extent, thanks to the strong export of grain...agriculturalists paid and paid thousands for steam-powered threshing machines, which presently are distributed everywhere in Kherson province, yet complained about spending hundreds on rams: many agriculturalists presently employ machinists for a high wage, but can't be bothered to look for herd supervisors.[85]

Shchepkin was aware that some estate owners had attempted to adjust to the simultaneous challenges of life after serfdom, the collapse of the wool market, and the steady rise in grain prices, and had done so by investing in the most advanced agricultural implements available. Faced with perennial shortages in labor, they reasoned that these capital investments would yield immediate profits. Unfortunately, enterprising estate owners often outran their capital and found themselves unable to continue. A representative case is that of A. N. Bulatsel′, who owned Arkhanhelsk (Arkhangelskoe), a 3,000-desiatina estate in Bakhmut district, Katerynoslav province. In 1870 he attempted to work his own land with the most advanced equipment and with the best hired labor available. But it was clear that he would not be able to achieve adequate results. Bulatsel′ then adopted another approach. In a formal arrangement with his former serfs from the village of Arkhanhelsk, Bulatsel′ agreed to give over his entire estate—with the exception of his main buildings, the yard, and a few fields—to the villagers for a six-year period. During that time, the peasants had the right to sow up to 300 desiatinas of wheat, but were also obligated to sow an additional 300 desiatinas for Bulatsel′, and to bring in his harvest. Finally, the lessees were allowed to use the rest of the estate as hay meadow and pasture, though Bulatsel′ reserved the right to have his own livestock pasture under their supervision.[86]

New Russia's nobility began to sell or lease out their lands at a frenzied pace after 1861. Members of the Agricultural Society and provincial officials viewed such practice with dismay, fearing that lessees would be careless in their agricultural practices and risk the exhaustion of the soil.[87] However, official appeals to curtail such arrangements went unheeded. Faced with the unprecedented opportunities and pressures of the post-reform era, nobles intent on procuring an income from their lands had to decide whether to develop cash economies, to lease out their lands, or to arrange some manner of sharecropping. They overwhelmingly chose to lease the land. A contemporary investigation of landholding in Kherson province during the 1870s suggested that the nobility managed no more than 15 percent of all privately held lands.[88] These were not merely short-term trends, since nobles continued to lease out between one-quarter and one-half of all their holdings into the 1880s.[89]

In 1871, the Kherson zemstvo commented on the lethargic state of estate-managed agriculture that had prompted this shift:

> Thanks to the climatic conditions of this region on the one hand, and the insufficient capital, labor, implements, and the most elementary information necessary for the proper managing of one's business on the other, agriculture in Kherson province still finds itself in a completely unsatisfactory state…[with the] majority of gentry giving their estates to leasers.[90]

In 1875, an agent for the Kherson province zemstvo, N. K. Kalaeorgi, was sent to Illinske (Ilinsk) volost in Odesa district to complete a study of estate agriculture there. The first three estates he considered were entirely leased out to peasants, who were charged up to seven rubles a desiatina if the land was used for intensive gardens, and only four rubles if it served as a pasture.[91] How accurately does this finding depict peasant-noble land relations in the immediate post-reform era? Unfortunately, it may be impossible to know, since the leasing arrangements that nobles made with their peasants were generally informal. But whatever the exact percentage, the supply of noble lands in the 1860s and 1870s remained large enough to assure relatively low lease rates and in Katerynoslav province actually led to a drop in land values to levels predating the Emancipation Manifesto.[92] The trend toward large-scale leasing was further encouraged by the collapse of European wool markets in the 1860s and the fall of grain prices in the 1880s, both of which reinforced the tendency of estate owners to avoid an active involvement in estate management.[93]

Former serfs were among the prime beneficiaries of the glut of lease land, especially since the scale of estate abandonment kept land values remarkably low at a time when rising grain prices made tillage more attractive.[94] In fact, former serfs found themselves in a remarkable situation in the 1860s and 1870s. During this time, they were disillusioned with the allotments that had been awarded to them, which they deemed too small to sustain their households, given the relatively poor condition of the soils as well as the high redemption payments expected for them. Not surprisingly, many peasants actually turned their back on the lands allotted to them after 1861 and opted instead to lease the more fertile adjoining estate lands at far lower rates. V. E. Postnikov, author of a magisterial study of New Russian peasants published in the late nineteenth century, noted: "former serfs do not regard their allotment lands as the dainty treat that they are in other places, on account of the small income derived from them and the possibility of relatively inexpensive leased lands beyond the commune." In one representative former serf village, Makedonivka (Makedonovka), in Slov'iano-Serbiia district, Postnikov observed that "recently the quarrels [for allotment land] have declined, as peasants prefer to lease land adjoining Kamensk volost in the Don oblast, where they can take large parcels (of 200 to 300 desiatinas), and are not left with scraps, as on allotment lands. And it is even cheaper, at 2 to 3 rubles a desiatina and less, when for allotment land one has to pay 12 rubles per soul."[95]

Leasing arrangements in the 1860s and 1870s were ideally suited to former serfs, because they were short-term and involved a modest combination of payment in cash and kind. The example noted earlier of the Bulatsel′ estate is representative. Even the landless *desiatinshchiks* lived well under these arrangements. Many established villages on leased land in exchange for fixed labor dues and a modest lease rate that was lowered if the size of leased land increased. As a result, *desiatinshchiks* were able to focus their energies on livestock acquisition and grain cultivation, which allowed them to develop fixed household economies that were relatively more prosperous than those found among allotment peasants. The one concession *desiatinshchiks* made was that all immovable property, including buildings, would revert back to the estate owner at the end of the lease.[96] But that did not seem likely in the first two decades following the Emancipation Manifesto.

The availability of seemingly endless amounts of lease land also had a profound impact on landed relations within former serf villages. Although village allotment lands were divided up among all registered male souls in 1861, in the early 1870s no one was calling for a repartition of those lands that would take into account the new generation that had come of age—but had not been registered—or the older generation that was dying off. Indeed, a study of Slov'iano-Serbiia district, Katerynoslav province, in the mid-1880s revealed that 56 of 134 former serf communes had not had a partition of any kind in over a generation. Even those that had been repartitioned had made only minor adjustments. All agreed that the new generation of former serfs did not want the allotment lands and the financial obligations that came with them. Instead, they preferred to lease non-allotment holdings from private estates. If anything, it was the discovery of coal deposits in Slov'iano-Serbiia district that may have led to a regionally high demand for allotment lands, given the increased opportunity for financial remuneration. As a case in point, in Kherson province former serfs firmly rejected radical repartition, and only 4 of 1,522 former serf communes had repartitioned by the end of the 1880s.

Meanwhile almost all former serf households leased land. In Berdiansk district, Tavriia province, for instance, 90 percent of former "full-allotment" serfs leased estate lands in the 1880s, compared with only 50 percent of former state peasants.[97] Indeed, it is worth noting that former serfs were highly dependent on this access to inexpensive lands for lease. They were not alone—others also took advantage of the new opportunities to lease estate lands, including "former" German and Mennonite colonists. Nor were only nobles involved in leasing out their estates, as can be seen by the examination of land sales in table 4.3 below. This table suggests that the amount of land sold by New Russian nobles was consistently high for the entire period. It is also apparent that the average number of sales per year rose steadily and, finally, that the average size of land sold steadily decreased from the 1860s to the 1880s.

Table 4.3. Land sales in New Russia, 1863–1892.

Province	1863–1872	1873–1882	1883–1892
	Average number of desiatinas sold per year		
Katerynoslav	73,517	97,993	105,893
Kherson	118,966	110,721	111,124
Tavriia	81,574	97,553	80,206
New Russia (provincial avg.)	**91,352**	**102,089**	**99,074**
European Russia (provincial avg.)	**44,736**	**77,149**	**63,250**
	Average number of transactions per year		
Katerynoslav	191	298	293
Kherson	323	365	506
Tavriia	159	348	644
New Russia (provincial avg.)	**224**	**337**	**481**
European Russia (provincial avg.)	**250**	**487**	**578**
	Average number of desiatinas per transaction		
Katerynoslav	385	329	361
Kherson	368	303	220
Tavriia	513	280	125
New Russia (provincial avg.)	**422**	**304**	**235**
European Russia (provincial avg.)	**179**	**158**	**109**

Source: *MSDZ*, tables 1–3.

Germans, Mennonites, and the "Great Dispute over Land"

Nobles in New Russia were quick to sell off their estates after the emancipation and did so at a pace that was faster than elsewhere in the empire. The amount of land sold each year in New Russia also far exceeded empire-wide averages, as did the average size of each transaction. These trends reflect a significant social revolution that was underway in the post-emancipation countryside; one in which peasants, estate owners, and colonists all participated. Although peasants purchased a small portion of these lands, most went to a new landowning elite—especially former Mennonite and German colonists—who took a more active part in the management of their estates. This new landed elite dramatically altered the shape of the New Russian countryside by implementing agricultural practices that made less land available for lease, thereby compelling former state peasants and serfs to reexamine their own land-use patterns.

The rapid sale of noble estates after 1861 might have benefited former serfs more had they had become actual buyers of the estates or if they had not become dependent on those lands through various leasing arrangements. In fact, the most active purchasers were former German colonists and Mennonites, Jewish entrepreneurs, merchants, and other nobles, whose acquisitions reduced the amount of land available for peasants to lease or purchase.[98] Of the new owners, the Germans and Mennonites stood out. By 1900 they owned as much as half of all peasant private holdings in Kherson province. By a different measure, they owned almost a fifth (involving 18 percent, or 493,243 desiatinas) of all private lands in the province at the end of the nineteenth century.[99] Such a statistic is all the more remarkable because, according to the 1897 census, only 4.52 percent of the province's population identified itself as German, which by that date officially included Mennonites, and many of these lived in towns and cities.[100]

What accounted for the red-hot activity in estate purchasing? The involvement of German and Mennonite colonists in aggressive land purchasing should be seen against the background of economic and social developments in the first half of the nineteenth century, especially the state-imposed land inheritance structure that did not permit them to redivide their farmsteads. At the same time, many members of successive generations were unable to obtain farmland in the settlements, which left them angry and frustrated. They were unable to utilize even the reserve land within the colonies that had specifically been set aside for this purpose, because almost all that land had been claimed by the full farmers (the 65-desiatina holders). As early as 1841, a distinct gap between landed and landless Mennonites was noted in the largest settlement of the Molochna in Tavriia province, where landless families numbered 1,700 of a total of 2,733. The problem was exacerbated by the fact that the landless were also disenfranchised and therefore unable to have their voice heard at village assemblies.[101]

Still other factors contributed to this crisis. Many of the landless Mennonites who did not engage in artisanal work depended on land leased from Tatars in the adjoining region, but after the Crimean War a majority of Tatars emigrated and the state settled Bulgarian colonists and state peasants on the land.[102] As a result, long-brewing internal tensions among Mennonites came to a boil in the early 1860s. Initially, the Mennonite landless sought access to the existing unallocated lands within the Mennonite colonies, but their landed co-religionists turned them down.

In the words of historian Harvey Dyck:

> The cottagers and renters then flooded the Guardianship Committee in Odessa and the St. Petersburg Ministry of State Domains with petitions in a tightening spiral of social and political protest. Appealing equally to the principles of Mennonite religious brotherhood and of the Great Reforms, the landless leadership drafted proposals, organized mass meetings, and mobilized the support of some influential Mennonite merchants and landholders (including Johann Cornies's influential son-in-law Philip Wiebe) with government contacts in St. Petersburg.[103]

The landless proposed solutions that ranged from moderate to radical, and included the introduction of a system whereby all Mennonite lands would be repartitioned, similar to the classic system used by peasants. Wealthier Mennonite farmers were aghast, and tensions continued to mount as all Mennonites waited to see whether St. Petersburg would intervene. Jacob D. Epp, a Mennonite minister and landholder who supported the landless, recorded in his diary on 31 December 1867: "We anxiously await the response of our beloved government to the petition that our entire community sent to His Excellency the Lord Minister. The Khortytsia [Mennonite] community is embroiled in a great dispute over land, involving land-owners, cottagers, and officials at the District level. This will not be a blessing for the community."[104]

Finally, in 1866 all parties came to an agreement through the mediation efforts of the Ministry of State Domains. It provided for an enfranchisement of the landless, permission to divide 65-desiatina farms in half, and the distribution of the settlement's reserve lands to families with houses, or house and garden plots, but no land. Finally, settlements as a whole—there were by now more than sixty of them—were provided with a mechanism that made possible the collective purchase of lands elsewhere in the empire. There they were to establish new, so-called "daughter" colonies for those families that had neither houses nor land. Dyck has identified the collective formation of the new settlements as "the crowning piece of the agrarian reform of the 1860s." To help pay for them, a portion of the original Mennonite settlements was set aside in perpetuity as lease lands, from which the proceeds went directly to the purchase of additional lands. These lands amounted to approximately 3,000 desiatinas in the Khortytsia settlement, and almost 12,000 desiatinas in Molochna.[105] As a final step, the government imposed this arrangement on all other German and Mennonite settlements in New Russia. In this way German and Mennonite colonists found a solution to their landless crisis at a time that was propitious, as it coincided with the larger changes within the region that had prompted many large estate owners to sell or lease out their lands. For its part, the state was pleased that a potentially debilitating crisis involving New Russia's most prosperous agriculturalists had been averted without the concession of additional state or crown lands.

Germans and Mennonites quickly became active in land purchases through the formation of village-based cooperatives.[106] Their gains were evident throughout New Russia. For example, in the northern district of Bakhmut, in 1891 they alone purchased 43,467 of the 45,152 desiatinas sold by nobles.[107] By contrast, the vast majority of peasants lacked the collective capital for such purchases and received only minimal assistance from the state-sponsored Peasant Land Bank.[108] Mennonites established about six new villages a year in the half-century after 1865.[109] They almost immediately began to purchase private estates in New Russia, beginning with the founding of Zahradivka (Zagradovka) in Kherson province. Zahradivka, the first daughter settlement of the Molochna Mennonites, comprised 21,276 desiatinas. It was purchased from Count Kochubei at the cost of 23.5 rubles a desiatina, a price that permitted the establishment of seventeen additional new settlements. The Mennonite, Wilhelm Kroeker, purchased the massive manor house, with its stone house and green-tinned roof, as a separate farmstead. A surviving account indicates that Kochubei had first offered his former serfs as much of the land as they desired. But they declined, preferring instead to cultivate their own lands, and to lease where available.[110] It is far more likely that former serf villages were unable to compete with the Mennonites in finding the necessary financial resources. Other permanent settlements appeared at this time throughout the region, including seventy in the Crimea. However, by the 1880s Mennonites had begun to look to the Volga River and beyond for their new daughter colonies, since land there was less than half the price of land in New Russia.[111]

New Russia's Jews also undertook major land acquisitions in New Russia. From 1869 to 1891, for example, they purchased almost 140,000 desiatinas in Kherson province, compared to 350,000 by Germans and Mennonites (and almost 380,000 by peasants). Thereafter, their own net gain in the province diminished, and from 1896 to 1905 amounted to less than 6,000 desiatinas.[112] By contrast, former serfs and state peasants purchased from 35 to 40 percent of private lands after 1861, an amount insufficient to support their extensive agricultural practices.[113]

The Mennonites occasionally leased entire estates in order to "plant" their daughter colonies. Often, the estate owners themselves sought out these arrangements, especially those who had served as officers in the Crimean War and had observed firsthand the prosperity of the Khortytsia and Molochna Mennonite settlements.[114] Mennonites were especially desirable as leasers because, unlike peasants, they tended to make cash payments for leased land. Consequently, they were often awarded land for longer terms. For example, Khortytsia Mennonites established six separate villages on leased lands in Dnipro district, Tavriia province, between 1864 and 1868. Of the 11,413 desiatinas, more than 7,000 were leased continuously until 1917. On another estate in Kherson province, an estate owner permitted German colonists to settle 135 families in five separate villages on his 12,000-desiatina estate. The land was leased to them for a ten-year period, during which the annual lease rate went from 3 rubles for the first five-year period to 3 rubles, 50 kopecks in the second. In addition, the colonists agreed to construct stone homes, which would revert back to the lord at the end of the lease. Normally, the tenants were expected to pay all of the land taxes. The twelve German settlements founded on the estate of a Major-General Popov in 1862 were also expected to cultivate a half-desiatina of woodlot for each household in the course of the ten-year agreement.[115]

Finally, some Mennonites responded to the sudden availability of estate lands by establishing private estates of their own. As noted in chapter 3, Mennonites had begun to purchase estates before 1860, though it took an enormous amount of wealth for individuals to purchase an entire estate. A more popular practice in this era involved the corporate purchase of large private estates by clusters of prosperous Mennonites. They then subdivided the lands among parties according to the original investment. Perhaps the most remarkable collection of private Mennonite estates was located in Oleksandrivsk district, Katerynoslav province. This 5,324-desiatina estate had been in the possession of Dmitrii Brazol, a Russian noble who had come into contact with Mennonite agriculturalists during the Crimean War. Prior to 1861, Brazol had managed a large, fine-fleeced sheep breeding operation with the help of his serfs. However, by the mid 1860s, he was ready to sell, and offered it to his Mennonite contacts at the very time they were seeking to expand their horizons. In an agreement signed on 20 July 1868, Dmitrii Brazol sold his entire estate to six "Russian subjects, Mennonites," who established individual estates on these lands. Another eleven families purchased an adjoining estate in the following year, though there they settled in two newly constructed villages: Schönfeld and Weisenfeld. By 1873, additional purchases had resulted in the formation of a distinct volost, known as Schönfeld [Schoenfeld], with four villages, more than two hundred estates, and almost 50,000 desiatinas.[116]

Conclusion

The middle decades of the nineteenth century were a time of revolutionary change in New Russia, and nowhere was this more apparent than in the management of the region's large landed estates. From the 1840s onward the burgeoning grain trade persuaded many estate owners to limit their extensive sheep-breeding operations and to increase their involvement in grain cultivation. To do so, they relied heavily on serf labor, especially on smaller estates where hired laborers could be entirely avoided. Although the largest estate owners were compelled to enter the labor market, almost all sought to stretch the serf laborers to the limit, even if it meant denying them access to otherwise vacant lands. Thus, a people associated with a tradition of freedom, whether as Cossacks or as serfs who had fled to New Russia to escape their bondage, found themselves in increasingly difficult straits.

Estate serfs responded in a number of ways, from direct protests to flight, and they were especially susceptible to rumors of freedom—rumors that legitimized their actions. The potential for unrest increased after 1853 when the Crimean War brought a new kind of devastation to the region. At the same time, the state's need to buttress its fighting force seemed ideally suited to the belief, nurtured within countless peasant communities in the empire, that they would be given freedom if they aided in the cause. New Russian serfs observed hundreds of runaway peasants enter the south upon that basis, and they soon joined in the movement themselves. Thus, the end of the war and the eve of reform was a time of considerable uncertainty and anxiety for serfs and nobles alike.

The terms of the Emancipation Manifesto bewildered the region's serf population; that is, until they were given the proper "interpretation" of its meaning. Thereafter, they attempted to implement their own "reform package" by refusing to fulfill any of the labor demands still placed on them. How could they be expected to work for free if they themselves were now supposed to be free? Even if the former serfs were persuaded to accept the conditions of the Manifesto, it was doubtful that peasants would forget the far more glorious opportunities they had imagined, even if those were based only on rumors of their own making. It is perhaps most surprising, then, that the post-reform era proved to be so bewildering to the estate owners. "Like ships at sea without a rudder," they first returned to increased fine-fleeced sheep breeding, and, when that market collapsed, they sought to lease or sell as much of their land as they could. Former serfs were the initial beneficiaries of the practice of leasing, especially since it blurred the actual impact of the land charters that had left them with relatively expensive lands of poor quality. The situation of confused nobles making relatively inexpensive and vast lands available for lease was not to last long, however. One immediate threat—at least from the perspective of former serfs—came from former colonists in the region.

The Mennonites and Germans played an important role in the turbulent decades following the emancipation. The sudden availability of massive estates within New Russia provided a welcome outlet for both the disadvantaged and the prosperous among them. At the same time, their large-scale purchases of estates often meant that lands leased to former serfs were suddenly removed from the market. Although Mennonites may have viewed themselves as "agricultural innovators" in their new holdings, it is quite likely that many neighboring peasants viewed them as threats to their livelihood. Thus, the relations between Mennonites and their neighbors on land acquired after 1860 was far less cordial than relations involving the original settlements of Khortytsia and Molochna.[117] In following chapters we will examine the long-term economic and social impact that these changes would have on New Russia's rural population.

5

CITIES, RAILS, AND MARKETS

New Russia's Transformation beyond the Fields, 1850–1900

THE RUSSIAN EMPIRE EXPERIENCED a welcome period of stability in the second half of the nineteenth century. The absence of major international conflicts on the scale of the Crimean War allowed St. Petersburg to focus on extending rudimentary services to its rural inhabitants. Village schools were constructed, and agronomists and various health practitioners made their first appearance in the New Russian countryside. Thanks to the energetic activity of an emerging civil society, the advances resulted in per capita increases in living standards.

New Russia's Demographic Explosion

Improving conditions led to a decline in mortality rates and a corresponding increase in natural growth rates.[1] The historian A. G. Rashin suggests that the population increased faster between 1863 and 1885 than between 1885 and 1897—proportional increases of 33.6 and 14.3 percent respectively.[2] The most dramatic growth within the empire occurred in Siberia, the Caucasus, and the southern steppe—all frontier, or at least former frontier regions.

Population changes for New Russia during these years are presented in table 5.1.

Table 5.1. Population figures for New Russia, 1863–1897.

Province	1863	1885	1897
Katerynoslav	1,204,751	1,792,800	2,113,674
Tavriia	606,783	1,060,000	1,447,790
Kherson	1,330,138	2,202,690	2,733,612
New Russia	**3,141,672**	**5,055,490**	**6,295,076**
European Russia	**60,909,309**	**81,725,200**	**93,442,900**

Source: *SVR66*, 12–13, 26–27, and 30–31; Rashin 1956, 44–45; and *PV97*, vol. 13, 1; vol. 47, 1; and vol. 41, 1.

Taken as a whole, New Russia's population doubled between 1863 and 1897, a reflection of ongoing migration patterns into the region as well as natural increases. New Russia's greatest demographic advance occurred between 1863 and 1890, a time when immigration continued to respond to the availability of inexpensive lands and the lack of rail transport made relocation to Siberia difficult. By the 1890s, however, governors in the region regularly reported about the petitions of local peasants who wished to resettle in less populous regions of the empire.[3] As one might expect, Tavriia province experienced the most rapid rate of growth. Large-scale settlement there was prompted by the emigration of thousands of Tatars in the immediate aftermath of the Crimean War. Melitopol and Dnipro districts experienced the greatest growth. From 1863 to 1885, the population of Tavriia increased by almost 75 percent—a rate unparalleled within the empire. Kherson and Katerynoslav provinces also experienced impressive growth, at 52.4 and 48.8 percent respectively.[4] Still, proportional increases in these two provinces were significantly lower than in others because they lacked the open lands still available in either Tavriia or in the more easterly regions along the Don and Volga rivers. A population density in New Russia of thirty-two inhabitants per square kilometer in 1897 continued to place it midway between the Ukrainian provinces to the north and the newly opened frontiers to the east.[5]

Odesa and the Cities of the South

Dynamic population growth affected the manner in which peasants and estate owners regarded and worked the land, as subsequent chapters will demonstrate. It is equally important to note the impact that the population growth had on New Russia's urban centers, and the markets it created for agricultural goods. Moscow and St. Petersburg dominated Russia's urban landscape up to the mid-nineteenth century, and although these cities remained dominant thereafter, the economic and social reforms inaugurated after the defeat in the Crimean War stimulated renewed urban developments in New Russia. The nature and function of urban space underwent a revolutionary transformation there.[6] The earliest urban centers had been established either as port cities along the Black and Azov seas or as administrative centers in the interior. Of the former, only Odesa had blossomed by midcentury. Kherson, Berdiansk, and Mykolaïv continued to struggle in its wake. Oleksandriia, Ielysavethrad, and Katerynoslav were the only substantial urban centers in the interior, and each served as an important trading and marketing center.

Although the proportion of urban dwellers in New Russia from 1856 to 1897 only increased from 16.4 to 19 percent, the actual changes were qualitatively enormous.[7] In 1897 almost half of the region's urban dwellers resided along the shores of the Azov and Black seas, where Odesa continued to dominate with 403,815 people, up from 118,000 in 1864.[8] By the latter date almost one in four of New Russia's urban dwellers (up from 19 percent in 1860) lived in this picturesque city overlooking the Black Sea, even though inadequate access to water power, coal, or wood impeded its industrial development until after 1900. Still, it had two deep and well-sheltered harbors that were suitable both for smaller boats destined for travel inland and sea-bound vessels. By 1881 Odesa had emerged as the empire's dominant port in terms of overall trade.[9]

Although Odesa continued to expand during the next two decades, its relative share of international trade would actually fall as rival southern ports grew, especially Kherson and Mykolaïv. Of these Kherson had been more important at midcentury, because its location on the Dnipro allowed it to profit from the importance of river transport, and it was situated at a logical transition point from river to sea shipping. Kherson's relative position suffered at midcentury with the rising prominence of Mykolaïv and the Crimean port of Sevastopol, but after 1895 Kherson's port facilities were improved and a new boom period began.[10] In a similar way, the improvement of water transport around Mykolaïv after 1887, and its placement at the end of one of the earliest rail lines in the region, enabled that city by 1904 to rise to fifth place in the empire in the ruble value of its exports—a stunning achievement in an empire that was generally making rapid gains. By 1900, the Black Sea ports of Odesa, Mykolaïv, and Kherson together accounted for one-third of all Russia's agricultural exports.[11]

On the Sea of Azov, the ports of Rostov, Taganrog, Berdiansk, Mariupol, and Henichesk (Genichesk) accounted for another 21.7 percent of all Russian grain exports from 1902 to 1906. This activity occurred despite the fact that the sea's shallow waters hindered the easy passage of ocean-bound vessels. These cities benefited, however, from a rich agricultural hinterland and the close proximity of the region's emerging mining centers. The importance of Rostov and Taganrog to New Russia diminished with the expansion of Berdiansk and Mariupol. The relatively late arrival of rail lines had delayed developments in both of these port cities, but they soon profited from the close proximity of the successful Mennonite and German colonists engaged in grain production. Of the Crimean ports, only Henichesk was of even modest importance as an outlet for producers in the northern steppe districts. Feodosiia (population of 26,496 in 1897), and Ievpatoriia (17,913), served more as local markets than regional trade rivals.[12] The Crimean port of Sevastopol remained unique in all of New Russia, functioning not only as a trading center but also as the empire's preeminent southern naval base.

A second category of cities, containing 12 percent of New Russia's urban population in 1897, fulfilled diverse functions as administrative centers, major depots for the expanding railroad network, and food processors and distributors with relatively modest industrial bases. These older centers were located mainly in the northern districts of Katerynoslav and Kherson provinces, and in 1897 included Ielysavethrad (61,488), Tiraspol (31,616), and Oleksandriia (14,000) in northern Kherson; Pavlohrad (15,775), Novomoskovsk (12,883), and Bakhmut (19,316) in Katerynoslav; and, lastly, Simferopol (49,078), capital of Tavriia province.[13]

New Russia's Industrial Revolution: Katerynoslav and the Donbas

Though all of the cities mentioned thus far played important roles in New Russia's overall rural development, none of them matched the rate of growth found in the region's industrial and mining centers, especially the Donbas and Kryvyi Rih (Krivoi Rog), as well as the "Dnipro bend" cities of Katerynoslav and Oleksandrivsk. Katerynoslav, with roots as an early trading center and transshipment point on the Dnipro, had grown to a population of almost 113,000 inhabitants in 1897 and become the second largest city in New Russia. Much of this expansion had occurred in the industrial boom ignited by the empire's decision to broaden its industrial base after the Crimea War, which made it possible for state officials and private entrepreneurs to exploit New Russia's rich coal and iron ore deposits.[14] Located in a broad diagonal swath from the southeastern corner of Kherson province to the northwestern counties of Katerynoslav province, these deposits were enormous in size and rich in quality. The Donets coal basin in Katerynoslav province covered some 24,000 square versts, though as late as 1860 a mere fifty small deposits had been mined. All of this changed with the implementation of ambitious plans for rail construction during the 1860s.[15]

Rail transport was deemed to be especially important to New Russia's development because of the difficulties that the existing network of water and land routes presented for the movement of people and goods. Travel conditions worsened in the late fall season, at the precise time that agriculturalists wished to move their goods to market. Describing road travel in Katerynoslav province at midcentury, V. Pavlovich wrote:

> In general, one can say that during the dry times of the year, not only post, but indeed all main roads are well suited to travel, not only in the case of dikes and corduroy roads, but even in the low places, along river valleys. Indeed none of the roads, whether small or large, present any difficulty for the movement of even large loads. But with the onset of late fall, when the heavy rains come, travel along these roads becomes more difficult. In the districts of Verkhnedneprovsk, Novomoskovsk, Pavlograd, and parts of Aleksandrovsk, these roads, which are composed of black-earth soil mixed with clay, are in a muddy state after the rains. All travel is difficult as the mud from this ooze clings to the wheels.[16]

Though in their lower reaches the river systems were important for the movement of goods, the upper sections contained numerous sets of rapids and shoals that prevented the establishment of a reliable system of transport from the interior. Even along the lower reaches travel was often impeded by sudden storms that kept ferry operators off the river for days at a time.[17]

Despite the obvious need for something more reliable, insufficient resources had long delayed rail construction in the region. The empire's first push in rail construction had required the import of rails from England. Before 1859, almost all railroad construction relied on similarly imported metals, and as late as the 1870s imports still comprised more than 60 percent of rails in use in the empire.[18] Meanwhile, coal imports as a proportion of the total required in the empire averaged 40 to 45 percent in the 1870s (down from 54 to 60 percent in the 1860s).[19] The pace of railroad construction in New Russia is shown in table 5.2.

Table 5.2. Railroad construction in New Russia, 1861–1910.

Years	Versts
1861–1870	8,598
1871–1880	11,146
1881–1890	7,373
1891–1900	19,022
1901–1910	12,865

Source: Bakulev 1953, 73.

The first railroads constructed in New Russia operated as two disconnected north-south lines, and were situated with strategic and military rather than commercial considerations in mind.[20] The first, a western line, was begun in 1863 and completed in the early 1870s. It joined Kyiv to the port of Odesa on the Black Sea. The second, an eastern line which ran to Rostov on the Sea of Azov, was completed in 1869.[21] An important east-west line, stretching across the northern counties of New Russia, was finished in the 1870s, and was followed by the construction of adjoining secondary lines running to the Black Sea ports of Mykolaïv (1872–73), and the Crimean naval base of Sevastopol (1875).[22] This latter line ran north-south through the heart of New Russia along the eastern edge of Katerynoslav province.[23] Ongoing construction in the 1880s and 1890s—the latter decade being the single greatest period of rail development before 1910—established additional north-south connections to the Crimean ports of Feodosiia and the Azov port of Mariupol, as well as several other connecting lines. By 1903, New Russia contained 3,618 versts of rail, of which over half were located in Katerynoslav province, an indication of its central location between Ukrainian grain fields to the north and international ports to the south, as well as of the province's abundant mineral wealth.[24]

Despite these impressive quantitative advances, problems remained with rail transport. For one, the demand continued to outpace its growth. Although the New Russian rail system represented only 19 percent of the empire's rail lines in the late nineteenth century, 40 percent of all goods passed over them.[25] Also, the unequal distribution patterns and distances between depots led to chronic congestion and delay. In 1889, a petition to the Ministry of Transportation claimed that a third of Kherson province lacked either adequate water or rail links, a fact that led to extreme crowding during peak times of the year. Many agriculturalists saw their hard-won harvests rot at rail depots while they waited for train cars to appear.[26] Others expressed consternation with state tariffs that raised the cost of rail transport and the lack of grain storage and sorting facilities at depots.[27] Livestock breeders complained that their beasts were often transported to markets for days at a time without adequate supplies of fodder and water.[28]

In 1902 an especially harsh critique of the region's rail system was contained in Katerynoslav province's report to the Local Commission on the Needs of the Agricultural Commission (the so-called Witte Commission). It condemned the system as impractical for grain cartage because of its slowness, the great distances between depots, the poor condition of access roads, high trade tariffs, and the limited supply of rail wagons.[29] In fact, the problem was deemed to lie less in the rail links themselves than in the obstacles that continued to separate local depots from the fields. As late as 1900, most agriculturalists remained dependent on ox- and horse-drawn carts for the overland shipment of their goods. The picture here had not improved during the previous half century, since many roads continued to be impassable for much of the spring and fall.[30] In fact, it is likely that road conditions actually deteriorated during the last half of the nineteenth century, since the dramatic increase in land tillage and soil exhaustion had accelerated and prolonged the spring and fall runoffs, thereby increasing the time that roads were unusable. Rapid runoffs also swelled rivers and increased the necessity for bridges at a time when few permanent ones had been constructed. In 1891 an observer complained that not one permanent bridge was found on the ninety-verst distance between the village of Berezivka (Berezovka) and the town of Ananïv, despite the fact that this was a vital and busy grain route.[31] Owing to such poor and undependable transportation links, farmers also received lower prices for goods sold at local bazaars that were far from the railway depots.[32]

The picture was not entirely hopeless, however. Although the New Russian rail system was still unable to satisfy the demands placed upon it in 1900, its impact on local agriculture was already enormous. More than half of all grains delivered to Odesa after 1880 arrived by rail. The cartage of coal proved to be even more impressive. It reached approximately seven billion kilograms by 1900, by which time it had become an essential component of the empire's industrial revolution.[33] By that year New Russia had emerged as a leader in rail transport, far outstripping gains made elsewhere in the empire. Katerynoslav province led the way, as table 5.3 suggests. With 37.9 versts of rail lines for every thousand square versts of land, its density was exceeded only by Moscow. New Russia's overall average of 23.2 versts of rail lines per square verst was more than double the empire-wide average of 9.9. Further, with 79 versts of rail for every 100,000 inhabitants, Katerynoslav was only exceeded by the Baltic province of Estland (103.1 versts).

Table 5.3. The Railroads of New Russia in 1904.

Province	Total versts	Rail lines (versts per 1000 sq. versts of land)	Rail lines (versts per 100,000 inhabitants)
Katerynoslav	2,109	37.9	79.0
Tavriia	737	13.9	44.0
Kherson	1,115	17.9	35.4
European Russia	44,132	9.9	40.1

Source: *Ezhegodnik Rossii 1904 g.* (1905): 338–40. For comparative statistics with European nations and the United States, see ibid.; and *Ezhegodnik Rossii 1905 g.* (1906): 67.

Railroads thus had an enormous impact on New Russia's agriculturalists. Their construction allowed peasants in the interior to move goods relatively quickly to southern ports and international markets, and led to a greater uniformity of prices within the region. Railroads also benefited peasants in the northern parts of New Russia, who were no longer captive to local markets and the high-priced goods sold there. As we shall see, increased access to urban markets prompted peasants to initiate intensive market-gardening operations. Moreover, railroad construction brought a host of modernizing benefits related to agriculture. For instance, in one district in Kherson province it was noted that peasant literacy was higher in villages close to the rail lines.[34]

Not everyone viewed these developments with the same enthusiasm, however. Increased rail transport altered or eliminated many of the carting routes upon which local peasants had traditionally relied to supplement household incomes. The era of the *chumaks* now faded away, and with it an important source of supplemental income at a time when it was most needed. Railroads also increased the numbers of migratory laborers from the central provinces who annually flooded the region in search of seasonal agricultural work on New Russian estates. Although they benefited their employers, the local peasants viewed the migrant workers as bitter rivals and held them responsible for a reduction in wages and employment opportunities. These tensions would become a major grievance for peasants during the politically stormy years of 1905 and 1906.[35]

The railroad boom that occurred in New Russia after 1860 was facilitated by the exploitation of rich coal and iron deposits and the genesis of a vibrant local industrial sector centered in the coal of the Donets basin and the iron ore of Kryvyi Rih. Rail transport was both a stimulus to and beneficiary of this development. The rail connection of the Donets basin with the iron ore deposits of Kryvyi Rih in 1884, along with the opening of the Donets railroad in 1897, allowed for the movement of extracted coal from the Donets basin.[36] Although state initiatives in coal extraction were already evident before 1860, significant headway was not made until the government signed a contract in 1869 with John Hughes, the London-based industrialist.[37] When steel production finally began in 1872, his company, Iuzovka, together with the state firm of Pashikhov in the neighboring Don oblast, significantly expanded coal mining in the Donbas. Hughes employed more than three thousand workers at his factory and coal mine—one of the largest industrial enterprises in the empire.[38] The growth in coal production before 1905 is outlined in table 5.4.

Table 5.4. Coal extraction (in millions of poods) in New Russia, 1860–1905.

Year	Donbas	Russian Empire
1860	6.0	7.4
1865	9.8	12.6
1870	15.6	22.3
1875	51.4	79.4
1880	86.3	122.4
1885	114.9	151.3
1890	183.2	216.4
1895	298.3	330.7
1900	671.7	734.7
1905	785.3	922.0

Source: Bakulev 1955, 128, 657–58.

Coal extraction and iron ore smelting were closely connected. The production of one ton of iron at the dawn of the twentieth century required 1.8 tons of rich ferrous deposits (Kryvyi Rih deposits were 60 to 65 percent pure—far in excess of all other Russian deposits) and 2.8 tons of coal. In addition, smelting required large amounts of limestone deposits. These were found in the immediate vicinity as well as further south in the Crimea.[39] New Russian industrial development benefited further from the fact that minerals located and extracted in the region were also processed there. The growth of New Russian iron ore smelting reflected the rapid pace with which coal and iron ore were mined. Although none was smelted in 1860, annual production rates thereafter rose to 320,000 poods in 1870, 1.3 million in 1880, 13.4 million in 1890, and a remarkable 91.4 million in 1900.[40]

New Russia's industrial development in the late nineteenth century benefited greatly from its proximity to mineral rich Kryvyi Rih, as well as its access to good rail or water transport. Many cities in New Russia attempted to become industrial centers during the period of frenzied growth between 1885 and 1900. By 1900 three centers dominated: the Donbas region itself, smelting 58 percent of the region's iron by the turn of the century; the industrial centers of Katerynoslav and Oleksandrivsk on the so-called Dnipro bend (26 percent of the region's output); and the Sea of Azov centers of Kerch and Mariupol (12.6 percent).[41] The rapid pace with which the rich iron ore and coal deposits in New Russia were exploited after 1870 provided more employment opportunities, stimulating local industrial initiatives and steady immigration.[42] The population of the Donbas region grew from 34,500 in 1864 to 153,200 in 1897, and Kryvyi Rih grew from 8,800 to 25,600.[43]

How did industrialists utilize the newly mined coal and produced steel? As suggested above, much of the region's earliest industrial production went into the manufacturing of rail lines and the provision of fuel for locomotives, but some factories were built to produce agricultural implements.[44] While only five such firms were reported by the Valuev Commission in 1872, the number of enterprises had grown considerably by 1900 (see table 5.5 below).[45] These statistics confirm that the production of agricultural machinery was centered in the provinces of Katerynoslav and Tavriia, close to the Donbas coal fields and the iron ore of Kryvyi Rih, and accessible to good water or rail transport. The average factory producing agricultural equipment in 1909 had slightly over seventy workers, with an annual production in excess of 88,000 rubles.

Table 5.5 also points to the important role that these enterprises played in the provincial economies of Katerynoslav, and especially Tavriia, where they comprised almost one-fifth of the province's annual industrial production. They played a smaller role in Kherson province, which had developed a larger, more diverse industrial base concentrated in the large urban markets of the Black Sea coastline. In 1900, for example, almost half of Kherson province's total production came from the production of foodstuffs (*obrabotka pitatel'nykh veshchestv*).[46] Many agriculturalists preferred locally produced implements that were designed specifically for local conditions and thus often better suited to the region than imported ones. The flourishing of a local manufacturing sector also provided a need in the region for replacement parts and skilled artisans to repair and maintain the growing inventory of modern farm technology.[47] Even so, in

Table 5.5. Production of agricultural machinery in New Russia after 1900.

	Factories	Production (in rubles)	Percent of overall provincial industrial production	Workers
Katerynoslav	33	2,757,000	14.2	2,076
Tavriia	19	2,097,000	19.0	1,516
Kherson	16	1,162,000	2.8	1,244
Total	**68**	**6,016,000**	--	**4,836**

Source: Morachevskii 1910a, 404.

the late nineteenth century some powerful and influential estate owners in the south made certain that tariffs on imported equipment were kept low, since they preferred American and British products.[48]

Thus, during the half century before 1905, the world beyond the fields in New Russia was fundamentally transformed. Its urban centers grew at a remarkable rate, especially the important coastal cities, including the empire's most lucrative port in Odesa, but also such significant regional centers of industry and trade as Katerynoslav and Ielysavethrad. By 1897 the Dnipro city of Katerynoslav had jumped from the seventh largest (in 1864) to the second largest city in New Russia and one of the ten largest in the empire, with a population of 112,939.[49] Cities like Katerynoslav were now important centers of industrial production, markets for locally grown products, and vital transshipment points for regional and international markets. They also served as popular magnets of immigration, as demonstrated in the 1897 Imperial Russian census. In that year only 12 percent of Katerynoslav province's rural inhabitants had been born outside of the province, compared with 40 percent of its urban inhabitants. Similarly 7 percent of Kherson's rural, but 35 percent of its urban inhabitants had been born outside that province's borders.[50]

Katerynoslav's emergence as a vital and dynamic center in New Russia reflected the degree to which its industrial sector had grown. The nearby iron ore and coal deposits were not just extracted in the region: much of the raw mineral wealth was also processed in what had become the region's second largest city. Once known primarily as an administrative center, Katerynoslav had become a giant through its smelting operations, the production of rails, and the manufacture of agricultural implements. In 1905 a commentator noted:

> Ekaterinoslav produces a very different impression to that of most other Russian towns, even including the industrial centres. As a rule industrialism appears rather incongruous in Russia.... But at Ekaterinoslav one feels oneself at once in an authentic up-and-coming industrial city.... There is no beauty and no picturesqueness in Ekaterinoslav, but there is an air of genuine activity and business which...may already stand comparison with some of the great industrial centers of Germany or England; it is a business town existing solely for business. We are in the real "New Russia," the Russia that will some day occupy an assured place among the modern and industrial counties of Europe.[51]

New Russia in 1900 was at the industrial core of the Russian Empire: a cornerstone of the empire and a far cry from a half century earlier, when most of its commercial activity derived directly from agricultural produce. As one measure of this development, the proportion of ruble earnings coming from animal or plant products in Katerynoslav province had plummeted from a high of 87 percent in 1860 to 31 percent by the dawn of the twentieth century. The transformation was less dramatic in Kherson and Tavriia provinces, but signs of the dawning new world were also present there. At the same time, important questions remained about the manner in which agriculturalists would respond to the industrial revolution.[52]

6

WEEDS IN THE WHEAT FIELD

Peasants and the Struggle toward Intensive Agricultural Economies in the Late Nineteenth Century

Observers of the late imperial era have long disagreed about the health of peasant agriculture in the second half of the nineteenth century. Was it improving or declining, or was it doing both, but at different times and in different locations? In 1874 Anton I. Umiss despondently described the course that New Russian peasant agriculturalists had recently taken:

> The old timers of New Russia would be astonished at the profound transformation that has occurred in the past five decades. In this comparatively short period of time, the rich grasses have been destroyed and replaced with plowed fields and emaciated hay meadows.... Trees, scattered in the ravines, which occasionally served as a conductor for predators and the protection from wind, have been destroyed; rivers have become shallow, and water sources for the most part have dried up....The entire region has taken on a sorrowful character....The number of working oxen and horses have increased, but the pedigrees have become emaciated and weak.[1]

Umiss warned that peasants were headed for disaster because of their inability to manage their economies properly. Subsequent historians picked up the theme of increased peasant poverty and broadened its application to the entire empire in the half-century before 1917. Such conditions were summed up in Geroid Robinson's famous depiction of "The Hungry Village," in which he noted that "during the decades that followed the Emancipation, the Russian peasantry carried on a desperate struggle with a desperate situation."[2] Robinson believed that insufficient land holdings and communal structures, coupled with a crippling debt load and the dogged application of old practices to new conditions, resulted in agricultural collapse, and made revolutionary turmoil all but inevitable.

Yet, however persuasive that argument, contemporary sources also revealed a very different picture of peasant initiative and energy. One example is the case of Andrei Gorlov, who at some point in the 1850s planted several fruit trees on his farmstead. His neighbors in the village of Velyki Kopani (Bolshoe Kopanoe), situated on the land mass bordered by the Crimea to the south and the Dnipro River to the north, responded with disbelief, envy, and ill will. As they walked by, villagers broke off his saplings or otherwise damaged the trees as much as possible. Still others threatened to gather the entire village assembly and destroy his orchard. But sheer perseverance enabled Gorlov to surmount his difficulties, and his steady success won the begrudging respect of his peers. Soon neighbors appeared at his door for advice on how best to plant and manage their own orchards. By the 1880s almost every one of the 457 villagers had small orchards that averaged sixty trees each. Such impressive orchards attracted merchants from distant cities. They purchased the harvested fruit and sold a portion of it in the expanding urban markets of the southern Ukraine.[3]

Ultimately, in order to assess the health of peasant agriculture, we will need to understand how extraordinary the village of Velyki Kopani was before 1900. What motivated Gorlov to engage in commercial fruit production when he did, and what accounted for the initial ill will shown by his fellow villagers? Does this episode accurately reflect larger peasant attitudes about experimentation and innovation? Recent historians believe that peasant agriculturalists were more innovative and productive than previously thought, a fact demonstrated by the introduction of new crops and the doubling of grain yields, all within communal village structures. Although historians have recently acknowledged that peasants made these gains in the late imperial period, few have explored the limits of these gains or the degree to which peasant economies had become intertwined with those of other agriculturalists in the area.[4] Moreover, historians who stress the gains made by peasant farmers have yet to account adequately for contemporary assertions that peasant agriculture was in a state of crisis during the second half of the nineteenth century.

This chapter explores the main agricultural developments of the second half of the nineteenth century in New Russia. It argues that a very real crisis erupted in the third quarter of the century when peasant agriculturalists continued to apply agricultural practices designed for conditions that no longer existed. However, we must also examine the manner in which peasants adjusted their practices to correct this situation. In fact, as part of this process, and unlike the era of sheep breeding in the early part of the century, the peasant, colonist, and noble economies became considerably intertwined before 1900, in a manner that held forth promise as well as peril.

Peasant Economies at Midcentury: "Safety First"

In his path-breaking study of peasant villages in contemporary Asia, James Scott concluded that "precapitalist" societies were reluctant to risk and introduce innovations for fear that they might threaten existing incomes. Instead, such societies stressed the importance of "safety first." Ironically, much of the initial expansion and innovation attempted by New Russian peasant agriculturalists reflected this cautious approach. Their conservative attitude to agricultural innovation did not mean that their practices were entirely static, however.[5]

New Russian peasants maintained extensive, largely pastoral economies before midcentury, with minimal capital and labor requirements. In addition to sheep breeding, discussed in chapter 3, peasants also pursued cattle breeding, vegetable production, and grain production. The large amount of land available meant that agriculturalists did not need to choose among agricultural systems. Land was deemed plentiful enough in 1838—the region was so immense—for contemporary observers to conclude that the local population was "destined for a wandering and pastoral people, rather than for a settled and agricultural population." How could it be otherwise when the vast steppe made everything within it wild, including herds that often roamed at will?[6] In the 1850s peasants from Tavriia province nostalgically remembered this bygone era:

> Our land was formerly freely available. People plowed where they wanted, though mostly the sections close to the settlement because [the peasants] were too lazy to travel further. Only the best agriculturalists worked right to the boundary markers. Sown areas were small at first, because they were occupied with livestock. The wealthy peasant sowed 15 to 20 desiatinas,

> the average from 5 to 8. Grain was not sown for sale, but for domestic consumption. They [the peasants] were more concerned with livestock, and maintained simple plows and harrows. And there were fewer weeds then. Both rich and poor peasants worked with oxen.[7]

Both state peasants, with their abundant holdings, and serfs, who had almost unlimited access to demesne lands, utilized extensive agricultural practices. Although peasants were essentially clothed, fed, and warmed by the sheep they bred and the by-products that they sold, they regarded cattle, specifically oxen, as no less important. Peasants at midcentury favored hardy, indigenous breeds that were more likely to survive under the open sky with only minimal protection from the continental winds and sudden climatic shifts. The most popular breeds had been developed within the region over centuries and reflected the interplay of Cossack, Tatar, and Bulgarian livestock. Of these, the so-called Cherkass (also known as the Ukrainian, or Little Russian) breed was the most common. Its size made it an excellent source of meat and tallow, both of which were invaluable as household products and export commodities.[8] In addition, its large frame, accented by prodigious horns, made it a highly valued beast of burden. Peasants relied upon cattle for field cultivation in the spring and fall, and at all other times for carting, which remained an important supplemental source of income until late in the century.

Cattle were also a source of milk, and their hides provided the raw materials necessary for clothing. Although their market value declined with the rapid expansion of sheep breeding after 1820, cattle continued to play an important role in both peasant and estate economies. The German and Mennonite colonists were the only agriculturalists to switch to horses before midcentury, despite the vulnerability of horses to disease. The vast majority of peasants maintained extensive economies more suited to oxen. In the 1850s the average peasant household possessed approximately four cattle, twenty sheep, and no horses.[9] Cattle were usually sold at village and town fairs, or driven to major centers such as Kharkiv, St. Petersburg, and Moscow. Since cartage was so costly and risky—a high proportion of cattle died en route or contracted contagious diseases that dramatically reduced their market value—many cattle were often sold and butchered within the region. The Black Sea fleet provided an important, immediate market for salted beef, and tallow was processed into numerous consumer goods, including soap and candles. In 1816 sixteen tallow-melting firms were located in Katerynoslav province; by 1860 the number had risen to over forty, in which almost a thousand workers were employed.[10]

Vegetable gardens and fruit orchards also played a vital and multifaceted role in New Russian peasant household economies before midcentury. Melons and a variety of fruits were highly desirable as sources of water in a region where groundwater was often of poor quality in spring and altogether absent by mid-July. The consumption of cabbages and other vegetable greens in either their fresh or fermented (*kvashenye*) form was considered an effective hindrance to a variety of diseases, including scurvy. Also, the cultivation of fruits and vegetables provided peasant households with an important way to utilize surplus labor supply, especially that supplied by the very young and old. Hence peasants designated garden work as either "grandma's work" (*delo bab'e*) or something done in "one's spare time" (*mezhdu delom*).[11]

The dramatic population increases of the late nineteenth century expanded the demand for fresh fruits and vegetables and also required a greater surplus labor force in the villages. Fruit, vegetable, and even tobacco cultivation expanded accordingly. Peasants normally planted gardens and orchards in marginal lands. Ravines and river valleys seemed ideal, since they were protected from the region's harsh winds. In the process, peasants managed to utilize otherwise worthless holdings. Peasants in the southeast portion of Ielysavethrad district, in New Russia's northern reaches, initially confronted a system of ravines which flowed into the Berezivka, Vysun, and Sagaidachek rivers. These had previously seemed to be an economic liability and of only limited value for pasture. However, through intensive manuring village peasants eventually transformed these small fields into valuable land for growing cabbages that were primarily intended for household consumption.[12] Most New Russian peasant households maintained at least modest gardens and orchards throughout the nineteenth century.

If the benefits were this obvious, why did peasants not expand more aggressively into these forms of agricultural specialization? New Russia's climate was surely an important factor. The predominant northeast winds in spring and summer brought unrelenting heat and dryness to tender fruits and vegetables. But there were also widespread frosts in late spring and early summer that damaged the freshly planted gardens and exposed orchards. Snow and rainfall were normally too meager to provide gardens and orchards with the moisture required. And crops that survived the summer months frequently succumbed to unpredictable fall frosts, which ruined many promising harvests. Not surprisingly, New Russian peasants first developed fruit and vegetable operations in places that provided natural protection from the year-round searing winds. These included the region's many river valleys, the southwest slopes of any hilly area, and, of course, the Crimea's famed southern slopes.[13] Finally, owing to the lack of extra-communal incentives and support, peasants were more reluctant to engage in agricultural experimentation and diversification before the late nineteenth century. Rural sociologist Bogusław Gałęski has focused on the role played by stimuli outside of the village in making agricultural specialization feasible:

> When discussing the process of specialization in farming, one cannot but draw attention to the fact that it begins outside of farming itself. The market and industry create the basic stimuli for the transformation. State intervention, too, plays an important role, some of the manifestations of this being a ban on break-up in landholding; social insurance and retirement pensions; the demand that heirs should receive agricultural education; the extension of agronomic and veterinary services to agriculture.[14]

Supporting Gałęski's thesis, the world beyond the actual farms had long played a role in New Russian peasant agriculture. For generations seaports and river cities had fostered market gardens and fruit orchards in their immediate hinterland, among which the finest recorded were in the environs of Odesa and scattered along the river valleys of the southern part of Kherson province. Beyond these isolated islands, however, the rich interaction between peasant agriculturalists and the external stimuli Gałęski identifies seems to have been absent, and most peasants at midcentury were left with little incentive to expand or diversify their holdings. Instead, and with only limited exceptions, peasants geared their fruit and vegetable production to limited, immediate, and vital household dietary needs.

The picture was not all that different in peasant grain production, which involved less than a tenth of all lands in 1800. Decades later peasants were still reluctant to plant grains beyond protected, low-lying areas with reliable water supplies.[15] Market-oriented grain cultivation first expanded after 1830, coinciding with a crisis in sheep breeding and the assurance in 1829 of safe passage of Russian grains through the Ottoman-controlled straits. By 1833, the governor of Katerynoslav was already claiming that grain cultivation provided an invaluable source of livelihood for his province's population. As mentioned earlier, England's abolition of the Corn Laws in 1846 and the movement of other European countries in the direction of free trade further stimulated New Russian grain cultivation. Grains were first cultivated to a significant degree in the northern districts of Kherson province, where favorable weather conditions and a greater population density demanded more intensive land use. With a harsher climate and little population pressure, peasants in the southern districts were less likely to shift from pastoral to grain economies, though the close proximity of the Black Sea ports eventually provided too powerful an incentive to ignore. Grain production also enjoyed a solid beginning in the southern districts of Katerynoslav, given the short distance to markets either overland to ports on the Sea of Azov or by barge down the Dnipro River to the Black Sea.[16]

Thus, for reasons of market and/or population pressures, New Russian peasants increased their grain cultivation by the mid-nineteenth century, even though their economies continued to reflect the reality of plentiful holdings, mixed agricultural economies, and the limitations of labor and capital. In his midcentury investigation of Kherson province, Aleksandr Shmidt wrote:

> Land on the steppe is in abundance, and the population small. . . . The proximity of the Black Sea and the familiarity of the markets of western Europe with the port of Odesa give special value and significance to agricultural production here. In Kherson province one even meets those estates which are exclusively in grain production for external markets. Besides that, there is still not one economy in which working strength and capital correspond with the land available. From this it follows that agriculture here is wholly extensive.[17]

Most peasants at midcentury practiced two- or three-field systems, in which lands were commonly divided into sown area and pasture (*toloka*), with a parcel often left as a separate hay meadow (*senokos*). Farmers worked the same field for several years in a row, after which it was allowed to regenerate naturally for twenty or more years.[18] Such enormous time frames were still possible because virgin lands seemed to be in endless supply. An account from a state peasant village on the eve of the reforms describes how peasants selected land to cultivate:

> Once the peasant decides to plow, he travels to the field and selects a place which he wishes to sow as long as, by his own judgement, it is not in use. According to established custom, the land is then considered to be his, until his harvest has been removed... After the removal of the crop, it [the land] remains in the possession of the one who first plowed it. Thus, the land can belong to the same person for several years in a row. Uncultivated lands, upon which there is no sign of any grain stalks, are deemed to be common hay meadows [and available for the taking].[19]

In this way, peasants worked the land on the assumption that once exhausted, it would convert easily to pasture for at least a decade, during which time a process of natural regeneration would occur.[20] Nothing else was required, and even agronomists concluded that the natural fertility of the soils, coupled with the length of time soils had to regenerate, made the application of fertilizer unnecessary, if not altogether harmful. Even the use of manure as a fertilizer was discouraged, since it could scorch and destroy fragile wheat crops if applied excessively or prematurely.

The rural settlers who entered New Russia in the late eighteenth and early nineteenth centuries had from the start been compelled to modify their agricultural practices in a number of ways. Peasants quickly discovered that the light construction of their plows (the famed *sokha*), which tilled to depths of four and one-half inches and widths of six inches, may have been sufficient for the sandier, looser soils of the north, but was unacceptable for the hard-baked virgin lands of the southern prairie. Here shallow plowing left soils vulnerable to drought. In contrast, the "Little Russian plow" brought to the region by Ukrainian settlers proved far superior and became the ubiquitous means of tillage in the first half of the nineteenth century.[21] Also known as the two-wheeled plow, its heavier wood frame supported a plowshare that could cultivate to a depth of nine inches, if sheathed in steel. Five pairs of cattle were needed to pull such a heavy plow on the hard-packed virgin soils, compared to the three pairs considered sufficient to use with a *sokha* on previously tilled soils, and the heavier plow required other adjustments as well.[22]

Experience with wood-based plows prompted some peasants to acquire Ukrainian plows that local firms had adapted to increase durability and reduce the draft power needed. For example, the Potemkin firm in Kremenchuk constructed a Ukrainian plow that required no more than three pair of oxen for the cultivation of virgin lands. Although its predominantly cast iron construction and iron cutters and plowshares gave it increased durability over earlier models, most peasants prior to the last third of the nineteenth century sought less expensive labor-saving equipment that they could manufacture and repair by themselves. The *ralo* and extirpator (*ekstirpator*) were the most common substitutes for the "Little Russian" plow. Functionally akin to harrows, the simplest of these consisted of saplings that were dragged behind oxen with their root system intact. More sophisticated *ralo*s consisted of a thick timber beam pierced by three, and sometimes five or more, wooden teeth. Steel-tipped teeth were not uncommon by the mid-nineteenth century. Peasants used *ralo*s and extirpators in spring either to level the soils and cover the seeds of fall crops or as the sole means of tillage for lands that had been plowed in previous years.[23]

Almost all peasants broadcast seed onto their fields and then left them untended until the harvest, at which time they cut and bound the grain, leaving it shocked in large piles until all other field work had been completed. Peasants reaped their grains either with sickles or scythes throughout the first half of the nineteenth century. As late as 1853 the historian Skal′kovs′kyi wrote that "New Russian agronomists continue to argue among themselves as to which of these implements is better." The labor-saving qualities of the scythe, with cradle attached, increased its popularity over time, especially as it also allowed peasants to harvest the stalk for use as feed or litter.[24]

With the onset of autumn, peasants transported their shocked and dried grains to the village threshing floor (*tok*) on three-meter-long carts consisting of wooden axles and wheels that lacked steel-reinforced rims. Thereafter the grains were threshed and winnowed under the open sky as time and weather permitted. Peasants spread the harvest over the ground or—if one was available—over a specially constructed wooden floor where it would be struck with chains or else trampled by oxen and cart. V. Pavlovich observed at midcentury that "peasants [at threshing] normally harness a pair of oxen to a cart in which is placed a predetermined weight. They then trample the grain until the legs of the oxen and the wheels of the cart cannot thresh out any more."[25] On windy days peasants cleaned the grains by casting them into the air in the hope that weed seed and other impurities would be blown away.[26] Contemporaries also observed villages where grains destined for the mill or market were first manually washed and dried in the sun. Other grains were normally stored in sheds and shelters of various shapes and sizes.

Although peasants occasionally modified their farm inventories to meet new challenges or demands, numerous shortcomings remained at midcentury. The wooden construction of most tools was insufficient for local conditions and resulted in numerous breakdowns and a generally high replacement rate. One investigation of Slov'iano-Serbiia district, in the hilly, northern reaches of New Russia, noted that the Ukrainian plow lasted for varying times, depending upon the village, but it "generally does not exceed two years. In *obshchinas* with inferior, stony soils, peasants will often end up paying twice over for their plows. In addition, they are often being repaired due to the poor soil conditions."[27] Wooden-toothed harrows were not expected to last beyond a single springtime, and even iron-toothed ones rarely survived a fifth season. Peasant carts also failed to withstand the test of time, as a travel account from the time of the Crimean War (1853–56) noted: "It is not difficult to find the war theatre in the Crimea, for such a large number of broken Russian wagons lie along the military roadway, that they serve as signposts, even though all drivers had used broken wheels, axles, hubs, spokes, etc. to boil coffee or cook their porridge."[28]

Although peasants were keenly aware of these shortcomings, they continued to rely upon wooden implements until the second half of the nineteenth century. Self-made and -repaired wood-based products allowed village peasants to maintain a greater degree of control over their own mixed economies and avoid the financial costs and risks that accompanied technological innovation. It was for good reason that at midcentury New Russia's peasants, like their French counterparts, still relied on age-old implements that, in the words of one commentator, had been used by the ancient Egyptians.[29] Because of such conservatism and other forces beyond their control, agriculturalists still had to confront major difficulties, such as the 1830s crisis in sheep breeding. Poor harvests were not uncommon, and were often attributed to conditions ranging from drought to hail damage or the periodic infestations of locusts and grasshoppers. For example, in 1843 hailstones "bigger than the largest egg," with many weighing more than three-quarters of a pound, caused considerable devastation in Katerynoslav and Novomoskovsk districts.

A hailstorm on 16 June 1844 destroyed up to fifteen thousand desiatinas of vegetables, potatoes, and various grains in the center of Katerynoslav provinces.[30] Nonetheless, despite the devastation of these losses, they were not seen as part of a larger systemic crisis, nor were they sufficient to provoke a revolution in the manner in which peasants undertook their agriculture. That was soon to change.

Peasant Acquisition of New Implements after 1870

Perhaps the most dramatic agricultural innovation of the late nineteenth century was the near universal abandonment of Ukrainian plows after peasants acquired such manufactured tillage equipment as the steel plow and the scarifier (*bukker*).[31] The deeper and more thorough cultivation made possible by steel-shared plows had the double advantage of increasing moisture preservation while burying weed seeds, which had become a steadily increasing problem. The "Anglo-Bulgarian" plow was the most desirable of the new generation of plows being sold in Katerynoslav district. Its shorter, more cylindrical moldboard not only turned soil over (as was the case with other imported plows), but also loosened it so as to increase drought resistance. Its heavier steel shares were not as brittle as the earlier cast-iron ones, and made tillage possible to a depth of nine inches.[32]

Other peasant acquisitions reflected their desire to reduce the necessity of excessive draft power from their animals while minimizing the time required for soil preparation. Not surprisingly, by the 1870s peasants living in close proximity to the region's German and Mennonite colonists had followed the latter in acquiring an entire generation of lighter, less expensive implements. The reduction in virgin lands in all but the leased estate lands, together with the steady expansion in grain cultivation over livestock grazing, diminished the need for heavier plows, and led to the widespread use of the *bukker* by the region's colonists and peasants.[33] Functionally a hybrid of the *ralo* and a multishared plow, the *bukker* was initially manufactured with three or four shares, though seven-share *bukkers* were common in New Russia by the 1870s. Historian David G. Rempel has identified some of the *bukker*'s advantages:

> The single-furrow plow which had been in use until then had cut a furrow of only about ten inches in width in comparison with eighteen inches by

> the three-share *bukker* and twenty-four to twenty-six and thirty-two to thirty-six inches respectively for the two types of four-share *bukkers*. The five-, six- and seven-share *bukkers* plowed a correspondingly wider strip of land. Consequently the use of the new plow enabled a farmer, with no additional manpower, to practically double the size of his planted area. The price of these plows was low enough to make them easily procurable even by a poor farmer. Though cheap in price, they were durably and simply constructed, two of the most important prerequisites of any machinery to be of use to the average Russian farmer.[34]

Although shared like a plow, the *bukker* resembled a *ralo* in that it did not turn the soil over. Peasants used it to grind and loosen topsoil (*rastirat´ v poroshok*) sufficiently to cover the previous year's stubble. Thus, they managed to forgo plowing altogether and double the speed of soil preparation. Local manufacturers introduced a further time-saving innovation in the 1880s when they attached seeding machines (*razbrosannye seialki*) to the front of the *bukker*. Peasants also selected the *bukker* as a cost-saving measure. At first glance, cost would appear to have favored the acquisition of plows, which ranged in price from 28 to 32 rubles in Katerynoslav district at the end of the nineteenth century, whereas simple *bukkers* sold at 45 rubles, or 55 rubles when the seeding machine was attached. Yet, when zemstvo statisticians in Oleksandrivsk district, Katerynoslav province, did a more careful calculation—one that considered the added demands of time and draft power for peasants using the heavier steel plows—they concluded that overall tillage costs were a third less with the *bukker*.[35]

The results of the Oleksandrivsk district zemstvo survey provides a picture of peasant tillage inventories at the end of the nineteenth century (see tables 6.1 and 6.2).

Approximately half of all peasant households in Oleksandrivsk district owned their own *bukkers* or plows by 1899, a fact which reflected their proximity to prosperous colonist agricultural and manufacturing enterprises in the same district. At first glance, these inventories appear to correspond with those compiled in the mid-1880s for Ielysavethrad district in the northern reaches of New Russia, where plows were found in slightly less than half of all former state peasant households. However, peasants from this northern district continued to rely on the wood-based

Table 6.1. Distribution of tillage implements (in percent) among peasant households in Oleksandrivsk district, 1899.

	Without plow or *bukker*	With plow only	With *bukker* only	With plow and *bukker*
Former state peasants	45.7	13.8	10.8	28.3
Former full serfs	48.4	7.6	15.0	25.6
Former household serfs	47.3	4.4	20.9	25.4
German and Mennonite colonists	76.3	--	7.9	15.8

Source: *MOZE* 1902, pt. 2, p. 14.

Table 6.2. Peasant means of cultivation (in percent) in Oleksandrivsk district, 1899.

	Not working land	In 'yoked' manner	With rented implements	With own implements	Hiring workers
Former state peasants	9.0	66.6	13.3	18.7	1.4
Former full serfs	8.0	60.3	17.7	19.7	2.3
Former household serfs	13.2	58.3	16.3	22.7	2.7
German and Mennonite colonists	76.4	--	11.1	88.9	--

Source: *MOZE* 1902, pt. 2, p. 15.

Ukrainian plow and eschewed innovations such as the *bukker*. Here the transfer to predominantly steel implements had only just begun.[36]

Table 6.1 shows that most peasant households lacked tillage inventories sufficient to farm independently, since barely more than one in four households had both a plow and a *bukker*. The data found in table 6.2 reveal that only approximately one in five peasant households from Oleksandrivsk district did not need to either hire out or share the inventories of fellow villagers, including draft power. Two-thirds of all former state peasant households worked cooperatively, as was the case with approximately the same proportion of all former serf households. Although evidence has not been found to suggest that the commune formally established these working relationships, their very existence suggests that purchased implements may have reinforced informal cooperation among peasant households. Shared inventories made it possible to share expenses. The most common practice was known as yoking (*supriaga*), by which two to three households that lacked complete inventories would plow each household's allotment at a ratio determined by relative contributions. For example, a peasant owning a pair of oxen who yoked together with a peasant owning three pair might not only cultivate his own land but also spend a specified amount of time cultivating his fellow villager's allotment. Equally proportioned households received an equal number of days for plowing. Finally, households without livestock or implements were entirely dependent on the inventories of more prosperous fellow villagers. In exchange for the use of their inventories, they received free labor at a predetermined rate. Investigators believe that payment between villagers was on a cash basis only if more expensive reapers and threshers were involved.[37]

Steady changes in equipment were also evident during the grain harvest, the busiest time of year for peasant agriculturalists. Although foreign imports had played a leading role in the introduction of self-binding grain reapers, local demand mushroomed only when Mennonite industrialists near Oleksandrivsk on the Dnipro River began production of the famed reaping machine called the *lobogreika* ("forehead-heater" or "brow-sweater"). The elimination of the expensive and weighty self-binding mechanism made the *lobogreika* not only affordable, but more suited to the relatively small horses found in the region. The *lobogreika* required two laborers: one to serve as driver and one to rake the cut grain off of the reaper's platform.[38]

Purchases of the *lobogreika* quickly spread from the Mennonite colonies to neighboring peasant communities and beyond, and it became, by one assessment, the "predominant mechanical harvester in Russia until 1910." Peasants alone owned over 5,300 reapers in Katerynoslav district at the end of the nineteenth century, an undetermined number of which were *lobogreika*s. Even so, less than a quarter of peasant households would have been able to afford any kind of reaper. The most prosperous peasant households—those cultivating at least thirty desiatinas of land—were inclined to purchase a *lobogreika* for between 180 and 200 rubles, and then lease it out to fellow villagers for 1 to 2 rubles per desiatina.[39]

The adoption of new implements coincided with the large-scale replacement of oxen with horses, a process that resulted from an equally complex process. The rapid transformation of virgin pastures into wheat fields in the 1880s and 1890s steadily decreased the appeal of oxen, which consumed more hay than horses and were able to work fewer hours in a day. Peasants were especially apt to switch to horses after seasons with poor harvests, as was the case among the peasant farmers of Slov'iano-Serbiia district in 1901.[40] As a rule, peasants living in large villages were quicker to acquire horses, an especially important factor in a region where former state peasant villages often numbered above five hundred households and where it was common for the fields to be fifteen kilometers from the village. Under those conditions, peasants realized that they had everything to gain from reduced travel time. "With horses you can travel to the fields and back two times [in a day], the peasants say, though only once with oxen." Peasants also acquired horse power more quickly when they farmed in regions of high agricultural innovation, close to the main lines of communication, or in locales where the hard-baked virgin soils had given way to tilled fields. Indicative of these trends, fully three-quarters of all peasant households living near colonist agriculturalists in the three mainland districts of Tavriia province relied on horse power by the mid-1880s, whereas the figure dropped to 52 percent in the Crimean steppe lands immediately to the south, where virgin lands still predominated.

Wealthier peasant households were more reluctant to switch to horses than poorer ones because oxen were less costly to maintain and hardier, and therefore better able to endure rough handling by unsupervised, hired laborers. Even so, most New Russian peasants had made the shift to horse power by 1900 at a more rapid pace than had occurred on private estates, where larger landholdings allowed nobles to retain their larger and slower pastoral animals. One representative survey of working livestock is found in table 6.3.[41]

Table 6.3. Working livestock in Katerynoslav district, 1897.

	Horses	**Oxen**
Peasants	59,584	7,757
Estate owners	4,819	9,112

Source: *MOZE* 1899, pt. 2, p. 131.

By the end of the nineteenth century peasants in Katerynoslav district were relying on horses for 88 percent of their draft power, whereas the 4,819 horses owned by estate owners accounted for only 35 percent of their draft power. A report of the Special Conference on the Needs of Agriculture from Kherson province refers to the replacement of oxen among the peasantry: "Oxen, having lost their significance in peasant agriculture, nevertheless still play a major role as beasts of burden within estate agriculture." Peasants in that province in 1900 owned over 450,000 horses and fewer than 100,000 oxen, and the latter figure dropped steadily in the following years.[42]

Finally, peasants had begun to acquire more efficient means of conveyance before 1900, especially light carriages (*brichki*) and wagons (*mazhari*). Either purchased directly from Mennonite manufacturers or from local fairs, where they were sold in large numbers, the wagon's design utilized a single undercarriage of two sets of wheels connected by an adjustable beam. In its most elongated form the *mazhara* featured railings placed on the sides for grain cartage from the fields, which was an especially important feature when peasants wished to reduce the number of trips between the distant fields and the village. The *brichka*, an undercarriage that peasants shortened and secured with side planks, provided them with an effective means for human transport as well as carting threshed grains to the market.[43]

In short, New Russian peasants modified their agricultural inventories throughout the nineteenth century, but especially in the second half. A survey of the artisanal trade in Kherson province in 1904 noted that the wooden plows and ox carts which had been commonplace twenty to twenty-five years earlier were rarely to be seen.[44] Similarly, in his study of Katerynoslav province in 1900 the anthropologist V. A. Babenko concluded that:

> Universally here in the province peasants and settlers have adopted improved methods of cultivating fields and gardens by means of steel manufactured agricultural implements. Everywhere plows, *ralos*, harrows, winnowers, cutters, threshers, and so on have been acquired. Homemade wooden implements have already departed into the realm of legend.[45]

Although Babenko's enthusiastic report may have been somewhat lacking in objectivity, it provided accurate testimony to the changing nature of peasant agricultural inventories. In his study of peasant agriculture in New Russia at the end of the 1880s, V. E. Postnikov recorded typical peasant agricultural inventories (see table 6.4). The first inventory belonged to a prosperous peasant, Emel′ian Sakhnov. Sakhnov lived in Rivne (Rovnoe) village, in Ielysavethrad district of Kherson province with his wife, two sons (ages thirty and eighteen), and sixteen-year-old daughter. He, along with a live-in hired laborer and seasonal workers, cultivated 16 of his 20 desiatinas of allotment land, and leased an additional 19 desiatinas from a neighboring estate owner. A second, "middle" peasant household comprised a husband and wife along with two sons, of whom one was an adult. Together they had 15 desiatinas of allotment land, and along with leasing arrangements the family cultivated 20 desiatinas annually. Finally, the third, peasant family was that of forty-five-year-old Efim Vergun, who together with his wife and three sons (ages sixteen, three, and one) annually raised crops on 4 of his 5-desiatina allotment. Implement inventories for all three households are listed below in table 6.4.[46]

A small but significant innovation occurred in the late nineteenth century in the type of actual crops sown: a drop in wheat and rye prices encouraged a move to other grains. At first, the price decline was masked by the simultaneous, steady increase in exports from Black Sea ports, which belied the declining proportion of foreign market sales going to Russian producers. However, the increased European preference for American grains in the 1880s and 1890s was clearly reflected in depressed prices throughout all of European Russia. New Russia was especially hard-hit since its grain prices had been disproportionately high in the

1870s, and because it had remained highly dependent on foreign markets.[47] Table 6.5 provides wheat and rye prices from 1876 to 1900 in New Russia.[48]

With only occasional shifts upward, after the early 1880s New Russian grain prices remained depressed for some fifteen years. Although prices did rise from time to time in this period, overall the collapse was severe.[49] Peasant producers responded to the depression in grain prices by altering the proportion of land allotted to their various crops, as table 6.6 indicates (though unfortunately it combines information for estates and

Table 6.4. Selected peasant agricultural inventories (ruble value in parentheses) in Ielysavethrad district, 1885.

	Prosperous farm	Average farm	Poor farm
Draft power			
Horses	3 (150)	4 (170)	2 (50)
Oxen	6 (330)	--	--
Implements			
Plows	2 (30)	1 (11.5)	1 (12)
Bukkers	1 (30)	--	--
Harrows	5 (15)	5 (19)	2 (6)
Wooden roller	--	1 (1.5)	--
Winnower	1 (40)	1 (30)	--
Grain sorter	1 (25)	--	--
Horse-drawn thresher	1 (450)	1 (300)	--
Mazharas	4 (80)	3 (39)	1 (20)
Brichkas	2 (95)	--	--
Horse harness	(30)	(40)	(20)
Shovel, hoe, etc.	(10)	(6.4)	(5)
Total value	**(1285)**	**(617.4)**	**(113)**

Source: Postnikov 1891, 219–21.

peasants). Wheat, with its relatively high market value, continued to be sown on fifty percent of all arable lands, though significant changes were noted in the proportions of rye and barley sown. Rye experienced the

Table 6.5. Fixed prices (kopecks per pood) of wheat and rye in New Russia, 1880–1905.

Years	Wheat	Rye
1876–1880	--	67
1881–1885	101	77
1886–1890	86	52
1891–1895	64	60
1896–1900	82.8	57
1901–1905	79	60

Source: Mironov 1985, appendix, tables 11, 16.

Table 6.6. Major crops sown (in thousands of desiatinas) in New Russia, 1881–1899.

	1881		1899	
	Total	Percent	Total	Percent
Winter rye	1,105.2	17.2	892.9	10.5
Spring rye	38.2	5.9	8.0	0.1
Winter wheat	468.6	7.3	750.3	8.8
Spring wheat	2,722.8	42.3	3,636.2	42.6
Oats	306.5	4.8	407.1	4.8
Barley	942.4	14.6	2,188.0	25.7
Potatoes	90.5	1.4	199.1	1.4
Other grains	760.8	11.8	529.2	6.2
Total	**6,435.0**	**100.0**	**8,530.8**	**100.0**

Source: *SSXIX* 1902, vol. 1, 56–58.

greatest decline, as its share fell from 23.1 percent in 1881 to 10.6 percent. By the latter year, only one district in all of Tavriia still regarded rye as an important market crop. Instead, peasants favored barley, as its consistently sound harvests compensated for its lower market values.[50]

Although it is clear that New Russian peasants introduced significant agricultural innovations during the late nineteenth century, we have yet to account for what motivated them to do so. We take as our starting point the fact that the majority of New Russia's peasants at midcentury had little incentive to expand or diversify their holdings. This was largely so because the agricultural practices of the early nineteenth century appeared to be more than adequate to meet their needs at midcentury. If the system was not broken, why should the peasants have fixed it? Part of the reason also lay in the lack of extra-communal incentives and support, as Gałęski has indicated. Thus, with the exception of those peasants who had direct access to attractive markets, most peasants hesitated to introduce agricultural innovations, and for good reason. Internal needs, rather than external forces, such as expanding markets, were paramount. But beyond market-driven considerations, other changes were also on the horizon.

A Crisis Unfolds

During the last decades of the nineteenth century, after their existing practices had produced crisis-like conditions, New Russian peasant agriculturalists modified their agricultural practices. The crisis itself was the natural result of the dramatic increase in grain cultivation over time and space, and can best be observed by contrasting trends in New Russia with those found empirewide. In all Russia the area sown by peasants changed very little, a mere 1 percent, rising from 44.0 to 44.4 million desiatinas from the 1860s to the turn of the century (see table 6.7). A more impressive increase of 16 percent was observed among peasants in the adjacent Ukrainian provinces of Volynia, Podolia, and Kyiv. All of this notwithstanding, the expansion undertaken by New Russian peasants was of an entirely different order. Within New Russia as a whole, the amount of cultivated peasant lands under cultivation in the second half of the nineteenth century increased by 50 percent, from 2.8 to 4.4 million desiatinas.[51] Tavriia province experienced the greatest increases within the region, as countless households more than doubled their arable fields. On average, by the 1890s peasant households in that province cultivated as much land as their counterparts in Katerynoslav and Kherson. Tavriia was also unique in that the greatest expansion came in the 1860s and 1870s, when its sown area increased from 610,000 to over a million desiatinas.

Several factors accounted for this unprecedented expansion within New Russia: favorable market conditions, the availability of previously

Table 6.7. Peasant lands (in thousands of desiatinas) in grain production, 1860–1900.

Province	1860s	1870s	1880s	1890s	pct. increase 1860–1900
Katerynoslav	1,003.8	1,036.8	1,136.4	1,430.5	43
Tavriia	610.0	1,008.0	1,116.9	1,370.9	125
Kherson	1,213.6	1,320.5	1,232.9	1,450.6	20
New Russia	**2,827.6**	**3,365.3**	**3,486.2**	**4,251.7**	**50**
European Russia	**44,006.0**	**43,850.8**	**43,718.8**	**44,376.8**	**1**

Source: *MVU01*, vol. 1, 170–71.

uncultivated lands, and the persistence of extensive practices. Only the Baltic and far western provinces of the empire matched the degree to which natural location tied New Russian producers to foreign markets. Such a connection was especially attractive in the 1860s and 1870s, when rising grain prices coincided with improved rail transport and the expansion of port facilities on the Black and Azov seas. At the same time, the population base expanded steadily because of the continued immigration from the more crowded Ukrainian and Russian heartlands.[52] Combined with natural increases, this immigration actually resulted in a per capita decline in the area sown within the region, despite the fantastic increases identified above (see table 6.8 below).

By 1900 average peasant holdings planted in crops in New Russia was almost double that of European Russia, with 1,051 desiatinas per

Table 6.8. Peasant grain production (in desiatinas) per thousand souls (male and female), 1860–1900.

Province	1860s	1870s	1880s	1890s	pct. change 1860–1900
Katerynoslav	1,020	854	772	792	-22
Tavriia	1,478	1,981	1,697	1,573	+6
Kherson	1,194	1,099	847	787	-34
New Russia	**1,231**	**1,311**	**1,105**	**1,051**	**-15**
European Russia	**825**	**717**	**616**	**547**	**-34**

Source: *MVU01*, vol. 1, 170–76.

1000 people. By contrast, the Ukrainian provinces to the north had fewer than 400 desiatinas in crops per 1000 people.[53] Table 6.8 also shows the degree to which peasant grain production, as a proportion of the population, expanded in Tavriia over a longer period than in Katerynoslav and Kherson, where it was in steady decline after 1860. In other words, while the amount of land tilled increased steadily and dramatically throughout the entire region before 1900, it could keep up with population increases only in Tavriia. Demographic increases at this time were significant. New Russia's population doubled between 1863 and 1897, increasing from 3,141,672 to 6,295,900, with the greatest growth occurring before 1885. Katerynoslav province had an average of 40.2 inhabitants per square verst by the latter date, up from 15.9 inhabitants in 1863. Although almost 20 percent of this population were urban dwellers by the turn of the century, the demographic increase in the countryside meant that less land was available for increasing numbers of peasants. Former state peasant allotments in Kherson province, for example, decreased on average from 9.6 desiatinas in 1858 to 4.7 in the mid-1880s, at which time former serf allotments averaged a mere 2 desiatinas per soul, well below the level required to maintain basic subsistence levels from grain cultivation.[54] Thus, the average peasant allotment decreased in size at the very time that a greater portion of it was under cultivation.

Initially, peasants had expanded their grain cultivation through the application of previously successful extensive practices to ever increasing amounts of land. With less land and without any other modifications, something had to give; in this case, it was the number of years that peasants were prepared to rest fields exhausted by overcultivation. It was not uncommon for peasants to work ever greater proportions of their land continuously, and any remaining reserves of virgin and pasture lands were also put under the plow. The following description of events for peasant villages in Bakhmut district, Katerynoslav province, can be applied to almost every corner of New Russia between the late 1850s and the early 1880s:

> Plowland for peasants has risen by at least 50 percent in the last twenty years. Among former state peasant villages, in which not so long ago there were still significant portions of untrammelled virgin land, and vast stretches of hay meadows and other long-fallowed lands, now the greatest portion of arable has been turned under the plow. Virgin land and fallow have almost completely disappeared. In Andreevsk volost, for example, in the last 35 to 36 years the cultivated area of allotment land has increased by 200 percent at the expense of the hay meadow and virgin lands. Up to the middle of the 1870s, this rank of relatively land-rich peasants managed their allotment land in such a way that allowed for both grain cultivation and livestock breeding. But in the past decades, insufficient land allotments have been experienced here, and peasants have been compelled to lease land on the side. Former serfs, who plow all of their allotments with the exception of pastures (though in many villages even the pasture is plowed under) already long ago have undertaken the main portion of their economies on leased land. All of the increased demand in land for cultivation means that almost without exception peasants allow less time for the land to rest, and in many of the former serf *obshchina* allotments have already been sown for ten to fifteen years without a break.... Land in which only the thin upper layer is worked has long ago been exhausted by annual sowings. Yet these are constantly worked until it is impossible for them to give a satisfactory harvest as the fields are choked with weeds, couchgrass, spurge (*molochai*) and wild oats (*ovsiug*). To plow more deeply, and bring lower areas of soil to the surface, is not possible with peasant plows.[55]

In retrospect, it is not altogether surprising that the fabled fertility of New Russian soils, and their supposed ability to produce fine harvests with only minimal input, had clearly been exposed as false by the mid-1870s. At the time, however, the fact dropped like a bombshell. The Fifth Congress of the Union of Russian Agriculturalists, held in 1878 in Odesa, was entirely devoted to this problem. In his opening address, Valerii Ivanovich Mazarakii, president of the Imperial Agricultural Society of New Russia, concluded soberly:

> In Russia, and especially in the south, agriculture is managed not according to a fixed system, but by the judgments and means of each separate agriculturalist. Our agriculture up to the present time consists, with few exceptions, of the desire to plow and sow more and more. But this passion for excessive plowing, this demand for quick profits is not at all advantageously reflected in our economies. Insufficient workers, unproductive expenditure of capital, obtained not from the surplus of produce but from the mortgaging of property, unpleasant climatic conditions, harmful insects, the difficulty in marketing products, and other disadvantages have caused our agriculturalists to hesitate, and [forced us] here to listen to the loud cries about the exhaustion of the soil, rapacious economies, and about the necessity of replacing it all with new, rational, intensive, more careful, and overall more orderly economies.[56]

As Mazarakii pointed out, the reckless increase in grain production left New Russian agriculturalists—peasants as well as estate owners—exceedingly vulnerable to a host of problems. Of these, the main concerns facing peasants in the 1870s centered on environmental changes, the repeated and mass appearance of harmful predators, and excessive weed damage. Weather was able to bless or damn the best efforts of all the region's agriculturalists, and both outcomes had been in evidence over the years. Dramatic shifts in temperature and precipitation were not uncommon. For instance, a prolonged drought in 1863 in Oleksandrivsk district was severe enough to require grain imports from Poltava, Kharkiv, and Kursk. Peasants in the more densely settled northern districts of New Russia appear to have found climatic conditions increasingly hostile after 1860. This was, in no small part, because the rapid increase in poorly managed lands for grain production depleted what little moisture was available in the region at precisely the time when more was required (grain production required more moisture than did pastoral farming). The New Russian steppe had also become less hospitable due to the destruction of forests to the north and northeast of the region, a development that allowed drier and stronger winds to make their way south unimpeded.[57] Even within New Russia moisture levels had decreased from the destruction of what few trees did exist in the ravines, along with the plowing under of the rich prairie grasses of the virgin steppe. Anton I. Umiss, in the 1874 address that began this chapter, concluded: "The climate has become dry and unhealthy; summers unbearably sultry; winters inconstant; and the whole region has taken on something of a gloomy character."[58]

Insects were also a cause of concern for the region's peasants, though until the 1850s they had appeared only in random, infrequent waves. In 1823, for example, locusts destroyed an entire area of forty square kilometers. Still, while there were considerable losses the next year as well, locusts did not reappear in such large numbers until 1852, and then again in 1858.[59] Thereafter, they were reported with increasing frequency, especially in places where peasants had transformed pastures bursting with natural vegetation into poorly cultivated and exhausted plowland. All farmers found that insects such as locusts, beetles, grasshoppers, and cockroaches were extremely difficult to control or eliminate once they arrived in the region. Locusts flourished in the estuaries and river flats, as well as on the banks of the Black and Azov seas. Laying from sixty to seventy eggs annually, they consumed a wide range of foodstuffs, including wood, tree leaves, dry straw, and even wool. Their preference, though, was for grasses and grains, to which they turned with devastating ferocity. From morning until evening they fed, at which time the cold or occasional rains forced them to seek shelter in wooded areas or on north-facing slopes.[60]

Agronomists soon realized that locusts, and generally all insects, could only be controlled with the rigorous cultivation of soils in the fall and early spring, at which time the insects were in their most vulnerable state. The careful rotation of crops, and the introduction of new ones, were able to rob these predators of a stable and preferred diet. Unfortunately such careful husbandry in the 1860s and 1870s was rarely seen, since agriculturalists—whether peasant or noble—remained committed to extensive labor-saving practices. Instead, the rapid expansion of grain production in the 1860s increased the potential for insect damage and led to the destruction of hundreds of square kilometers of grain crops. One contemporary observer claimed that grain beetles alone consumed a third of the empire's entire grain harvest.[61]

Damage became more generalized and pronounced in the 1860s, and was first observed in the more densely settled northern districts of New Russia, where grain production had first developed. In 1862 an estimated 17,800 desiatinas of drought-afflicted land were destroyed by insects in Pavlohrad district alone, and earlier, in 1855, there were so many beetles in the rye, wheat, and barley fields in Ielysavethrad district that their collective sound mimicked swarms of bees. Often entire fields were destroyed and needed to be resown. At other times, grain was simply cut green and used for cattle feed, as happened to more than 1,400 desiatinas of wheat on the Karpov estate in Bakhmut district in 1878. Concomitantly, livestock frequently became diseased from eating grains "infected" by beetles and grain cutters (*khlebnye pilil'shchiki*).[62]

Finally, gophers were a major source of damage for the grain fields of New Russia. To give an indication of their destructive force, Pavlovich noted that the harvests of 1862 were not particularly unusual, despite the fact that gophers had destroyed up to half of all crops grown on private estates. Harvests were only truly bad, he noted, if there was barely enough grain gathered to assure a seeding for the following year. One account of harvest conditions in Katerynoslav for 1866 claimed that billions of gophers had devastated the countryside, and eighty-desiatina fields of previously good wheat could yield no more than five stacks after the wheat had been cut and gathered.[63]

Peasants initially contributed to these problems through their own inactivity, their anachronistic cultivation practices, and their unwitting elimination of potential allies. Regarding the latter, a St. Petersburg professor of agriculture who had toured Kherson province in the summer of 1872 observed:

> In the time of Pallas, i.e., in the last quarter of the previous century, in all of south Russia there were many wild birds of prey whereas gophers, by contrast, were few in number. With my travels in the province in the present summer, I was struck by the limited appearance of birds of prey. In enquiring of the peasants about the birds and the wild animals, I realized that they had all persecuted and feared the fox; the polecat (*khorek*) had been almost completely exterminated in several areas. The *pereviazka* (*Mustela sarmatica*) had been completely exterminated and even the name of it was unknown, though in the time of Pallas it had been most common. In several localities I was told of peasants and gentry who zealously

> exterminated foxes and polecats. I was even told that there were peasants who were almost exclusively engaged in the killing of foxes.[64]

The dramatic reduction in pastures and hay meadows had a direct impact on peasant livestock breeding and anticipated the shift from oxen to horses. Per capita numbers of cattle decreased steadily in all three provinces of New Russia from 1870 to the end of the century, reflecting the peasants' decreased interest in livestock breeding as grain economies developed.[65] The desire to sow more of their allotment lands had reduced the portion devoted to pastures or hay meadows. In the early 1860s former serfs had compensated for these trends by leasing pastures and hay meadows from adjoining estates, but the subsequent escalation in lease rates made many look elsewhere. New Russian peasants then sought to cut corners in the care of their livestock by reducing pastureland—and at the very time that the animals were required to do more field work. At the same time, peasants resisted leaving fields fallow, which left pastures choked with weeds and able to provide fodder of only minimal nutritional value. The results were not surprising, especially in the more densely settled provinces of Kherson and Katerynoslav.

Contagious diseases, the result of overpasturing, now prevailed every three to four years and resulted in massive losses. In 1873, fully 16 percent of all cattle in Kherson province, or almost 120,000 of 735,000, died of rinderpest when this highly contagious, viral disease swept in from Tavriia. Such devastating losses were now judged to be among the hardest of the burdens faced by peasants. Once cattle contracted it, there was little that peasants could do: the high fever began a process in the animals that within days culminated in uncontrolled diarrhea and death. Over 40 percent of all cattle that became ill from rinderpest in Katerynoslav province in 1874 did not recover.[66] In 1868 the governor of Kherson province succinctly summed up the basic problem, declaring that peasants

> work the land with the cheapest means possible. They do not sow feed grasses, in the hopes that the natural hay meadow will suffice. Yet with the wasteful collapse of meadows under the pasturing methods of cattle, and especially sheep, the hay crops are often small. In spite of the breadth of the steppe, the livestock often collapse from insufficient feed.[67]

It is clear that large sections of New Russia, including almost all of Katerynoslav province and the northern districts of Kherson, experienced mounting difficulties in the 1870s. There were low or declining grain yields in all three provinces owing to the rapid increase of poorly cultivated lands and a corresponding decrease in the time fields were allowed to regenerate naturally. The widespread persistence of practices ill-suited to intensive grain cultivation had a negative effect on the physical geography of the region itself and increased both the probability of, and vulnerability to, harsher climatic cycles, depleted water sources, and the increased frequency of invasions by gophers and harmful insects.

The Turnaround in Peasant Agriculture

Faced with such difficulties, it seems improbable that peasant agriculturalists could have rebounded by the 1890s, and yet they did. Harvest information for the entire period is presented in table 6.9. This table shows that grain harvests in New Russia rose steadily from 19 poods per desiatina in the 1860s to 34 poods in the 1890s, an overall increase of almost 80 percent. Tavriia province, with an average of 41 poods per desiatina in the 1890s, had the highest yields within New Russia itself,

Table 6.9. Peasant grain harvests (poods per desiatina) in the Russian Empire, 1860–1900.

Province	1860s	1870s	1880s	1890s
Katerynoslav	18	16	25	38
Tavriia	21	23	28	41
Kherson	18	20	23	31
New Russia	**19**	**20**	**25**	**34**
Little Ukraine	25	30	33	40
Southwest Russia	31	36	41	47
European Russia	**29**	**31**	**34**	**39**

Source: *MVU01*, vol. 1, 171, 177.
Note: "Southwest Russia" refers to the provinces of Volhynia, Kyiv, and Podillia. "Little Ukraine" refers in this instance to Poltava and Chernihiv.

followed by Katerynoslav and Kherson with 38 and 31, respectively. From the 1860s to the 1870s, yields increased by 5 percent in New Russia, (though dropping from 18 to 16 poods per desiatina in Katerynoslav). Yet regionwide increases from the 1870s to the 1880s and the following decade amounted to 25 percent (20 to 25 poods) and 36 percent (25 to 34 poods) respectively. This contrasts with more modest increases for the same period in central Ukraine or Southwest Russia. What changes in New Russian peasant agriculture during the 1870s and 1880s accounted for this upsurge in productivity? Secondly, why is it that yields by 1900 were still relatively low? Despite increases, yields in the region remained similar to rising harvests in European Russia, which themselves were significantly lower than those found among European agriculturalists. What accounted for these trends?

Peasants were especially motivated by the increasing scarcity of arable land and the need to extract a better harvest on reduced per-capita holdings. However, demographic necessity is unable to account for the manner in which New Russian peasants before 1900 had shifted from agricultural involution to innovation, nor can it account for the limits to that innovation. It also does not follow, as one study has concluded, that "the least densely populated and least industrialized provinces had the most primitive method of maintaining soil fertility, and the most densely populated and most developed provinces had (for nineteenth-century Russia) the most advanced method."[68] To cite one example that challenges monocausal population-based explanations, peasant villagers living in the northern, densely settled districts of Kherson province were less inclined to switch to steel plows than were peasants found in the less populous villages bordering on the Mennonite colonist villages in the southern rim of New Russia.[69] In another instance, it is clear that the development of intensive vegetable gardening operations had more to do with marketing possibilities than with population pressures. This suggests that innovation resulted not only from population pressures, as in the case of New Russia's northern districts, but also from emerging markets, or from the influence of neighboring agriculturalists who had introduced new technologies on their own lands, as was the case in the southern areas.

A more promising approach in explaining agricultural innovation is that taken by historians Eugen Weber, Roger Price, and David Grigg, and recently endorsed by Judith Pallot.[70] In his study of French agriculture, Price succinctly describes the factors leading to the transformation of peasant agriculture:

> Whereas the two prime inputs of traditional agriculture were land and labour, and productivity was thus limited by the quality of the land and the amount of labour, in a modern agriculture productivity is substantially increased by inputs of working capital in the form of fertilizers, improved hand tools, and mechanical power. This change appears to have been determined by the evolution of three basic groups of variables—product prices, the prices of the factors of production (land, labour and capital) and development of the economic infra-structure, i.e. of transport and marketing facilities—an evolution which intensified the commercialization of agriculture by means of a 'two-way tie' to the market economy, i.e. through the sale of products and the purchase of equipment and fertilizers.[71]

Technological innovation occurred first among those French agriculturalists who were not consumed with meeting subsistence needs.[72] By the end of the century, French peasants had begun to acquire new agricultural implements in response to new market opportunities and an expanded economic infrastructure in which they could take part. Thus, technological innovation reflected the increased confidence of French peasants to interact with the larger world and marked a significant transition point in their development as capitalist farmers. Where does New Russia fit into this theoretical framework?

The Example of Others

Consistent with Price's conclusions, technological innovation in the region was initially undertaken by wealthier Mennonite agriculturalists who were inclined to risk and innovation. Neighboring peasants followed their lead only after it had proven to be successful. As noted previously, the origins of Mennonite industry in the nineteenth century were directly tied to an inheritance system that left the majority of heirs landless. As a result, Mennonite villages soon developed a significant proportion of landless offspring. Many were compelled to serve as an inexpensive source of labor for Mennonite farmers; others turned to artisanal trades. This combination of labor supply, artisanal support, and nondivisible landholding was the basis for Mennonite prosperity in Russia. The inclination to adopt and profit from locally manufactured and newer agricultural implements led Mennonites to an age of true prosperity and provided neighboring peasants with a powerful demonstration of alternative agricultural practices, so much so that local peasants would say, "We will not do it this particular way, because the [Mennonites] do not. We will follow the [Mennonites]."[73]

Mennonites were but one part of an unusually polyglot population base, however, and any consideration of gains made in New Russian agriculture has to take into account the region's rich cultural and ethnic diversity. Non-Russian and non-Ukrainian peoples comprised almost 15 percent of Katerynoslav province's population in 1900, and at least 25 percent of Kherson and Tavriia provinces. Included in this sizable share were both indigenous peoples, such as Tatars, and foreign agriculturalists, whom the state had invited into this region in the late eighteenth and early nineteenth centuries. Many of the latter sought to replicate the agricultural practices of their homelands. Though at times unsuccessful, the application and adaptation of previously acquired methods resulted in a rich patchwork of widely differing agricultural practices within the Black Sea region. One contemporary observer, writing about Kherson province for the Imperial Free Economic Society in 1878, claimed "we do not know of any province, besides this one, where the population is more ethnically diverse, and where it would be as possible to find the same wealth of information for the study of economic relations and life of such diverse peoples."[74]

Many colonists proved to be exceptional market gardeners, among them the Moldavians of the Dnister River valley who excelled in fruit, vegetable, grape, and tobacco production. Bulgarians were noted for having among the best vegetable gardens in the region. Aiding them was a self-designed means of irrigation, known as the "Bulgarian wheel," which lifted water up from a river or pond by pails attached to a large wheel and then poured it into specially designed wooden troughs. The steadfast care given by Bulgarians to their fields diminished the likelihood of drought and resulted in magnificent harvests.[75]

Opportunities for interaction between peasants and the various foreign colonists were many. Russian and Ukrainian peasants often came face to face with Bulgarian agricultural techniques within the confines of their own villages, where Bulgarians came annually to lease and manage whatever lands were available for their market gardens. In this manner, peasants had the opportunity firsthand to observe Bulgarians cultivate cabbages, turnips, onions, sugar beets, carrots, and other vegetables for sale.[76] Mennonites also made significant contributions to the development of vegetable and fruit production in New Russia. Many of their forebears had migrated from the Netherlands to the Danzig (now Gdansk) region in the eighteenth century, where they established intensive agricultural economies geared to local markets. Not surprisingly, they pursued similar ventures when they immigrated to New Russia after 1789. Mennonites, and to a lesser degree the German Lutherans and Catholics who also immigrated to New Russia at that time, established enviable reputations for their vegetable gardens and orchards as well as mulberry plantations and vineyards.[77]

Foreign colonists greatly stimulated peasant agricultural specialization and diversification. Vegetables such as tomatoes were introduced to the region for the first time. Superior varieties of potatoes were brought by German and Mennonite farmers from their European homelands. The Bulgarians' practice of leasing out village lands significantly stimulated peasant market gardening in the lands along the Dnipro and Dnister rivers. In all such cases, peasants observed the cultivation of unfamiliar crops, sampled the produce in local markets, and then purchased seeds and nursery stock at markets so as to improve their own production.[78] In his memoir of life in the Mennonite settlement of Zahradivka, Kherson province, Gerhard Lohrenz presents an account of the interaction between Mennonites and their peasant neighbors:

> Our watermelons were large and very delicious. When I was a boy every farmer had a very large watermelon patch. My father had about nine acres of watermelons. In the fall, the Russians from far and wide came to buy these melons and we had no difficulty selling them all at a good profit. But in the course of time this changed. The Russians learned to plant watermelons themselves and it became more difficult to sell them.[79]

Colonists were as likely to benefit from these processes as were peasants. For example, the Bulgarians' successful cultivation of vineyards in Berdiansk district caught the attention of neighboring Germans in the villages of Veinau, Durlakh, and Altenau. Here they soon established vineyards, which in turn stimulated peasant experimentation. Il′ia Kopych of the nearby village of Pishchane (Peshchanoe) planted over one hundred vines in the 1860s and established a winemaking operation by 1884.

Foreign colonists were not the only models for agricultural specialization available to New Russia's peasants. The Crimean Tatars, who had long led the way in the region's tobacco cultivation, owned two-thirds of all land in Tavriia province that was under tobacco cultivation in the 1880s. They also leased additional lands for that purpose.[80] Contemporaries were also quick to note the agricultural contributions made by the region's many Orthodox sectarians. In this regard, Skal′kovs′kyi recorded in the mid-nineteenth century that

> *Raskolniki* and Old Believers, who arrived here from Starodubovskii district in Chernihiv province, were the first founders of market gardening here. In [Ukraine], they were already considered to be respectable agriculturalists, and many of them knew of vegetable and fruit production and were passionately involved in it.... So as to judge the relative success of these settlers, it is enough to glance at two main regions: to the villages of Znamenskaia volost (Melitopol district, Tavriia province), and to the settlements of Ploskoe, Krasnoe, Lysaia-gora, and even the towns of Elisavetgrad, Tiraspol, Dubossara, and so on (in Kherson province), where they grow enormous gardens and orchards. They immeasurably fill our markets and bazaars with their own vegetables, greens, fowl, and eggs.[81]

At this time, Old Believers were responsible for the very best gardens located on a ten-kilometer stretch of the Moscow Road near the regional center of Ielysavethrad. The *raskolnik* villages of Velyka Znam'ianka and Kam'ianka also initiated the expansion of market gardening all along the southern banks of the Dnipro River in the Dnipro and Melitopol districts of Tavriia province. Almost three-quarters of the 1,611 households located in Velyka Znam'ianka were engaged in viticulture in the late nineteenth century, where they planted approximately half a million vines on 170 hectares.[82]

Expanding Markets

Peasant acquisition of new agricultural implements coincided with more favorable market conditions, or improved "product prices." Rising market prices for New Russian grains, most especially wheat, motivated the region's agriculturalists to increase their incomes through horticultural expansion. Historian Boris Mironov has shown that grain prices in New Russia increased more than tenfold during the period from 1707–10 to 1910–14.[83] The most spectacular increases occurred in the 1870s when the region benefited from its immediate access to expanding European markets through the Black Sea and Azov ports. And even though the region was hard-hit by the worldwide grain depression of the 1880s, wheat prices in Katerynoslav province rebounded from an average of sixty kopecks a pood in 1891–95 to eighty kopecks in the next five-year period. New Russian peasants cultivated over four thousand desiatinas of their allotment lands in the 1890s, an increase of 50 percent since the 1860s, as agriculturalists responded to rising prices with sharp increases in grain production.

New Russian peasant economies were especially responsive to price fluctuations because of the degree to which their efforts were market driven. Nowhere was this more evident than in Katerynoslav district, where peasants at the end of the nineteenth century realized yields of 10.8 million poods from spring wheat, barley, and rye. Of this amount, an estimated 4.7 million poods (44 percent) reached the market, leaving 1.6 million poods for seed, and 4.5 million poods for household needs.[84] The responsiveness of New Russia's peasants to rising prices supports previous work undertaken by the European agricultural historian, B. H. Slicher van Bath, who wrote:

> In general, market prices of agricultural products will influence farmers in the purchase of improved tools or new machinery. The farmer will purchase when the prices of the products are relatively high; he will postpone his purchases when the prices are relatively low. As a consequence of the difficulty of obtaining exact knowledge of the financial situation of the farm and to overcome the problems of bookkeeping, farmers will be inclined to consider high prices as identical with his profits.[85]

Of course, if rising prices stimulated agricultural innovation, collapsing market prices could discourage it, as peasants in Tavriia province discovered. They returned to more labor-intensive means of reaping during a time of low market prices in the 1880s. Nor were international markets the only ones that mattered. Important local markets opened up as urban residents in New Russia consumed increasing amounts of the region's produce and contributed to the steady demand for wheat and other grains. Local markets safeguarded grain prices at a time of collapsed European prices, and may have been the reason why the demand for local grains in Katerynoslav district rose annually from 1875 to 1893.

Despite the depression in prices during the 1880s, the local grain trade served as a powerful incentive for farmers to bring more crops to the marketplace, and in that same decade peasants responded by plowing most of their remaining pastures and hay meadows to plant more wheat. Though increased weed damage and soil exhaustion required additional adjustments, the process nevertheless demonstrated peasant inclinations to gear their economies to prevailing market conditions.[86]

The appeal of these expanding market opportunities in the late nineteenth century only partially accounted for the increased peasant acquisition of new agricultural implements. Equally important is an understanding of trends in the costs of production, especially as it pertained to land, labor, and time. Of these, historians of European agriculture have emphasized that a diminished labor force in the nineteenth century forced rural wages upward and compelled estate owners to introduce labor-saving implements. This initially resulted in a two-tiered rural economy in which labor-saving estate owners were separated from labor-intensive peasant farms. Gradually, however, changing attitudes to work and the growing appeal of the market motivated peasant agriculturalists to acquire labor-saving technology.[87] Although concerns about an adequate labor supply figured prominently in the Mennonites' acquisition of implements at midcentury, as it did for Russian estate owners from the 1890s onward, among peasants such concerns were initially restricted to those living in the Tavriia province districts of Melitopol and Berdiansk. Approximately one in five peasants living in these districts cultivated from twenty-five to fifty desiatinas of land in the late 1880s, enough to require hired laborers. Known as "Tavrichinin," they were among the first peasants in New Russia to rely on labor-saving technology.

Although only a minority of peasants tested the labor market as employers, all contended with rising land values, which varied greatly depending on the soil type and location. Even so, the upward trend was universal. For example, lands in one northern district of Katerynoslav province (Novomoskovsk) rose from 70–80 rubles a desiatina in the early 1880s to 350 rubles in 1905.[88] Such increases resulted from both the dramatic population increase noted earlier and the region's dramatic shift to grain production in the late nineteenth century. Wheat and barley cultivation comprised 76 percent of all crops sown in 1899 (50 and 26 percent respectively) and reflected the increased profits being realized by peasant agriculturalists. Costs were also on the rise. It is not surprising that by 1900 estate owners often required cash payment for land leased to peasants, whereas payment in kind had previously been the norm.[89]

The peasants' decision to expand their activity in grain cultivation further increased the value of time as a unit of production. They had to prepare soils rapidly in autumn if winter crops were to survive and experience enough growth in late fall to withstand the hot dry weather of late spring and early summer. Spring crops needed to be sown quickly so as to preserve as much winter moisture as possible. Yet those peasant producers who expanded their tillage operations also had to confront other challenges, since the increased time required for the summer harvest shortened the time available for fall field preparation. Thus, peasants had choices to make. They could expend more capital on their farms by hiring more laborers or purchasing more efficient equipment, or they could sow more crops less thoroughly than before. Not surprisingly they often chose a little of both. It was during the busy agricultural season of the late summer and early fall that innovations were first observed. Peasants had become acutely aware that their profits were determined, in large part, by the speed with which grains could be cut, threshed, and carted to market, and another crop sown.[90]

Markets and the Development of Intensive Garden Economies

Nowhere was the importance attached to increased markets more evident than in the steady expansion of peasant fruit and vegetable production. By 1900 almost one in five New Russians, or more than 1.5 million inhabitants, were urban dwellers. Within the space of three generations this former frontier had been transformed into one of the industrial and urban cornerstones of the empire. Odesa, with almost a quarter of the region's dwellers, still dominated, and had become the fourth largest city in the empire. Other important centers included the Black and Azov seaports of Kherson, Mykolaïv, and Berdiansk, the rapidly expanding mining and heavy industrial centers of the Donets-Dnipro bend,[91] and the administrative centers of Ielysavethrad (over sixty thousand inhabitants in 1897) in the north and Simferopol in the south (almost fifty thousand). The latter two cities were among several that had gained commercial significance with the development of new rail lines after 1870.

The peasants, along with German and Bulgarian colonists living in the hinterlands of these expanding urban centers, had long profited from these markets. Travelers in the early nineteenth century commented favorably on the abundance of fruit and vegetable gardens in the environs of Odesa. The German traveler Johann Kohl observed as early as the 1840s that "in these gardens are cultivated melons, cucumbers, and all plants of this species, besides onions, beet-root, and other vegetables." Yet not all appeared to be in Odesa's favor. The great city's appeal as a vibrant market for fruits and vegetables was partially offset by its location on a high, arid plain, which made it difficult for any gardens more than five kilometers away from the city limits to obtain the necessary water supply. Enterprising market gardeners had dug wells by hand and constructed wood-framed irrigation machines. Others manually transported water to their sites. The dramatic increase in Odesa's market gardening was directly linked to the construction of a long-awaited water pipe from the city, which was completed in 1870. Almost three-quarters of the 2,025 hectares used for vegetable and fruit production by the turn of the century were cultivated only after its completion.[92]

People living at still greater distances from urban markets required an efficient transportation network in order to reach the markets. Easy access to markets was especially important in New Russia because the region's peasants lacked the means to preserve their produce. As a result, peasants sold the fruit in its fresh form or else pickled it in an acidic brine. Either way, great distances reduced the profitability of hauling vegetables to market, especially when the fall rains made the region's dirt roads impassable.[93] As a result, many within the region sought other means to reach urban markets, including travel by New Russia's main river systems, which served both as a means of irrigation and conveyance. The most important market gardens were situated in the valleys of the Dnister River, which entered the Black Sea west of Odesa. The Dnister, with its fertile, silt-laden soils on the flood plains and a climate moderated by deep, meandering valleys, was able to provide a rich natural setting for market gardening. The Dnister River valley was especially noted for its viticulture. Almost 95 percent of all grapes grown in Kherson province in 1900 (47,501 of 51,372 hectares) were grown by small-scale peasant agriculturalists along its banks, the majority of whom lived in Tiraspol district.[94] An article describing these developments for the *Journal of the South Russian Agricultural Society* in 1895 claimed that it was "possible to state categorically that at the present time in Tiraspol district there is not one settlement, excluding the temporary ones on leased lands, where there has not already been one attempt—indeed one could say a completely successful one—to cultivate fruit orchards and vineyards."[95]

Like Odesa's environs, the Dnister River valley began to flourish only in the late nineteenth century, before which time it had been dominated by forest and meadow. Its transformation into a center for intensive gardening was initiated by Moldavian, Bulgarian, and German colonists, but Russian and Ukrainian peasants soon followed their lead. The lands of Dnipro district, which jutted out westward between the Crimea and the southern banks of the Dnipro River, provided a third concentration of market gardens in New Russia. Here peasant agriculturalists, such as Andrei Gorlov, whose story began this chapter, utilized plentiful water supplies, adequate soils, and water transport to Kherson, Odesa, and Mykolaïv in order to establish thriving market-oriented economies. A special place within this district was occupied by the village of Oleshky (Aleshka), where less than a quarter of its eight hundred households were still cultivating grains in 1885. By contrast, almost three-fifths of the households relied exclusively on market gardening. Zemstvo investigators determined that the average peasant gardener in Oleshky volost with a plot of 2.7 hectares could expect an impressive annual income of 230 rubles.

By 1900 peasants had developed successful concentrations of market garden operations in the lower Dnister and Dnipro rivers, as well as in the environs of Odesa. Meanwhile, operations dependent on long distance land transport continued to develop, despite the seasonal difficulties experienced on the region's dirt trails and roads. Caravans of more than a hundred carts laden with watermelon, for example, had been commonplace at fall bazaars for decades.[96] Such caravans opened up the gardens of the Crimea to the heartland of the empire. But they also prompted peasants and foreign colonists living elsewhere in New Russia to adopt intensive gardening practices wherever soils and climactic conditions permitted. Peasants from the villages of Dobrovillia (Dobrovolia), Oleksandrivka, Sofiïvka, and Varvarivka (Varvarovka) in the heart of Katerynoslav province acquired an impressive reputation as intensive market gardeners, and attracted buyers from the regional centers of Katerynoslav, Rostov, and Taganrog. The peasants of Kam'ianka and Velyka Kam'ianka (Bolshaia Kamenka) in Melitopol district, immediately to the north of the Crimean peninsula in Tavriia province, together possessed more than 450 orchards. Harvested grapes, fruit, and berries were either sold on site to buyers, carted to the villages along the Dnipro, or else transported to the towns of Nikopol, Katerynoslav, Kherson, or even the more distant centers of Poltava and Kharkiv.[97]

The Emergence of an Economic Infrastructure

With rare exception, peasants began to innovate only after the requisite economic infrastructure had been created, especially as it pertained to rail construction, implement manufacturing, and zemstvo activity in the countryside. The acquisition of agricultural implements, upon which peasant grain producers were so dependent, was stimulated by the emergence of a vibrant New Russian manufacturing sector that was closely connected to the region's boom in rail expansion during the 1870s and 1880s. This boom had a direct impact on peasant agricultural specialization in New Russia, to the benefit of some and the detriment of others. By 1900 within the entire empire Katerynoslav province was second only to the Baltic province of Estland in per capita rail lines.[98] Railway stations followed. Ten stations were placed along the line between Odesa and Balta that opened in 1867, and these almost immediately stimulated the expansion of market gardens in the surrounding countryside. Rail transport also allowed for the rapid shipment of goods into the Russian industrial heartland during precisely those times of year when cartage on mud-clogged roads was impossible. A zemstvo investigation on the transformation of Simferopol district, in the heart of the Crimea, concluded that "without a doubt the greatest stimulus to market gardening in the Crimea has been the opening up of the Lozovo-Sevastopol railroad. Now the Crimea can compete with its produce against foreign producers, and even has a chance in the capitals of Moscow and St. Petersburg."[99]

Not all of the region's market gardens benefited equally from improvements in rail, land, and sea transport. Some previously secure regional markets were now flooded with imported goods. By 1900 farmers living in the outskirts of Odesa faced fierce competition from goods produced in central Russian and Ukrainian provinces. This competition was in addition to the longstanding rivalry with market gardeners from the Ottoman Empire, where the shorter growing season had long allowed Turkish producers to monopolize the Odesa market days before New Russian produce had ripened, and when prices were at their highest. The increased rail connections also led to the collapse of modest market garden initiatives around cities in the northern reaches of New Russia, as goods from the southern reaches began to flood north.[100]

Zemstvos, Teachers, and Depots

To produce new crops or implements was one matter, but for peasants to acquire them was another, given the onerous financial demands already put upon them. Here zemstvos played a vital role in making implements available in the countryside, especially by providing needed subsidies and loans. First, however, the zemstvos required a change of heart. Before the late 1880s those zemstvos that sought to make agricultural implements available were solely interested in supporting estate agriculture. Peasant agriculturalists were dismissed out of hand. Indicative of this mood was a remark uttered by a Tavriia zemstvo member, identified only as Polutov, in 1873: "Agricultural implements are required by the wealthy landowners, as peasants have absolutely no need for them."[101]

By the 1880s, however, zemstvo assemblies had rejected this approach, and they began instead to focus more attention on peasant agriculture. A few went so far as to establish zemstvo depots in order to sell peasants improved agricultural implements and seed varieties. Most zemstvos took no such action, however. Their activity within New Russia remained sufficiently weak to earn the censure of zemstvo historian, B. B. Veselovskii. Only three district agricultural depots had been constructed in New Russia by 1890—one in Katerynoslav province and another two in Kherson, though by 1904 the number of depots had surged to eighteen. Of these, the most active were in Ielysavethrad and Oleksandrivsk districts in Kherson and Katerynoslav provinces respectively. Each had an annual turnover of more than 150,000 rubles at the turn of the century. Several depots were established by the Oleksandrivsk district zemstvo, which also encouraged the sale and distribution of smaller implements through its fourteen village libraries. By dramatic contrast, three districts within the same province had sales of less than 20,000 rubles each, though even here the trend was toward greater involvement. Another era dawned after 1900 when growing numbers of zemstvos began to place joint orders for new equipment, and even invited competition between firms so as to lower the costs.

By 1900 peasants had more options available to purchase a wider range of new agricultural implements and to do so under more favorable conditions. The data available suggests that peasant capital expenditures exceeded the absolute total spent by private estate owners. The difference was a modest one within the empire as a whole and a dramatic one in New Russia. These figures obscure the fact that the population of the countryside was overwhelmingly peasant and that peasant purchases were heavily weighted to smaller, less expensive items such as one-horse plows, scythes, and improved seed, but Veselovskii was still able to conclude that zemstvo depots were making a positive contribution to the general improvement of peasant agriculture.[102]

Finally, zemstvos and other state-related agencies also played an increasingly important role in the diffusion of agricultural education among New Russia's peasants. State involvement in this area dated back to the establishment of the School for Viticulture and Vineyards in Sudak in 1804, and to the renowned Nikitskii Botanical Garden in Yalta in 1811.[103] Yet these early efforts were modest in scale and had little impact on the region's rapidly expanding population. The provincial and district zemstvos founded in the 1860s initially placed little emphasis on agricultural education, focusing instead on medicine and basic education. A report published as late as 1903 claimed that "many students completed their formal education at the age of 13 or 14 without ever having thought about agriculture."[104] But by that time many others had begun to actively combat these deficiencies. Village teachers became noticeably active in agricultural affairs even though their reasons for doing so are not always easy to identify. Teachers were compelled, by virtue of their low salaries, to cultivate gardens and orchards for their own subsistence. Some sought, altruistically, to provide an example of improved agricultural practices for peasants and estate owners alike. One such "demonstration field," located in the village of Veseli Terny (Veselii Tern), was managed by a teacher named G. I. Vartminskii. Contemporaries described him as "a mature teacher of 23 years who had a desire to assist peasants in agricultural development." Though he initially sowed wheat on this field, Vartminskii later experimented with a variety of other crops before eventually producing a thriving vineyard and tree nursery in less than ideal soil conditions.[105]

Local zemstvos strongly endorsed the individual efforts of such teachers as Vartminskii, and encouraged others to follow in their paths. In 1890, the Mariupol district assembly (Katerynoslav province) adopted a resolution that gave preference in future hirings to teachers with an agricultural education. It also agreed to subsidize the establishment of school nurseries, and called upon teachers to attend special classes at forest reserves in the district where they could familiarize themselves with "the planting, inoculation, and grafting of fruit trees." The Tavriia Zemstvo Teachers' Council urged its teachers in 1892 to attend summer courses in such institutes as the Odesa School of Gardening and the Nikitskii Botanical Garden. An annual subsidy of fifteen hundred rubles was created to that end, and eleven teachers took advantage of this opportunity in 1894.

These efforts bore fruit, and a promising trend was evident by the end of the century. In Oleksandriia district 13 of 65 schools had begun gardens by that time, as had 9 of 39 in Odesa district, and 9 of 57 in Ananïv. Likewise, peasants were prepared to introduce innovations when their success could be demonstrated, and especially when seedlings were provided. A zemstvo tree nursery in the village of Velyki Kopani, Dnipro district, distributed fifty thousand trees annually (grafted stalks were offered at ten kopecks a shoot; wild stalks were free).[106] Not only had peasants gained access to an improved stalk by 1900, their children had also been exposed to new techniques, as the following report from Ielysavethrad district makes clear:

> In several schools the scholars are taking active part in the maintenance work of these school gardens; they dig holes for planting new trees, help the teacher with the planting, study inoculations under the leadership of the teacher, and in this manner acquire the proper care for fruit and leaf trees. In order to encourage the scholars and begin to interest them in garden work, teachers of several schools have begun to distribute wild and inoculated trees to the scholars.[107]

What can be said of the parents' reaction to these innovations? In Ben Eklof's study of peasant schools, peasants are seen to endorse a narrowly restrictive view of education. Eklof recorded peasant objections to the teaching of agriculture in school: "But the peasants objected strongly to such trivia (*pustiaki*) and said that with time their children 'would learn these skills at home…that [the teacher's] job was to teach them to read and write!'" Similar reactions were recorded by many teachers living in Ielysavethrad district as parents responded cautiously to the innovations. Obviously social mores were at issue as much as economic concerns. If garden work was women's work, how would it appear to have young male scholars actively engaged in it? Such transitions would take time, though the end result seemed clear. Even the Ielysavethrad report had an optimistic conclusion about the growing peasant appreciation for agricultural innovation.[108] A more positive attitude was evident in Tavriia province, where local peasants had long observed the various agricultural innovations successfully introduced by Bulgarian and Mennonite colonists. In a report prepared for the Berdiansk district zemstvo, a peasant named Marchenko urged village schools to go beyond basic literacy and to teach the practical skills required for the household economy. "A new time is dawning, when peasants will send their children to school with the goal that along the way they will receive practical information and practical advice on one or another facets of agriculture."[109]

Conclusion

At the dawn of the 1890s, statistician V. E. Postnikov presented an optimistic assessment of trends in New Russian agriculture. He believed that the use of more efficient implements during seedtime and harvest provided peasants with enough time to further improve their agricultural practices, including proper soil preparation and the application of natural fertilizers. The utilization of time- and labor-saving equipment during the harvest permitted more fall plowing, reduced the necessary tasks for the following spring, and decreased the waste caused by leaving grains unthreshed well into the winter months.[110] By 1900 other observers were less optimistic in their evaluation of peasant agricultural change in New Russia. They identified outstanding problems, concerning in particular the *bukker*, whose reputation had lost some of its luster. Widespread peasant use of the *bukker* and the general neglect of the steel-shared plow had indeed resulted in rapid exhaustion of the topsoil and increased vulnerability to weed infestation. One study had already noted in 1889 that:

> In most villages, peasant field economies are in a terrible state! It can be said that peasant lands are exhausted, but I would answer that it is not completely so: the top layer, from 2–3 *vershka*, is perhaps that way, but further down the soils have still not been touched. With deeper plowing and with the destruction of weeds, peasants will still be able to obtain good harvests without fertilization.[111]

Ironically, the very acquisition of labor-saving technology, when coupled with the enormous tracts of estate lands available for lease, may have convinced peasants that there was no need to cultivate village allotment lands more effectively.[112]

Whatever the drawbacks, New Russian peasant agriculturalists made great strides in the acquisition of new technologies and pursuits in the late nineteenth century. Increased market opportunities played an important role in this development, as did peasant reevaluation of production costs in terms of land, labor, and time. Much of this was prompted by the sudden realization that earlier practices geared to mixed economies were ill-suited to land-use patterns in an era when crop cultivation predominated. This reevaluation was also dictated by an emerging infrastructure that included an improved rail network, a thriving implement industry, and a constantly improving distribution system for the products. Peasants were also challenged to modify their practices when they observed productive innovations in neighboring colonist economies. Individual peasant households, rather than communal organizations, appear to have been responsible for such innovations; however, I support Esther Kingston-Mann's conclusion that the "village as a whole" was often quick to adopt them. At times the innovations created new problems; for example, the weed infestation that resulted from shallow plowing with the *bukker*. It should not be surprising that the adaptations failed to solve all of the problems facing agriculturalists. Of course, the fact that changes produced new problems was not unique to pre-revolutionary peasant societies. "Modern" society faces similar challenges as it confronts the environmental crisis brought about by the industrial-technological revolution.

The fact that peasants were acquiring implements and experimenting with new crops, as we have shown in this chapter, supports the view that they were actively engaged in shaping everyday aspects of their lives before 1900.[113] These findings correspond to patterns found elsewhere in western Europe. Peasants' willingness to risk their very livelihood by incorporating new agricultural technologies provides evidence that they were not all tradition-bound and opposed to change. As cautious agricultural innovators, they contributed directly to the economic development of New Russia and the empire. Perhaps the most important adjustments the peasants made involved a willingness to diversify along with the widespread replacement of oxen with horses, rye with barley cultivation, and the use of steel instead of wooden implements. These changes helped peasant harvests increase by 25 percent from the 1870s to the 1880s and by a further 36 percent in the following ten years (see table 6.6 above). Peasant agriculturalists were matching the estate owners, industrialists, and colonists of the region in their ability to adjust to the post-frontier and modern era of agriculture.

The full picture is hardly this glowing, however, for whereas in 1900 New Russian peasant yields were almost in line with those found in adjoining provinces in the empire, they continued to lag far behind international levels. Peasants in New Russia averaged 34 poods per desiatina in the 1890s, whereas the European Russian average was 39. Even adjoining Ukrainian regions had yields in excess of those found in New Russia. Yields in the empire as a whole continued to compare badly with those of other European nations. At the end of the 1880s the average harvest was 83 bushels a desiatina in England, 68 in France and Prussia, 57 in Austria, but a mere 27 bushels in Russia. England, it was claimed, had not had harvests as low as Russian ones since the fourteenth and fifteenth centuries.[114]

The average harvest in New Russia at the end of the century proved unable to sustain most peasant households, which were working substantially less land than a generation earlier. By one estimate, peasant harvests in Kherson province in 1891 averaged 16.5 poods per inhabitant at a time when 24 poods was required. Agricultural experts as late as 1905 acknowledged that allotment lands continued to be insufficient to sustain peasants, who were forced to lease out additional lands or else seek seasonal employment on neighboring estates.[115] Why was it that yields did not improve enough to sustain peasant households? Why did technological innovations in agriculture not fundamentally alter the manner in which land was worked? Why were lands cultivated annually in an unsystematic manner, without careful rotation or the use of natural fertilizers—in other words, with little regard for the future?[116] The following chapter will address these questions by focusing on the reassertion of social controls over economic freedoms in peasant society.

7

NEWLYWEDS IN REVOLT

The Peasant Commune and "Land Hunger" after 1870

Peasant Life after "The Great Reforms"

STATE OFFICIALS WERE DELIGHTED with the social peace that prevailed in Kherson province in the mid-1870s. Gone was any trace of the instability that had characterized landed relations during the 1850s and early 1860s, and even though economic gains were still modest in a province where annual grain yields continued to fluctuate wildly, peasant loyalty to the tsar seemed secure. In his report for 1876, the governor of that province reported:

> In spite of the harsh crop failures recently, which have deprived the [province's] inhabitants of the means to even feed themselves, the incidents of major crimes against individuals and property, such as, for example, murder, theft, and assault, are relatively rare given the size of the population. In general, all of the inhabitants peacefully labor in their respective walks of life, enduring adversity calmly and with conviction, and not losing hope in the kindness of our mighty sovereign.[1]

How accurate was this picture of a peaceable kingdom? Had rural New Russia turned the corner by the 1870s? Had decades of social instability been overcome by a hopeful, patient, and loyal peasantry?

Any student of 1905, much less the whirlwind unleashed in 1917 and its aftermath, knows that that was not the case. Only one generation later, officials routinely described a New Russian countryside teetering on the brink of revolutionary chaos. In his annual report for 1903, another governor for Kherson province expressed alarm about the all-pervasive threat that the peasant commune [*obshchina*] posed within his jurisdiction:

> Overall, with each new generation and with every repartition, *obshchina* land use unquestionably weakens the idea of property in the peasant midst, and therefore respect for other people's property also is diminished. But the main threat (*ugroza*) of such collective land use is found in the fact that the constant redivision of land belonging to the *obshchina* reinforces in peasants—in spite of all the efforts of authorities—a dangerous fear about what will happen to them in a future repartition of all non-allotment lands."[2]

The governor's fears of future instability were entirely well founded. But why? This chapter considers why New Russian peasants, who had been entirely peaceful in the mid-1870s, were in such an agitated state by 1900, despite their steady gains in overall agricultural productivity. To that end, I will consider the separate paths taken by former serf and state-peasant communities in the second half of the nineteenth century. Both communities confronted an internal social crisis in the late 1870s, and their responses to these crises unwittingly laid the groundwork for revolutionary unrest after 1900.

By almost any measurement, former serfs and state peasants continued to exist as two distinct groups well into the second half of the nineteenth century. According to the great landholding survey of 1877–78 undertaken by the Ministry of Internal Affairs, peasant allotment lands—which included those owned by colonists—comprised slightly less than 40 percent of all lands in New Russia. This proportion was lower than the empirewide average proportion of allotment land by almost 15 percent, and remained virtually unaltered throughout the late nineteenth century.[3] These lands, in relation to the closest available population census, were divided up as seen in table 7.1.

State peasants continued to dominate the region in both their share of the population (63 percent of the total) and in the land they held (66.7 percent); however, the congruity that existed between the share of the population and allotment lands disappeared entirely for the other two sectors of the "peasant" population. Former serfs comprised 24.7 percent

Table 7.1. Peasant population and allotment landholding proportions in New Russia: percent population as of 1858; percent landholding as of 1877.

	Serfs		State Peasants		Colonists	
Province	**Pop.**	**Land**	**Pop.**	**Land**	**Pop.**	**Land**
Katerynoslav	30	13	61	67	9	19
Tavriia	8	4	75	71	17	24
Kherson	36	21	53	62	11	18
New Russia	**24.7**	**11.5**	**63**	**66.7**	**12.3**	**20.3**

Source: *SPSNM*, 18–26, 52–58, 62, 63, 84–89, 92.

of the rural population, yet possessed only 11.5 percent of allotment lands, whereas former colonists were at 12.3 and 20.3 percent respectively. It follows from this that former serf allotments were significantly smaller than those held by former state peasants (see table 7.2). By this measurement alone, former serfs were clearly disadvantaged, as their average allotments of 6.7 desiatinas were 60 percent lower than that of the average former state peasant household. But was this difference significant? Perhaps surprisingly, it was not very significant in the 1860s and 1870s, when former serfs were able to lease additional lands from their former lords at very attractive rates.

Table 7.2. Average household allotment sizes (desiatinas per household) in New Russia, 1877.

Province	Serfs	State Peasants	Colonists
Katerynoslav	5.6	16.3	37.2
Tavriia	11.5	21.5	40.0
Kherson	7.2	14.0	33.1
New Russia	**6.7**	**16.8**	**36.6**

Source: *SPSNM*, 18–26, 52–58, 62, 63, 84–89, 92.
Note: For European Russian totals, see Khodskii 1891, vol. 1, tables 2, 20–21; and *SZ1905*, 14:31; 16:28; 42:31.

Former state peasants were only occasionally attracted to the rental market in the 1860s, despite the sudden availability of inexpensive estate lands for lease. Instead, they continued to rely on their own holdings, which seemed plentiful well into the nineteenth century. In a typical case, households from the state peasant village of Shulhivka (Shulgovka), Melitopol district (Tavriia province), were permitted to plow up as much land annually as they wanted. Once cultivated, that parcel remained in the household's possession until such time as it was no longer worked, whereupon it returned to the general fund. This practice, known as possession by "squatters' rights" (*zakhvatnii prav*), was still widespread among former state peasants at midcentury and helps account for the sprawling nature of their villages, as households were easily able to expand beyond the original settlement.[4] Although poorer peasants occasionally initiated this expansion, it was more common for wealthier peasants to do so. They physically distanced their farming operations to avoid paying the tax arrears owed by poorer households in the original village. Wealthier households were also better able to muster the livestock needed to break through the hard virgin soils on distant lands that had previously served exclusively as pastures or hay meadows.

Prosperous peasants typically worked these former virgin lands for up to six years—the normal length of time before they began to lose their vitality, whereupon they relocated to lands even further away from the original village. For example, state peasants initially founded the village of Mykolaïv on a high plain in Berdiansk district, Tavriia province. Gradually, however, those with the means relocated to an adjacent river, where they planted gardens and maintained orchards. In this particular case a separate, legally recognized, discrete unit (the *obshchina*) was eventually formed, though often the end result was a complex, legal, and communal entity (*obshchestvo*) that included the original village settlement and several distant hamlets and farmsteads (*khutora*).[5]

State peasants in the adjoining district of Melitopol had developed similar practices:

> With the abundance of land and the weak development of field crops collisions between peasants were not possible.... The ones who were richer and found it too confining to manage their households on the fields closest to the village departed to the farthest *obshchestvo* fields or to "reserve" state

> lands where they constructed a *khutor*, dug a well, and plowed and sowed what they wanted.[6]

In this manner, former state peasant settlements in the 1860s and 1870s expanded their holdings and absorbed population increases. In only rare exceptions were concerns about land limitations expressed. Normally, children became heirs, inheriting these same lands on the condition that they remain under continuous cultivation. Households were limited only by the technology employed. For example, the widespread use of inefficient Ukrainian wooden plows and a shortage of labor prevented even the wealthiest peasants from sowing more than ten desiatinas in any one year.[7]

At first glance, former serfs and state peasants seem to have taken quite different paths in the 1860s and 1870s. The former serfs emerged with sharply circumscribed allotments and had to adjust to a new relationship with their erstwhile lords, although the adjustment was eased by easy access to inexpensive lease lands. The state peasants, for the most part, continued to farm lands that vastly exceeded their needs.[8] In addition, the sheer size differences in their respective settlements assured that some differences, at least, would continue. (Former serf villages in New Russia continued to average fewer than one hundred revision souls in the period immediately following their emancipation, compared to almost seven hundred souls among former state peasants.) Former serf villages were simply more efficient than former state peasant settlements.

Yet, despite different approaches to village land use, size, and regulation, there were also striking parallels. During the 1860s and 1870s, all peasant households functioned on the assumption that additional lands were available either on existing *obshchina* lands, or by leasing non-allotment lands at favorable terms and conditions. Hence, there was little need to work existing allotment lands more intensely. All peasants also maintained at least a minimal commitment to multi-field agricultural systems (*cherespolnosti*) intended to distribute allotment lands among all members according to quality and location. As a result, former serf households usually held their allotments in two or three separate parcels. State peasants adopted the same principle, though they generally worked several more.[9] Within the confines of this system, former state peasants still managed to make agricultural improvements, though they first needed to overcome the burden of more travel time between fields, more space wasted between boundaries, and the prospect that land worked now might eventually pass into another's hands through the communal system of redistribution.

At the same time, peasants placed a high value on fair and equitable inheritance systems. The fate of the next generation was largely dependent on the manner in which property rights (both movable, such as livestock and implements, and immovable, including land and buildings) were determined and disposed of. Furthermore, inheritance customs assured that those who did not receive land allotments would not be left destitute. Detailed information on peasant inheritance patterns in New Russia was preserved by an imperial investigation of local district (volost) courts in Katerynoslav province during the early 1870s. The investigation revealed that peasants rarely relied upon formal, written wills because of the abysmally low levels of literacy among peasants, elected elders, and even district court officials.[10] To their relief, however, investigators concluded that existing oral traditions revealed certain inheritance practices that were universally held despite the commonly found differences. The investigators' findings gave an indication of how weak the central government's authority was in the countryside.

Households either divided the property when the male household head was alive or after his death. The former practice was more common, and normally took place by mutual agreement among household members, often after a period of intense quarrelling. Quarrels erupted most frequently when married sons wished to establish their own economies—a situation that was frequently aggravated by feuding mothers and their new daughters-in-law. Regardless of when the household was divided, however, all sons appear to have had equal access to it. There was only one peasant commune in which the youngest son inherited the family home (*izba*) in its entirety. Even so, inheritance arrangements were often highly contentious. One case brought before a local court in Katerynoslav district in 1870 involved a man whose oldest brother had seized the father's home, land, and livestock after his parents had died.[11] More frequent complaints came from men who returned from military service to find their father's lands divided up among their other brothers.

In an age when high mortality rates resulted in a wide range of marital relations, stepfamily disputes arose often, such as when a peasant returned from his tour of duty to discover that his stepmother had assumed sole possession of the property following his father's death.[12] In fact the area of stepfamily relations was one place where inheritance practices differed among peasant communes: some granted stepsons equal portions if they had lived with the family for "a long time"; others did not. In most instances, however, inheritance rights were determined by whether the son or stepson had aided in the payment of taxation and redemption dues. Such obligations were normally divided up with the property, and only those who agreed to share financial responsibility were granted use of the *izba* and its lands (*usad'ba*). In other communes, however, stepsons were entitled to only a half-share of the property. Such exclusions also occasionally threatened stepfathers, as one elderly male peasant belatedly realized when he found himself entirely bereft of land upon the death of his wife, whose sons he had raised over the previous sixteen years.

Local inheritance customs also protected those not eligible for full inheritance rights, such as orphans and women. In the case of the former, allotments were controlled in trust by guardians who were usually close neighbors or relatives. At other times, the commune-appointed guardian held funds in trust that had been acquired through the sale of household possessions. Allotment-inheritance arrangements assured mothers of perpetual care by their sons. Some widows even received a portion of the allotment in order to assure them of a means of livelihood. Similarly, although daughters received no more and often less than one-fourteenth of all immovable, and one-seventh of all movable property, they were placed in the charge, and under the care, of a brother until they married.[13]

In the final analysis, and in the immediate aftermath of the Great Reforms, New Russian peasant communes recognized property claims if the household head had been identified in the last census of male souls, which had been undertaken in 1858. Thereafter, the disposal of household lands was ultimately the subject of communal rather than household decision making. The village assembly (*skhod*) settled property disputes between quarrelling family members more frequently than did state-appointed courts. It was the assembly that assigned guardians for children and held their monies in a common trust until they became adults.[14] In the words of one submission to the investigation of volost courts: "All matters concerning inheritance, for the most part, begin and end with the *skhod*." For the most part, matters proceeded smoothly—certainly when compared to the period that followed.

Storms and Solutions in Former State Peasant Villages

A new generation of peasants came of age in the late 1870s, and their insistence that they be provided with adequate landholdings led to a stormy period in New Russia's villages. As noted in chapter 6, peasant frustration grew when previously available lands were removed from the rental market owing to the estate owners' increased use of agricultural implements, the fracturing of estates, and the purchasing of these large landholdings by colonist agriculturalists and others.[15] Under these circumstances, peasants turned increasingly to their own village lands, which themselves had become scarcer due to mounting population pressures. Smaller allotments per household were the inevitable consequence of these trends. By one estimate for 1887, household allotments in state-peasant and former serf villages were half of what they had been at the time of the tenth revision in 1858. Moreover, this reduction occurred at a time when access to individual holdings had actually begun to matter to peasants because of the ongoing massive shift to grain cultivation. The desire to plant wheat compelled household heads to clarify access rights to village lands in a way that the grazing of sheep never had. Renewed peasant interest in their allotment lands was further increased by a series of imperial legislative initiatives in the 1880s that substantially lowered the redemption payments owed to the government.[16] Thus, at the same time that allotment lands had become fiscally attractive, non-allotment lands were more expensive and less viable.

The conflict that erupted within peasant communes in response to these trends was generational in nature. It had its origins in the 1858 revision of male souls. All male state peasants and serfs born up to that moment were registered, and received a corresponding right to an allotment. By the same measure, males born after 1858 were denied similar rights pending a new revision. The desire for another revision increased as the post-1858 generation came of age in the late 1870s. Hence, many communes hesitated to redistribute land after 1858 in the belief that a new registration, or revision, would soon be forthcoming. Yet it was not, and its delay meant that allotments became increasingly unequal. In cases where allotment holders (revision souls) had died with one or two sons, the land was easily divided. But those with many sons confronted more complicated situations. Still others acquired allotments by means deemed questionable, if not improper, yet no mechanism existed to correct the situation. The most common complaint involved peasants born in the early 1860s who had married by the 1880s yet still had no allotments. They now demanded that the situation be addressed immediately.[17]

State-peasant and serf communes responded to this crisis in distinctly different manners. Among the former, with traditions of strong communal enterprise before the 1860s, generally egalitarian concepts were now reasserted, though only after a struggle. Examples abound of conflicts that emerged between young and old, between those with and those without allotments, and between those with larger and smaller allotments and family sizes. In 1890 an investigation of Kherson district concluded that a large proportion of landless in the state peasant villages were the so-called "newlyweds" (*novozhentsy*)—families who had already separated from their parental households but had not yet registered. One zemstvo investigator observed: "These non-revision souls, already now thirty years old with a family, only received a household plot [*usad'ba*] from the division of their father's property that was undertaken by the *obshchina*, and sometimes not even that much."[18] A report from the same period for Slov'iano-Serbiia district reported:

> In all villages of former state peasants bitter quarrels over garden land [*usadebnoi zemli*] are now occurring. Everywhere peasants are complaining about the unequal distribution of this land and, having recognized the unjustness of such methods, loudly express the need to change it.[19]

Yet another type of conflict pitted members of main settlements and villages against splinter settlements or farmsteads that had formed on more distant allotment lands. Previously congenial relations were suddenly upset by the land squeeze. Such disputes were reported to be on the increase among former state-peasant households in Melitopol district, and were usually described as struggles between rich and poor. "[A]nd this agitation was not always peaceful, but often ended with fists." Incidents of intervillage hostilities in Melitopol district were among the earliest in the region. They dated back to the early 1860s, when the transition from pastoral breeding to grain cultivation was well underway. In one instance, both "squatters" and separate farmsteads observed an uneasy truce with the original settlement of Nyzhni Sirohozy (Nizhnii Serogakh) until 1863, when quarrels erupted and the more distant properties were seized.[20]

In all instances, former state-peasant villages managed to restore a social truce only after the commune had reasserted the principle of collective decision making by offering its control over matters far beyond inheritance disputes. Conflicts between main villages and wealthier farmsteads almost always had one of two outcomes. Most frequently the village peasants destroyed or dismantled outlying dwellings and farmsteads and forcibly resettled those households back into the main village. Wells that had been dug on the distant farmsteads were seized for the general use of the entire *obshchina* without compensation of any kind to the industrious peasants who had dug them. At times this forced relocation involved even the destruction of small villages that former state peasants had formed on the large holdings available at the time. The second outcome occurred when outlying hamlets and clusters of farmsteads managed to separate themselves totally from the "parent settlement" to form their own, independent *obshchina*. Normally, the main settlement's support was required for such a development, as was the case in 1870 when a second *obshchina* was formed from the village of Pokrovske in Dnipro district, Tavriia province, at a distance of fifty-two versts from the original village.[21] In such instances, however, the new commune usually functioned on strong collective principles, and the first partition of plowland normally followed soon thereafter.

Former state peasants partitioned and redistributed their lands in a number of distinct ways in the 1870s. The most far-reaching involved the radical repartition of all plowland according to either the number of revisions (as of 1858) or the number of available male souls (as of the actual year). But even earlier, peasants had also utilized a wide range of partial redistributions that involved only a part of a given *obshchina*. The date at which radical repartitions began in a given district serves as an indication of when land was first perceived to be in short supply. As mentioned above, the earliest appearances of such a situation in New Russia appears to have been in the mainland districts of Tavriia—especially Berdiansk and Melitopol districts—where 91 percent of all state-peasant communes had already radically redistributed their lands by the end of the 1860s. Its earlier occurrence here was doubtlessly connected to the close proximity of colonist settlements and the almost total absence of estates—factors that curtailed leasing possibilities drastically and placed the focus squarely on the *obshchina*. Elsewhere former state peasants first made the call for repartition in the second half of the 1870s and after. Such was the case in the village of Novyi Buh (Novyi Bug) in Kherson district, with 25,000 desiatinas, which had existed on a household allotment system until urgent appeals led to a radical redistribution in 1883.[22]

By 1900, two districts in Katerynoslav province reported that almost all former state-peasant communes had experienced a radical repartition since 1858. More conclusively, the 1905 land survey for that province listed only one former state-peasant village, situated in Novomoskovsk district, as having maintained household tenure. And a study of the same district completed in 1906–7 revealed that nineteen of twenty-two former state-peasant communes (for which information existed) had undergone a partial repartition of lands since 1900, many as recently as during the previous year.[23]

While former state-peasant communes regularly redistributed portions of their collective holdings before 1900, several factors may have delayed the frequency of radical (wholesale) re-partitions. For one, many who settled on state lands in New Russia during the 1860s and 1870s had previously been serfs in the heartland provinces of central Russia, where the radically repartitioning *obshchina* was as weakly developed as among former serfs in the south. This may also account for why twenty-six of seventy former state-peasant communes in Kherson district—a popular destination for immigration given its relatively sparse settlement—did not experience any kind of redivision before 1900.[24]

The sheer size of former state-peasant communes in New Russia also worked against the introduction of radical repartitions, since it made any kind of all-encompassing collective agreement extremely difficult to achieve. The 1905 land census for New Russia listed 388 individual households in the average state-peasant *obshchina*. The largest one, in Katerynoslav, comprised nearly two thousand families, or more than ten thousand people! In 1902, no less a figure than the governor of Kherson province stressed the difficulties caused by these massive settlements: "To gather a village assembly of several thousand individuals, and to bring such a large crowd to a definite agreement in practice, is an extremely complicated and difficult matter."[25] It was almost impossible to obtain the necessary support of two-thirds of the household heads when heads often did not even know each other.

Thus, even though one study maintained that radical partitions occurred every twelve years, former state peasants were more inclined to divide their holdings among a smaller, preselected group of households within the given *obshchina*.[26] Lands in the more populous communes could be divided into six or seven parcels, whereupon each portion was redistributed among those households that immediately adjoined it. In the process, former state peasants managed to decrease the travel distances between home and field.[27] These repartitions almost always involved only plowland, and garden plots remained in the permanent possession of the households residing there.

Lastly, differences also existed within former state-peasant villages as to the shares that males were entitled to. Initially, only those males identified in the 1858 census were eligible to an allotment, although the common practice was soon modified to include all males, even those born after 1858. Even so, a minority of peasant communes continued to employ unequal practices, and struggles continued to the end of the century. Most often such conflict involved the making of a distinction between those males listed in the 1858 revision and those not, either because they had not yet been born, or because they had been absent from the village at the time of the revision. In Zherebets village of Oleksandrivsk district (Katerynoslav province), for example, the fifteen thousand desiatinas of land were divided among the 1,136 families on three separate occasions before 1890. In 1891, however, the *obshchina* struck a new course when it granted each household on the 1870 registry lists permanent possession of five desiatinas. Males born thereafter received only a single desiatina. Nor did changes stop there. In 1897 the commune agreed to grant a minimum of five desiatinas to all males. Although such uneven divisions were only observed in six of forty-nine state peasant communes in Oleksandrivsk district, they nevertheless alert us to the ongoing tensions over land distribution rights within communities of former state peasants. Overall, by 1900 the prevailing opinion among former state peasants was unambiguously in support of the periodic redistribution of all lands. That this redistribution occurred with varying degrees of frequency and scale does not diminish its importance in shaping former state-peasant understandings of property, especially its redistributive nature, and the right all males had to it.[28]

Former Serf Villages, and Alternate Strategies

Former serfs also confronted a land squeeze at the end of the nineteenth century, although, unlike their former state-peasant counterparts, they did not opt for the communal redistribution of their lands. As a result, household tenure retained its dominance, and although generationally based quarrels erupted in their midst, they did not have the same ferocity as those dividing former state peasants.[29]

Former serfs realized that the terms of their emancipation had left them in a vulnerable state. With allotments so small in this new era, however, differences between rich and poor landholders were normally insignificant. In addition, former serfs entered the reform era unfamiliar with communal forms of land use and instead remained committed to the principle of household tenure. Although former serfs continued to value the *obshchina*, it now functioned less as an agent for radical land redistribution than as the arbiter of land disputes between individual households. Whereas a new generation of former state peasants entered the 1880s seeking a radical redistribution of holdings among available souls, former serfs in that same time supported the reversion to allotments based upon shares established at the time of the emancipation.

Former serfs occasionally reapportioned land among all male souls, as in Melitopol district, though their motivation for doing so was to share the tax burden more equitably. Yet even in these isolated instances, by the 1880s there was enormous pressure from 1858 revision males to return to household tenure, something that the vast majority of former serf households had practiced consistently. By the late 1880s, 185 of 206 former serf communes in Kherson district had still not undertaken a major redistribution of land, and the same was true for 38 of 40 former serf communes in Oleksandrivsk district.[30] Instead, the most common disputes originated in perceived injustices from inheritance arbitration. Typical quarrels involved those who had held land in trust as guardians but refused to surrender control of it, an act which compelled the *obshchina* to intervene. In other cases, households that had seized pastureland improperly and cultivated it for years were confronted and required to return it to general use.

Perhaps a more telling type of dispute involved former serfs who wished to reclaim the use of allotment lands that had been given to other peasant households in the 1860s, a time when high redemption payments and ready access to lease lands had encouraged household heads to divest themselves of their holdings. But could they reclaim their allotments? In many cases they did, as the primacy of household tenure within former serf communes, and the overarching authority of the collective commune, added a sense of ambiguity to any subsequent land transfer. In response, such transactions often carried stipulations penalizing those households that wished to reclaim their lands. One such agreement stated: "If the seller or his descendants claim the 'purchased' allotment lands, then they must, besides paying back the purchase price (30–60 rubles), return in full the land taxes paid, and above that a penalty of 200–300 rubles."[31]

The continued primacy of household tenure and the threat of stiff financial penalties for allotment reclamation discouraged many former serfs from allotting lands to anyone not entitled to them at the time of their emancipation. Exceptions to this practice were rare, but included a case in Kherson district where 4 of 206 former serf communes chose to incorporate "new souls" as allotment holders, albeit with smaller parcels. They now received 3.5 desiatinas, whereas revision souls were granted 5. But those males reaching adulthood in the vast majority of former serf communes confronted a limited number of possibilities within the village. One common response was simply to remain in the original household and not divide the allotment lands among the extended family. There is reason to believe that many took this route, because the average household size among former serfs remained high until the end of the century. More importantly, desiatinas per household in former serf communes well exceeded desiatinas per allotment, which suggests that often two or more former males eligible for allotment lands chose to live as a single household. The 1901 imperial land commission determined that former serf allotment sizes (per male soul) for Katerynoslav, Tavriia, and Kherson were 2.0, 6.5, and 2.3 desiatinas respectively. However, the 1905 land survey suggested that average respective household sizes for the three provinces were 6.2, 6.7, and 5 desiatinas. Thus, former serf households averaged no fewer than two allotment souls in Katerynoslav and Kherson provinces.[32]

The reluctance of former serfs to divide their households is better understood when their situation is compared to simultaneous developments in the relatively land-rich former state-peasant communes. There the periodic redivision of land among available male souls, and the corresponding division of households, yielded the obvious benefit of increased access to village lands. By contrast, such incentives disappeared in former serf communes after 1861, because the minuscule holdings available dramatically reduced any potential gains from their communal reallocation. Former household serfs (*darstvenniki*) who had received half-sized allotments after 1861 were even less inclined to redistribute holdings than were full-allotment serfs (*sobstvenniki*).[33] The differing trends between former state peasants and serfs are clearly evident in the statistics on household changes in Katerynoslav district from 1858 to 1900 (table 7.3).

Table 7.3. Changes in household size and population growth (percent increase) in Katerynoslav district, 1858–1898.

Category	Household units	Population
Former state peasant	191.4	161.0
Former serf (*sobstvennik*)	99.7	134.8
Household serf (*darstvennik*)	88.4	156.4

Source: *MOZE* 1899, pt. 1, 76.

Table 7.3 reveals the dramatically differing trends underway in former serf and state-peasant communes during the second half of the nineteenth century. The pace of household repartition among former state peasants far exceeded the population increases for the same period, as household units increased by 191 percent, and the population by 161 percent. Family units were getting smaller. By contrast, former serfs with full allotments, who from 1858 to 1898 had a total population increase of 134.8 percent, had by the latter date increased the number of households by only 99.7 percent. While this was itself a substantial increase for former serfs, it nevertheless reflected a strong disinclination to separate from the original household. The fact that even fewer new households were being formed among former household serfs—those who had not received full allotments—confirms my conclusion: before 1900 former serf households were increasing in size as their communes resisted the further division of allotment lands, whereas the opposite was true within former state-peasant communes. Thus, only a small portion of former serf households sought the subdivision of their collective holdings, although occasionally several households undertook partial and mutually agreeable reallocations depending on the ages and number of children on hand.[34]

The final option available to former serfs who had reached adulthood and wanted to remain within their villages was for them to receive no more than a household plot, and sometimes less. As a result, there were a number of landless peasants—an average of around 10 percent of all households up to 1905. Many of these men were deprived of even adequate garden space and were therefore obliged to become wholly dependent for their livelihood on non-allotment lands. In time, their numbers were augmented by the *desiatinshchik*s, who themselves had been deprived of allotments in the emancipation of 1861, at which time they were legally identified as *meshchane* (members of the petty bourgeoisie). Former *desiatinshchik*s were especially noticeable in the western half of Kherson province, where 376 of 1,101 revision souls had been denied a land allotment in one district alone.

Initially, such deprivations did not pose any difficulties given the availability of lease land at advantageous rates. Freed from all redemption dues, the *desiatinshchik*s concentrated their energies on livestock grazing on long-term lease land. This allowed them to develop "temporary" household economies on private estate lands that were relatively prosperous.[35] But *desiatinshchik*s were hard-hit by the gradual decrease in per capita lease lands available and the corresponding increase in rental rates in the 1880s and 1890s. Thus, on one estate of Ananïv district, Kherson province, the *desiatinshchik*s suddenly found themselves with lease costs of nine to ten rubles a desiatina—equal to one-half of the average harvest.[36] In 1900 the governor's report for Katerynoslav province concluded that *desiatinshchik*s were in a state of near bondage because of their virtual entrapment on private estate lands from which they could realize little gain. In addition, stiffer leasing terms robbed their households of the opportunity to establish themselves as truly viable agriculturalists, especially since many were now compelled to relocate every five years.[37]

Faced with small holdings and mounting arrears, a steadily increasing number of former serfs with allotments responded by selling their lands. On 21 April 1885 two peasants from Dnipro district signed an agreement that typified these arrangements:

> We, the undersigned former full-allotment serfs [*sobstvenniki*] of Dnipro district, Kalanchak volost, in the village of Novo-Aleksandrovka, Epifan

> Markelov Morozov and Gavril Mochalin, have come to the following agreement: (1) I, Epifan Markelov Morozov, have sold in permanent possession [*v vechnoe vladenie*] to my fellow villager, Gavril Mochalin, the property belonging to me of 6.5 desiatinas inherited by me as an allotment upon the death of my father-in-law, for a cost of 40 rubles (the sale excludes the house [*dvor*]). (2) We both are obligated to pay for the poll taxes this year and then, (3) I, Gavril Mochalin, am obligated to pay for all other obligations for two souls: for a soul without an allotment, and for one with an allotment. (4) This title to Mochalin's land cannot be challenged by anyone, not my children nor any other relative.[38]

In most instances, former serf communes were required to give their approval to such transactions, which may have limited their number. In sum, however, such sales made it possible for hundreds of peasants to depart from their commune, either in search of land in the recently opened Siberian frontiers or in the emerging industrial centers in New Russia. The flow of local peasants into the mining and manufacturing enterprises of the Dnipro bend were significant enough to prompt the governor of Katerynoslav province to propose a complete division of the province in two: a western section that was still devoted to agriculture, and an eastern one where peasants were abandoning agriculture in unprecedented numbers. A cycle of crop failures after the mid-1890s added additional incentive to former serfs to unload their small holdings, shift off of the land, and seek employment in the region's emerging industrial sector.[39]

In short, conditions for the *desiatinshchik*s became more desperate at the very time that their numbers were increased by the inclusion of new generations of landless serfs. Tiraspol district alone possessed almost fifty settlements of *meshchane-desiatinshchik*s by the late 1880s, which comprised a staggering 15 percent of all peasant settlements in the district. Reports for 1904 estimated that there were more than two hundred thousand *desiatinshchik*s in Kherson province alone. The problem of landless and increasingly vulnerable peasants after 1900 was felt throughout the entire region. The governor's report for Tavriia province in 1906 claimed that up to 40 percent of all peasants were landless, and that most of these were sharecroppers whose survival depended on the mercy of local estate owners.[40] Relationships of mutual respect were clearly unlikely under these volatile conditions, as the revolution of 1905 would soon make clear.

Social Relations on the Eve of Revolution

By 1900 New Russia's peasants lived in villages that varied tremendously in size and internal organization. Former state peasants, long accustomed to govern their internal affairs independently, maintained and actually strengthened the *obshchina*'s ability periodically to redivide all landholdings among its members. Such a pattern was reinforced by the existence of truly large villages, averaging more than four hundred households, in Katerynoslav and Kherson provinces. The former state-peasant settlements in Tavriia provinces were also very large, yet with an average of 269 inhabitants were still smaller than in the other two provinces.[41] The sheer scale of these villages worked against household tenure by making the connection between household and allotment land less clear. How could it be otherwise if plowland was located twenty kilometers and more from their homes, or if some huts did not even border on open lands? Under such conditions, it is easy to see why the sense of land shortages in the 1870s and 1880s actually reinforced the commune's role in allotment land, along with the belief that all males found within a given village should have access to its lands.

Former serfs, by contrast, had developed a system of landholding grounded in household tenure. Such a practice emerged naturally from the experience of serfdom, during which peasant communal decision making had always been tempered by the estate owners' decrees. In addition, the fact that both the villages and the land allotted to them were smaller in the post-reform period made it possible—if not essential—to define one's land in relation to a given household, and to do so immediately. As land became scarcer, that connection was strengthened. This explains why household tenure among former serfs was most evident among the household serfs (*darstvenniki*), who had normally received only half-allotments under the terms of emancipation.

Ironically, the single phenomenon of growing land shortages forced former state-peasant and serf-peasant villages into opposite directions: one toward communal, and the other toward household, systems of land tenure. As a result, the principle of equality was also more strongly maintained in state peasant communes than among former serfs. We are able to measure the degree to which this was the case in the 1904 survey of peasant households in Slov'iano-Serbiia district of Katerynoslav province. For the sake of comparison, only former state peasants and serfs who had received full allotments (*sobstvenniki*) are included (see table 7.4).

Table 7.4. Household allotment sizes in Slov'iano-Serbiia district, 1904.

	Former state-peasant households		Former serf households	
Desiatinas per household	**Total**	**Percent**	**Total**	**Percent**
No allotment	483	5.7	1,303	10.0
< 1 desiatina	483	5.7	1,556	12.0
1–3 desiatinas	379	5.0	5,157	40.0
3–5 desiatinas	3,275	39.0	3,171	25.0
5–10 desiatinas	2,947	35.0	1,414	11.0
10–15 desiatinas	672	8.0	95	1.0
> 15 desiatinas	160	2.0	19	--
Landless	45	1.0	222	2.0
Total	**8,444**	**100.0**	**12,937**	**100.0**

Source: *MOZE* 1906, pt. 1, 421.

This table, which shows that households were distributed in a wide range of allotment sizes, accurately reflects empirewide patterns. For example, 39 percent of state peasant households possessed from 3 to 5 desiatinas, whereas another 35 percent had from 5 to 10 desiatinas. By contrast, only 25 percent of former serf households had from 3 to 5 desiatinas, whereas 40 percent had from 1 to 3 desiatinas. Thus, it is clear that former serf peasants were in a less advantageous position with respect to overall absolute landholdings. But is it possible to measure differences within each grouping of peasants? Were inequalities higher among former serfs, as we have suspected?

A study of the 1904 survey confirms this thesis. The proportion of households without allotments among full-allotment serfs (at 10 percent) was nearly double that of former state peasants (5.7 percent), whereas half-allotment serfs possessed even more landless people (24 percent).[42] In short, landless peasants in New Russia were more apt to come from former serf villages than from state peasant villages. A more sophisticated measurement of inequalities can be obtained by using the Gini index, which allows us to gauge the degree to which landholdings were unequally distributed among peasants. Using table 7.4, above, this calculation assumes that peasants averaged holdings at the median point for each of the categories. For example, the 379 state-peasant households with 1 to 3 desiatinas laid claim to an average of 1.5 desiatinas each.[43] For that reason, it was also necessary to eliminate those holdings listed as more than 15 desiatinas, which only accounted for 1.89 percent of state peasant households (160) and 0.146 percent of serf households. With the Gini index, the lower the number, the lower the degree of inequality; hence the significance of the gap between former state peasants and serfs, with the index for each being 30.9 and 49.1 respectively. The maximum inequality possible using this index would be 50.

Inequality within the commune was greatest, then, within former-serf communes in New Russia. Given their emphasis on household tenure, this should not be surprising, although it would be misleading to extrapolate from this that stratification was widespread. A mere 0.88 percent of all households enjoyed allotments in excess of ten desiatinas, which was considered to be the minimal amount for a household wishing to avoid leasing other lands. In neither grouping is there any evidence to suggest that a substantially rich peasant (*kulak*) class had emerged.

More worrisome for state officials in 1900 was the realization that almost all peasants in New Russia continued to nurture a sense of landholding that placed them at odds with private estate lands and state officials in the region. At the heart of all peasant societies was the understanding that land worked today could be reallocated tomorrow, either to a family member or to another member of the commune. This sense of impermanence concerned officials because it discouraged those who might otherwise seek to improve their holdings by such means as planting orchards or vineyards.[44] Instead, peasants sought to exploit their lands just enough to sustain their households. As late as 1910 a scholar of New Russian peasants noted that:

> For the majority of peasant families, the ideal success is served not in the accumulation of the largest possible number of material possessions...but in the satisfaction of the most essential needs; all with the greatest amount of calm [*pokoi*] and the least expense of labor.[45]

Long compelled to shoulder the main tax burden of the countryside, New Russia's peasants had reconciled themselves to low incomes. Hence the notion of accumulating "private" property was alien to them. Land, after all, had been claimed and worked by "squatter's rights" within the lifetime of many peasants in 1900. Under these conditions the right of the collective *obshchina* to regulate village life and tenure, either through direct and all-village systems (as with former state peasants) or through the household (as with former serfs), was rarely challenged before 1900.[46] Indeed, evidence suggests that it was actually strengthening in New Russia, Siberia, and elsewhere.

The commune's resilience as a controlling agent in the countryside can be partly explained by the state's inability to enter into or alter village life before 1900. The state was never far away when it came to the collection of taxes, but they were collected in a manner that solidified communal guardianship. And education, which contemporaries considered to be the most positive way to influence the peasant world, was still in a rudimentary state. A report submitted to the *Vestnik Ekaterinoslavskogo Zemstva* in 1905 noted that only 3 percent of Russia's subjects were in schools, compared with 15 percent in France, 16 percent in England, and 28 percent in the United States. The investigations of the Witte Commission of 1903–4 concluded that parts of Kherson province still possessed barely more than one school for every two thousand inhabitants, and the Tavriia report noted that Russia was spending only 12 kopecks per person on education. By contrast, annual commitments elsewhere ranged from the equivalent of 1 ruble, 50 kopecks in France, to 2 rubles, 50 kopecks in England, to 3 rubles, 75 kopecks in the United States.[47] What is more, peasants were often unimpressed with the education offered and therefore reluctant to endorse it. One report for Kherson province in 1890 concluded:

> Primary education in the province is not located in the high position which it ought to be: schools here are comparatively few, and for the most part children of school age do not gain literacy.... Unfortunately the population does not always see the need for such instruction.[48]

Peasant reluctance to support the few schools in existence can be attributed at least partly to their normally ineffectual performance. The first schools often consisted of little more than informal gatherings in the hut of a literate male in the village. Such schools not infrequently were drafty or poorly ventilated. Smoke from a primitive stove would cloud teachers and students alike. At other times,

> Drinking buddies [*druz'ia-sobutyl'niki*] would drop in on the teacher. Then a bottle of vodka and a snack [*zakuska*] would suddenly appear on the table over which the heads of the students were inclined, and the "temple of science" would be transformed into a tavern.[49]

While the number and quality of New Russian schools steadily increased in the years before 1900, they remained inadequate by all official standards, and their impact on New Russian peasant society was far less than had been hoped for.[50]

By 1900 state administrators feared that the failure to penetrate the traditional peasant village had resulted in the perpetuation of customs and understandings that were contrary to official policy. One troublesome area where this discontinuity was observed was in the realm of civil law. Peasants almost always settled internal matters at the village level according to traditional convention and not formal law.[51] However much this concerned officials, however, it paled in comparison to their alarm over persistent peasant attitudes to property rights. Peasants, they reasoned, could be counted on to respect the property of private estate owners and the state if their own lives were governed by this principle. Yet their investigations showed that such was clearly not the case. Instead, communal understandings of land tenure, as distinguished from state notions of privately owned lands, had prevailed in the years since 1861. In fact, it had strengthened. Whether land was divided by former serfs among the family, or distributed more broadly by former state peasants, such practices resulted in the strong conviction that the land that a household worked today would likely not be theirs in the near future.

Even more alarming to officials was the manner in which peasants came to view the property rights of those who lived beyond their commune's borders. This does not mean that peasants had no understanding of "property," as the governor's report for Kherson province mistakenly concluded in 1902.[52] Rather, given the manner in which peasant laborers had long worked estate lands as part of their own economies, they could not be counted on to understand, much less honor, the notion of inviolable and permanent land tenure. Private estate owners continued to lease out large portions of their lands, including up to 60 percent in Oleksandrivsk district in 1900, and a staggering 90 percent of all private lands in neighboring Katerynoslav district. Although the latter figure included land leased by colonists, it serves as the clearest indication of how former serfs had maintained a close connection with estate lands in the post-emancipation era. In a representative instance, former serfs in Bakhmut district sowed 71 percent of their crops annually on leased land, and less than 30 percent on their own allotment land. This stood in sharp contrast to former state peasants, who sowed less than a quarter of their crops on leased land.[53]

The volume of estate lands leased by New Russian peasants in 1901 was without equal in European Russia. It involved almost 346,000 desiatinas in Katerynoslav province, a figure which was more than double the total leased by peasants immediately to the north in Poltava province. In some districts the increase in recent years had been astronomical. Peasants leased more than 52,000 desiatinas in Pavlohrad district in 1904, up from 4,000 desiatinas in 1886. Peasants in Tavriia province leased 337,000 desiatinas.[54]

This widespread leasing in the late nineteenth century was a clear indication of the extent to which peasants had integrated estate lands into their own economies. Nowhere was this more apparent than in Dnipro, where almost half of all households leased land by the early 1890s. More than three-quarters of all land leased by peasants in Dnipro was on a sharecropping basis. In some cases peasants worked entire estates but were compelled to surrender a significant portion of the harvest as rental fee. To make matters worse, by 1900 estate owners had driven lease rates up and stiffened the terms as a response to the increased demand for those lands and as they themselves were beginning to introduce labor-saving implements into their own economy. Peasants from the Dalmatovka estate, who annually leased 3000 desiatinas of a 5,700-desiatina estate, were suddenly required to pay their fee of ten rubles a desiatina in advance of the harvest. Other estate owners were quite content to leave their lands as virgin pasture for their merino flocks.[55]

The P. N. Trubetskoi estate was typical. His 26,000-desiatina domain was located on the banks of the lower Dnipro River in Dnipro district, across from Kherson district. Trubetskoi's herd of thirty thousand sheep grazed freely on 10,600 desiatinas of land, whereas approximately 6,000 desiatinas were leased out to peasants on a sharecropping basis. Slightly more than two thousand estates were worked with hired labor and the estate's own equipment. Although the land was poorly farmed, an 1899 investigation of the estate revealed that the lease rate of ten rubles was double what peasants could reasonably be expected to pay, and well in excess of the actual land value. Yet such exorbitant rates could be charged because of the desperation with which peasants sought land. For their part, peasants realized that if they refused these inflated terms, these lands could simply be offered to neighboring peasants, equally in need of it.[56]

Before 1900, as the shape of private landholding changed in Dnipro district, peasant vulnerability increased there, as it did throughout all of New Russia. The steady selling-off of noble estates from 1863 to 1892, noted in chapter 4, continued into the twentieth century. On average, between 1893 and 1902, more than eight hundred estates were sold annually in the region, compared to fewer than five hundred annually in the previous decade.[57] But whereas private landholding at midcentury had been typified by massive estates owned by hereditary nobility, the estates sold by 1900 were much smaller. At the same time, land ownership passed out of the exclusive control of the nobility. In this process the nature of private landholding, and the manner in which those lands were managed, was transformed. A comparison of the two great imperial land surveys completed in 1877–78 and in 1905 reveals the distinct emergence of smaller private estates as well as a decline in the proportion of private lands (that is, lands other than allotment, church, and state lands) owned by the nobility (see table 7.5).[58]

Noble landholding underwent a dramatic decline in the space of less than thirty years. By 1905 New Russian nobles had sold off 41 percent

Table 7.5. Noble landholding in New Russia, 1877–1905.

	Average size of holding (in desiatinas)		Noble holdings as a percent of all private holdings	
Province	**1877**	**1905**	**1877**	**1905**
Katerynoslav	1,252.8	748.1	84.5	42.2
Tavriia	1,288.2	594.0	58.3	31.4
Kherson	963.0	719.0	75.7	39.2
New Russia	**1,168.0**	**687.0**	**72.8**	**37.6**
European Russia (provincial avg.)	**638.0**	**488.0**	**79.8**	**61.9**

Source: *SPSNM*, 2–5, 36–39, 70–73; *SZ1905*, 16:30–37, 14:33–36, 42:33–38. See also *Svod dannykh po 50-ti guberniiam Evropeiskoi Rossii* 1907, 15–17.

of properties that had been in their possession in 1877. During that same period, the average-sized noble estate shrank from 1,168 to 687 desiatinas. Tavriia, with a 54 percent decline, suffered the greatest loss. Only in Kherson province, with sales of 25 percent of noble lands, was the decline comparable to the average for European Russia of 24 percent. Overall, the sale of noble estates in New Russia was significantly greater than in the empire overall. This dramatic drop in the average size of nobles' estates in New Russia was accompanied by the rise of a new landed elite at a rate that was unmatched elsewhere in European Russia. In 1905, 62 percent of all private lands in European Russia were still owned by nobles, whereas New Russian nobles only owned 37.6 percent of all private lands, a drop of almost 50 percent over twenty-eight years. All three New Russian provinces experienced declines, though by 1905 the authority of nobles was the weakest in Tavriia, where they owned less than one-third of all private lands. These trends mirrored a profound transformation of economic patterns within rural New Russia before 1905. A new private landowning elite had clearly emerged during these years, one that took a more active part in the management of their estates and sought to increase their efficiency and profitability.

The shift of estate lands away from the New Russian nobility might have benefited communal peasants if *they* had purchased most of the properties. But they had not. On the contrary, the new landed elite comprised a mixture of German and Mennonite colonists, Jewish entrepreneurs, merchants, and other nobles. Together, they sharply reduced the amount of land most peasants could afford.[59] By 1905 perhaps half of all peasant private holdings in Kherson province were owned by German colonists; this involved 18 percent (493,243 desiatinas) of all private lands. These energetic agriculturalists had increased their holdings in that province by 125,003 desiatinas between 1896 and 1905, while all other peasants combined had obtained only 123,437 desiatinas. Such a statistic is especially remarkable because, according to the 1897 census, only 4.52 percent of the population of Kherson province was German, and many of these people lived in towns and cities. Still, by that time they had acquired 14 percent of the province's land. Their active entry into the land market was deemed to be a central factor in the escalation of land values, which went from 30 rubles a desiatina in 1884 to 180 rubles by 1900.[60]

The large-scale purchase of private estates in Kherson province had an immediate impact on local peasants, because the Mennonites and

Germans brought capital-intensive economies to their new holdings. As a result, they rarely made land available for lease and thereby deprived peasants of land that had long been accessible to them. Even more difficult was the plight of the *desiatinshchiks* in villages found on these estates, whose claim to the land dated back "to time immemorial," but whose fate suddenly became noticeably worse.[61]

New Russian estate owners were in a decidedly better position at the dawn of the twentieth century than they had been a generation earlier. The transition to smaller estates had stripped away many of the previously massive and unmanageable holdings, a number of which had simply been leased out to neighboring peasants. The new, smaller estates could be managed more efficiently. Also, many estate owners (or their heirs), who had been caught off guard by the 1861 Emancipation Manifesto and the subsequent depression in wool prices, had adjusted by the late 1880s to the new social and market conditions. Aiding them in this process was the steady increase of agricultural machinery, itself a spinoff of the region's industrial boom.[62]

By the 1890s most estate owners were in an even more advantageous position when it came to deciding how to manage their properties. Those who still chose to lease out their lands could demand higher rates and choose from a growing body of potential lessees. Not surprisingly, peasants were the least able to meet the new rates. A growing number of estate owners also decided to pull their lands off of the rental market entirely. Some took this route because of the unsatisfactory leasing arrangements of the 1860s and 1870s, when peasants had greater control over the process. Moreover, the introduction of better, more efficient implements, including better plows, scarifiers, reapers, hay rakes, winnowers, and threshing machines, made a crucial difference. Estate owners were able to circumvent a problem as old as their own history on the New Russian steppe: the scarcity and high cost of seasonal labor.[63]

Estate owners maintained that the perennial problem of labor shortages had long hampered agricultural development in New Russia, especially the spread of grain production. This problem became more acute after the emancipation in 1861 as former serfs turned their energies toward their own allotments.[64] Faced with a shortage of laborers, especially at peak times of the year, estate owners relied on the annual arrival of laborers from the more densely settled provinces to the north, especially from Kharkiv, Poltava, Chernihiv, and Kyiv.[65] These workers were hired under several different kinds of cash payments: cash payment by the day, season, or year; or on terms under which labor was exchanged for a specified share of the harvest. Day laborers, by far the largest portion of all groups, were most commonly hired during haying and reaping, and seasonal workers were involved in all summer activities, including weeding, herding, and carting. Only a small percentage of workers were kept over winter, though often estate owners would be forced to pay workers nominally during this period if they wanted to retain their services for the following year.[66]

Employers faced a number of challenges. First, estate owners were required to anticipate the number of laborers required for the coming harvest, since hiring often began well before. Given the manner in which promising harvests were regularly ruined by sudden fierce rain storms or unrelenting hail, this was a difficult choice, in view of the fact that low harvests could double the losses for an owner who had already paid out advanced wages. By one estimate, the number of laborers required by estate owners in Katerynoslav province in the early 1890s might range from 36,000 to 80,000 depending on the harvest. No wonder estate owners found the business of forecasting to be a very difficult one when it came to the labor market.[67]

Even workers who had been hired and had received partial wages in advance might not honor their agreements. Often peasants who had previously agreed to work for relatively low wages in exchange for a cash advance in winter found better bargaining opportunities under the warmth of the summer sun. At times, estate owners could be their own worst enemies, since parties of workers might abandon one estate for another overnight on the promise of higher wages. One noble from Pavlohrad district regularly assumed that one-half of the 500 to 600 workers employed in early spring (often with cash advances) would not appear when needed in summer. Estate owners also complained about the astonishingly high number of holidays taken by laborers in the region, which ranged from 106 to more than 180 days. Averaging 2 to 3 days a week, including Sundays, such occasions were concentrated in the winter months, although at least 4 holidays were identified in June, and another 5 in July (not including Sundays).[68]

Under these conditions, employers needed to pay vigilant attention to their laborers to ensure that they would honor the negotiated terms. More established and prosperous employers, such as the colonists in Berdiansk and Melitopol districts, provided wages and conditions liable to attract workers back annually. Records indicate that by 1900 some of these had returned to the same farm for twenty-five years or more. Finally, estate agriculturalists who had acquired labor-saving implements were at an obvious advantage, as their labor requirements were significantly reduced.[69]

The difficulties experienced by estate owners in the hunt for sufficient laborers during the 1860s and 1870s diminished significantly thereafter. In a striking departure from the immediate post-emancipation era, the annual reports that New Russian estate owners submitted to the Ministry of State Domains between 1882 and 1905 noted serious labor shortages in only two years: 1888 and 1903. In fact, by the 1890s most estate owners had begun to comment favorably on the annual surpluses of available labor.[70] Although the region's rapid population increase was clearly a factor in this shift in relations between estate owners and laborers, no less important were the various attempts the zemstvos made to regulate the movement of labor. Perhaps the most important step was the formation of medical-provisioning stations during the 1890s. Established in Kherson and Katerynoslav provinces, these stations provided migratory laborers with inexpensive lodging, nourishment, and medical care while they were en route to their summer destinations. The stations were also able to monitor local crop and climate conditions, and assure a more efficient movement of laborers to the fields.[71]

Information gathered by these stations toward the end of the 1890s confirms the fact that the position of estate owners in New Russia was steadily improving. In 1899, V. V. Khizhniakov, a zemstvo doctor in Kherson province, noted an important aspect of this change:

> Having strongly developed in recent times, mechanized agriculture [*mashinoe khoziaistvo*] has caused an increase in the demand for, and in the supply of, child and female laborers and the hiring of "half-wage earners" to the disaster of full-wage earning males.[72]

At a time when more workers were appearing on the market, the adoption of new technology—especially reapers—allowed estate owners consistently to hire lower-paid workers (the so-called "half-wage earners") such as women and youth. Thus, peasant household incomes were reduced, and estate economies were strengthened and made more efficient. Although wages in New Russia remained among the highest in the empire, the gap with laborers elsewhere had begun to diminish to the benefit of estate owners and the chagrin of the laborers. Moreover, this happened at the very time that New Russia's peasants were being drawn into this "workers' turf" with renewed vigor. The percentage of local workers registered at zemstvo sanitation points leapt from approximately 8 percent of the total in the early 1890s to 20 percent a decade later as New Russians sought to supplement their increasingly meager incomes. Thereafter, laborers continued to arrive annually in the tens of thousands, drawn in part by dreams of wealth and prosperity.[73]

As employment opportunities and conditions worsened, tensions between the migratory laborers and local peasants in search of supplemental work worsened considerably. One account from 1896 states:

> Local workers blame the lowering of wages on workers coming from other provinces. This harmful relationship was manifested with special intensity in the action of local workers at the hiring market in Bobrinets [Ukr. Bobrynets; northern Kherson province]. In 1896, the manager of that employment center reported that on the 30th of June, between three and five in the afternoon, landless local peasants appeared at the station, and with threats, fists, and stones drove the migratory laborers from Poltava [*Poltavtsy*] away. These migrants scattered to other centers, while the largest portion returned home.[74]

Local workers were also unhappy with the practice of allowing soldiers to be requisitioned for agricultural work. By 1900 approximately 14,000 soldiers worked annually in Kherson province alone.[75]

Faced with limited possibilities as hired laborers, former serfs sought with each new year to extract the greatest yield possible from their allotments. The most obvious way to do this was to completely stop the practice of leaving cultivated lands fallow. There are countless records about the peasants' practice of continuous plowing and haphazard crop cultivation around the year 1900. Once-profitable gardens were plowed under, and even "old timers" could not recall a time when many of their fields had not been cultivated.[76] Peasant agriculturalists utilized a new generation of implements in their work, but with very little change in actual techniques. A representative report completed for the Agricultural Bureau of the Katerynoslav Provincial Zemstvo in the late 1890s concluded:

> If we were to determine a household's well-being simply by its inventory, taking into account that the mass of peasant households are exclusively using improved plows and steel harrows to cultivate the soil, and for the hay and grain harvest they use mowers and horse-rakes, then agricultural progress would appear to be everywhere. In reality, however, productivity is not only not rising, but actually falling, since all of this is being done not to increase the yield per desiatina, but so as to expend the least amount of labor and capital in order to be able to exploit the greatest amount of space.... In general, agriculture in the province is at the very point where the old system has died, but the new system has yet to be born.[77]

Conclusion

By 1900 peasants themselves knew that the widespread application of practices suited to frontier-like conditions could no longer sustain their household economies. In the absence of a true revolution in agriculture, the only alternative was to increase the amount of land at their disposal, even if it meant going outside of the village to get it. Thus, it is not surprising that tensions were on the rise in the New Russian countryside before 1900. How could it be otherwise when land values had more than doubled during the last twenty years of the nineteenth century and when the German and Mennonite colonists were continuing to buy up estate lands that the peasants had long cultivated themselves?[78] In his assessment in 1904 of these various trends, the governor of Katerynoslav province expressed alarm:

> There has been a considerable rise in peasant demands for more land. Land values have sharply risen in recent times and are reaching 300 rubles a desiatina in several districts. The appearance of these [inflated prices] can be attributed to the enormous competition that exists in the business of obtaining land among not only local peasants, but more especially, from the countless colonists, as well as from industrial firms.[79]

Other reports pointed to increased tensions when estate owners denied peasants access to pasture lands that had long been theirs to use. Together, these emerging disputes pointed to the largest question of all: If peasants had no firm understanding of private property on their own lands, how could they be counted on to recognize the abstract legal claims to land made by estate owners, foreign colonists, or the state?[80] And even if they did have an appreciation for household tenure, would they still claim non-peasant lands if those had been integrated into their own economies for more than a century? These questions would be conclusively answered in 1905–7, and again after 1917. Early results did not provide property owners or administrators with cause for optimism, however. In this regard, in 1903 the governor for Tavriia province recorded:

> The *obshchina* nourishes in peasants a vague and improper understanding of property rights with the belief that if not today, then tomorrow, there will again be a re-division [*peredel*], and they will again be given land, even if it will be taken away from the gentry. I have personally had to hear repeatedly complaints from peasants that they have small landholdings, but the nobility have large ones; only the fear of authority restrained them, for they expressed the necessity of seizing all gentry lands and transferring them to peasants.[81]

This report, and the one from Katerynoslav province that began this chapter, correctly identified a phenomenon that must have utterly confounded local officials. They had overseen the transformation of the New Russian countryside in the half-century following the Crimean War, yet had failed to alter substantially the social cohesiveness and separateness of the traditional New Russian peasant commune. Indeed, there was every reason to believe that peasant society had become more unified over the past generation and more at odds with their non-peasant neighbors.

While former serf and state-peasant villages had undergone an organizational transformation, there were few indications that the fundamental sense of the collective had diminished in New Russia. In addition, no new groups of wealthier peasants had emerged—groups that might have stressed individual economic initiative alongside a fundamental respect for the privileges and position of elite society.[82] To that end, beginning in 1906 with the so-called Stolypin reforms, Russian administrators would make a concerted attempt to create such a rural ally. But those reforms came only after the collision between peasants and the state—and between peasants and estate owners—in the revolution of 1905.

8

A FITTING CONCLUSION?

1905 in New Russia

On 9 May 1905 peasants from the village of Komisarivka (Kommisarovka), in Slov'iano-Serbiia district, approached the manor house of the neighboring Komisariv (Kommisarov) estate. A collision of worlds was about to begin. The peasants proceeded to inform the lord, Depreradovich, that a recent examination of their documents had revealed a shocking truth. The survey upon which their forebears had determined the boundary between village and demesne lands at the time of the Emancipation Manifesto had deprived the villagers of one hundred desiatinas. They now wanted the land back. They also asked Depreradovich for a copy of the original "emancipation" land charter from 1862, as theirs had disappeared.

Depreradovich declined on both counts. Two days later a stack of his cut hay from the disputed land was set ablaze. That same evening a shed located some distance from the stack, but on the same parcel of land, also went up in flames. Three months later, on 21 August, the peasants of Komisarivka—spurred on by reports of labor disorders in nearby mines—drove away the migratory laborers whom Depreradovich had hired to plow the disputed lands. The very next day villagers again repulsed the hired laborers, this time with stones, and two days later they intimidated a lone police officer who had been summoned to restore order. Finally, on 25 August a regiment of Cossacks arrived and order was restored, more than four months after the first troubles had been recorded.[1]

Two months later, harsher demands were made by peasants from the village of Bohdanivka (Bogdanovka) in Ananïv district, who declared that serfdom had been possible only because "dishonorable and cunning enemies of the people" had surrounded the tsar. They went on to declare that these nobles, along with all district and provincial officials, held all land within the empire hostage. Therefore, the Bohdanivka village assembly resolved that "the old order of Russian life must be once and for all destroyed…so that life can, as it must, be founded on the basis of fraternity, equality, and freedom for all peoples in Russia." To that end, they demanded

> the transfer of all lands, henceforth to be cultivated by the labors of all people, the destruction of social estates, bureaucratic rank [*chin*], and the police in their present form, and their replacement by truly popular forces. We demand an amnesty for all who have been accused of crimes, the abolition of martial law and the death penalty. We demand universal and free education for our children, and that the demands of our laborers be satisfied.[2]

The unrest initiated by peasants in Komisarivka and Bohdanivka occurred throughout much of New Russia and beyond in 1905. In part, this revolution reflected an immediate, widespread, and profound lack of confidence in the Russian Empire following its disastrous war with Japan in 1904. Hopes for a "short victorious war" faded quickly, and morale sagged further with each naval and military defeat. Social tensions appeared in both the city and countryside, and at many levels within each. Virtually every sector of Russian society had become disillusioned with the Romanov state by the start of 1905, and especially after 9 January, when imperial troops in St. Petersburg fired on the peaceful demonstrators who had converged on the Winter Palace to present their petitions to the tsar. The senseless death of hundreds quickly gave that day its notoriety as Bloody Sunday and prompted a wide range of opposition movements to burst forth throughout the empire. In the months that followed, periods of relative stability were gradually overshadowed by mounting protests.

State officials had long recognized that a prosperous and peaceful countryside was essential to the empire's longevity. They reasoned that a prosperous peasantry would be a loyal one, one which would more readily adopt the values of elite society, including a respect for the property rights of estate owners in their midst.[3] Many officials before 1900 increasingly supported initiatives ranging from increased educational opportunities for peasants to better medical care, in hopes that peasants would become more productive, and social stability more secure. However, so as to not put all of their eggs into this one basket, by 1900 New Russian governors were also calling for an expanded local police force and a complete overhaul and expansion of regional prison facilities.[4]

Ultimately, it was the failure of elite society to understand, much less transform, peasant society that led to the rural revolutionary crisis. Peasants resented the state's call to serve in an army and to die in distant lands for a cause that meant nothing to them. Many wondered openly why they should perish in distant lands if there was no adequate compensation on the home front. In that vein, and in a scene that would be repeated countless times in the succeeding months, on 20 July 1904 sixty peasants from the village of Petrove (Petrova), in Oleksandriia district, began to pasture their livestock on the Einzidel estate, located near their village. They ignored the estate supervisor's demand that they immediately remove their livestock. Instead, they declared that "the land is the Tsar's. Why doesn't the baron forfeit the land, and we ourselves will pay for it." The supervisor's utter failure to remove the peasants prompted the estate owner to intervene directly. He rode out to the disputed fields on horseback, whereupon he was quickly surrounded, and a boisterous exchange ensued. Peasants responded to his challenge with sneers, and declared that "the baron has much land, but [we] have nowhere to pasture [our] livestock." In consternation, they continued: "what kind of order [*poriadok*] is this? They take us to serve in the war, but won't give us land. What on earth are they doing with us?!" The baron later complained that these peasant trespassers freed him only after he took his revolver and fired several shots into the air. The peasants allowed him to retreat, but they continued to use the lands as though they were no longer his, but theirs.[5]

Peasants in New Russia also initiated large assemblies where discussions moved from a consideration of the empire's faltering war effort to the call for more radical acts against local estate owners. Amid such moves the peasants continued to proclaim their loyalty to the tsar. One noble, instructed by Nicholas II to prepare a report based upon an investigation of events in Kherson province in June 1905, concluded: "From my discussions with peasants I personally came away with the assurance that the mass of peasants still hold Your Majesty in complete devotion, that their relationship to their sovereign can up to the present moment still be described as patriarchal." Perhaps it was. The peasants from the village of Papelnastovskoe were by no means alone when they sang "God Save the Tsar" before torching a neighboring estate owner's home and grain-filled shed.[6]

We noted earlier that in the immediate aftermath of the emancipation of 1861 the peasants refused to hold the tsar responsible for their perceived misfortune. Instead, they clung to the myth of the "good tsar" and identified the nobles and the tsar's officials as the real villains.[7] A striking parallel can be found between the post-emancipation unrest and the empire's disintegration in 1905. Once again, peasants identified the tsar as someone who had been unwittingly manipulated by his closest advisors. Peasants were especially determined to link Nicholas's October Manifesto with the legislative initiatives of the early 1860s. Many, including the villagers of Komisarivka, demanded a reconsideration of their "emancipation" well before October.

The nature, scale, and location of peasant protest changed dramatically with the issuance of the October Manifesto. The final two months of 1905 came to represent the most critical phase of the revolution. Many insisted that the manifesto actually contained more radical reforms, including permission for peasants to seize all estate lands as of January 1906. Peasants were now encouraged to initiate such seizures with the assurance that the tsar fully blessed their deeds. As we mentioned at the start of this chapter, peasants from the village of Bohdanivka called for the destruction of the nobility's social privilege and rank, as well as for the seizure of all estate lands, in the name of the tsar.[8] At approximately the same time, on the evening of 8 December 1905, some three hundred peasants in Verkhn'odniprovsk district raided the neighboring Filipov estate, where they told terrified estate representatives:

> A decree has been issued from the Tsar, which states that it is necessary for peasants to go to the nobles and other landowners and invade and burn these estates, and then to go to the towns to invade and burn them, and for all of this there will be no punishment of any kind, because there is now complete freedom, and the Tsar has given his blessing to this endeavor.[9]

Once again, peasants relied heavily upon rumors to determine and justify a wide range of actions.[10] As the year progressed, mass evening meetings became frequent and brought hundreds of peasants together from the surrounding countryside. Occasionally crowds reached a thousand and more, which was not difficult given the massive villages scattered throughout New Russia.

Agitators in the Village: Myths, Rumors, and Outsiders

Contemporaries often commented on the role outsiders played in these deliberations. In one case, peasants from the village of Kurysove (Kurisova), near the port of Odesa, congregated in a "very large gathering" on 27 November 1905. Here, according to the police report, a local teacher welcomed "two Jewish students," whose call for mass agitation found a receptive audience. Other accounts also highlighted the role played by teachers, including Gustav Kleinshmidt, who was charged with distributing revolutionary proclamations in the village of Ploske (Ploskaia) in Tiraspol district.[11] In that same district, Mikhail Volkov, a teacher from the village of Slov'ianoserbske, gathered peasants together for regular meetings and informed them that peasants in other provinces had begun to raid private estates. Such reports made a strong impression on local peasants, who soon declared that they too would take what they wanted from neighboring properties. Still, not all village teachers encouraged the peasants to forcibly seize property. Most were reluctant to incite agrarian terror. One teacher, identified only as Vazhnenko, urged peasants in Katerynoslav province to assume more "cultured forms" of protest and to eschew the use of force. By the end of 1905, however, officials had seen enough to link village teachers directly to the collapse of societal order, and they brought large numbers of teachers to trial. By January 1906 even the arrest of priests for their role in peasant agitation was no longer considered especially newsworthy.[12] Socialist Revolutionaries and Social Democrats also traveled throughout the countryside spreading the gospel of insurrection, and many took positions as village teachers in order to legitimize their presence within a village. Others traveled freely in the summer of 1905, as was reported from northern Kherson province:

> The disorders that occurred among the peasants in June of this year were without a doubt prompted by the influence and under the leadership of

> revolutionary organizations which, at this time, discourage peasants from taking extreme measures. They have persistently advised them not to commit murder, plunder, or other acts of violence, but rather to present en masse the most impossible demands to estate owners and back up their demands with threats.[13]

Not surprisingly, outside agitators were most active in the hinterlands of New Russia's major cities, including Odesa, Ielysavethrad, Katerynoslav, and Ananïv. When not personally represented in the countryside, revolutionary organizations distributed illegal newspapers and other correspondence to Ananïv and other inland towns from a regional center in Odesa.[14] Reports, including the one from the village of Kurysove, often identified Jews as the leaders of these movements. Jewish revolutionaries were also blamed for almost all of the disturbances in Verkhn'odniprovsk district from early September 1905 to the spring of 1906, when peasant unrest reached a fever pitch.[15]

The Imperial Russian Free Economic Society was interested in the role played by these outsiders in the revolution of 1905. It sent out a questionnaire to all corners of the empire in early 1907. Of the seventy-four individuals from New Russia who responded, seventeen identified outsiders as central to peasant unrest, whereas nine rejected the idea outright. Most of the positive references vaguely referred to "the unifying role among the people [*narod*] played by agitators, Jews, and students," or "the leadership of the organization from Geneva." A communication from the police department in Kherson province in June 1905 warned that peasants had already formed their own revolutionary Social Democrat societies.[16] Such links were especially important in the eastern portions of Katerynoslav province, where local peasants had increasingly sought supplemental employment in the various mining and industrial enterprises of the Donbas. Peasant unrest in Slov'iano-Serbiia and Bakhmut districts closely overlapped with incidents of labor unrest in the mines and with the increasingly frequent outbreak of pogroms.[17]

How important, then, was the role played by outsiders? Can it account for the lion's share of the unrest experienced in the New Russian countryside in 1905? It is not surprising that Soviet historians stressed the "direct and decisive impact of the Bolshevik party." Nobles and state officials also stressed the role of outsiders: to do otherwise threatened their belief in the passive and loyal peasant *muzhik*, the mainstay of the new state.[18] Peasants themselves reinforced the role of outsiders in the aftermath of the 1905 revolution. In report after report prepared after the state had regained firm control of the countryside, New Russian peasants proclaimed their innocence and placed the blame on outsiders. Peasants from Melitopol district who had plundered a nearby estate on 10 December 1905 later blamed their actions on the "dark" people who had persuaded them that the time had come to seize gentry lands. Others later spoke vaguely of "unknown people" who had suddenly appeared in their villages in late 1905 and claimed that an overthrow of estates was entirely legitimate and timely. Still other peasants portrayed themselves as a "poor and ignorant people" who had simply followed the trends of the time in 1905—something that officials were eager to believe. One report from Tavriia province opined that peasants had naively fallen for simple slogans like "free land for all" and did not understand why such transfers were impossible. Finally, and not surprisingly, in subsequent years convicted outsiders minimized their own role, portraying themselves as voices of reason that had urged peasants to avoid random acts of violence.[19]

In sum, it is likely that outsiders played an important role in the spread of ideas and news from regional and imperial centers. They were especially valuable in interpreting the events of the day to their village audiences or formulating petitions and demands. Finally, their value reached beyond the era of revolutionary instability, since peasants could use the influence of outsiders as an alibi. But outsiders were only able to play the role they did play because the peasants themselves were inclined to rebel by 1905. In the words of Scott Seregny,

> Peasants were able to manoeuver within the complex web of relations that had evolved by the turn of the century between peasant communities on the one hand, and local elites, officials, and other outsiders, on the other. Relations between peasants and outsiders were complex, symbiotic, and, particularly in the heated atmosphere of 1905, fluid.[20]

There is every indication that peasants utilized the skills and views of outsiders only when these coincided with their own previously established goals. In a similar manner, as in the aftermath of the 1861 Emancipation decree, rumors served as an effective means for peasants to advance ideas that they themselves believed. After all, did most peasants actually believe that the tsar had ordered them to seize noble estates? Anand Yang has aptly concluded from his investigation of colonial India that rumors were "the utterances of a people sharing common preoccupations" that gave them "the capacity to speak in a common voice loud enough to be heard by their superordinates."[21]

Thus, to cite the most extreme case, peasants spread rumors that the tsar wanted them to seize private estates, and they welcomed outsiders who carried the same message. Teodor Shanin's argument that peasant dreams directly shaped their actions in 1905 is clearly borne out throughout much of New Russia, where the "dreams" stretched into the past and future.[22] Peasant delegates to the All Russian Peasant Congress in November 1905 grounded their aspirations in a tradition of freedom that dated back to the region's independent Cossack bands: "In our people there lives to this very day that sense of freedom which was found among the Zaporozhian Cossacks."[23]

These same peasants also believed that the terms imposed at the time of their "emancipation" had been immoral because they had driven a wedge between those who owned land and those who used it. In early December 1905 peasants in Pokrovske volost of Dnipro district began to cart hay away from the estate of Peter and Nikolai Shmidt. When challenged, they declared that such was their right given that they had long been the principle estate harvesters on a sharecropping basis.[24] Similarly, former serfs from Tashino, Kherson province, petitioned the tsar in May 1905 to grant them what they clearly deserved:

> Our needs are great, Your Majesty! For many centuries we peasants have endured all the adversities, all the blunders of the state: our ancestors spilled their blood for the expansion of Russia; for two and a half centuries we endured servitude and thereby made it possible for the privileged classes to live in clover; we alone carried the burden of harsh military service. For many centuries we have had to pay an unbearable amount in taxes and duties. For our unfailing centuries-old service to the state we received a wretched allotment of land with high redemption dues, [and] we were deprived of all rights; for centuries we stagnated in ignorance, and we remain in that condition today.[25]

The fact that New Russian estate owners had regularly leased out a high proportion of their lands to neighboring peasants reinforced peasants' beliefs that the land was theirs already, or about to become so. In this way rumors, myths, dreams, and historical reconstructions fused into one. The resulting crisis was especially acute in the western reaches of Kherson province, where landless *desiatinshchiks* had been compelled for decades to lease land from estate owners. Here clashes had intensified between owners and lessees in the years before 1905. Nor was unrest limited to the *desiatinshchiks*. Even when former serfs retained their own land, the intermingling of estate and village holdings after 1861 blurred the distinction between the two, especially when the peasants were cultivating both.[26]

Even though the blurring of estate and village lands had been initiated by estate owners, it ironically reinforced what had long been a particular revolutionary dream. Peasant society had previously experienced considerable tension in the 1880s, when the first generation born after the administrative reforms of the 1860s came of age. At that time both former serfs and state peasants responded to those new demands for lands in a manner that had temporarily alleviated the crisis. By the turn of the century, however, yet another generation had come of age, and had left New Russian officials wondering if peasants might alleviate their internal land crisis by unilaterally expanding their holdings at the expense of nearby private holdings.[27]

Observers at the local level also reported on peasant land hunger:

> Year after year the local population is growing steadily and, naturally, the demand for land increases as well. At the present time one can everywhere hear complaints from peasants about their crowded conditions. The desire to possess as much land as possible is very great among local peasants.[28]

Under these conditions, peasants viewed 1905 as a year when they could set the ledger straight and correct generations of unfair treatment.[29] That said, it remained to be seen how this goal might be realized.

1905 in New Russia: An Overview

Although 1905 was clearly a tumultuous year in the New Russian countryside, it is more difficult to determine the actual degree of the unrest, or how the region fared relative to the empire as a whole. There is reason to argue that, however difficult the New Russian experience may have been, it remained an island of stability when compared to other regions in the empire. In his study of the Russian countryside from 1905 to 1907, Soviet historian S. M. Dubrovskii argues that only the Lower Volga provinces, Latvia, the Urals, and the far and desolate north experienced fewer disturbances than did New Russia.

Peasant disturbances were first reported in the central Russian provinces in January 1905, and only thereafter spread to the empire's periphery. And yet the truth may have been otherwise. As Dubrovskii points out, the difficulty in determining degrees of instability lies in measuring the strength of "the peasant movement" within any given region.[30] Thus, historians have weighed reported disturbances equally, even though there were large differences: on one end of the scale, several peasant households might simply have pastured their livestock on estate lands; on the other, crowds numbering in the hundreds burned down outbuildings and manor houses. Furthermore, the incidents themselves were not even recorded unless reported to police authorities, or recorded in response to the 1907 questionnaire sent out by the Imperial Free Economic Society. While that questionnaire was a valuable source—one that Dubrovskii himself relied heavily upon—its reliance on a relatively small number of correspondents limits its value for the measurement of disturbances in any given region. There were only 46 respondents to the society's questionnaire in New Russia. Of these, 25 limited their responses to the immediate district in which they resided. Another 10 focused exclusively on events that transpired within a single village, and 12 claimed to cover *all* of Katerynoslav province (14 were located in Tavriia, and 20 in Kherson).[31] Such limited coverage makes it difficult to present a statistical measurement of events in 1905 in the New Russian countryside.

Although statistical certainty remains elusive, we can reach a more informed assessment of 1905 in New Russia by referring to a rich archival record not available to earlier investigators. It is now possible to reach some tentative conclusions about the links between agricultural development and rural disturbances. For example, we can ask how the number of peasant disturbances was related to the degree to which estate agriculture was capitalized. A brief overview suggests that the earliest indications of peasant unrest in the form of strikes and demands for better conditions were found in villages scattered throughout New Russia. Peasants in the northern districts of Kherson, especially Ielysavethrad and Oleksandriia, were first off the mark in the spring of 1905, and from then on unrest spread rapidly and intensively into the summer months. Thereafter it appears to have diminished significantly. That was not the case, however, in the districts of all three provinces that bordered on the lower Dnipro. Here the last two months of 1905 witnessed a crucible of terror for estate owners as peasant hostility toward them reached its boiling point. Disturbances were strongest in the eastern portion of Kherson, western Verkhn'odniprovsk, northern Melitopol, and almost all of Dnipro. More than eighty estates were destroyed in Verkhn'odniprovsk alone, and another seventeen in Dnipro. Although estate owners and colonists elsewhere in the region were equally fearful of what might unfold, the dreaded peasant war did not materialize, at least not yet.[32]

In their initial confrontations with estate owners in the spring of 1905, New Russian peasants adopted practices similar to those found elsewhere in the empire. They demanded better lease rates for land and higher wages for labor, and they were reluctant to accept no for an answer. Peasants in Novomoskovsk district of Katerynoslav province seized adjoining estate lands when financial obligations had not been altered to their satisfaction. On 24 June 1905 a representation of peasants from the village of Ivanivka, in Melitopol district, gathered at a neighboring estate and verbally threatened the owner. In response, he provided a written guarantee to immediately halve lease rates to 4 rubles, 50 kopecks a desiatina.[33] Similar disturbances occurred in the spring of 1905 in Dnipro district, where peasants threatened to seize estate lands if the owners did not immediately and significantly reduce lease rates for land. Peasants who lived near the Kniazev estate in Pavlohrad district demanded that five hundred desiatinas of land be leased to them for no more than three rubles a desiatina, a dramatic decrease from current rates.[34]

As the foregoing makes clear, peasant "requests" for better terms and conditions were often accompanied by acts of intimidation. Peasants insisted that they would simply begin working the land for free if better rates were not immediately forthcoming. The request made at the Kniazev estate in December 1905 was preceded by several days when hay and straw stacks were burned at four estates in the region. In other instances peasants began, without prior notice, to pasture their livestock on estate lands and cut timber for household needs. Peasants in Dnipro district were especially responsive to the rapid loss of land for lease because of the increasingly vigorous estate purchasing by German colonists. Crowds of landless *desiatinshchiks* gathered to obstruct these transactions and block the necessary land surveys, thereby serving notice that local peasants would not accept the changed status of these holdings.[35]

New Russian peasants also reacted strongly in 1905 to the annual influx of migratory laborers. Hundreds of thousands of these so-called "foreigners" appeared in the south annually, and local peasants blamed them for a curb in agricultural wages and the removal of estate lands from the rental market. Furthermore, anxiety over the local labor market had intensified in the lower Dnipro River districts because of the recent large-scale adoption of labor-saving machinery on estate lands, which significantly curtailed the need to hire more highly priced adult male laborers. Under these circumstances, local peasants clearly understood that a diminished labor supply would be immediately advantageous to them. In 1905 they did what they could to fight against laborers from outside. Threats and attacks against migratory laborers, which had been part of the New Russian landscape for at least a decade, became noticeably more pronounced when "foreign" laborers first appeared in the spring of 1905.

The vast majority of these laborers arrived on foot, traveling in collectives (artels) most commonly formed by association with their home region (*rodina*). In the revolutionary year of 1905, their welcome suddenly became a hostile one. In June 1905 peasants from the village of Troiantsovo, in Ielysavethrad district, bullied all hired laborers on the adjoining sugar-beet estate and forced them to leave. The noble realized that he would face crippling losses if he did not improve the situation for local peasant laborers. Acts of arson and theft directed against estate owners became commonplace on New Russian estates and only ceased after migrant workers had been banished. One account noted that local peasants had been so successful that no migratory laborers were hired in Kherson province after the first half of June.[36] At the same time, peasants relied heavily on strikes. After first denying estate owners access to migratory laborers, they themselves then refused to work until wages had been increased. In a more direct challenge to the established order, on the night of 19 June peasants from Katerynoslav district ransacked and torched the zemstvo depot that had been established for migratory laborers in the village of Grushevo-Ruditsino.[37]

Yet, apart from violence directed toward migratory laborers and occasional threats of unilateral actions against the estate owners, New

Russian peasants generally conducted themselves in a peaceful manner in the spring and summer of 1905. They often assembled in numbers of four hundred and more to make their demands, which occasionally were addressed to multiple numbers of estate owners. In June 1905 peasants from Sviato-Troitskoe volost informed all area estate owners that annual lease rates needed to be immediately lowered to six rubles a desiatina from previous rates that had ranged up to eighteen rubles. Other peasants, who had lately been compelled to accept sharecropping arrangements under which they received only a fifth of the harvest, now pressed their demands to receive no less than a third.

Yet despite this show of peasant force, there is little to suggest that these petitions and demands, even the expulsion of migratory laborers, significantly altered conditions for local peasants beyond a modest increase in wages and a significant, but short-term, decrease in lease rates.[38] For that reason alone it is hardly surprising that the pace and scale of peasant protest soon changed dramatically.

In the autumn of 1905 disturbances escalated throughout the empire's countryside, including in New Russia itself, and they reached a staggering crescendo in November and December when the pillaging of estates became widespread, especially in Verkhn'odniprovsk district. Crowds of a thousand and more—often from surrounding districts—arrived at estates, where they seized and carted off thousands of kilograms of grain. More than four hundred carts were observed in some of these caravans, as peasants took the law into their own hands.[39] Such pillaging was most commonly initiated by large assemblies of peasants who had gathered earlier in the day to elect a committee that was then dispatched to warn the estate owner or bailiff that a larger assembly was on its way. The committee called for the immediate surrender of all estate lands and possessions, or at least what was left of them, as countless peasants had already removed estate herds, carted away implements, haystacks, grain, and straw, and destroyed immovable property, including sheds and other outbuildings. Speaking to the owner of the Khankovo estate in Verkhn'odniprovsk district, peasants from the village of Novostarodub expressed the new mood: "We will destroy the long-held nests [*gnezda*] of the nobles, and they will not return here anymore, and their days of running these lands are over. Then we will receive more land, and be able to live as free women and men."[40] Some estate owners managed to gain a partial reprieve by offering substantial concessions even at this late date.

For instance, a noble living near the village of Dudchyna (Dudchino), in Kherson district, immediately reduced lease rates from ten to four rubles per desiatina. In most cases where peasants gathered, however, concessions were not made during the final weeks of 1905. Owners had long since fled the countryside.[41]

The peasant revolution of the lower Dnipro districts in November and December involved a broad cross section of villagers, including poor, middle, and prosperous (*zazhitochnye*) peasants. Only the wealthiest (*bogatye*) were said to have declined involvement;[42] indeed, on rare occasions they themselves became, along with the estate owners, the target of mass action. Several New Russian correspondents to the Imperial Free Economic Society reported that "peasants turned on fellow villagers who were wealthy," especially those who had previously purchased modest private holdings. In exceptional cases, tensions erupted within villages between those eager to participate in disorders and those opposed to them. Threats of murder flew back and forth within the village as nerves frayed and the stakes increased. Nonetheless, most reports to the society declared that peasants acted peaceably and in solidarity.[43]

Several factors account for the dramatic radicalization of the New Russian countryside in the early winter of 1905. Peasants who returned from the war theater in Manchuria following the end of hostilities in August 1905 played a destabilizing role, as did the widespread expectations that followed the issuance of the October Manifesto. Peasants claimed that the latter, in which Tsar Nicholas II agreed to some form of representative government, actually included the tsar's wish that peasants seize all estate lands.[44] Peasant actions were also facilitated by the fact that many estate owners fled their lands in November, when all signs pointed to increasingly frequent and intense peasant disturbances. Estate owners in Dnipro district, along with many estate managers, fled their lands during the third week of November as rumors of an imminent attack peaked.[45] The daughter of a Mennonite estate owner in Dnipro district later recalled the panic that ensued as estate owners gathered at local train stations:

> No one except the estate manager...knew of our departure. When we arrived at the station, I remember the large crowd of people consulting to see which train would be allowed to cross the border. There was an atmosphere of anxiety among the passengers on the train. It was a relief when, after a long period of uncertainty, the train began to move.[46]

Peasants were also inspired to act by their dawning awareness that the traditional means of social control in the village had evaporated by the fall of 1905. Both the police and the army failed to halt the violence, albeit for different reasons. The police force in Russia had long been ineffectual, the subject of scorn from local inhabitants, and lacking almost entirely in support from above.[47] Although these shortcomings were masked in times of relative peace, they were suddenly exposed during the last months of 1905 when peasants saw that local police officers were consistently overmatched. When disturbances were reported, the police often arrived too late, and they commonly described themselves as powerless to stem the tide of peasant unrest. Officers were ignored, pelted with stones, and knocked from their horses. Even the limited success of authorities in one region seemed only to lead peasants to refocus their energies. When local police managed to protect an estate from attack in Slov'iano-Serbiia district, the crowd simply redirected its efforts, whereupon an even larger peasant gathering looted and destroyed the buildings on the nearby Popov estate.[48]

Local authorities were no less alarmed by the terrifying truth that the army's intervention could not be relied on in this time of crisis. Even making an appeal for external intervention proved difficult in December because striking telegraph workers refused to transmit the necessary communications. Once troops were summoned, the skeletal framework of rail lines and the seasonal degeneration of county roads made a successful intervention all but impossible. Worse, as John Bushnell has clearly shown, after the release of the October Manifesto the Imperial Russian army contributed directly to the disintegration of power. Soldiers in Odesa took part in the October pogroms. Weeks later, at the start of December, three regiments and a squadron of Cossacks mutinied in the central industrial and administrative center of Katerynoslav. By this time, authorities had been forced to appeal to St. Petersburg for troops to restore order among the ranks themselves.[49]

The Restoration of Order

Many officials, estate owners, and colonists feared during the late months of 1905 that the peasants would prove victorious in this struggle. Hundreds of estates were looted and destroyed in a region where the presence of private estates had been weak to begin with.[50] Yet privileged society was not destroyed—at least not then. The state responded to the threatening situation with several severe measures, including military courts and corporal punishment. At times, the government's actions had little more than a punitive intent, as when troops came and burned the huts of peasants assumed to have taken part in disturbances. At other times, the newly established military courts carried out their task with a zealousness that earned the censure of local provincial governors.[51] Other officials, including the governor of Tavriia province, excused military excesses and declared the importance of showing peasants "the danger in acting badly."[52]

The return of order in the Russian military, and the army's willingness to intervene in the countryside, were central to the state's success. Mass arrests were made from the middle of December 1905 on, and sentences were passed on the most circumstantial of evidence. The transition from lawlessness to order was often a dramatic one. In Verkhn'odniprovsk district, for instance, peasants had free rein from mid-November to the second week of December. Then suddenly, on 30 December soldiers descended on a crowd of a thousand peasants who had seized the Baidakov estate. After the peasants refused to withdraw, troops opened fire on the stunned masses until they surrendered.[53]

Arrests followed, often on the most fragmentary evidence. For example, an estate owner who had been "visited" by a thousand peasants in the middle of the night might allege that he recognized four peasants who were later arrested as ringleaders. Others were identified and arrested simply by the sounds of their voices. Inevitably, peasants declared that they had been wrongly accused and sentenced, with some claiming to have been hundreds of kilometers away from the disturbance at the time. Others questioned the authenticity of crown "witnesses."[54] Even when peasants did not deny the accuracy of the charges, they maintained that the effect of sending them to prison for several years only worsened the situation in the countryside, since it left young families impoverished. As one appeal noted: "Our families remain for many months without workers, and our economies will become utterly disordered."[55] Those members of the rural intelligentsia, including teachers and zemstvo workers thought to have been involved in the movement, found themselves under increased supervision with decreased mobility. On occasion, village peasants rallied around village teachers on the verge of arrest and facilitated their escape. Finally, authorities ordered that all aid in seed grain and food be stopped in regions where peasants were involved in disturbances, thereby bringing those villages to the edge of what they could endure physically.[56]

Thus, a number of factors led to the restoration of order in the countryside after the December uprising of 1905. Although there were further disturbances the following summer, they did not duplicate the scale of the previous winter. In the struggle between peasant and elite society, the 1905 disturbances showed that peasants could at least for the moment be controlled militarily, even if utterly against their wills.[57] A decade later, and in the midst of a much larger war than the empire had faced in 1904, the countryside would again explode in revolution. This time the hostility would be more widespread and the outcome different—and more terrible than most people could imagine.

Conclusion

"OF ALL THE PROVINCES in the Russian Empire there is probably not one that has undergone as many all-encompassing transformations as Ekaterinoslav."[1] With these words, I. Khmirov, the author of a late-nineteenth-century school textbook on Katerynoslav attempted to sum up the bewildering pace of change that his province had experienced in the past century. Russian conquest had resulted in new administrative structures and the eventual formation of three provinces north of the Black Sea. European colonists from central and western Europe had settled there alongside Russians and Ukrainians who had relocated from locales to the north. All of these new settlers joined Cossacks and Tatars whose roots there dated back centuries to when their ancestors had first arrived in the river valleys and arid plains of the lands that would become "New Russia." Against this backdrop, Khmirov described a province where the earliest agricultural gains of the first half of the nineteenth century had been augmented in the second half by the work of energetic merchants and industrialists. Together, agriculture and industry shaped a province in which grains, coal, salt, ore, and flour were exported, and grains, tallow, horses, sheep, oxen, hogs, wool, vegetables, fruits, and all manner of metallurgical and manufactured goods were traded at stores, markets, and bazaars within.[2]

Khmirov's depiction, which could easily apply to the other New Russian provinces of Kherson and Tavriia, was not entirely optimistic in outlook. He also observed that peasants were cultivating ever greater portions of their holdings annually, often with diminished results. Locust, grasshopper, and other insect infestations were all too prevalent, as was the occurrence of rinderpest among cattle. Tertiary means of sustenance, such as fish breeding, were in collapse, and areas of promise, including tobacco cultivation, were not living up to their potential.[3] Khmirov, and countless others, found it difficult to assess New Russia's potential as it entered the twentieth century, and it remains a puzzling question for scholars today. Clearly, the era of Russia's conquest of the south had long passed, and over time the giant herds of sheep had been replaced by grain fields. It was also a century in which peasants, estate owners, and colonists had all weathered a series of crises, and it remained unclear as to whether the solutions would be good for all or merely serve as the terms upon which future grievances would rest.

If some questions about New Russia in 1900 remain unanswerable, however, others no longer need remain so. Of these, we might begin by asking again: was there, in fact, a legacy of freedom among New Russian peasants that was waiting to burst in 1900? It is worth recalling that most historians of the Ukrainian peasant movement in the early twentieth century have emphasized the independent traditions that defined Zaporozhian Cossack society until its Sich was dissolved in 1775. Clearly the legacy of freedom embodied by Cossack society carried on into the nineteenth century. What has received far less attention, however, is the manner in which peasant expectations of their eventual freedom were nurtured throughout the nineteenth century.

For example, even the briefest of overviews of the settlement period makes it clear how much the empire's policies encouraged the expectation that those who settled in New Russia would be free. Estate owners dependent on the rapid settlement of their lands welcomed fugitive settlers, and the state itself was eager to make special arrangements for Dukhobors, Molokans, and other groups that previously had been persecuted or declared unwelcome. Fugitives who agreed to settle in the south initially had only minimal labor obligations imposed on them, and in return they received unlimited access to land for their own pursuits.

Long before the memory of those times disappeared, the conditions of the early settlement period changed, and first of all, for the estate peasants. They began to face new restrictions, yet even then they maintained their belief that the land around them was rightly theirs and that their freedom was nonnegotiable. Thus, well into the nineteenth century rumors continued to allege that the tsar himself supported peasant claims to freedom. The linkage between such rumors and the strong memory of the Cossack Sich in New Russia was not merely coincidental. It represented a voice of freedom in a region that had not forgotten its legacy.

The steady movement of peasants from the north in search of their freedom also played an important role, especially immediately after the outbreak of the Crimean War in 1853. Hundreds of serfs made their way to the south then, believing that full civil freedom would be granted to all who had volunteered for even a brief period of military service. Serfs from the most northerly districts of Katerynoslav and Kherson provinces responded positively to these rumors: "The tsar sits in a gold palace and to all who come he grants their freedom, but to those who do not appear, or are late, they will remain as before in bondage."[4] The war's end in 1856 further fueled peasant unrest: rumors circulated that personal freedom was available for all serfs who voluntarily relocated to the Crimea and helped its shattered economy. Now entire villages, comprised of large and intact extended families, left the lands of their former lords for the south.

By all accounts, New Russian peasants consistently resisted the attempts of estate owners to enserf them. Even the admonition of estate owners and local authorities against rumors promising personal freedom was offset by the reality that peasants from various provinces in the Ukrainian north had relocated as free settlers in the lands recently vacated by the Nogai Tatars in the Molochna basin.[5] By the late 1850s, the New Russian serfs had good reason to believe that better times lay ahead, even as estate owners feared the idea of emancipation. Peasant resistance to their reduced status continued into the post-emancipation period. Available information suggests that former serfs were vociferous in voicing their disillusionment with the reform process of the early 1860s and repeatedly compelled the state to restore civil order in the New Russian countryside with armed force. Up to fifteen thousand people from Tavriia province were involved in disturbances between 1861 and 1863. Official reports from Katerynoslav province declared that, at its peak, entire volosts of peasants were united in an opposition movement.[6]

Yet in almost all cases, order was restored with the visible threat of physical force and the arrest of those deemed to be instigators. Already by 1864 provincial governors reported that disturbances were negligible, as these former serfs—now called "temporarily obligated" peasants—had adjusted to their new circumstances. For our purposes, it is important to note that the lack of peasant freedom remained an issue. In short, the answer to our first question as to whether peasants treasured their legacy of freedom is a resounding "yes." In 1905 peasants had a clear sense that they had rights to land and liberty that had not been fully realized. And when they expressed their grievances in that year, it was often with reference to the reforms of the 1860s, when so many had felt badly served.

If a legacy of freedom remained strong among New Russian peasants, to what extent did issues of nationality determine relations between peasants and colonists in the years leading up to the revolution of 1905? There is little to suggest that nationality issues played a significant role in these relations. In fact, there is significant reason to believe that in a host of cases the multiethnic composition of southern Ukraine was of considerable benefit to various parties. In previous work I have attempted to demonstrate that for much of the nineteenth century relations were positive, and the benefits went both ways.[7] Peasants close to the Mennonite colonies were relatively quick to introduce more efficient agricultural implements, in part because Mennonite colonies contained artisans who were able to repair them. Reports from the revolutionary disturbances in 1905 do not suggest that foreign colonists were a major target for peasant protests and disturbances unless their activities as estate owners were a factor, in which case they might be treated like the Russian landowners. Even then, it appears that not all estate owners were equally involved in the peasant uprising. Areas within New Russia where capitalist agriculture had long been established, such as Melitopol district of Tavriia province, were less likely to be targets of peasant unrest in 1905.

Instead, peasants concentrated on estates that had recently and enthusiastically made the shift to capital-intensive agriculture. On those estates, due to the adoption of a new generation of labor-saving implements, peasants found themselves with less land available for lease and lowered wages. Under such circumstances the peasants targeted Mennonites in places where the latter had become major agents in this process of rapid change, particularly in a cluster of districts situated on the lower Dnipro River. This economic factor was especially relevant in December 1905, when peasants throughout the empire decided the time had come to bring about their true "emancipation." In all of my research, I have yet to find a credible source to suggest that ethnicity played a significant factor in the 1905 peasant uprisings. Indeed, the main villains for New

Russian peasants in 1905 were the hundreds of thousands of migratory Ukrainian and Russian peasants who sought annual agricultural work in the south. In short, the struggle in 1905 was clearly between locals and outsiders over local economic privileges, and not between Ukrainians and Mennonites, unless the latter had recently and aggressively entered a new district.

A final question flows from the first two: How do we square peasant agricultural progress with the revolutionary unrest after 1900? Let me suggest a possible approach to this problem. There are clear indications that before 1900 New Russia's peasants had made significant adjustments and adaptations in order to better their state. Although the variations were considerable depending upon location within the region, the overall pattern and direction was clear. Crop yields were showing a steady increase, in part because of improved implements, the shift from oxen to horse power, and the introduction of new crops. Yet even these gains were insufficient to reduce peasant reliance on supplemental forms of income, and herein lies the problem. The primary sources of extra income required peasants to lease additional land or seek employment as laborers on adjacent estates. Peasants found it increasingly difficult to rely on either of these possibilities. Estate owners had come to use their lands more efficiently—all the more so if these lands had been taken over by Mennonite or German colonists. Even nobles who resisted innovations knew that they could demand far higher lease rates given the increased demands on land. Increased mechanization allowed owners to hire fewer laborers, and at lower wages. In response, local peasants did what they could. In eastern Katerynoslav province they sought employment in the burgeoning mining industry of Donetsk, a development that prompted the provincial governor to recommend that the province simply be divided in half.

Most peasants did not have that option. Instead, they adopted one of two strategies. The first was to adapt where possible and otherwise make ends meet. Occasionally, as when they substituted horses for oxen, they acted wisely. At other times, they did not, an example being the almost catastrophic cultivation of wheat without fallow or adequate soil preparation. The second strategy emerged from the peasant belief that the land was theirs, or at least deserved to be; and that in a just society they would have unlimited access to the lands around them. For former state peasants, who comprised two-thirds of the rural inhabitants in New Russia, this dream was manifested in the context of the repartitional commune and the conviction that all lands should be included in future repartitions. Former serfs, meanwhile, followed another logic to claim that the land they had leased for decades was really their land; that "ownership" could not be determined by deed but by precedent of use.

In both former serf and former state-peasant societies, these views were most passionately held by people who lived in places that had recently undergone rapid change. Even so, it remained an open question in 1900 as to which of the two peasant strategies would win out. Would New Russia become a place of peasant adaptation or peasant revolution?

It is clear that peasants in southern Ukraine had a legacy of freedom that was in part rooted in the Cossack past. But no less important was the actual experience of settlement in a sparsely settled frontier and the seemingly limitless portions of land available to those who relocated here. This legacy of freedom was rekindled by events growing out of the Crimean War and a host of rumors associated with the peasant emancipation of 1861. It is also clear that peasants were still clinging to that legacy in 1905, when a host of circumstances briefly persuaded them that civil order in the empire had disintegrated. They knew that the collapse had occurred because troops rarely appeared when summoned, and those that did were generally ineffective. Estate owners were absent even more than in previous times. Furthermore, popular resentment to the established order was especially high due to the empire's military losses in Manchuria during the Russo-Japanese war. Many peasants within New Russia concluded that there was an opportunity to be exploited. Those most inclined to take action were found in one of two areas. Many were located in villages near the coal fields of the Donets basin or other urban centers such as Odesa. Another area of peasant unrest involved peasants who lived in entirely rural settings, such as the Dnipro River districts of Verkhn'odniprovsk and Dnipro, where the pace of change had recently been fast, leaving many local peasants feeling disadvantaged and disoriented.

Colonists were part of the larger, complex society caught between social stability and rapid change. Many—including most Germans and Mennonites—were comparatively wealthy and were viewed this way later, when local unrest became regional and social. Nonetheless, when that did occur after 1917, it did not diminish the fact that in most instances the relations between colonists and their peasant neighbors had been mutually beneficial. Even to describe the situation in this manner almost assumes the worst outcome, but that was not necessarily the only route open to the region's inhabitants by 1900. Indeed, there is every reason to believe that by 1900 a significant part of the New Russian countryside had made the adjustments necessary for social stability. New Russia was not the same place then that it had been in 1860, and by no means were the changes entirely for the worse. By the same token, the revolutions of 1905 and 1917 were complex and unpredictable phenomena. It was impossible for any single group to command or be responsible for its own destiny. In all cases, local relations were as variable as the individual people involved, and one should be wary of generalizations.

At every turn, the reliance on stereotypes to depict colonists, estate owners, and peasants is anything but helpful. It simplifies the complex relations of the New Russian countryside to the point of absurdity. Any one of these sectors had multifaceted relations with the region and empire in which they existed and to speak of their "isolation" relies on stereotypes that are too simple for academic discourse.

Taking new findings and perspectives into account, revolution in New Russia was by no means a certainty as late as 1900. In that sense, we are left with the oldest of questions, the one that defies an easy answer: what, but for the Great War, might have transpired in the Russian Empire in general, and in New Russia specifically? The answer closest to the mark would be one that stresses the possibility of an emerging civil society—one based on a century's progress during which Ukrainians, Russians, Greeks, Bulgarians, Germans, Mennonites, and countless others all made valued contributions. It was a world within reach as late as 1900, and might yet be worth reclaiming.

Appendix

Correspondence of Ukrainian and Russian Place Names

Throughout this book, names of cities, towns, and villages located within the modern borders of Ukraine have been transliterated from the Ukrainian spelling. The primary sources for the book are almost exclusively Russian, however, and utilize Russian spelling in all instances. This appendix provides a guide for correlating the Ukrainian names to the spelling used in the original, Russian sources.

Ukrainian	Russian
Adzhamka	Adzhamskoe
Ananïv	Ananev
Annivka	Annovka
Arkhanhelsk	Arkhangelskoe
Berezivka	Berezovka
Beryslav	Berislavl
Bilozerka	Belozerka
Bobrynets	Bobrinets
Bohdanivka	Bogdanovka
Chervone Ozero	Krasnoe Ozero
Dnipro district	Dneprovsk
Dobrovillia	Dobrovolia
Dudchyna	Dudchin
Fedorivka	Fedorovka
Henichesk	Genichesk
Hromokliia	Gromokle
Hrykor'ïvka	Grigorevka
Ielysavethrad	Elisavetgrad
Ielyzavetivka	Elizavetovka
Ievpatoriia	Evpatoriia

Ukrainian	Russian
Illinske	Ilinskoe
Ivanivka	Ivanovka
Kafa	Kaffa
Kam'ianka	Kamenka
Katerynivka	Ekaterinovka
Kenehez	Kenigez
Komisarivka	Kommisarovka
Kovalivka	Kovalevka
Kremenchuk	Kremenchug
Kryvyi Rih	Krivoi Rog
Kurysove	Kurisova
Kushkivka	Kushkovka
Makedonivka	Makedonovka
Mala Katerynivka	Malaia Katerinovka
Mala Znam'ianka	Malaia Znamenka
Malaieshty	Malaeshta
Mykhailivka	Mikhailovka
Mykolaïv	Nikolaev
Neihofnunh	Neuhoffnung
Nohaisk	Nogaisk
Novosilka	Novoselka
Novospaske	Novospasskaia
Novovavylivka	Novovavilovka
Novyi Buh	Novyi Bug
Nyzhni Sirohozy	Nizhnii Serogakh
Oboznivka	Oboznovsk
Obytochna	Obitochnaia
Ochakiv	Ochakov

Ukrainian	Russian
Odesa	Odessa
Oleksandriia	Aleksandriia
Oleksandrivka	Aleksandrovka
Oleksandrivsk	Aleksandrovsk
Oleshky	Aleshka
Pavlohrad	Pavlograd
Petrove	Petrova
Pishchane	Peshchanoe
Ploske	Ploskaia
Pokrovske	Pokrovsk(oe)
Rivne	Rovnoe
Shulhivka	Shulgovka
Slov'iano-Serbiia	Slavianoserbsk
Slov'ianoserbske	Slaviano-Serbka
Sofiïvka	Sofievka
Ustynivka	Ustinovka
Varvarivka	Varvarovka
Vasylivka	Vasilievka
Velyka Bilozerka	Bolshaia Belozerka
Velyka Kam'ianka	Bolshaia Kamenka
Velyka Katerynivka	Bolshaia Katerinovka
Velyka Znam'ianka	Bolshaia Znamenka
Velyki Kopani	Bolshoe Kopanoe
Velykyi Tokmak	Bolshoi Tokmak
Verkhn'odniprovsk	Verkhnedneprovsk
Verkhnii Rohachyk	Verkhnii Rogachik
Veseli Terny	Veselii Tern
Zahradivka	Zagradovka

Abbreviations

AHFP	Archive of the Historical Faculty
Braun	Peter Braun Archive
DAOO	Derzhavnyi arkhiv Odes´koï oblasti, Odesa, Ukraine
DZhK	*Doklad, zhurnali kommissii dlia issledovaniia nyneshnego polozheniia sel´skogo khoziaistva i sel´skoi proizvoditel´nosti v Rossii*. 1873. 7 vols. St. Petersburg.
EAIVE	*Ezhegodnik po agrarnoi istorii Vostochnoi Evropy*
GSKh	*God v sel´skokhoziaistvennom otnoshenii, po otvetam, poluchennym ot khoziaev*. 1881–1917. St. Petersburg.
ISOP	Timiriazev, D. A., ed. 1883–. *Istoriko-statisticheskii obzor promyshlennosti Rossii*. St. Petersburg.
ISPT	*Issledovanie sovremennogo polozheniia tonkorunnogo ovtsevodstva i Iuga Rossii*. 1882. Edited by A. P. Perepelkin and N. N. Deriagin. Moscow.
ISSO	*Issledovanie sovremennogo sostoianiia ovtsevodstva v Rossii*. 1884. Vol. 4. St. Petersburg.
ITUAK	*Izvestiia Tavricheskoi uchenoi arkhivnoi kommissii*
IVILZ	*Istoricheskii vestnik: istoriko-literaturnyi zhurnal*
JMS	*Journal of Mennonite Studies*

KA *Krasnyi Arkhiv*

KISOT "Kratkoe istoriko-statisticheskoe obozrenie Tavricheskoi gubernii." 1867. In *PKTG*, 144–247. Simferopol.

Listki *Listki Obshchestva sel´skogo khoziaistva iuzhnoi Rossii*

MDIKP *Materialy dlia istorii krepostnago prava v Rossii: Izvelecheniia iz sekretnykh otchetov ministerstva vnytrennikh del za 1836–1856 gg.* 1872. Berlin.

MOZE Materialy dlia otsenki zemel´ Ekaterinoslavskoi gubernii. 1899–1911. 6 vols. Ekaterinoslav.

MOZKh *Materialy dlia otsenki zemel´ Khersonskoi gubernii.* 1883–1890. 6 vols. Kherson.

MQR *Mennonite Quarterly Review*

MSDZ *Materialy po statistike dvizheniia zemlevladeniia v Rossii.* 1902. Vol. 13, *Pogubernskie itogo mobilizatsii zemel´ i srednye tseny za 40 letie 1863–1902 gg.* St. Petersburg.

MVU01 *Materialy vysochaishe uchrezhdennoi 16 noiabria 1901 g. Komissii po issledovaniiu voprosa o dvizhenii s 1861 g. po 1900 g. blagosostoianiia sel´skogo naseleniia srednezemledel´cheskikh gubernii, sravnitel´no s drugimi mestnostiami Evropeiskoi Rossii.* 1903. Vol. 1. St. Petersburg.

MVZS *Materialy po voprosu o zemskoi statistike v Khersonskoi gubernii.* 1874. Kherson.

MZSKh *Materialy po zemskoi statistike Khersonskoi gubernii.* 1875. Kherson

NDOKh *Nekotoriia danniia o khode i razvitii sel´skogo khoziaistva v Khersonskoi gubernii.* 1896. Vol. 1. Kherson.

OEGZ *Otchet Ekaterinoslavskoi gubernskoi zemskoi upravy po agronomicheskomu biuro.* (See reference list for specific volumes.)

OKPU *Otmena krepostnogo prava na Ukraine: Sbornik dokumentov i materialov.* 1961. Kyiv.

PDSV *Protokoly delegatskago soveshchaniia Vserossiiskago Krest´ianskago Soiuza 6–10 Noiabria 1905 g., v Moskve.* 1906. Moscow.

PKTG *Pamiatnaia kniga Tavricheskoi gubernii.* 1867. Simferopol.

PNSP *Polozhenie i nuzhdy sel´skokhoziaistvennoi promyshlennosti,*

	na osnovanii vsepoddanneishikh otchetov general-gubernatorov, gubernatorov i nachal′nikov oblastei
PSZ	*Polnoe sobranie zakonov Rossiiskoi imperii.* 1830–1916. St. Petersburg.
PV97	*Pervaia vseobshchaia perepis′ naseleniia Rossiiskoi Imperii 1897 g.* 1903. Vols. 13, 41, and 47. St. Petersburg.
RGIA	Rossisskii gosudarstvennyi istoricheskii arkhiv
RM	*Russkaia mysl′*
SEOKh	*Statistiko-ekonomicheskii obzor Khersonskoi gubernii*
SKh	*Sel′skii khoziain*
SKhL	*Sel′skoe khoziaistvo i lesovodstvo*
SKhZ	*Sbornik Khersonskogo zemstva*
SNM	*Spisok naselennykh mest po svendeniiam 1864 gody.* 1865. Vol. 41, *Tavricheskaia guberniia.* St. Petersburg.
SPSNM	*Statistika pozemel′noi sobstvennosti i naselennykh mest Evropeiskoi Rossii.* 1885. Vol. 8, *Gubernii Novorossiiskoi gruppy.* St. Petersburg.
SSSE	*Sbornik statisticheskikh svedenii po Ekaterinoslavskoi gubernii.* 1886. Vols. 2 and 3. Ekaterinoslav.
SSSM	Sel′skokhoziaistvennyia i statisticheskiia svedeniia po materialam, poluchennym ot khoziaev. 1884–1905. 12 vols. St. Petersburg.
SSSTG	*Sbornik statisticheskikh svedenii po Tavricheskoi gubernii. Statisticheskiia tablitsy o khoziaistvennom polozhenii selenii.* 1885–1889. 9 vols. Simferopol and Moscow.
SSXIX	*Svod statisticheskikh svedenii po sel′skomu khoziaistvu Rossii k kontsu XIX veka.* 1902–1906. 3 vols. St. Petersburg.
STR56	*Statisticheskie tablitsy Rossiiskoi imperii za 1856 god.* 1866. St. Petersburg.
STS	Semenov-Tian-Shanskii, V. P., ed. 1910. *Rossiia: Polnoe geograficheskoe opisanie nashego otechestva.* Vol. 14, *Novorossiia i Krym.* St. Petersburg.
SVR66	*Statisticheskii vremennik Rossiiskoi Imperii.* 1866. St. Petersburg.
SZ1905	*Statistika zemlevladeniia 1905 g.* 1906. Vols. 14, 16, and 42. St. Petersburg.

TIVEO	*Trudy Imperatorskogo vol´nogo ekonomicheskogo obshchestva*
TKPV	*Trudy kommissii po preobrazovaniiu volostnykh sudo*. 1874. Vol. 5, *Ekaterinoslavskaia guberniia*. St. Petersburg.
TMKN	*Trudy mestnykh komitetov o nuzhdakh sel´sko-khoziaistvennoi promyshlennosti*. 1903. Vols. 12, 40, and 46. St. Petersburg.
TOSP	*Trudy oblastnogo s″ezda predstavitelei zemstv i sel´skikh khoziaiev iuga Rossii*
TPS	*Trudy piatogo s″ezda Russkikh sel´skikh khoziaistv v Odesse, v Dekabre 1878 goda*. 1879. Odesa.
VEZ	*Vestnik Ekaterinoslavskogo zemstva*
VGI	*Voprosy germanskoi istorii*
VISKh	*Voprosy istorii sel´skogo khoziaistva, krest´ianstva i revoliutsionnogo dvizheniia v Rossii*
VKK	"Volneniia krest´ian na Khersonshchine v 1905 g." 1935. *KA* 71:17–38.
VRSKh	*Vestnik Russkogo sel´skogo khoziaistva*
VSKh	*Vestnik sel´skogo khoziaistva*
VSORI	*Voenno-statisticheskoe obozrenie Rossiiskoi imperii*. 1849–1850. Vol. 11, pts. 1, 2, and 4. St. Petersburg.
VTZ	*Vestnik Tavricheskogo zemstva*
Zhizn´	*Zhizn´. Literaturnyi, nauchnyi i politicheskii zhurnal*
ZhMGI	*Zhurnal ministerstva gosudarstvennykh imushchestv*
ZhSKhL	*Zhurnal sel´skogo khoziaistva i lesovodstva*
ZIOS	*Zapiski Imperatorskogo obshchestva sel´skogo khoziaistva iuzhnoi Rossii*

Notes

Introduction

1. Noted, for example, in Edelman 1987, 41.
2. Druzhinina 1981.
3. Harvey 1938.
4. Herlihy 1963.
5. Herlihy 1986. See especially the treatment of Odesa's hinterland in chapters 3, 5, and 8.
6. Kuromiya 1998; Wynn 1992; McCaffray 1996; and Friedgut 1989–1994.
7. *VGI* 1995; *VGI* 1998, vol. 1; *VGI* 1999; Rempel 1933; Urry 1989; and Dyck 1991. See also Brandes 1993.
8. Shcherbina 1880. Cf. Kuromiya 1998, 65; and Martin 1992.
9. Cf. Brower and Lazzerini 1997, xv.
10. Braudel 1977, 5; Wallerstein 1989; and Mironov 1999.
11. Wolf 1982.
12. See, especially, Grigg 1992.

Chapter One

1. Pallas 1812, 528; Scott 1854, 204–5; Stavrovskii 1910, ch. 4; Haxthausen 1856, vol. 2, 84–85, 96; and Beauplan 1959, p. 452.
2. Skal′kovs′kyi 1850–1853, vol. 1, 35–36, 50; and *VSORI*, pt. 1, 11–12.
3. Iavornyts′kyi 1888, 78.
4. See, for example, Holderness 1823, 75.
5. Kohl 1842, 409; Lyall 1825, 153–55; and Armstrong 1831, 24.

6. Gogol 1971, 33.
7. Pavlovich 1862, 85–87; Shmidt 1860–1863, vol. 1, 380–416; and Kohl 1842, 473–76.
8. *VSORI*, pt. 2, 16.
9. The paraphrase is found in Druzhinina 1970, 49, 66. For a map of elevations in the Crimea, see *Encyclopedia of Ukraine* 1984, vol. 1, s.v. "Crimean Mountains."
10. Kohl 1842, 449.
11. Shmidt 1860–1863, vol. 1, 162.
12. Ulissov 1910, 420–24.
13. Skal′kovs′kyi 1850–1853, vol. 1, 88.
14. Ibid., 101.
15. Karpov 1910, 12.
16. Iavornyts′kyi 1898b, 202.
17. See Skal′kovs′kyi 1850–1853, vol. 1, 113–14, for a listing of islands in the Dnipro River. See also Iavornyts′kyi 1898b, 88; and Martin 1992, 188.
18. *VSORI*, pt. 4, 24–25.
19. The Black Sea's greatest distances were measured at 1,133 kilometers from east to west, and 626 kilometers from north to south. See *VSORI*, pt. 1, 16.
20. Herlihy 1986, 11; and *VSORI*, pt. 1, 20.
21. Beauplan 1959, 456.
22. Skal′kovs′kyi 1885, vol. 1, 29; and Magocsi 1996, 175.
23. Skal′kovs′kyi 1850–1853, vol. 1, 306–7. On the various Nogai hordes, see Skal′kovs′kyi 1885–1886, vol. 1, 26–28.
24. *Ukrainian Dumy* 1979, 23. See also Subtelny 1981, 121.
25. Fisher 1972, 17, 23.
26. This site would later serve as the base for Moscow's assault on the Cossacks themselves, as well as the Crimean Tatars. See Iavornyts′kyi 1888, 60, 62; Subtelny 1988, 108; and Magocsi 1996, 178. For a discussion on the etymology of "Cossack," see Omeljan Pritsak, forthcoming.
27. Iavornyts′kyi 1898b, 125. Cf. Avanas′ev-Chuzhbinskii 1861, 53ff.
28. Beauplan 1959, 48; and Bahalii 1889, 20.
29. Golobutskii 1957, 350. Estimates for the eighteenth century range from 60,000 to 100,000 Zaporozhian Cossacks. See Iavornyts′kyi 1898b, 232–33; and Bahalii 1889, 28.
30. Shaw 1976, 169.
31. Trade links between the Ottoman Empire and Europe in the mid-eighteenth century principally connected Balkan agriculturalists with French and Austrian markets. Herlihy 1963, 27–28; Jones 1981, ch. 9; and Kasaba 1988, ch. 2.
32. Menning 1980, 130–61.
33. Skal′kovski 1836–1838, vol. 1, 20ff.

34. Kabuzan 1976, 52.
35. Brandes 1993, 16–24; Kabuzan 1976, 84–89; and *VSORI*, pt. 1, 89, 91. See also Skal′kovs′kyi 1850–1853, vol. 2, 18–19.
36. Skal′kovs′kyi 1885–1886, vol. 1, 30, 33–37; and Fisher 1972, 597; *MOZE* 1899, pt. 1, 50.
37. Shmidt 1860–1863, vol. 1, 35–39; and Bartlett 1979, 19–20, 109–16.
38. Golobutskii 1957, 344; and *VSORI*, pt. 1, 80.
39. Skal′kovs′kyi 1887, 772; and Shmidt 1860–1863, vol. 1, 33.
40. Druzhinina 1959, 48–51. The same position is taken in Subtelny 1988, 179–80.
41. Golobutskii 1957, 352–53, 364–65.
42. Skal′kovs′kyi 1850–1853, vol. 2.
43. Holderness 1823, 100.
44. Golobutskii 1957, 351, 364–65.
45. Skal′kovs′kyi 1885–1886, vol. 1, 220.
46. Golobutskii 1957, 365; and Stavrovskii 1910, 147–48. The quotation is from Beauplan 1959, 448–50.
47. Christian and Smith 1984, 27.
48. Pallas 1812, vol. 2, 469.
49. Ulissov 1910, 435–36.
50. Golobutskii 1957, 361–62; Skal′kovs′kyi 1885–1886, vol. 1, 223–27, 238. On the importance of the carters to the Cossack economy, Skal′kovs′kyi wrote: "Listen to Ukrainian folk songs; eighty out of a hundred will be about *chumaks*, and ten about love."
51. Skal′kovs′kyi 1850–1853, vol. 1, 85ff.

Chapter Two

1. DAOO, fond 1, op. 192, d. 12, fols. 288ff.
2. Madariaga 1981, 359.
3. LeDonne 1984, 269.
4. *VSORI*, pt. 2, appendix, 2; *VSORI*, pt. 4, 2; and LeDonne 1984, 275. On the choices confronting the Catherinian state regarding serfdom and settlement, see Melton 1998, 238–39.
5. Madariaga 1981, ch. 18; LeDonne 1984, 270ff; and Kabuzan 1976, 142–43.
6. Madariaga 1981, 360; and Druzhinina 1959, 53.
7. *PSZ*, vol. 20, no. 14354. See also Stavrovskii 1910, 162; and Druzhinina 1959, 54.
8. Pisarevskii 1909, 212. Some 30,000 Greeks migrated from the Crimea to the north shore of the Sea of Azov at this time. See Dubrovin 1885–1889, vol. 2, 634–37.
9. Kabuzan 1996, 52.

10. See *PSZ*, vol. 22, no. 15925 for the ukase of 8 April 1783; Madariaga 1981, 364; Druzhinina 1959, 92; and Fisher 1972.
11. *VSORI*, pt. 1, 6.
12. Skal′kovs′kyi 1850–1853, vol. 2, 25; and LeDonne 1984, 303.
13. *PSZ*, vol. 27, no. 20449; and Druzhinina 1970, 174–75.
14. Druzhinina 1959, 69. These figures are inflated as they apply to the provinces of New Russia and Azov in 1782, which at the time included portions of Poltava province. Kabuzan 1976, 264; Druzhinina 1970, 70; and Rashin 1956, 28–29.
15. *SPSNM*, 26, 63, and 92; and Druzhinina 1981, 14.
16. Rempel 1933, ch. 4.
17. For this argument in detail, see Wirtschafter 1997.
18. Bahalii 1889, 72; Kotsievskii 1962, 247.
19. Bahalii 1889, 71.
20. Kabuzan 1976, 131.
21. Borovoi 1964, 373.
22. Bahalii 1889, 72–75.
23. DAOO, fond 1, op. 1, d. 1584, fol. 290v.
24. Borovoi 1964, 373.
25. *PSZ*, vol. 24, no. 17638, 233–34; and Kabuzan 1976, 149, 167–68.
26. Borovoi 1964, 376; and Kotsievskii 1962, 224–25.
27. Kotsievskii 1962, 226; Bahalii 1889, 71; and Sekirinskii 1964, 351.
28. Ignatovich 1910, 200.
29. Druzhinina 1966, 577–78. The ukase is found in *PSZ*, vol. 28, no. 21458.
30. Druzhinina 1966, 574; Shmidt 1860–1863, vol. 1, 477; Kotsievskii 1964a, 362; and Kotsievskii 1962, 246–47.
31. Kotsievskii 1964a, 363–65.
32. Quoted in Sekirinskii 1964, 414–15; see also Sekirinskii 1963, 358–59; and *VSORI*, pt. 2, 121.
33. Borovoi 1964, 375.
34. Sekirinskii 1963, 359; cf. *MOZKh* 1886, 139.
35. Kolchin 1987.
36. Lavrentov 1867, 381–82.
37. Druzhinina 1981, 14. Druzhinina lists 801,868 male souls living on state lands, and 344,213 on private estates.
38. Druzhinina 1970, 79–81.
39. Bahalii 1889, 26–28; and Kabuzan 1976, 131–32.
40. *VSORI*, pt. 4, 8–9.
41. Bahalii 1889, 63, 66; Kotsievskii 1964b, 420–21; Druzhinina 1970, 94; and Druzhinin 1946–1958, vol. 1, 89–90. On the emergence of land shortages in Katerynoslav province, see Druzhinin 1946–1958, vol. 1, 322.
42. Livanov 1872, vol. 2, 52. Source is found in *PSZ*, vol. 4, nos. 1591 and 1826.

43. Skal′kovs′kyi 1887, 771–82. The law itself is found in *PSZ*, vol. 27, no. 20123.
44. Skal′kovs′kyi 1887, 778; Druzhinina 1970, 98; and *VSORI*, pt. 4, 168.
45. Skal′kovs′kyi 1887, 778; Bahalii 1889, 67; Pinkerton 1833, 167.
46. KISOT, 208; Skal′kovs′kyi 1887, 781; and Sekirinskii 1963, 358.
47. Bahalii 1889, 66, 85. Settlements established between 1752 and 1770 included Zlynka, Lysuiu-Goru, Peshchanyi Brod, Nikolskoe, Krasnoe, Klintsy, Pokrovske, and Zubkoe (Skal′kovs′kyi 1887, 772).
48. *VSORI*, pt. 2, 93; Skal′kovs′kyi 1887, 772, 775. On Old Believer interest in Tavriia province, see A. Ivanov 1885, 71.
49. Klibanov 1965, 122–23. The villages of Novo-Vasylivka, Astrakhanka, and Novospaske were formed in the 1820s. Information from this section comes from *VSORI*, pt. 2, 93; Sekirinskii 1963; *SSSTG* 1889, pt. 2, 5–6; Livanov 1872, vol. 2, 220–21.
50. KISOT, 207–8; *VSORI*, pt. 2, 93. Some 36,000 sectarians were thought to live in New Russia in the 1830s, though the figure includes Bessarabia province. See Skal′kovs′kyi 1850–1853, vol. 1, 215.
51. Keep 1985, 277–79; and Pallot and Shaw 1990, 48–49.
52. Skal′kovs′kyi 1836–1838, vol. 1, 65; Druzhinina 1959, 58; and Kabuzan 1976, 143–56.
53. Druzhinina 1970, 86; Keep 1985, 276–79; and Kohl 1842, 407.
54. Lyall 1825, 151–52; and Kohl 1842.
55. Druzhinina 1981, 15.
56. Pavlovich 1862, 188, 269–70; and Druzhinina 1981, 19–20.
57. These privileges could be repealed if eligible males in any given family failed to assist in navigation for a period of three years. See Druzhinina 1981, 21.
58. L. P. 1888, 124–25; *VSORI*, pt. 4, 12.
59. L. P. 1888, 126; and Pavlovich 1862, 271–72. For a different statistical breakdown, see Druzhinina 1981, 21.
60. Skal′kovs′kyi 1867b, 365–79; and *SSSTG* 1889, pt. 2, 1–2.
61. Skal′kovs′kyi 1867b, 379–80, 384–85.
62. Pallas 1812, 532–33.
63. Skal′kovs′kyi 1867b, 385.
64. Ibid., 386, 396, 398–99.
65. Ibid., 400.
66. *VSORI*, pt. 2, appendix, 13–14; and Skal′kovs′kyi 1867b, 407–8.
67. Demidov 1853, vol. 1, 349. Cf. Skal′kovs′kyi 1867b, 407–8.
68. Kohl 1842, 410–12. Cf. Webster 1830, vol. 1, 48–49.
69. *VSORI*, pt. 2, 94–95.
70. *VSORI*, pt. 2, 93, 115–17; Skal′kovs′kyi 1850–1853, vol. 2, 9–10; and Postnikov 1891, 70.
71. Skal′kovs′kyi 1850–1853, vol. 2, 10.

72. DAOO, fond. 1, op. 192, d. 12; and Druzhinina 1970, 79–80. Velyka Bilozerka had 2,832 souls, Verkhnii Rohachyk had 2,241, and Mikhailivka had 2,209 inhabitants. For slightly earlier figures, see Sekirinskii 1963, 357.
73. Webster 1830, vol. 1, 48.
74. *VSORI*, pt. 4, 101.
75. On Catherine's motivation for the settlement of foreigners, see Bartlett 1979, ch. 2; and Brandes 1993, 19–21. The translation for Musin-Pushkin is found in Bartlett 1979, 34.
76. *MDIKP*, 69–70.
77. The English translation is found in Bartlett 1979, appendix 1. The 1762 manifesto is found in *PSZ*, vol. 16, no. 11720. The manifesto of 1763 is found in *PSZ*, vol. 16, no. 11880. The subject of the colonization has previously been addressed in detail by Rempel 1933, Bahalii 1889, Klaus 1869, Bartlett 1979, Brandes 1993, Auerbach 1965, and others.
78. Bahalii 1889, 85–86. The manifesto is found in *PSZ*, vol. 28, no. 21163.
79. The English translation is found in Bartlett 1979, 197.
80. Ibid., 230, appendix 6.
81. RGIA, fond 383, op. 29, d. 964, fol. 248v; Skal'kovs'kyi 1848, 6, 34–35; and Brandes 1993, 33.
82. Klaus 1869, appendix 7. Cf. RGIA, fond 383, op. 29, d. 964, fols. 55r–55v, 248v.
83. Klaus 1869, 321; Bahalii 1889, 88; Skal'kovs'kyi 1848, 38; and *VSORI*, pt. 1, 89.
84. Brandes 1993, 34; Klaus 1869, 322; and Derzhavin 1908, 59, 60–65.
85. Derzhavin 1908, 60; and Skal'kovs'kyi 1848, 89–90.
86. There were 598 landless male souls in Kishlau according to the tenth revision, as opposed to 250 souls with land. The figures for Staryi Krym were 251 and 133 respectively (Derzhavin 1908, 298).
87. Skal'kovs'kyi 1848, 102–7, 118; Skal'kovs'kyi 1850–1853, vol. 1, 227; Druzhinina 1959, 57–68; and Brandes 1993, 34.
88. Urry 1989, 45–47; and Rempel 1933, ch. 3.
89. Pisarevskii 1909, 263–64. Emphasis is in the original.
90. Stumpp 1957, 39–42.
91. Rempel 1933, 58.
92. RGIA, fond 383, op. 29, d. 159, fols. 95r–98v.
93. Bahalii 1889, 88–91; and "Über die Gründung und Entwicklung einiger Kolonien" 1958: 65–67.
94. For an excellent overview of this topic, see Dyck 1982a, 318–41; and Dyck 1982b, 307–18.
95. *PSZ*, vol. 14, no. 12095; and Rempel 1933, 102.

96. Rempel 1933, 105–6, 138.
97. Postnikov 1891, ch. 3.
98. Geisinger 1974, 67–68.
99. Kabuzan 1976, 166–67; Druzhinina 1970, ch. 3; Druzhinina 1981, ch. 1; and Herlihy 1986, 27–28. One reason why Kherson's population was able to expand so quickly was that Bessarabia, to the west, was secured after the war with the Ottoman Empire from 1806–12, and Kherson was no longer left on the frontier's edge. See Stavrovskii 1910, 163–64.
100. Urban dwellers comprised 26.8, 18.8, and 10.9 percent of Kherson, Tavriia, and Katerynoslav provinces respectively (Theide 1970, 49).
101. Holderness 1823, 77.
102. Theide 1970, 186.
103. Webster 1830, vol. 1, 46.
104. Demidov 1853, vol. 1, 289.

Chapter Three

1. DAOO, fond 22, op. 1. d. 580, fols. 32r–32v, 34v, 190r–190v. Herlihy 1986, 19, 97, 123; and Morachevskii 1910b, 462. For the early history of port cities in New Russia, see Thiede 1970, 81–88.
2. Kahan 1985, 197; and Braudel 1982, 462–66. For a systematic treatment of this expansion, see Wallerstein 1989, vol. 3.
3. Harvey 1938, 85. Harvey assumed that wheat production spread out in concentric circles from the Black Sea northward, but there is no substantive source to support this claim.
4. Haxthausen 1856, vol. 2, 54, 63–64; Kohl 1842, 409; and Bremner 1840, 356.
5. Morachevskii 1910a, 262; Bremner 1840, 356; Iavornyts′kyi 1898a, 291; Golobutskii 1957, 347; and Grigg 1974, 116–18.
6. Conditions could also be quite harsh on the livestock, as was the case in 1833, 1834, 1846, and 1847. See Skal′kovs′kyi 1850–1853, vol. 2, 347.
7. Skal′kovs′kyi 1850–1853, vol. 1. For his comments on New Russia's climate, see 30–31. An indication of how little agricultural technology had developed to compensate for the varying climatic conditions can be found in the published reports of the Ministry of State Domains. For the entire series of publications, consult *GSKh*. Cf. Borovoi 1964, 369.
8. RGIA, fond 383, op. 29, d. 159, fol. 86r; and DAOO, fond 1, op. 248, d. 1580, fols. 113r–113v: "Those peasants who settled from central Russia brought with them the agricultural practices of that land. Therefore there is a need to adjust."

9. Herlihy 1986, 101–6, 114–17. See, for comparison, Turner 1920, 11; and the comments of Boserup 1973, ch. 1.
10. Skal′kovs′kyi 1850–1853, vol. 2, 341; and Herlihy 1986, 53.
11. Druzhinina 1970, 222, 264; Herlihy 1986, 53; and Druzhinina 1981, 96.
12. DAOO, fond 270, op. 1, d. 16, fols. 2v–3r; Iavornyts′kyi 1898a, 291; Golobutskii 1957, 347; and Skal′kovs′kyi 1885–1886, vol. 1, 181–82.
13. DAOO, fond 22, op. 1. d. 580, fols. 32r–34r; *MOZKh* 1883, pt. 1, 207; Druzhinina 1981, ch. 2; Herlihy 1986, 49–52; and Morachevskii 1910a, 322.
14. *Odessa* 1895, xxix; Zablotskii 1841, 11–13; and *SSSTG* 1889, pt. 4, 17.
15. *Odesskii Vestnik*, no. 40 (25 May 1827): 1590; Pavlovich 1862, 158; *SSSE*, vol. 3, 247; Kotelnikov 1883, 51–52; Skal′kovs′kyi 1850–1853, vol. 2, 364; and Teetsman 1838, 83–84.
16. RGIA, fond 1284, op. 223, d. 202, fol. 27r; Shmidt 1860–1863, vol. 2, 240; and Morachevskii 1910a, 326. This rounded cheese had a loose, slightly sweet texture. Peasants were able to obtain 3 *funt* (1.2 kg) of the cheese from a single sheep, and the product was used domestically or sold at 3 to 4 kopecks a *funt*. *MOZKh* 1883, pt. 1, 220.
17. DAOO, fond 1, op. 248, d. 1590, fol. 80v; *ISPT*, appendix 1, 44; "Zapiski o soderzhanii ovets i ikh bolezniakh pomeshchika Bakhmutskogo uezda" 1860, 13; Oleksenko 1889, 70; Shchepkin 1869, 142 and 145; *MOZKh* 1883, pt. 1, 224; and Shmidt 1860–1863, vol. 2, 233.
18. M. K. 1837, 262; and Shchepkin 1869, 145.
19. Mordovskii 1889, 351; *SSSE*, vol. 3, pt. 1, 233–37, and pt. 2, 71.
20. For example, sheep in 1873 were able to pasture almost all year in Tavriia province because of the mild, moist winter (RGIA, fond 1284, op. 69, d. 265, fol. 47v). The northern districts of Kherson province appear to have required dry feed for an average of five months each winter. See Gulak 1865, 508; and Shmidt 1860–1863, vol. 2, 228. In his account Mordovskii (1889, 351) identified the period when pasturing was impossible as lasting from approximately the third week in November to the third week in March.
21. See Shmidt 1860–1863, vol. 2, 85; Lozinski 1875, 378; and "Zapiski o soderzhanii ovets i ikh bolezniakh pomeshchika Bakhmutskogo uezda" 1860, 9–10. Pictures and information on these weeds can be found in Mulligan 1976, 14, 31–34, 59–62, and 87. The overworking of these fields and the related reduced fallow periods led directly to a decline in the quality of the hay crops and, as we shall see, an increase in livestock diseases.
22. Shmidt 1860–1863, vol. 2, 220 and 228; Morachevskii 1910a, 325; Mordovskii 1889, 35; and *SSSE*, vol. 3, pt. 2, 74, 229. On the daily routines of feeding, see Lutkovskii 1862, 105.
23. Gulak 1860a, 98; "Mnenie odnogo iz chlenov obshchestva na stat′y I. A. Petrova" 1864, 289–94, esp. 289–90; and "Mnenie deistvitel′nogo chlena I. A.

Petrova o predotvrashchenii pasezhei rogatogo skota" 1864, 280–89. "Doklad kommissii po voprosu o nuzhdakh sel′skogo khoziaistva v Novorossiiskom krae" 1872, 10. On the administration of salt, see Kuzmin 1863, 50; and Shchepkin 1869, 49.

24. Shchepkin 1869, 147; and Shmidt 1860–1863, vol. 2, 230; "Zemledel′cheskii s″ezd v Elisavetgrade 20, 21, i 22 Aprelia 1860 goda" 1860, 93; "Doklad kommissii po voprosu o nuzhdakh sel′skogo khoziaistva v Novorossiiskom krae" 1872, 10; and Kuzmin 1863, 50.
25. "Zapiski o soderzhanii ovets i ikh bolezniakh pomeshchika Bakhmutskogo uezda" 1860, 18; Shchepkin 1869, 147; and Shmidt 1863, 230. *MVZS*, 51–52. On the construction of wells, see "Zapiski o soderzhanii ovets i ikh bolezniakh" 1860, 18; also Oleksenko 1889, 71. For examples, see *DZhK*, vol. 1, pt. 2, 121.
26. Kuzmin 1863, 67; *SSSE*, vol. 3, pt. 1, 247; *ISPT*, appendix 1, 46; and Shchepkin 1869, 148.
27. Kotelnikov 1883, 48; Shmidt 1860–1863, vol. 2, 225; *SSSTG* 1889, pt. 4, 17; and Sokalskii 1869, 25. On the Gypsy sheep, see also Kuleshov 1949, 133–39. Compare *SSSTG* 1887a, 104.
28. Shchepkin 1869, 131–32; and Kotelnikov 1883, 47.
29. *VSORI*, pt. 2, 153.
30. Shchepkin 1869, 135–36, 139; Druzhinina 1970, 222; Morachevskii 1910a, 324. Chervinskii (1951, vol. 2, 80) states that the average length of wool was 8 to 9 centimeters.
31. Kiriakov 1837, 262–63; Vassel 1855, 90–91.
32. *PKTG*, pt. 4, 18; and Bartlett 1979, 225–26.
33. Skal′kovs′kyi 1850–1853, vol. 2, 353–54; and *PKTG*, pt. 4, 19.
34. *MOZKh* 1883, 215–16; Bartlett 1979, 226–28; and Skal′kovs′kyi 1850–1853, vol. 2, 354–57.
35. Skal′kovs′kyi 1836–1838, vol. 2, 132–33; and Bartlett 1979, 228.
36. RGIA, fond 383, op. 29, d. 159, fols. 87r–87v; and Oleksenko 1842, 16.
37. Urry 1989, 88–89; Rempel 1933, 124.
38. Stumpp 1957, 40–42; and Brandes 1993, 204–24.
39. Jenkins and Ponting 1982, 43–44; and Randall 1991, 13–14.
40. With respect to the Canadian experience, see Owram 1980, 119–20. The role of transportation networks to eliminate distance as a factor is the central theme of Blainey 1982.
41. DAOO, fond 22, op. 1. d. 580, fols. 32r–32v, 34v, 190r–190v; Veselovskii 1846, 152–53; and Herlihy 1986, 123.
42. DAOO, fond 22, op. 1, d. 511, fol. 11r. In 1816, wheat prices in Odesa reached 45 rubles a chetvert at a time when laborers received no more than 4 rubles a day, or 8 rubles when accompanied by their own oxen ("Istoricheskii ocherk

torgovli chernogo i azovskogo moria" 1841, 69–77; and Druzhinina 1970, 206).

43. DAOO, fond 270, op. 1, d. 16, fols. 3r–3v; and DAOO, op. 1., d. 580, fols. 32r–32v; Skal′kovs′kyi 1850–1853, vol. 2, 363–64; and Grotto-Slepikovskii 1897, 40. Cf. Pavlovich 1862, 131; and Druzhinina 1981, 65, 70, and 90.
44. Compare "Sostoianie tonkorunnogo ovtsevodstva v Rossii" 1843, 23; Shchepkin 1869, 3; and Veselovskii 1846, 118–20.
45. DAOO, fond 22, op. 1, d. 580, fols. 89r–122r; and Passek 1839, 185.
46. Cornies 1843, 75; and Rempel 1933, 125.
47. RGIA, fond 1281, op. 6, d. 83, fol. 4r; Grotto-Slepikovskii 1897, 42–43; and V. Borisov 1877, 3.
48. "Izvestie o Ekaterinoslavskikh iarmarkakh i v osobennosti o Petropavlovsk uchrezhdeniia dlia sbyta shersti" 1838, 236–45; and M. K. 1837, 264. For an excellent article on the Kharkiv market (*iarmarka*), the predominant market for wool produced in Bakhmut, Pavlohrad, and Katerynoslav counties of Katerynoslav province, see Passek 1839, 177–87.
49. *Odesskii vestnik* (19 January 1827): 18–19; *Odesskii vestnik* (23 March 1827): 90–91; Brandes 1993, 224; and Krestling 1845, 109. By July 1826, G. Rouvier had already sold over 5,000 ewes and 800 rams from his Tavriia province estate to buyers throughout the empire.
50. Lincoln 1977.
51. DAOO, fond 22, op. 1, d. 1, fols. 98r–101r; DAOO, fond 22, op. 1, d. 584, fols. 7r–8r; and *Listki* 1833, 198.
52. Oleksenko 1842, 9; Urry 1989, 108–11; Dyck 1984a, 35–36; and Haxthausen 1856, 430. For a critical review on Cornies see Dyck 1984b, 9–28.
53. DAOO, fond 22, op. 1, d. 580, fols. 190r–190v; and Shchepkin 1869, 26, 30, 33.
54. RGIA, fond 1281, op. 6, d. 31, fols. 7r–9r; RGIA, fond 1281, op. 6, d. 67, fol. 11v; and DAOO, fond 1, op. 248, d. 1575, fols. 482r–482v (Kherson province, 1848).
55. Von Pantser 1861, 35; Shmidt 1860–1863, vol. 2, 237; Kabeshtov 1869, 166; *SSSE*, vol. 3, pt. 2, 74; and Pavlovich 1862, 296. Kuzmin (1864, 218) gives the exaggerated figure of one million sheep dying in Katerynoslav province in 1862 and 1863.
56. Felibert 1863, 213–14; *VEZ* (6 November 1903): 27; and von Pantser 1861, 35.
57. RGIA, fond 1284, op. 69, d. 187, fol. 6r; Pavlovich 1862, 296; Felibert 1863, 212–13; and Kuzmin 1863, 50. The first vaccination in Kherson province was administered for smallpox as early as 1828 (Shmidt 1860–1863, vol. 2, 237).
58. "Zapiski o soderzhanii ovets i ikh bolezniakh pomeshchika Bakhmutskogo

uezda" 1860, 25–26; *ISPT*, appendix 1, 49–50; Iaron 1873, appendix, 14–15; *SSSE*, vol. 3, pt. 1, 255–56. More complete lists are found in Shmidt 1860–1863, vol. 2, 237–40; and Pavlovich 1862, 296.

59. *ISPT*, appendix 1, 49–54; RGIA, fond 1284, op. 67, d. 252, fol. 20r; Shmidt 1860–1863, vol. 2, 237; and Gorskii 1871, 206. For an account of a similar problem in Australia, see Fyfe 1983, 65–67. Scab does not seem to have affected herds in Kharkiv, Poltava, or Voronezh provinces (*ISPT*, appendix 1, 52).
60. RGIA fond 1284, op. 69, d. 187, fol. 6r; *Odesskii Vestnik* (28 January 1828): 31; and Kuzmin 1863, 50; "Otchet o deistviiakh Imperatorskogo Obshchestva sel′skogo khoziaistva iuzhnoi Rossii v 1870 godu" 1871, 251. See also the tables being circulated at this time in "Vedomost′ ob epizooticheskikh bolezniakh i obshchem kolichestve rovshogo skota…" 1864–74. An unidentifiable disease, linked to the decline in adequate pastures for sheep, is noted in RGIA, fond 1281, op. 7, d. 76, fols. 33r–33v.
61. DAOO, fond 22, op. 1, d. 583, fols. 30v–31r.
62. DAOO, fond 22, op. 1, d. 580, fols. 154r, 190r–190v; RGIA fond 1281, op. 7, d. 76, fol. 31r; "Iz Novorossiiskago kraia" 1871, 1; and Gorskii 1871, 206. Fleece washing, it should be noted, developed into an important secondary industry at this time, with its greatest concentration found in the towns of Kharkiv and Belgorod (Kursk province), as well as throughout Kherson province. Eight washing plants (*sherstianye moiki*) were located along the Dnipro River by 1880. Of these, the largest had washed a high of 70,000 poods in a single year (1870). Most of these washing facilities appear to have been located on estates, with some establishments devoted solely to their own flocks. See "Sherstianye Moiki na iuge Rossii," in *ISPT*, 11–22; Skal′kovs′kyi 1850–1853, vol. 2, 369–370; and Shmidt 1860–1863, vol. 2, 246.
63. M. K. 1837, 264. *Peregonnaia,* not surprisingly, characterized wool sales in central Ukraine, where water for washing would have been more plentiful. See Kotelnikov 1883, 54. Prices of wool in Katerynoslav province in 1863 ranged from 8 rubles to 8 rubles 50 kopecks a pood for muddy wool, and 13 rubles to 15 rubles 50 kopecks a pood for half-clean wool. See Kuzmin 1864, 219. On the declining market value of Russian wool, see N. Strukov 1870, 219.
64. DAOO, fond 22, op. 1, d. 584, fols. 7r–15r; Shchepkin 1869, 58; and Gorskii 1871, 199–200.
65. Wallerstein 1989, vol. 3, ch. 3.
66. Grigg 1974, 251; Blainey 1982, 124–37; and Irving 1974, 154.
67. Jenkins and Ponting 1982, ch. 5.
68. DAOO, fond 22, op. 1, d. 580, fol. 155r; and *ZIOS* 1847, 25.

69. *Odesskii vestnik* (28 January 1828): 29; and Sokolov 1837, 73.
70. DAOO, fond 22, op. 1, d. 584; DAOO, fond 1, op. 192, d. 91; *ZIOS* 1840; and *ZIOS* 1846, 11.
71. Gulak 1843, 236; and Shchepkin 1869, 23.
72. DAOO, fond 22, op. 1, d. 586, fols. 13r, 76r–77r, 81v, 108r–11r, 119r–22r; and DAOO, fond 1, op. 152, d. 67, fols. 8r–8v.
73. *Listki* 1835, 6.
74. Cornies 1843, 75. For a slightly different calculation, see Rempel 1933, 127.
75. Cornies 1843, 75.
76. Urry 1989, 116–17.
77. RGIA, fond 89, op. 1, d. 406, fol. 1v. One such agreement between Johann Cornies and Duiungul, a Tatar from the village of Kichildino, is found in the Braun archive, fond 89, op. 1, d. 313, fol. 1r. See also Cornies 1844, 140.
78. Braun, fond. 89, op. 1, d. 1408, fol. 1r; Braun, fond 89, op. 1, d. 314, fol. 2r; and Braun, fond 89, op. 1, d. 1261.
79. Zablotskii 1841, 35.
80. Skal′kovs′kyi 1850–1853, vol. 2, 366; and Klaus 1869, appendix 7; Cornies was unique in that 500 desiatinas of his estate lands were found within the Molochna settlement itself, and were the only exception to the village settlement pattern found there. His remaining lands were found on three parcels scattered throughout New Russia. See J. C. Toews 1954, 4.
81. Billington 1971, 38–39.

Chapter Four

1. Markevich 1912, 48–51.
2. Eklof, Bushnell, and Zakharova 1994; Taranovski 1995; and Lincoln 1990.
3. DAOO, fond 22, op. 1, d. 511, fol. 11r; DAOO, fond 1, op. 152, d. 67, fols. 6v–8r; DAOO, fond 22, op. 1, d. 580, fol. 32r; "Istoricheskii ocherk torgovli chernogo i Azovskogo moria" 1841, 69–73; Kahan 1985, 197; Braudel 1982, 462–66; and Herlihy 1986, 103–8. For a systematic treatment of this expansion, see Wallerstein 1989, vol. 3, ch. 3.
4. RGIA, fond 1281, op. 6, d. 83, fol. 4r; and RGIA, fond 1284, op. 67, d. 540, fol. 2r; and Leshchenko 1959b, 194.
5. Shmidt 1860–1863, vol. 2, 297–98.
6. RGIA, fond 1284, op. 67, d. 540, fol. 2r; and Pavlovich 1862, 172.
7. Dyck 1991, 42 and 120.
8. Postnikov 1891, 167–68. A. A. Klaus (1869, 162) has similar statistics for Molochna Mennonites, whom he felt cultivated almost 22 of their 65 desiatina farmsteads in 1851.
9. Rempel 1973–1974, 51–52.

10. Postnikov 1891, 36–37; and Rempel 1973–1974, 64. An interesting overview of changing historiographical perspectives on Mennonite farming is found in David G. Rempel, "Mennonite Agriculture and Model Farming as Issues of Economic Study and Political Controversy, 1870–1917," David Rempel Collection, box 4, series 2:4, 1–45, Thomas Fisher Rare Book Library, University of Toronto.
11. Troinitskii 1861, 45.
12. RGIA, fond 1281, op. 6, d. 52, fol. 5v; and Sekirinskii 1964, 353.
13. Sekirinskii 1964, 355–56.
14. Ignatovich 1910, 205–7; Maksimenko 1957, 22–24; and Sekirinskii 1964, 354–56. On the significance of *barshchina* in shaping peasant attitudes to agricultural work, see Mironov 1978, 121–23. For the argument that nobles were unable to justify the enserfment of their serfs, see Mironov 1996, 323–47.
15. Sekirinskii 1964, 357–58.
16. Cited in Borovoi 1970, 291–92.
17. Sekirinskii 1964, 358; and Alferakii 1863, 102. Most of the seasonal laborers for hay cutting and grain harvesting were said to come from Kyiv, Poltava, and Kursk guberniias. See Benedskii 1861, 99; and "Iz Novorossiiskogo kraia" 1871, 1.
18. DAOO, fond 5, op. 1, d. 4, fols. 25v–26v; Borovoi 1970, 291–92; and Krstvtsv 1861, 2.
19. Borovoi 1970, 292–94.
20. "Vol′nonaemnye rabotniki v guberniiakh Volynskoi, Podol′skoi, Kievskoi i Khersonskoi" 1861, 129 and 138.
21. Dubrovskii 1975, 122.
22. Hamburg 1984, 24–26.
23. RGIA, fond 1281, op. 6, d. 51, fol. 2r; D. Strukov 1860, 89–90; and OKPU, 48. Almost two-thirds of all estates within the empire were already mortgaged on the eve of 1860. See Borovoi 1972, 198–202.
24. RGIA, fond 1281, op. 6, d. 97, fol. 8v; RGIA, fond 1281, op. 6, d. 86, fols. 5v–10r; and Maksimenko 1957, 41.
25. RGIA, fond 1281, op. 6, d. 48, fols. 5r–6v, 9r; *SSSTG* 1889, pt. 2, 14–17; and Rybkin 1873, 3.
26. Field 1976b; and Moon 1992. An important example from the Soviet era is Viola 1996. An influential work has been Scott 1985.
27. Maksimenko 1957, 24–25.
28. *MDIKP*, 69–70, 138–39; and Maksimenko 1957, 31, 40–41.
29. Moon 1992, 128–29.
30. Romanov 1901, 265.
31. Romanov 1901, 267; OKPU, 82; and Linkov 1940, 85–86.

32. Okun 1962, 284–85.
33. RGIA, fond 1281, op. 6, d. 48, fols. 6r–6v.
34. Field 1976a, 140–41.
35. RGIA, fond 1281, op. 6, d. 50, 53; Field 1976a, 88–89; and Saunders 1992, 232–33.
36. Zaionchkovskii 1960, 125–26; and Leshchenko 1959b, 192.
37. RGIA, fond 1284, op. 194, d. 89, fols. 5v–6r. Only 5 land charters in the guberniia, involving 654 revision souls, provided for an increase in holdings (Leshchenko 1970, 382–83; Maksimenko 1964, 458–59).
38. Leshchenko 1970, 385; Maksimenko 1964, 460.
39. DAOO, fond 91, op. 1b, d. 7, fol. 12v; DAOO, fond 91, op. 1b, d. 827, fols. 6r–6v; DAOO, fond 91, op. 1b, d. 826, fols. 2v–3r; and Leshchenko 1971, 429.
40. Leshchenko 1971, 425–26.
41. *MOZKh* 1883, 36; and V. Borisov 1876, 212.
42. Leshchenko 1970, 384.
43. On obligations, see Mironov 1985, 441. On the effect of these obligations on peasants, see Pakhman 1877–1879, vol. 1, 6.
44. DAOO, fond 1, op. 249, d. 416, fol. 9v; and Maksimenko 1957, 71.
45. Ibid.
46. DAOO, fond 1, op. 173, d. 9, fol 9r; DAOO, fond 1, op. 123, d. 13, fols. 1r–4v; DAOO, fond 1, op. 249, d. 416, fol. 150r; and DAOO, fond 1, op. 249, d. 407, fols. 1r–192r. On the myth of the tsar, see Field 1976b, 208ff.
47. See, for example, DAOO, fond 1, op. 249, d. 416; DAOO, fond 1, op. 123, d. 82, fols. 6r–7v; and Field 1994, 42–43.
48. Okun and Sivkov, 1963, 344.
49. DAOO, fond 91, op. 1b, d. 827, fols. 5r–5v; DAOO, fond 91, op. 1b, d. 826, fol. 1v; DAOO, fond 91, op. 1b, d. 7, fol. 11v; and Fortunatov 1892, 7–8.
50. DAOO, fond 1, op. 173, d. 10., fol. 3v.
51. RGIA, fond 1291, op. 52, d. 65, fol. 1r. See also DAOO, fond 1, op. 174, d. 15, fols. 5v, 11r–12r.
52. DAOO, fond 1, op. 173, d. 10, fols. 20v–21r.
53. DAOO, fond 1, op. 195, d. 219, fols. 2r, 93r; DAOO, fond 1, op. 123, d. 13, fols. 4r–4v; DAOO, fond 1, op. 123, d. 14, fol. 3v; DAOO, fond 1, op. 173, d. 9, fol. 27r; DAOO, fond 1, op. 173, d. 10, fols. 2r–3r; and RGIA, fond 1291, op. 52, d. 65, fol. 22r.
54. Leshchenko 1959a, 163–67; and Maksimenko 1957, 67–68. Although police were often brought in to quell disturbances, peasants were in almost all instances unarmed.
55. DAOO, fond 91, op. 1b, d. 826, fols. 1v–3v; and DAOO, fond 91, op. 1b, d. 807, fol. 11r.

56. DAOO, fond 91, op. 1b, d. 7, fol. 12v; and DAOO, fond 91, op. 1b, d. 832, fol. 8v.
57. DAOO, fond 1, op. 173, d. 10, fols. 26r–27r; and Leshchenko 1959a, 475. Leshchenko does not distinguish between the kinds of disturbances involved. Thus, for example, the pasturing of peasant cattle on estate lands without the owner's consent is given the same weight as the burning of buildings and stored crops. This approach was replicated by many Soviet historians. See also Naidenov 1955, 74–75.
58. DAOO, fond 1, op. 173, d. 10, fol. 5r.
59. RGIA, fond 1291, op. 52, d. 65, fols. 1v, 4v, 10r, 21v; DAOO, fond 1, op. 173, d. 10, fols. 24r–24v, 29v; and Maksimenko 1957, 85.
60. Maksimenko 1957, 90–95.
61. DAOO, fond 1, op. 249, d. 416, fols. 8v–9r, 15r.
62. DAOO, fond 7, op. 1, d. 642, fols. 1r–1v; DAOO, fond 7, op. 1, d. 761, fols. 1r–4r; and Kuzmin 1864, 236. One account noted the need for soldiers to maintain the peace as peasants "feared them" (DAOO, fond 1, op. 173, d. 9, fol. 22r).
63. RGIA, fond 1281, op. 7, d. 76, fols. 45r–46r.
64. DAOO, fond 1, op. 248, d. 1589, fol. 1r.
65. RGIA, fond 1, op. 248, d. 1593, fol. 2v–3r, 46v. Cf. Benedskii 1861, 99–104.
66. DAOO, fond 22, op. 1, d. 519, fol. 2r; and Borovoi 1970, 295.
67. Gr. 1863, 201–5; and Kuzmin 1863, 66–67.
68. See Manning 1982, 4–5.
69. "Khoziaistvennyia zametki" 1863, 252.
70. Gr. 1863, 249–51; Manning 1982, 4–5; "Khoziaistvennyia zametki" 1863, 206; and Lavrentov 1867, 381–82. The reference to Skal′kovs′kyi is found in AHFP, fond 200, op. 2, d. 13, fol. 1a.
71. For a sampling, see "Khoziaistvennyia zametki" 1863, 201–6; Krstvtsv 1861, 1–2; Gr. 1863, 264; and Skuratov 1863, 189. Cf. Leshchenko 1959a, 447.
72. Soviet historians have offered sharply differing assessments of this period. See the contrasting treatments offered by Druzhinin 1978, 114–15; and Ryndziunskii 1978, especially 101–2.
73. RGIA, fond 1281, op. 7, d. 76, fol. 49r; Keppen 1864, 495–96; *SNM*, liv; Avgustinovich 1865, 251; and Bulatsel′ 1866, 333.
74. A state investigation of sheep breeding in the empire, held during the early 1880s, considered all figures compiled for the 1870s and earlier to be unreliable. See *ISSO*, 3.
75. Gorskii 1871, 199.
76. This statistic includes Bessarabia and the Don oblast.
77. DAOO, fond 1, op. 249, d. 1593, fol. 271r; and Karnaukhova 1915, 38.
78. Lower prices were also experienced in Australia after the end of the American Civil War. See Barnard 1958, 229, table 27, and 200n56.

79. Kuzmin 1863, 50. "Otchet o deistviiakh Imperatorskogo Obshchestva sel′skago khoziaistva iuzhnoi Rossii v 1870 godu" 1871, 251. See also the tables being circulated at this time in "Vedomost ob epizooticheskikh bolezniakh i obshchem kolichestve rovshogo skota…" 1864–74.
80. RGIA, fond 1281, op. 7, d. 76, fol. 33r; DAOO, fond 1, op. 248, d. 1590, fol. 80v; "Iz Novorossiiskogo kraia" 1871, 1; Gorskii 1871, 206; and Lavrentev 1867, 119.
81. Grotto-Slepikovskii 1897, 44; and *ISSO*, 136–37.
82. "Zhurnaly zasedanii Khersonskago gubernskago zemskago sobraniia" 1870, 257–59.
83. *TPS*, 87; *DZhK*, vol. 1, 121–23 and appendix 6, pt. 1, 68 (Bakhmut uezd), 186–87 (Elisavetgrad uezd), 206 (Kherson guberniia), and 209 (Ekaterinoslav guberniia); and 230 and 277 (Kherson guberniia). Also Perepelkin 1882a, 40. A decline in numbers of sheep held in Kherson guberniia had already been noted in the early 1860s. See Avgustinovich 1865, 251. For a contrary opinion see Vassal 1870, 482, and Grotto-Slepikovskii's comment on it (1897, 53n7). See also Oganovskii 1922, 93.
84. Perepelkin 1882a, appendix 1, 2–3.
85. Shchepkin 1869, 33–34.
86. Dobrianskii 1871, 436–38.
87. RGIA, fond 1284, op. 69, d. 283, fols. 5r–7r; and Gulak 1866, 310.
88. *TPS*, 11; and Anfimov 1961, 160. More generally, see Hamburg 1984, 30.
89. L. Ivanov 1961. See also *SSSE*, vol. 3, 263–67; Karyshev 1892, 105; and Kutov 1906, 13.
90. "Khod zemskogo khoziaistva Khersonskoi gubernii za 1871 god" 1872, pt. 3, 4.
91. *MZSKh*, 72–74.
92. *TPS*, 10.
93. Zhurba 1891, 31; Shestakov 1924, 50; also *DZhK*, vol. 1, appendix 6, pt. 1, 67 and 78. The pressure placed on New Russian nobles to keep lease rates low so as to remain competitive appears to have been the greatest in the eastern half of Katerynoslav province, as rates offered in the adjoining Don oblast were always 50 percent lower than the regional average. See *DZhK*, vol. 1, appendix 6, pt. 1, 67. On collapsed prices, see Mironov 1985, 93.
94. RGIA, fond 1284, op. 702, d. 174, fols. 71r–71v.
95. Postnikov 1891, 49.
96. V. Borisov 1876, 212–13, 315–18; *MOZKh*, vol. 4, 155–56.
97. Oleksenko 1889, 51; *SSSE*, vol. 3, 65–66; and Postnikov 1891, 44.
98. Part of the problem in determining land ownership by "peasants" in late Imperial Russia is that the term by then included former colonists, some of whom were energetically involved in the purchase of former noble lands.

99. *SEOKh* 1908, 5; and *SZ1905*, vol. 16, 29.
100. *PV97*, vol. 47, vii. These figures indicate *net* gains in landholdings during these years. *Gross* gains by Germans between 1895 and 1900 were 196,087 desiatinas in Kherson guberniia; with peasants obtaining slightly over 140,000 desiatinas. It should be noted that Germans were also involved to some degree in land sales as well as purchases. See *TMKN*, vol. 46, 121.
101. Rempel 1973–1974, 69.
102. Ia. Boiko 1993.
103. Dyck 1991, 60. For examples of the petitions, see Isaac 1908, 27ff.
104. Dyck 1991, 241.
105. Dyck 1991, 61–62; and Rempel 1933, 217.
106. See *MOZKh*, vol. 4, 104; and vol. 5, 199.
107. *TMKN*, vol. 12, 64.
108. *TMKN*, vol. 46, 112. New Russian peasants may have been neglected by the Peasant Land Bank to a greater degree than other peasants in the empire. See the figures in *MVU01*, 108–11. Of thirty-one New Russian correspondents to a questionnaire from the Free Economic Society on the regional impact of the Revolution of 1905, twenty-four noted the failure of the Peasant Land Bank to effect developments in the region. The seven who did refer to it, did so negatively. See "Agrarnoe dvizhenie v Rossii" 1908, 436.
109. Dyck 1991, 62.
110. Lohrenz 1947, 9–12. Cf. Goerz 1957; and J. Friesen 1994.
111. Rempel 1933, insert between 228–29.
112. *SEOKh* 1908, 5; and Herlihy 1986, 174.
113. Peasants were also more limited geographically, often purchasing land adjoining their villages. See *MOZKh*, vol. 3, 185–88. and also Morachevskii 1910a, 237–38.
114. Rempel 1973–1974, 74.
115. V. Borisov 1876, 315–16; Rempel 1933, 235; Ehrt 1932, 77; and Postnikov 1891, 21–22.
116. Toews 1939, 11–26; and Urry 1989, 220–21. For photographs of Mennonite estates after 1860, see Quiring and Bartel 1974, 115–27.
117. L. Friesen 1992, 56–69.

Chapter Five

1. Rashin 1956, 25–26; Gregory 1994, 46; and Hoch 1994.
2. Rashin 1956, 42–43.
3. For the Governors' reports from Kherson guberniia for 1890 noting the continued immigration of peasants, see RGIA, fond 1284, op. 223, d. 159. For the reports of 1893 that give a contrary impression, see RGIA, fond 1284, op. 223, d. 200.

4. *SSSTG* 1889, pt. 2, 8, 12–16; Ia. Boiko 1993, ch. 3; and Rashin 1956, 44–45. Population figures are difficult to verify for this period. For a different count, see *MVU01*, vol. 1, 24–25.
5. Lorimer 1946, 13.
6. Hooson 1968, 257–59.
7. For detailed statistics on the urban population of New Russia from 1856 to 1897, see *STR56*, 39, 131, and 149; *SVR66*, 12–13, 26–27, and 30–31; *Novorossiiskii kalendar na 1892 god* (Odesa), 165–66, 174, 177, 179–85, 190–93; *PV97*, vol. 13, p. 1; vol. 41, p. 1; and vol. 47, p. 1.
8. *PV97*, vol. 47, 34–35; and *SVR66*, 135.
9. Ianson 1870, 283–87; Morachevskii 1910b, 461–62; and Herlihy 1986, 181.
10. Theide 1970, 430–35.
11. Ianson 1870, 81; *Ezhegodnik Rossii 1904 g.*, 324; Borinevich 1890, 14; and Theide 1970, 323.
12. *PV97*, vol. 41, p. 1; Kuntshevich 1964, 614; and Theide 1870, 349–51.
13. *PV97*, vol. 13, 1; vol. 41, 1; and vol. 47, 1. On the special role that Ielysavethrad was able to achieve as a trading and marketing center for the northern districts of New Russia, see Ianson 1870, 214–16.
14. McCaffray 1983, 35.
15. Pavlovich 1862, 176.
16. Ibid., 53–54.
17. Holderness 1823, 87–88.
18. Bakulev 1953, 72.
19. Ibid., 72.
20. Harvey 1938, 129–30; and Krutikov, 1971, 104.
21. Harvey 1938, 131–32.
22. Westwood 1964, 90. On the initial discussions in local zemstvos considering the merits of railroad construction, see *SKhZ* 1, no. 1 (1868): 78–84.
23. *SSSTG* 1889, pt. 6, ch. 3, 31.
24. Kherson and Tavriia provinces had 1075 and 699 versts, respectively. See Ulissov 1910, 445.
25. Bakulev 1953, 87–88.
26. "Zapiski predprinimatelei proektiruemoi zheleznoi dorogi ot st. Dolinskoi Khar´kovo-Nikolaevskoi i Ekaterinoslavskoi zheleznykh dorog, cherez Voznesensk, v Odessy" 1889, 5, 8.
27. Kabeshtov 1887, 263–67; Zertsalov 1891, 18, 23, and 54; and Fedorov 1894, 677. For an example of freight costs, see Zertsalov 1891, 55–56. See also "O zhelezno-dorozhnykh tarifakh" 1887, 131–33.
28. Zusman 1880, 18; and Iuzhanov 1889, 620. For those appealing for grain elevators, see "K voprosy ob elevatorakh v Rossii" 1887, pt. 3, 305; and Garris 1890, 12–13.
29. *TMKN*, vol. 12, 81ff.

30. RGIA, fond 1284, op. 69, d. 284, fol. 3v; and M. G. 1888, 168; Korolenko 1889, 21; and "Iz Dneprovskogo uezda" 1892, 283. The necessity of carting produce to markets and depots over distances of 25 versts and more on poor and slow roads meant that time needed for field work was curtailed.
31. Lonachevskii 1891, 95–97.
32. N. Borisov 1890, 67.
33. Herlihy 1986, 219–20; and Ulissov 1910, 450.
34. RGIA, fond 1284, op. 67, d. 257, fol. 6v; and *MOZKh 1888*, 90.
35. See, for example, "Agrarnoe dvizhenie v Rossii v 1905–1906 gg." 1908, 409–10. On the elimination of certain carting routes, see *Sel'sko-khoziaistvennoe opisanie Aleksandriiskogo uezda* 1888, 254.
36. Solov'eva 1975, 211.
37. On the excitement directed at Hughes's involvement, see RGIA, fond 1284, op. 67, d. 169, fols. 10v–11r.
38. Bakulev 1955, 130; and Friedgut 1989–1994, vol. 1, 56, 106. On the slow beginnings of the Kryvyi Rih iron ore industry, see Livshits 1955, 21; and McKay 1970, 121.
39. Bakulev 1955, 94–95.
40. Ibid., 657–58. The number of local blast furnaces in the region grew from 5 in 1887 to 53 in 1900. See Morachevskii 1910a, 376.
41. Bakulev 1953, 90.
42. By comparison, Russia produced slightly over one billion poods of coal in 1902, compared with 1.8, 9.2, 15.6, and 16.7 billion poods in France, Germany, Great Britain, and the United States respectively. While Russian steel output for that same year of 133.3 million poods exceeded that of France (99.8 million), it was dwarfed by the production occurring in Great Britain (311.4 million), Germany (475 million), and the United States (927.1 million). See *Ezhegodnik Rossii 1905 g.*, 365.
43. Theide 1970, 433–34.
44. Khromov 1963, 128.
45. *DZhK*, vol. 1, appendix 4. Three were found in Kherson province (De Spiller; Falk; and Zykov) and one each in Katerynoslav and Tavriia (Zaslavskii and Lepp respectively).
46. *Ezhegodnik Rossii 1904 g.*, 282–85.
47. Lavrentov 1867, 392–93. Mennonites in New Russia, located near the industrial centers of Katerynoslav and Oleksandrivsk, were especially noted for their strong local implement industry. For the entire series, see Epp 1911, nos. 51–96; and Rempel 1933, ch. 13. More generally on the value of local produced implements, see Palimpsestrov 1855, 38–49; and Grigorev 1864, 417.
48. On tariffs and agricultural implements, see Litoshenko 1910, 775–90.
49. *PV97*, vol. 13, 1.

50. *PV97*, vol. 13, xi; and vol. 47, 2.
51. The commentator is Luigi Villari, as quoted in Wynn 1992, 26–27.
52. During that same period the same proportions in Kherson province fell from 93 to 70 percent, while rising from 72 to 80 percent in Tavriia. Druzhinina 1981, 96–97, 148–49, and 165; *Ezhegodnik Rossii 1904 g.*, 278–85.

Chapter Six

1. Umiss 1874, 47–48.
2. Robinson 1932, 94.
3. *SSSTG* 1889, pt. 5, 69–70.
4. Loewe 1987; Bideleux 1990, ch. 12; Kingston-Mann 1991b, ch. 1; and Gregory 1994, ch. 3.
5. J. Scott 1976, 24–26. Cf. Hoffman 1996.
6. Kohl 1842, 466, 500. See, for comparison, Turner 1920, 11; and the comments by Boserup 1973, ch. 1.
7. Postnikov 1891, 164.
8. Skal′kovs′kyi 1850–1853, vol. 2, 3341–43. On the importance of the tallow trade, see Herlihy 1986, 53; and Druzhinina 1970, 264.
9. RGIA, fond 1281, op. 6, d. 86, fols. 11r–11v; RGIA, fond 1281, op. 6, d. 76, fol. 6v; and Kreits 1863a, 81.
10. Herlihy 1986: 53; Druzhinina 1970: 222, 264; and Druzhinina 1981, 96.
11. Shmidt 1860–1863, vol. 2, 103–7; and Morachevskii 1910a, 296.
12. RGIA, fond 1282, op. 3, d. 513, fol. 20r; and *MOZKh* 1886, 383.
13. *SSSTG* 1889, pt. 5, 69. and *VSORI*, pt. 2. Consult *SSSM*, vol. 2, 6; Oleksenko 1889, 22–27; Krstvtsv 1864, 335; Skal′kovs′kyi 1850–1853, vol. 2, 212, 304–5; and the annual examples in *GSKH*. This was the annual publication of the Department of Agriculture, St. Petersburg, between 1882 and 1916. The year of the publication is the first word in the title of each volume.
14. Gałęski 1972, 42.
15. Morachevskii 1910a, 262; Skal′kovs′kyi 1850–1853, vol. 2, 297, 316; and Bremner 1839, 356.
16. DAOO, fond 1, op. 152, d. 67; Herlihy 1963, 101–6, 114–17; Shmidt 1860–1863, vol. 2, 15; Druzhinina 1981, 52–53, 68; and Pavlovich 1862, 131.
17. Shmidt 1860–1863, vol. 2, 4.
18. *DZhK*, vol. 1, pt. 2, 46; Shimkin 1873, 273, and 277; and Pavlovich 1862, 132. Indeed, some claimed that there was no pattern, only irrational and poorly conceived planning. Bulatsel′ 1866, 340. For estate systems, see Bulatsel′ 1866, 343; Lutkovskii 1862, 84–85; and Pukhov 1878, 375–76.
19. Shmidt 1860–1863, vol. 2, 18.
20. See, for example, *SSSTG* 1889, pt. 3, 19; and Shmidt 1860–1863, vol. 2, 17.

21. Shmidt 1860–1863, vol. 2, 39; and Iasman 1970, 249. Ukrainians were referred to as "Little Russians" in the Imperial period.
22. A description of the Ukrainian plow, along with a sketch, are found in Saburova 1987, 192. Also Pavlovich 1862, 135; Shmidt 1860–1863, vol. 2, 39; and Skal′kovs′kyi 1850–1853, vol. 2, 66–67.
23. Shmidt 1860–1863, vol. 2, 41–42; and Saburova 1987, 194. In another instance, a German colonist, Konrad Bekhtol′d, constructed a plow almost entirely out of steel, for which he was awarded first prize in an 1840 competition of imperial Russian and foreign plows that the South Russian Agricultural Society sponsored. Still, peasants were reluctant to purchase these plows because of their higher purchase price, and also due to the absence of "skilled and reliable blacksmiths" required for their ongoing maintenance (Shmidt 1860–1863, vol. 2, 40–41; and "Usovershenstvovannyi malorossiiskii plug kolonista Bekhtol′da" 1868, 208).
24. Slicher van Bath 1963, 23–24. The quotation is from Skal′kovs′kyi 1850–1853, vol. 2, 68. Sickles were only rarely used. See also Pavlovich 1862, 136; Saburova 1987, 196–97; and *SSSE*, vol. 3, 220. Christine Worobec has suggested that the use of both the sickle and scythe reflected a "sexual division of labor" within the peasant household. See Worobec 1991, 184.
25. Pavlovich 1862, 136; and Shmidt 1860–1863, vol. 2, 42–43.
26. I observed the very same process still at work in a state collective farm near Velykyi Tokmak, Ukraine, as late as August 1989.
27. *SSSE*, vol. 3 (1886), Slavianoserbskii uezd, 185.
28. John Toews 1981, 297. David Epp argued in Toews 1981 that this very experience increased peasant demand for sturdier carts.
29. On the persistence of age-old practices and implements among French peasants, see Weber 1976, 118.
30. Cf. DAOO, fond 1, op. 220, d. 3, fols. 1–34; and Druzhinina 1981, 58–59.
31. For example, the zemstvo investigation for Melitopol district (along the Azov Sea) noted in the mid-1880s that "the awkward Little Russian plow and wooden harrow have ceased to be utilized" (*SSSTG* 1887a, 117). Cf. *SKhZ* 38 (February 1905): 11.
32. Postnikov 1891, 212–15; Babenko 1905, 731; *MOZKh* 1883, vol. 1, 103. Also Okushko 1890, 137. *MOZE* 1899, pt. 2, 18. On the significance of steel-shared plows for American prairie farming during the same time period, see Bogue 1963, 148–52.
33. Postnikov 1891, 5. On the origins of the *bukker*, see Rempel 1933, 248–49.
34. Rempel 1933, 249. Translated by David G. Rempel.
35. Anfimov 1980, 158; *MOZE* 1899, pt. 2, 20; Postnikov 1891, 214–15; *MOZE* 1902, 20; and *SSSTG* 1889, pt. 4, 59.
36. *MOZKh* 1886, 254–55, 59.

37. *MOZE* 1902, 15–16.
38. Rempel 1933, 251–52; Karatygin 1897; Carstensen 1984, 120; John Toews 1981, 309; and Hume 1914. A picture of the *lobogreika* can be found in Lohrenz 1977, 55.
39. *MOZE* 1899, pt. 1, 22–23; Carstensen 1984, 120; Postnikov 1891, 218; and *SSSTG* 1889, pt. 4, 59. Prices for reapers fluctuated from 140 rubles during years with low grain yields to 200 rubles or more when yields were high.
40. Kolesnik 1904, 1229; and Khizhniakov 1899b, 18.
41. *TMKN*, vol. 46, 75–76; *SSSTG* 1889, pt. 4, 10; and Zinov′ev 1900, nos. 7–8, 9, 11–12. See Postnikov 1891, ch. 3 for a detailed discussion of large peasant villages in New Russia.
42. *TMKN* 1903, vol. 46, 77; RGIA, fond 1263, op. 4, d. 52, fols. 43r–43v; and Postnikov 1891, 184.
43. Postnikov 1891, 215; and Oleksenko 1889, 56. For descriptions and sketches of these wagons, see Tiessen 1979, 32–33; and Kroeker 1981, 66–67. A photograph of the *mazhara* is found in Quiring and Bartel 1974, 55.
44. "Remesly i promysly Khersonskoi gubernii" 1905, 11. The article also comments on the growing number of villages with their own blacksmiths, itself an improvement over days when such artisans travelled from village to village, staying in each for several days.
45. Babenko 1905, 731.
46. Avgustinovich 1865, 459. For a discussion of the various factors leading to peasant poverty, as well as differing perspectives between peasants and "experts," see Wilbur 1991, 101–27.
47. Mironov 1985, 68–69 and 92–93; Zabarinskii 1893, 83–85; and Ganner 1890, 19. Russian exports to London were 8,682 chetverts (1861–65) and 13,784 (1881–85), whereas U.S. exports for the same periods were 13,882 and 44,722 chetverts. See Neruchev 1890, 83; also Liashchenko 1927, 6–8.
48. For another set of tables, see Egiazarova 1959, 75. Detailed pricing information for the 1880s can be found in *Vremennik* 3 (1888): 2–3; and *Vremennik* 4 (1889): 11–12.
49. Oleksenko 1889, 65–66. Parts of New Russia experienced a drop greater than 50 percent of wheat prices during the ten-year span from 1883 to 1893. See, for example, the report submitted by Ia. Raevskii, from Oleksandriia district in Kherson province, to *Sel′skii khoziain* (7 January 1894), where he compares prices from 1883 and 1893. Of all crops, oats was the most stable, only dropping from 60 to 40 kopecks per pood. See Raevskii 1894, 190–91.
50. See *Sel′sko-khoziaistvennyi obzor Tavricheskoi gubernii za desiatiletie, 1899–1908 gg.* 1911, 18–20; Mironov 1985, 51, 272–73; and *SSXIX* 1902, no. 1, 124–25; 136–37.

51. *MVU01*, vol. 1, 176.
52. Postnikov 1891, 164; and Mironov 1985, 93.
53. *MVU01*, vol. 1, 176.
54. SVR66, 12–13, 26–27, and 30–31; Rashin 1956, 44–45; and PV97, vol. 13, 1; vol. 47, 1; and vol. 41, 1; Alekseev 1910, 175; and Karyshev 1895, 50.
55. Postnikov 1891, 195–96.
56. *TPS 1879*, 1–2.
57. Kreits 1863b, 417; Zabudskii 1870, 11, 18–19; Shimkin 1873, 268; and Bezpomoshchnyi 1878, 119.
58. Umiss 1874, 47–48. On the negative effects of having plowed up the rich, natural, steppe grasses, see also RGIA, fond 1284, op. 223, d. 202, fol. 7v.
59. Mechnikov 1879, 26. According to Mechnikov, after 1794 complaints about the beetle did not arise again until 1857, 1862, 1875, and especially 1878. See also "O posledstviiakh mer k istrebleniia saranchi v iuzhnom krae Rossii v 1859–1860 godakh" 1861, 176–79.
60. Kushakevich 1865, 365; and "Rukovodstvo dlia istrebleniia saranchi" 1876, 44–47.
61. "Mnenie inostrantsev ob 'Anisoplia autriaca'" 1880, 566; and "Rukovodstvo dlia istrebleniia saranchi" 1876, 46. See, for example, Neruchev 1880, 259–61. Colonists, it should be noted, were reported to have had the same number of locust invasions, though they fared far better due to their vigilant response. See "O posledstviiakh mer k istrebleniia saranchi v iuzhnom krae Rossii v 1859–1860 godakh" 1861, 179. See the comments linking poor cultivation practices leading to soil exhaustion with the rise of insect devastation in Lavrentov 1870b, 556–57; and Lavrentov 1870a, 89–91. For early initiatives to contain the damage, see "O posledstviiakh mer" 1861, 176–94; and Kushakevich 1865, 365–66.
62. Kabeshtov 1870, 4–5; Kuzmin 1863, 59; Lavrentev 1867, 271; and "Vidy na urozhai" 1878, 295. The Governor's report for Ekaterinoslav guberniia in 1878 claimed that beetle damage during that year in the central districts of Oleksandrivsk, Pavlohrad, and Bakhmut had been the worst ever. See DAOO, fond 5, op. 1, d. 6, fol. 2v; also *GSKh* 1882, 7.
63. Pavlovich (1862, 173) claimed that most groundhogs were located on state lands, where peasants left them alone, claiming they were God's punishment. Groundhogs were especially harmful to melons. See Lavrentev 1867, 273.
64. Ballion 1873, 24–25. With respect to peasant inactivity in light of cockroach devastation, see "Ob istreblennii vrednykh zhivotnykh i nasekomykh" 1871, 106–7.
65. *MVU01*, vol. 1, 208; and Markovskii 1900, 10.
66. RGIA, fond 1284, op. 69, d. 192, fol. 23r; RGIA, fond 1284, op. 69, d. 187, fols. 4v–6r; and RGIA, fond 1284, op. 69, d. 246, fol. 5r.
67. RGIA, fond 1281, op. 7, d. 76, fol. 45r.

68. From Pallot and Shaw 1990, 122–24. For the argument that population densities directly affect technological change, see Boserup 1973, esp. 31, 41.
69. Rempel 1933, ch. 11; Urry 1989, chs. 4, 6, and 12; and Rempel, n.d., 50–51.
70. Weber 1976, pt. 2; Grigg 1992; Price 1983; Price 1987, 8–27; and Pallot and Shaw 1990, 131. Cf. Slicher van Bath 1963, 15.
71. Price 1987, 15.
72. Price 1987, 24–25; and Weber 1976, 122.
73. Postnikov 1891, 165. Among other sources dealing with Mennonite agriculture, industry, and inheritance practices, one should consult Rempel, n.d.; and Klaus 1869, esp. chps. 4 and 5.
74. V. Borisov 1878, 66. Cf. Klaus 1869; Bahalii 1889; Bartlett 1979; and Brandes 1993.
75. Borisov describes the villages in V. Borisov 1878, 67–69; Babenko 1905, 734.
76. *MOZE* 1902, 77–78; and Oleksenko 1889, 73.
77. L. Friesen 1994, 399–418.
78. Skal′kovs′kyi 1850–1853, vol. 2, 309, 318; *SSSM*, vol. 6, 126; and *SSSTG* 1889, pt. 5, 14. Pallot and Shaw (1990, 110–11) present a different view of the relationship between Mennonites and peasants. However, it should be noted that their study is of the Transvolga region, where the relatively late settlement meant that relationships had barely been established by the time of the zemstvo investigations in the 1880s. Even so, Pallot and Shaw also conclude that the contact between cultures increased with time, and went in many directions.
79. Lohrenz 1976, 28.
80. *SSSTG* 1889, pt. 5, 5–6, 14.
81. Skal′kovs′kyi 1850–1853, vol. 2, 305–6.
82. *SSSTG* 1889, pt. 5, 14–20.
83. Mironov 1985, 92–93, and appendix, table 16.
84. *MVU01*, vol. 1, 170–71. Domestic consumption was based upon the accepted annual per capita rate of 25 poods. *MOZE* 1899, pt. 2, 69.
85. Slicher van Bath 1963, 13.
86. *MOZE* 1899, pt. 2, 13–14. For detailed statistics on the urban population of New Russia from 1856 to 1897, see *STR56*, 39, 131, and 149; *SVR66*, 12–13, 26–27, and 30–31; *Novorossiiskii kalendar na 1892 god*, 165–66, 174, 177, 179–85, 190–13; and *PV97*, vol. 13, 1; vol. 41, 1; and vol. 47, 1.
87. Price 1983, 387–90; Collins 1969, 82–85; Weber 1976, 129; and Grigg 1989, 136–48, 155–56.
88. Postnikov 1891, 146, 165–66; "Po voprosu o peresmotre norm, opredeliniushchikh pravo uchastiia v zemskikh izbiratel'nykh sobraniiakh" 1905, 131.

89. *TMKN*, vol. 40, 100; *MOZKh* 1890, 160; *MVU01*, vol. 1, 170–76; and *SSXIX*, vol. 1, 56–58.
90. Postnikov 1891, 222, 227–28; Lozinski 1875, 367–70; and Shimkin 1873, 278.
91. *PV97*, vol. 13, 1; vol 41, 1; vol. 47, 1. The number is even higher if large economic centers officially designated as villages are included. See Thiede 1970, 236; Herlihy 1986; Wynn 1992; and Friedgut 1989–1994.
92. Bychikhin 1897, 11–12, 23; Kohl 1842, 432; and Herlihy 1986, 54.
93. *MOZKh* 1886, 384.
94. Others were in Ananïv district. See Morachevskii 1910a, 309; and Shmidt 1860–1863, vol. 2, 101.
95. Pogibka 1896, 38–39. The average garden in Oleshky comprised two equal thirds of cabbages and tomatoes, 11 percent of potatoes, and 22 percent cucumbers. For Tavriia province, see also *SSSM*, vol. 9, 174–78; and Pavlovich 1862, 142.
96. *SSSTG* 1889, pt. 5, 70–72.
97. *SSSM*, vol. 14, 293.
98. *Ezhegodnik Rossii 1904 g.* (1905): 338–40. Katerynoslav province had 84 kilometers of rail for every 100,000 inhabitants.
99. RGIA, fond 1284, op. 69, d. 284, fols. 3r–3v; Ianson 1870, 233; *SSSTG* 1889, pt. 5, 59; and "Verkhnedneprovskii uezd po otchetu uezdnoi zemskoi upravy za 1903 g." 1904, 558.
100. RGIA, fond 1284, op. 67, d. 257 (Governor's Report for Kherson province, 1871), fol. 6v; and *SSSM*, vol. 2, 5. More than 6 million kilograms of fresh vegetables entered the port of Odesa in 1897, up from 1.5 million in 1894. See *SSSM*, vol. 14, 292.
101. Veselovskii 1909–1911, vol. 2, 179.
102. Ibid., 180–88, 196–97; and Biriukovich 1903, 95.
103. *SSSTG* 1889, pt. 2, 13.
104. "Krest′ianskoe obshchestvo sel′skogo khoziaistva v sel′ Pokrovskom Aleksandriiaskogo uezda" 1903, 19.
105. Bertenson 1895, 775; see also Eklof 1986, 215–20; and Gokhgeim 1904, 706.
106. *SSSM*, vol. 9, 175; "Mariupol′skii uezd po otchetu uezdnoi zemskoi upravy za 1903 g." 1904, 410; and Sazonov 1896, vol. 2, 625, 645.
107. *Trudy s″ezda deiatelei agronomicheskoi pomoshchi mestnomu khoziaistvu* 1901, 59.
108. Ibid., 59; and Eklof 1986, 275.
109. Sazonov 1896, vol. 2, 639.
110. Postnikov 1891, 330.
111. P. K. 1889, 211–12. See also *MOZE* 1899, pt. 2, 18–19. There is evidence to

suggest that in 1900 peasants themselves were less enamored with the bukker than they had been a decade earlier. See *OEGZ* 1900, 10–11; and *OEGZ* 1899, 60.

112. Clear statements to this effect can be found in *OEGZ* 1897, 10–12; Markovskii 1900, 8; and Zinov′ev 1900, nos. 5–6: 34.
113. Seregny 1991, 342; and Eklof 1986.
114. Burakov 1892, 33–34; and *MVU01*, vol. 1, 171–77.
115. RGIA, fond 1284, op. 223, d. 168, fols. 3v–4r. See, for example, "Protokol zasedaniia sel′sko-khoziaistvennogo Soveta Aleksandrovskogo Zemstva" 1905, 1081; and RGIA, fond 1282, op. 3, d. 545, fol. 27r.
116. *MOZE* 1899, pt. 2, 13–14; RGIA, fond 1284, op. 194, d. 111, fol. 3v; RGIA, fond 1284, op. 223, d. 239, fols. 3r–3v; and RGIA, fond 1284, op. 223, d. 46, fols. 2v–3r.

Chapter Seven

1. RGIA, fond 1284, op. 69, d. 266, fol. 7r.
2. RGIA, fond 1282, op. 3, d. 526, fols. 4r–4v.
3. *SPSNM*, 2–3, 36–37, 70–71; *SSXIX*, vol. 1, table 2, 20–21; and *SZ1905*, vol. 14, 31; vol. 16, 28; and vol. 42, 31.
4. This form was also noted in Siberia and the northern provinces of European Russia—other areas with more spacious land holdings. See *SPSNM*, x, 3–4; and Kaufman 1897, 53–58.
5. *SSSTG* 1889, pt. 3, 19–20; and Shcherbina 1880, 42.
6. *SSSTG* 1885, 45.
7. DAOO, fond 1, op. 248, d. 1593, fols. 52v–53r; and *SSSTG* 1889, pt. 3, 8 and 35.
8. RGIA, fond 1284, op. 67, d. 540, fols. 2r–2v.
9. Kablukov 1899, 93; and *SSSE*, vol. 3, 104.
10. *TKPV*, 416 and 505; and RGIA, fond 1284 op. 223, d. 140, fol. 26v.
11. *TKPV*, 387, 389, 393, 396, 418, 499, 503; and Pakhman 1877–1879, vol. 2, 292 and 295.
12. *TKPV*, 386. The case was heard at the volost court on 5 April 1869. See also ibid., 532.
13. *TKPV*, 383–96, 415, 499, and 516–17; and Pakhman 1877–1879, vol. 2, 300.
14. Pakhman 1877–1879, vol. 2, 306; and *TKPV*, 390, 396, 414, 429, 503, 517, and 525.
15. RGIA, fond 1284, op 223, d. 140, fols. 26r–26v; *MOZE* 1902, 45; *TMKN*, vol. 12, 244; Osadchii 1894, 10; and *MOZKh* 1886, 473. Peasants in the mainland districts of Tavriia experienced land pressures even earlier. Berdiansk district, for example, had recordings of quarrels over land among peasants dating from the 1850s. See Fortunatov 1892, 8.

16. RGIA, fond 1284, op 223, d. 140, fol. 32r; and RGIA, fond 1284, op. 702, d. 174, fol. 73r; Karyshev 1895, 50; and Shcherbina 1880, 42.
17. Kablukov 1899, 98; *MOZKh* 1889a, 144; and *MOZKh* 1890, 27. Actually, such a situation of unequally sized holdings could also be to the disadvantage of existing allotment holders, who had limitations placed on the way they could extract financial or military obligations from non-allotment holders (*MOZKh* 1883, 45). The notion that the young were more disadvantaged with respect to landholdings also appears in Mironov 1972, 169–73.
18. *MOZKh* 1890, 188.
19. *SSSE*, vol. 3, 85–86.
20. Shcherbina 1880, 42–44. The quotation is from *SSSTG* 1885, 48.
21. Shcherbina 1880, 46; and Fortunatov 1892, 5.
22. See, for example, *MOZKh* 1888, 167–70; Fortunatov 1892, 13; and *MOZKh* 1890, 202.
23. *MOZE* 1902, 123; RGIA, fond 1290, op 6, d. 36, fol. 717r. Similarly, only one such *obshchina* was listed for Tavriia province. See also RGIA, fond 1290, op. 6, d. 86, fol. 280v; and *MOZE* 1911, 47.
24. *MOZKh* 1883, 43; and *MOZKh* 1890, 200.
25. RGIA, fond 1284, op. 194, d. 89, fols. 6r–6v; Karyshev 1895, 59, and RGIA, fond 1284, op. 194, d. 101, fol. 19r (on Tavriia province); RGIA, fond 1290, op. 6, d. 36, fols. 24v–25r; and *SZ1905*, vol. 16, 39; vol. 14, 41; and vol. 42, 43–44.
26. *MOZE* 1902, 123. For an example of the variations possible on partial divisions, see *MOZKh* 1888, 167.
27. Shcherbina 1880, 48. Shcherbina also maintained that peasants resisted a radical repartition in the hopes that a new revision of male souls would soon appear.
28. *MOZE* 1902, 123–25; and *MOZKh* 1890, 207. Even after 1900, many state peasant *obshchina*s were ignoring the state directive against dividing lands more than once every twelve years. See *MOZE* 1911, 47.
29. A similar point is made by Löwe 1990, 166–68.
30. *SSSTG* 1885, 50–54; *MOZKh* 1890, 109; and *MOZE* 1902, 123.
31. *MOZKh* 1889a, 144–45.
32. *MOZKh* 1890, 195; *SZ1905*, vol. 14, 47; vol. 16, 40; and vol. 42, 45; and *MVU01*, vol. 1, 78–79.
33. *MOZE* 1902, 47 and 127; and *MOZKh* 1886, 218 and 220.
34. This practice was found, for example, in 16 of 38 *obshchina*s in Oleksandrivsk district of Katerynoslav province. See *MOZE* 1902, 126–27.
35. RGIA, fond 1284, op. 702, d. 174, fol. 71v; *MOZE* 1906, pt. 1, 38; "Evgenievskaia volost′ (Tiraspolskogo uezda, Khersonskoi gubernii): Statistiko-ekonomicheskoi opisanie" 1888, appendix, 42–44; and *MOZKh* 1899a, 155–56.

36. RGIA, fond 1405, op. 108, d. 6988, fol. 15r. These rates were found on the estate of a Prince Gagarin, who was leasing out 4,000 of 13,000 desiatinas on his estate to *desiatinshchiks* before 1905.
37. RGIA, fond 1282, op. 3, d. 463, fols. 31v–33r; and *MOZKh* 1899a, 160–61.
38. *SSSTG* 1889, pt. 3, 29.
39. RGIA, fond 1284, op. 194, d. 84, fol. 3r; RGIA, fond 1282, op. 3, d. 463, fols. 1r–31r; and RGIA, fond 1282, op. 3, d. 545, fols. 24r–24v.
40. RGIA, fond 1263, op. 4, d. 57, fols. 1026r–1026v; RGIA, fond 1284, op. 194, d. 44; and *TMKN*, vol. 46, 379.
41. *SZ1905*, vol. 16, 39–40; vol. 14, 42; and vol. 42, 44–45.
42. *MOZE* 1906, pt. 1, 421.
43. I am indebted to B. N. Mironov for helping me understand this means of measurement. For a good introduction in English, see Dollar and Jensen 1971, 137ff.
44. RGIA, fond 1284, op. 223, d. 239, fol. 9r.
45. Oleksenko 1910, 40–41.
46. Ibid., 42–44.
47. *VEZ* (31 January 1905), 6; *TMKN*, vol. 46, 378; and vol. 40, 130.
48. RGIA fond 1284, op. 223, d. 159, fols. 11v–12r. On the peasant reluctance to support schools, see also "Proekt sel´skokhoziaistvennogo uchilishcha s. Bobrovskogo" 1869, appendix 1.
49. Borets 1903, 406.
50. One expressed concern was the low incentive given to teachers with inadequate salaries. See RGIA, fond 1284, op. 223, d. 239, fol. 28v.
51. RGIA, fond 1282, op. 3, d. 463, fols. 30v–31r. For an excellent overview of peasant justice in the late years of the Russian Empire, see Frank 1999.
52. RGIA, fond 1282, op. 3, d. 526, fol. 4r; RGIA, fond 1284, op. 194, d. 89, fol. 6r.
53. *MOZE* 1902, 68, 87; *MOZE* 1899, pt. 1, 133; and *SSSE*, vol. 2, 63.
54. 294,000 desiatinas were leased in Kherson province. See *MVU01*, vol. 1, 126–28; and Kutov 1906, 8.
55. RGIA, fond 1405, op. 193, d. 966, fol. 63r; Borovoi and Kotsievskii 1971, 273; Karyshev 1897, 318.
56. Bertenson 1899, 19.
57. *MSDZ*, tables 1–3.
58. For corresponding figures, see *MVU01*, vol. 1, 94–103. For an excellent overview of the 1877–78 land survey, see Tarasiuk 1981.
59. Part of the problem in determining land ownership by "peasants" in late Imperial Russia is that the term by then included former colonists, some of whom were energetically involved in the purchase of former noble lands.
60. *SEOKh* 1908, 5; and *SZ1905*, vol. 16, 29. *PV97*, vol. 47, vii; and *PNSP za 1902*

god 1904, 32. These figures indicate net gains in landholdings during these years. Gross gains by Germans between 1895 and 1900 were 196,087 desiatinas in Kherson province; with peasants obtaining slightly over 140,000 desiatinas. It should be noted that Germans were also involved to some degree in land sales as well as purchases. See *TMKN*, vol. 46, 121.

61. RGIA, fond 1284, op. 194, d. 84, fol. 3r.
62. *DZhK*, vol. 1, appendix 6, pt. 2, 66. See also Shestakov 1924, 50.
63. Pedunov 1889, 49–62; *NDOKh*, 25; L. Ivanov 1961, 324; and Kuntshevich 1964, 616.
64. Gulak 1860b, 98–101; Skuratov 1863, 190; Skal′kovs′kyi 1873, 51; and Armfeld 1872, 93–94.
65. Neruchev 1877, 135. On the movement of seasonal laborers, see Shimkin 1873, 310–11; and Dobrianskii 1871, 436; Alferakii 1863, 103; and "Trudy chetvertogo s″ezda Russkikh khoziaiev v Kharkove" 1875, 19.
66. Khliudzinskii 1880, 505–6; Rybkin 1873, 9; and Alferakii 1863, 104–9.
67. RGIA, fond 1290, op. 6, d. 414, fols. 6r–6v; Dobrianskii 1871, 436; and *TPS*, 20.
68. "Prilozhenie k dokladu kommissii po voprosu o rabochikh" 1872, 15; "Trudy chetvertogo s″ezda Russkikh khoziaiev v Kharkove" 1875, 21; Bunitskii 1866, 306; *DZhK*, vol. 1, 213–16; and Musin-Pushkin 1870, 612. For complete lists of specific years, see Bunitskii 1866, 306.
69. "Trudy chetvertogo s″ezda Russkikh khoziaiev v Kharkove" 1875, 18; Armfeld 1872, 95; Khristoforov 1865, 175; and Skal′kovs′kyi 1873, 54–55.
70. *GSKh* 1888, vol. 2, pp. 5, 10, and 14; and *GSKh* 1903, vol. 4, pp. 25, 27, and 29. See for example, *GSKh* 1886, vol. 2, pp. 7, 12, and 15; *GSKh* 1889, vol. 2, pp. 5, 7, and 9; *GSKh* 1895, vol. 4, pp. 36, 37, and 41; and *GSKh* 1901, vol. 4, pp. 27, 29, and 30.
71. L. Ivanov 1961, 325; Khizhniakov 1900, 128–29; and Arakcheev 1904, 1382. On the medical ailments of these workers, see Ivarov 1889, 9–11.
72. Khizniakov 1899a, 6.
73. Kablukov 1899, 42; *NDOKh*, 25; *TMKN*, vol. 40, 104; and Mixter 1991, 322–23.
74. Khizhniakov 1900, 166.
75. Khizhniakov 1899a, 43.
76. RGIA, fond 1284, op. 194, d. 89, fols. 2r–4r; RGIA, fond 1284, op. 223, d. 239, fols. 8v–9r, 33; and *MOZE* 1899, pt. 1, 13–15.
77. *OEGZ* 1900, 10–11.
78. DAOO, fond 1, op. 248, d. 1593, fols. 52v–53r; RGIA, fond 1284, op. 194, d. 111, fol. 3r; and Boiko 1899, 429–30.
79. RGIA, fond 1284, op. 194, d. 111, fol. 3v.
80. On peasants and the notion of private property, see Mironov 1984.

81. RGIA, fond 1284, op. 194, d. 101, fol. 16r. See also fond 1263, op. 4, d. 50, fol. 134v.
82. See, for example, RGIA, fond 1282, op. 3, d. 545, fol. 28r.

Chapter Eight

1. RGIA, fond 1405, op. 108, d. 6893, fols. 5r–9r.
2. DAOO, fond 634, op. 1, d. 620, fol. 3r.
3. This argument is found in the governor's report for Kherson province as early as 1880. See RGIA, fond 1284, op. 70, d. 248, fol. 5v. On the importance of agricultural questions to state policy makers, see Siminova 1987, 10.
4. RGIA, fond 1284, op. 223, d. 168, fol. 45r.
5. "*...na voinu berut, a zemli ne daiut. Kuda zhe nam det′sia?*" RGIA, fond 1405, op. 107, d. 9619, fols. 1r–2v.
6. "Agrarnoe dvizhenie v Rossii v 1905–1906 gg." 1908, 443. The quotation is from *VKK* 1935, 28.
7. Field 1976b, 14–17.
8. DAOO, fond 634, op. 1, d. 620, fol. 3r. Cf. Prokopovich 1912, 47–48.
9. RGIA, fond 1405, op. 194, d. 72, fol. 30r. Cf. RGIA, fond 1405, op. 246, d. 1067, fols. 1r–2r.
10. Moon 1992, 14–17.
11. DAOO, fond 634, op.1, d. 402, fol. 17r; and DAOO, fond 634, op. 1, d. 281, fol. 1r.
12. DAOO, fond 634, op. 1, d. 232, fol. 271r; and Seregny 1989, 182–83.
13. *VKK*, 22.
14. Ibid., 21–24; DAOO, fond 634, op. 1, d. 233, fol. 37r; and DAOO, fond 634, op. 1, d. 232, fol. 310r.
15. RGIA, fond 1405, op. 194, d. 72, fol. 38r.
16. "Agrarnoe dvizhenie v Rossii v 1905–1906 gg." 1908, 418.
17. RGIA, fond 1405, op. 194, d. 72, fols. 2r–10r.
18. Shanin 1986, 155. The changed attitude to peasants by the Russian state in 1907 was reflected in the new electoral law of 3 June 1907. See Hosking 1973, 42–43.
19. RGIA, fond 1263, op. 4, d. 57, fol. 1020v; RGIA, fond 1405, op. 246, d. 1067, fols. 1r–2r; DAOO, fond 634, op. 1, d. 402, fol. 13r; RGIA, fond 1405, op. 193, d. 1534, fols. 2v–3r; RGIA, fond 1405, op. 118, d. 2112; and "Agrarnoe dvizhenie v Rossii v 1905–1906 gg." 1908, 418.
20. Seregny 1991, 373.
21. Yang 1987, 500.
22. Shanin 1986, 120.
23. *PDSV*, 34.

24. RGIA, fond 1405, op. 116, d. 267, fols. 10v–11r.
25. Ascher 1988, 165. Translated by Ascher.
26. RGIA, fond 1284, op. 194, d. 84, fols. 3r–4r; and RGIA, fond 1405, op. 194, d. 72, fol. 10r; and RGIA, fond 1284, op. 194, d. 89, fols. 5v–6r.
27. RGIA, fond 1284, op. 194, d, 101, fol. 16r. See also RGIA, fond 1263, op. 4, d. 50, fol. 134v.
28. Smirnov 1904, 63.
29. "Prigovor Kalginskogo sel′skogo skhola Ivanovskoi volosti, postanovlen Noiabria 28 dnia 1905 goda" 1905, 165; and Enpe 1905, 33–34.
30. Dubrovskii 1956, 46, 59–60; and Ascher 1988, 161–63.
31. "Agrarnoe dvizhenie v Rossii v 1905–1906 gg." 1908, 399.
32. RGIA, fond 1405, op. 194, d. 78, fol. 17r; and "Agrarnoe dvizhenie v Rossii v 1905–1906 gg." 1908, 429.
33. RGIA, fond 1405, op. 107, d. 8970, fol. 1r; and RGIA, fond 1284, op. 194, d. 44, fols. 5v–6r. For a similar report dealing with Katerynoslav province, see RGIA, fond 1284, op. 194, d. 111, fol. 3v.
34. RGIA, fond 1405, op. 193, d. 966, fol. 63r; and RGIA, fond 1405, op. 194, d. 72, fos. 29r–29v.
35. DAOO, fond 634, op. 1, d. 840, fols. 18r–72v; and RGIA, fond 1405, op. 194, d. 72, fol. 29r.
36. *VKK*, 37; and *SEOKh* 1908, 115.
37. Kogon 1928, 182.
38. RGIA, fond 1405, op. 107, d. 8156, fols. 3v, 5r; RGIA, fond 1405, op. 107, d. 7936, fol. 4r; RGIA, fond 1405, op. 108, d. 6988, fols. 2r, 8v; and "Agrarnoe dvizhenie v Rossii v 1905–1906 gg." 1908, 432–33, 472.
39. RGIA, fond 1405, op. 108, d. 6988, fols. 8v; RGIA, fond 1405, op. 194, d. 54, ch. 1, fols. 89r, 109r, and 114r; and Dubrovskii 1956, 51–54.
40. "Agrarnoe dvizhenie v Rossii v 1905–1906 gg." 1908, 470.
41. Ibid., 469–70.
42. Ibid., 408–9. See also RGIA, fond 1263, op. 4, d. 52, fol. 15r.
43. "Agrarnoe dvizhenie v Rossii v 1905–1906 gg." 1908, 413–15, 440. Wealthy peasants were generally considered those with more than thirty desiatinas of purchased land.
44. "Agrarnoe dvizhenie v Rossii v 1905–1906 gg." 1908, 443.
45. DAOO, fond 634, op. 1, d. 620, fols. 3r–4r; DAOO, fond 634, op. 1, d. 233, fol. 84r; RGIA, fond 1291, op. 122, d. 123, fol. 34v; RGIA, fond 1405, op. 193, d. 966, fol. 63v; RGIA, fond 1405, op. 194, d. 78, fols. 17r–17v; and Prokopovich 1912, 47–48.
46. H. Friesen 1990, 21–22.
47. Starr 1982, 13.
48. RGIA, fond 1405, op. 194, d. 72, fol. 8r; RGIA fond 1405, op. 194, d. 78, fols. 3r–3v; RGIA, fond 1405, op. 116, d. 446, fol. 7v; and *VKK* 1935, 37.

49. RGIA, fond 1291, op. 122, d. 123, fols. 75r–76v; and Bushnell 1985, 78–79, 133–34.
50. RGIA, fond 1405, op. 194, d. 54, ch. 1, p. 7.
51. Prokopovich 1912, 66–69; and RGIA fond 1263, op. 4, d. 52, fol. 16v.
52. RGIA, fond 1291, op. 122, d. 123, fol. 77r; and Bushnell 1985, ch. 5.
53. RGIA, fond 1405, op. 194, d. 72, fols. 18r–19v.
54. RGIA, fond 1405, op. 194, d. 54, ch. 1, p. 114; and RGIA, fond 1363, op. 2, d. 1307, fols. 2r–2v; and RGIA, fond 1363, op. 3, d. 613, fol. 3v.
55. RGIA, fond 1405, op. 108, d. 8849, fol. 7v; and RGIA, fond 1405, op. 117, d. 907, fols. 2r–2v.
56. Prokopovich 1912, 70; *SKhZ* (February 1906): 58; and "Agrarnoe dvizhenie v Rossii v 1905–1906 gg." 1908, 445.
57. RGIA, fond 1284, op. 194, d. 63, fol. 12r; and "Agrarnoe dvizhenie v Rossii v 1905–1906 gg." 1908, 399.

Conclusion

1. Khmirov 1899, 90.
2. Ibid., 32–33.
3. Ibid., 16–24.
4. Romanov 1901, 265.
5. RGIA, fond 1281, op. 6, d. 48, fols. 6r–6v. For a recent study of the Molochna basin, consult Staples 2003.
6. DAOO, fond 1, op. 249, d. 416, fol. 9v; and Maksimenko 1957, 69.
7. L. Friesen 1992, 56–69.

Glossary

arshin. 71 centimeters or 28 inches.
barshchina. Peasant labor obligation.
brichki. Carts used by peasants for grain or human cartage.
brynza. Sheep's milk cheese.
bukker. A plowlike implement.
chetvert. 2.099 kilograms or 5.77 bushels.
chumak. Peasant ox-cart driver.
darstvennik. Former household serf.
desiatina. 1.09 hectares or 2.7 acres.
desiatinshchik. A category of landless peasant after 1861.
funt. 0.41 kilograms, or 0.9 pounds.
guberniia. Imperial province comprised of **uezd**s.
iarmark. Village or town fair.
khutor. Farmstead.
lobogreika. An animal-powered grain reaper.
meshchanin. Petty bourgeois; lower middle class.
mir. Peasant commune.
muzhik. Peasant male.
oblast. Administrative territory or province.
obrok. Peasant payment in cash or kind.
sel′skoe obshchestvo. Peasant village community.
obshchina. peasant commune as economic unit.
okrug. Administrative region or district.
pood. 16.38 kilograms or 36 pounds.
razdel. Peasant household division.

sazhen. 2.13 meters or 7 feet.
Sich. Fortified Cossack settlement.
uezd. District or county comprised of **volosts**.
ukase. Imperial edict.
usad′ba. Peasant yard, including buildings.
vershok. 4.45 centimeters or 1.75 inches.
verst. 1.065 kilometers or 0.663 miles.
volost. Smaller territorial administrative unit.
zemstvo. **Uezd** and **guberniia** assemblies established after 1864.

References

Archives

Archive of the Historical Faculty, Academy of Sciences, St. Petersburg, Russia
Conrad Grebel University College Archive, Waterloo, Canada
David Rempel Collection, University of Toronto Archive, Toronto, Canada
Dnipropetrovsk State Archive, Dnipropetrovsk, Ukraine
Odesa State Regional Archive (Derzhavnyi arkhiv Odes´koï oblasti), Odesa, Ukraine
Peter Braun Archive, Conrad Grebel University College, Waterloo, Ontario, Canada
Rossisskii gosudarstvennyi istoricheskii arkhiv, St. Petersburg, Russia

Published Sources

Aleksandrov, V. A. 1976. *Sel´skaia obshchina v Rossii (XVII–nachalo XIX v.).* Moscow.

"Agrarnoe dvizhenie v Rossii v 1905–1906 gg." 1908. *TIVEO* (July–October): 394–539.

Alferakii, Dmitrii. 1863. "O vol´non'aemnykh rabochikh v Novorossiiskom krae, a imenno vosle Taganroga." *TIVEO* (no. 2): 101–18.

Alekseev, V. V. 1910. "Raspredelenie naseleniia po territorii Novorossiiskikh gubernii, ego etnograficheskii sostav, byt´ i kul´tura." In STS, 172–227.

Andreevskii, I. E., ed. 1890–1907. *Entsiklopedicheskii slovar´*. 41 vols. St. Petersburg.

Anfimov, A. M. 1961. *Zemel′naia arenda v Rossii v nachale XX veka*. Moscow.

———. 1969. *Krupnoe pomeshchich′e khoziaistvo Evropeiskoi Rossii*. Moscow.

———. 1980. *Krest′ianskoe khoziaistvo Evropeiskoi Rossii, 1881–1904 gg*. Moscow.

———. 1984. *Ekonomicheskoe polozhenie i klassovaia bor′ba krest′ian Evropeiskoi Rossii, 1881–1904 gg*. Moscow.

Arakcheev, N. 1904. "Zemskie vrachebno-prodovol′stvennye punkty dlia prishlykh sel′skokhoziaistvennye rabochikh v Ekaterinoslavskoi gubernii (1899–1903)." *VEZ* (11 November): 1382–85.

Armfeld, A. 1872. "Nedostotatok i dorogovizna rabochikh ruk v Novorossiiskom krae." *ZIOS* (no. 1): 90–108.

Armstrong, T. B. 1831. *Journals of Travels in the Seat of War, during the Last Two Campaigns of Russia and Turkey*. London.

Ascher, Abraham. 1988. *The Revolution of 1905*. Vol. 1, *Russia in Disarray*. Stanford.

Auerbach, H. 1965. *Die Besiedelung der Suedukraine in den Jahren 1774–1787*. Wiesbaden.

Avanas′ev-Chuzhbinskii, A. 1861. *Poezdka v iuzhnuiu Rossiiu*. St. Petersburg.

Avgustinovich, Petr. 1865. "K voprosu ob uluchshenii tonkorunnogo ovtsevodstva na Rossii." *ZIOS*: 233–54.

Babenko, V. A. 1905. "Etnograficheskoe opisanie Ekaterinoslavskoi gubernii." *VEZ* (21 July): 731–46.

Bahalii [Bagalei], D. I. 1889. *Kolonizatsiia Novorossiiskogo kraia i pervye shagi ego po puti kul′tury. Istoricheskii etiud*. Kyiv.

Bakulev, G. D. 1953. *Chernaia metallurgia iuga Rossii*. Moscow.

———. 1955. *Razvitie ugol′noi promyshlennosti Donetskogo basseina*. Moscow.

Ballion, [first name unknown]. 1873. "O vrednykh v sel′skokhoziaistvennom otnoshenii nasekomykh Khersonskoi gubernii." *SKhZ* (pt. 1, March): 24–25.

Barnard, Alan. 1958. *The Australian Wool Market, 1840–1900*. Melbourne.

Bartlett, Roger P. 1979. *Human Capital: The Settlement of Foreigners in Russia, 1762–1804*. Cambridge.

———, ed. 1990. *Land Commune and Peasant Community in Russia: Communal Forms in Imperial and Early Soviet Society*. Houndmills.

Barykov, F. L., A. V. Polovtsov, and P. A. Sokolovskii, eds. 1880. *Sbornik materialov dlia izucheniia sel′skoi pozemel′noi obshchiny*. St. Petersburg.

Beauplan, Guillaume le Vasseur Sieur de. 1959. *A Description of Ukraine*. Translated by Andrew B. Pernal and Dennis F. Essar. New York.

Beckinsale, R. P., and J. M. Houston, eds. 1968. *Urbanization and its Problems: Essays in Honour of E. W. Gilbert*. Oxford.

Benedskii, Alexander. 1861. "O naime rabochikh liudei." *ZIOS*: 99–104.

Bertenson, V. 1895. "Po iugu Rossii." *Khoziain*, no. 39: 774–75.

———. 1899. "Po khoziaistvam iuga." *ZIOS* (December): 19–51.

Bezpomoshchnyi. 1878. "Iz Elisavetgradskogo uezda." *TIVEO*, no. 1: 116–21.

Bideleux, Robert. 1990. "Agricultural Advance Under the Russian Village Commune System," in *Land Commune and Peasant Community in Russia: Communal Forms in Imperial and Early Soviet Society*, ed. Roger P. Bartlett, 196–218. Houndmills.

Billington, Ray Allen. 1971. *The American Frontier Thesis: Attack and Defense*. Rev. ed. American Historical Association Pamphlet 101. Washington

Biriukovich, V. V., ed. 1903. *Spravochnaia svedeniia o deiatel´nosti zemstv po sel´skomu khoziaistvu (po dannym na 1902 god)*. St. Petersburg.

Blainey, Geoffrey. 1982. *The Tyranny of Distance: How Distance Shaped Australia's History*. Melbourne.

Bogue, Allan G. 1963. *From Prairie to Corn Belt: Farming on the Illinois and Iowa Prairies in the Nineteenth Century*. Chicago.

Boiko, G. 1899. "Iz Khersonskogo zemstva." *Zemledel´cheskaia gazeta 1899 goda* (no. 20, 15 March): 429–30.

Boiko, Ia. V. 1993. *Zaselenie iuzhnoi Ukrainy 1860–1890 gg. (istoriko-ekonomichesko issledovanie)*. Cherkassy.

Borets, I. 1903. "Ocherk deiatel´nosti zemskikh uchrezhdenii Ekaterinoslavskoi gubernii po narodnomu obrazovaniiu." *VEZ* (28 April): 406.

Borinevich, A. S. 1890. "Ocherk khlebnoi torgovli g. Odessy." *ZIOS* (no. 3): 1–16.

———. ed. 1895. *Sistematicheskii ukazatel´ statei, protokolov, otchetov i proch., pomeshchennykh v "Listakh" i "Zapiskakh" Imperatorskogo Obshchestva sel´skogo khoziaistva iuzhnoi Rossii*. Odesa.

Borisov, N. I. 1890. "Opyty, nabliudeniia i zametki po sel´skomy khoziaistvu Iuga Rossii." *ZIOS* (May–June): 49–68.

Borisov, V. 1876. "Desiatinshchiki Khersonskoi gubernii." *SKhL* (February): 212–20; (July): 317–27; and (December): 367–86.

———. 1877. "Posevy i urozhai khlebov za 50 let." *SKhL* (September): 1–22.

———. 1878. "Sel´skokhoziaistvennye i ekonomicheskie ocherki Khersonskoi gubernii." *TIVEO* 2 (pt. 1): 65–74.

Borisov, V., and N. Kalageorgi. 1875. "Ekskursia na reku Molochniiu." *SKhL* (January): 1–29; (February): 127–37; (March) 313–35; (April): 395–408.

Borovoi, S. Ia. 1964. "O nekotorykh osobennostiakh agrarnogo stroia stepnoi Ukrainy v predreformennyi period." *EAIVE*: 351–77.

———. 1970. "K voprosu o primenenii naemnogo truda v pomeshchichikh khoziaistvakh stepnoi Ukrainy v predreformennyi period." *EAIVE*: 290–96.

———. 1972. "K voprosu o zadolzhennosti pomeshchichego zemlevladeniia v predreformennyi period." *EAIVE*: 197–203.

Borovoi, S. Ia., and A.S. Kotsievskii. 1971. "K voprosu o kapitalisticheskoi evoliutsii iuzhnoukrainskogo sela v poreformennyi periode." *EAIVE*: 270–80.

Boserup, Ester. 1973. *The Conditions of Agricultural Growth: The Economics of Agrarian Change under Population Pressure.* Chicago.

Brandes, Detlef. 1993. *Von den Zaren adoptiert. Die deutschen Kolonisten und die Balkansiedler in Neurussland und Bessarabien, 1751–1914.* Munich.

Braudel, Fernand. 1977. *Afterthoughts on Material Civilization and Capitalism.* Baltimore.

———. 1982. *Civilization and Capitalism 15th–18th Century.* Vol. 3, *The Perspective of the World.* New York.

Bremner, Robert. 1840. *Excursions in the Interior of Russia.* London.

Brower, Daniel R., and Edward J. Lazzerini, eds. 1997. *Russia's Orient: Imperial Borderlands and Peoples, 1700–1917.* Bloomington.

Bulatsel′, S. 1866. "Zemledelie v Slav′ianoserbskom uezde, Ekaterinoslavskoi gubernii." *TIVEO* (no. 2): 333–49.

Bunitskii, K. 1866. "Vychislenie dnei prazdnyemykh v techenii goda, rabochimi liudmi v Aleksandrovskom uezde, Ekaterinoslavskoi gubernii." *ZIOS*: 306–11.

Burakov, P. 1892. *O vozmozhnykh merakh bor′by s zusychami.* Odesa.

Bush, M. L., ed. 1996. *Serfdom and Slavery: Studies in Legal Bondage.* London.

Bushnell, John. 1985. *Mutiny Amid Repression: Russian Soldiers in the Revolution of 1905–1906.* Bloomington.

Bychikhin, A. A. 1897. "Nastoiaschee polozhenie mest′nago ogorodnichestva i ego nuzhdy." *ZIOS* (July–August): 11–23.

Bykhovets, O. G. 1984. "'Prigovornoe' dvizhenie krest′ian v 1905–1907 gg. (metody izucheniia po materialam Samarskoi i Voronezhskoi gubernii)." Ph. D. diss., Moscow State University.

Carstensen, Fred V. 1984. *American Enterprise in Foreign Markets: Studies of Singer and International Harvester in Imperial Russia.* Chapel Hill.

Chervinskii, N. P. 1951. *Izbrannye sochineniia.* Moscow.

Christian, David, and R. E. F. Smith. 1984. *Bread and Salt.* Cambridge.

Chuprov, A. I., and A. S. Posnikov, eds. 1897. *Vliianie urozhaev i khlebnykh tsen po nekotoryia storony russkogo narodnogo khoziaistva.* 2 vols. St. Petersburg.

Collins, E. J. T. 1969. "Labour supply and demand in European agriculture 1800–1880." In Jones and Woolf, 61–94.

Cornies, Johann. 1843. "O sostoianii khoziaistva v Molochanskikh menonistkikh koloniiakh v 1842 gody." *ZhMGI* (no. 8): 64–78.

———. 1844. "O sostoianii khoziaistva v Molochanskikh menonistkikh koloniiakh v 1843 gody." *ZhMGI* (no. 11): 129–44.

Crowley, F. K., ed. 1974. *A New History of Australia.* Melbourne.

Demidov, Anatolii. 1853. *Travels in southern Russia and the Crimea through Hungary, Wallachia and Moldavia during the Year 1837.* 2 vols. London.

Derzhavin, N. 1908. "Bol′garskie kolonii novorossiiskogo kraia: Khersonskaia i Tavricheskaia gubernii." *ITUAK* 41:1–237.

Dobrianskii, Stepan. 1871. "Chto takoi Ekaterinoslavskaia stepi, otnositel′no zemledeliia." *TIVEO* (no. 4): 433–39.

"Doklad kommissii po voprosu o nuzhdakh sel′skogo khoziaistva v Novorossiiskom krae." 1872. *ZIOS* (no. 3): 3–12.

Doklad, zhurnali kommissii dlia issledovaniia nyneshnego polozheniia sel′skogo khoziaistva i sel′skoi proizvoditel′nosti v Rossii. 1873. 7 vols. St. Petersburg.

Dollar, Charles M., and Richard J. Jensen. 1971. *Historian's Guide to Statistics.* New York.

Druzhinin, N. M. 1946 and 1958. *Gosudarstvennye krest′iane i reforma P. D. Kiseleva.* 2 vols. Moscow.

———. 1978. *Russkaia derevnia na perelome 1861–1880 gg.* Moscow.

Druzhinina, E. I. 1959. *Severnoe prichernomore v 1775–1800 gg.* Moscow.

———. 1966. "Klassovaia bor′ba krest′ian iuzhnoi Ukrainy v pervoi chetverti XIX veka." *EAIVE*: 572–83.

———. 1970. *Iuzhnaia Ukraina v 1800–1825 gg.* Moscow.

———. 1981. *Iuzhnaia Ukraina v period krizisa feodalizma 1825–1860 gg.* Moscow.

Dubrovin, N. 1885–1889. *Prisoedinenie Kryma v Rossii.* 4 vols. St. Petersburg.

Dubrovskii, S. M. 1956. *Krest′ianskoe dvizhenie v revoliutsii 1905–1907 gg.* Moscow.

———. 1975. *Sel′skoe khoziaistvo i krest′ianstvo Rossii v period imperializma.* Moscow.

Dyck, Harvey L., ed. and trans. 1982a. "The German Conquest of Southern Russia." *MQR* 56:318–41.

———. 1982b. "Russian Mennonitism and the Challenge of Russian Nationalism." *MQR* 56:307–18.

———, ed. and trans. 1984a. "Agronomist Gavel's Biography of Johann Cornies (1789–1848)." *JMS* 2:35–36.

———. 1984b. "Russian Servitor and Mennonite Hero: Light and Shadow in Images of Johann Cornies." *JMS* 2:9–28.

———, ed. and trans. 1991. *A Mennonite in Russia: The Diaries of Jacob D. Epp, 1851–1880.* Toronto.

Edelman, Robert. 1987. *Proletarian Peasants: The Revolution of 1905 in Russia's Southwest.* Ithaca, N.Y.

Egiazarova, N. A. 1959. *Agrarnyi krizis kontsa XIX veka v Rossii.* Moscow.

Ehrt, Adolf. 1932. *Das Mennonitentum in Russland von seiner Einwanderung bis zur Gegenwart.* Langensalza.

Eklof, Ben. 1986. *Russian Peasant Schools: Officialdom, Village Culture and Popular Pedagogy, 1861–1914.* Berkeley.

Eklof, Ben, John Bushnell, and Larissa Zakharova, eds. 1994. *Russia's Great Reforms, 1855–1881*. Bloomington.

Encyclopedia of Ukraine. 1984–1993. 5 vols. Toronto.

Enpe. 1905. "S. Rozhdestvenskoe, Dneprovskogo uezda." *VTZ* (March): 33–34.

Epp, David H. 1911. "Aus der Kindheitsgeschichte der Deutschen Industrie in den Kolonien Sued-Russlands," *Der Botschafter*, nos. 51–96.

Etnografiia vostochnykh Slavian: Ocherki traditsionnoi kul′tury. 1987. Moscow.

"Evgenievskaia volost′ (Tiraspolskogo uezda, Khersonskoi gubernii): Statistiko-ekonomicheskoi opisanie." 1888. *SKhZ* (March): 30–108.

Fedor, Thomas Stanley. 1975. *Patterns of Urban Growth in the Russian Empire during the Nineteenth Century*. Chicago.

Fedorov, P. V. 1894. "Znachenie mashin v iuzhno-russkikh khoziaistvakh," *SKh* (10 June): 677–79.

Felibert, A. 1863. "O merakh k prekrashcheniiu chumy rogatogo skota." *ZIOS*: 211–18.

Field, Daniel. 1976a. *The End of Serfdom: Nobility and Bureaucracy in Russia, 1855–1861*. Cambridge, Mass.

———. 1976b. *Rebels in the Name of the Tsar*. Boston.

———. 1994. "The Year of Jubilee." In Eklof, Bushnell, and Zakharova 1994: 40–57.

Fisher, Alan. 1972. *The Russian Annexation of the Crimea, 1772–1783*. Cambridge.

Fortunatov, A. F. 1892. *Itogi ekonomicheskogo issledovanniia Rossii po dannym zemskoi statistiki*. Vol. 1, *Obshchii obzor zemskoi statistiki krest′ianskogo khoziaistva*. Moscow.

———. 1921. *O statistike. Uchebnoe posobie*. Moscow.

Frank, Stephen. 1999. *Crime, Cultural Conflict, and Justice in Rural Russia, 1856–1914*. Berkeley.

Friedgut, Theodore H. 1989–1994. *Iuzovka and Revolution*. Vol. 1, *Life and Work in Russia's Donbass, 1869–1924* and vol. 2, *Politics and Revolution in Russia's Donbass, 1869–1924*. Princeton.

Friesen, Helena Goossen. 1990. *Daydreams and Nightmares: Life on the Wintergruen Estate*. Winnipeg.

Friesen, John. 1994. *Against the Wind: The Story of Four Mennonite Villages (Gnadental, Gruenfeld, New-chortitza, and Steinfeld) in the Southern Ukraine, 1872–1943*. Winnipeg.

Friesen, Leonard G. 1992. "Mennonites and Their Peasant Neighbours in Ukraine before 1900." *JMS* 10:56–69.

———. 1994. "Bukkers, Plows and Lobogreikas: Peasant Acquisition of Agricultural Implements in New Russia before 1900." *Russian Review* 53:399–418.

Fyfe, Christopher. 1983. *The Bale Fillers: Western Australian Wool, 1826–1916*. Nedlands.

G., M. 1888. "Iz Ananevskogo uezda." *SKh* (1 January): 168.

Gałęski, Bogusław. 1972. *Basic Concepts of Rural Sociology*. Trans. H. C. Stevens. Manchester.

Ganner, A. V. 1890. "K voprosu ob upadke tsen na sherst′ i o merakh k ulushcheniia sherstianogo rynka." *ZIOS* (January–February): 15–24.

Garris, E. G. 1890. "Obiasnitel′naia zapiska k proektu zemskikh elevatorov v Odesse." *ZIOS* (May–June): 12–15.

Geisinger, Adam. 1974. *From Catherine to Khrushchev: The Story of Russia's Germans*. Winnipeg.

Gel′rot, M. 1899. "K mobilizatsii zemel′ krestianskikh obshchesv Ekaterinoslavskoi gubernii (1877–1897 gg.)." *Zhizn′* (August): 1283–1301.

God v sel′skokhoziaistvennom otnoshenii, po otvetam, poluchennym ot khoziaev. 1881–1917. St. Petersburg.

Goerz, H. 1957. *Die mennonitischen Siedlungen der Krim*. Winnipeg.

Gogol, Nikolai. [1971]. *Taras Bulba: Povest′*. Letchworth.

Gokhgeim, B. L. 1904. "Zemskiia pokazatel′nyia polia Verkhnedneprovskogo uezda." *VEZ* (no. 23): 703 6.

Golobutskii, V. A. 1957. *Zaporozhskoe kazachestvo*. Kyiv.

Gorskii, K. 1871. "K voprosu o vygodnosti soderzhaniia tonkorunnykh ovets." *ZIOS*: 199–207.

Gosudarstvennyi arkhiv Odesskoi oblasti. Putevoditel′. 1961. Odesa.

Gr., A. 1863. "Khoziaistvennyia zametki." *ZIOS*: 200–10, 249–64.

Gregory, Paul R. 1994. *Before Command: An Economic History of Russia from Emancipation to the First Five-year Plan*. Princeton.

Grigg, David. 1974. *The Agricultural Systems of the World: An Evolutionary Approach*. Cambridge.

———. 1989. *English Agriculture: An Historical Perspective*. Oxford.

———. 1992. *The Transformation of Agriculture in the West*. Oxford.

Grigorev, A. 1864. "Po povodu predstoiashchikh zemskikh uchrezhdenii." *ZIOS*: 413–42.

Grotto-Slepikovskii. 1897. "Ocherki iz istorii iuzhnorusskogo sel′skogo khoziaistva." *SKhL* 185 (April): 39–94.

Gulak, I. I. 1843. "O skotovodstve v iuzhnom krae Rossii." *ZhMGI* (no. 8): 233–40.

———. 1860a. "Sol′—kak neobkhodimaia pribava dlia kormu skota." *ZIOS*: 96–98.

———. 1860b. "Vopros, otnositel′no prilozheniia k khoziaistvo vol′nogo truda." *ZIOS*: 98–101.

Gulak, I. I. 1865. "Na statiu g. Avgustinovicha: k voprosu ob uluchshenii ton′korunnogo ovtsevodstva na iug Rossii." *ZIOS*: 505–16.

———. 1866. "Vzgliad na tepereshnoe zemledelie." *ZIOS*: 310.

Hamburg, Gary. 1984. *The Politics of the Russian Nobility, 1881–1905*. New Brunswick, N.J.

Harvey, Mose L. 1938. "The Development of Russian Commerce on the Black Sea and Its Significance." Ph.D. diss., University of California, Berkeley.

Haxthausen, August Freiherrn von. 1847–1852. *Studien über die innern Zustände, das Volksleben und Inbesondere die ländlichen Einrichtungen Russlands*. 3 vols. Hanover.

———. 1856. *The Russian Empire, Its People, Institutions, and Resources*. 2 vols. London.

Herlihy, Patricia. 1963. "Russian Grain and Mediterranean Markets, 1774–1861." Ph.D. diss., University of Pennsylvania.

———. 1986. *Odessa: A History, 1794–1914*. Cambridge, Mass.

Hoch, Steven L. 1994. "On Good Numbers and Bad: Malthus, Population Trends and Peasant Standard of Living in Late Imperial Russia." *Slavic Review* 53 (Spring): 41–75.

Hoffman, Philip T. 1996. *Growth in a Traditional Society: The French Countryside, 1450–1815*. Princeton.

Holderness, Mary. 1823. *New Russia. Journey from Riga to the Crimea, by way of Kiev; with some Account of the Colonization and the Manners and Customs of the Colonists of New Russia*. London. Reprint, New York, 1970.

Hooson, D. J. M. 1968. "The Growth of Cities in Pre-Soviet Russia." In Beckinsale and Houston 1968, 254–76. Oxford.

Hosking, Geoffrey A. 1973. *The Russian Constitutional Experiment: Government and Duma, 1907–1914*. Cambridge.

Hume, George. 1914. *Thirty-Five Years in Russia*. London.

Iaron, G. 1873. "Rukovodstvo prisoblennoe k raspoznavaniiu predokhranenii i lechenii poval′nykh i zarazitel′nykh boleznei domashnikh zhivotnykh iuzhnogo kraia Rossii," *ZIOS*, appendix, 1–23.

Ianson, Iu. E. 1870. *Statisticheskoe issledovanie o khlebnoi torgovle v Odesskom raione*. St. Petersburg.

Iasman, E. D. 1970. "Popytki vvedeniia uluchshennykh sel′skokhoziaistvennykh orudii v pomeshchich′ikh khoziaistvakh vtoroi poloviny XVIII v. (po materialam Trudov vol′nogo ekonomicheskogo obshchestva)." *EAIVE*: 246–55.

Iavornyts′kyi [Evarnitskii], D. I. 1888. *Zaporozh′e v ostatkakh stariny i predaniiakh naroda*. St. Petersburg.

———. 1898a. *Po sledam Zaporozhtsev*. St. Petersburg.

———. 1898b. *Vol′nosti zaporozhskikh kazakov*. St. Petersburg.

Ignatovich, I. I. 1910. *Pomeshch´i krest´iane nakanune osvobozhdeniia.* 2nd ed. St. Petersburg.

———. 1963. *Krest´ianskoe dvizhenie v Rossii v pervoi chetverti XIX veka.* Moscow.

Irving, T. H. 1974. "1850–1870." In Crowley 1974, 124–64.

Isaac, Franz. 1908. *Die Molotschnaer Mennoniten: Ein Beitrag zur Geschichte derselben.* Halbstadt.

Issledovanie sovremennogo polozheniia tonkorunnogo ovtsevodstva i iuga Rossii. 1882. Edited by A. P. Perepelkin and N. N. Deriagin. Moscow.

Issledovanie sovremennogo sostoianiia ovtsevodstva v Rossii. 1884. Vol. 4. St. Petersburg.

"Istoricheskii ocherk torgovli chernogo i azovskogo moria." 1841. *ZIOS*: 69–77.

Itogi ekonomicheskogo issledovaniia Rossii po dannym zemskoi statistiki. 1892. Vol. 1, *Krest´ianskaia obshchina.* Moscow.

Iuzhanov, P. 1889. "Ssudy pod khleb." *VRSKh*, no. 7 (1 April): 620.

Ivanov, A. 1885. "O poselenii raskol´nikov v predelakh nyneshnei Tavricheskoi gubernii." In *ITUAK* 7:70–80.

Ivanov, L. M. 1961. "O kapitalisticheskoi i otrabotochnoi sistemakh v sel´skom khoziaistve pomeshchikov na Ukraine v kontse XIX v." In *VISKh*, 312–37.

Ivarov, M. 1889. "Statistika dvizheniia naseleniia Khersonskoi gubernii v 1897 godu." *SKhZ* (May): 1–11.

"Iz Dneprovskogo uezda." 1892. *SKh* (28 February): 283.

"Iz Novorossiiskogo kraia." 1871. *Golos* 235, no. 9 (26 August): 1–2.

Izdanie zemstv 34-kh gubernii po obshchei ekonomicheskoi i otsenochnoi statistike, vyshedshchiia za vremia s 1864 g. po 1 ianvaria 1911 g. 1911. St. Petersburg.

"Izvestie o Ekaterinoslavskikh iarmarkakh i v osobennosti o Petropavlovsk uchrezhdeniia dlia sbyta shersti." 1838. *Listki*: 236–45.

Jenkins, D. T., and K. G. Ponting. 1982. *The British Wool Textile Industry 1770–1914.* London.

Jones, E. L. 1981. *The European Miracle: Environments, Economies, and Geopolitics in the History of Europe and Asia.* Cambridge.

———, and S. J. Woolf, eds. 1969. *Agrarian Change and Economic Development: The Historical Problems.* London.

K., M. 1837. "Sel´skoe khoziaistvo v Khersonskoi gubernii." *Listki*: 260–72.

K., P. 1889. "Iz Elisavetgradskago uezda, Khersonskoi gub." *SKh* (20 January): 211–12.

"K voprosy ob elevatorakh v Rossii." 1887. *ZIOS* (July–August): 302–25.

Kabeshtov, I. M. 1869. "Chto my dolzhny delat´ s nashim ovtsevodstvom." *ZIOS*: 166–74.

Kabeshtov, I. M. 1870. "Prus, ego razmnozhenie, zhizn′, i instinkty." *SKhZ* (February): 1–5.

———. 1887. "Vzgliad na sel′skoe khoziaistvo i na prichiny bezdokhodnosti ego." *ZIOS* (July–August): 246–67.

Kablukov, N. A. 1899. *Ob usloviiakh razvitiia krest′ianskogo khoziaistva v Rossii.* Moscow.

Kabuzan, V. M. 1976. *Zaselenie Novorossii (Ekaterinoslavskoi i Khersonskoi gubernii) v XVIII – pervoi polovine XIX veka (1719–1858 gg.).* Moscow.

———. 1996. *Russkie v mire.* St. Petersburg.

Kahan, Arcadius. 1985. *The Plow, the Hammer, and the Knout: An Economic History of Eighteenth-Century Russia.* Chicago.

Karatygin, E. 1897. "Orudiia i mashiny sel′skokhoziaistvennyia." In Andreevskii 1890–1907, vol. 22, 210–11.

Karnaukhova, E. S. 1951. *Razmeshchenie sel′skogo khoziaistva Rossii v period kapitalizma (1861–1914 gg.).* Moscow.

Karpov, B. G. 1910. "Formy poverkhnosti i stroenie zemnoi kory v predelakh Novorossii." In STS, 1–48.

Karyshev, Nikolai. 1892. *Krest′ianskie vnenadelnye arendy.* Vol. 2, *Itogi ekonomicheskogo issledovaniia Rossii po dannym zemskoi statistiki.* Derpt.

———. 1895. "Krest′ianskoe zemlevladenie i obshchina v Khersonskoi gubernii." *Russkoe bogatstvo* (no. 2): 38–61.

———. 1897. "Krest′ianskiia vne-nadel′nyia arendy v zavisimosti ot kolebanii khlebnykh tsen i urozhaev." In Chuprov and Posnikov 1897, vol. 1, 281–377.

Kasaba, Resat. 1988. *The Ottoman Empire and the World Economy: The Nineteenth Century.* Albany, N.Y.

Kaufman, A. A. 1897. *Krest′ianskaia obshchina v Siberii.* St. Petersburg.

Keep, John L. H. 1985. *Soldiers of the Tsar: Army and Society in Russia, 1462–1874.* Oxford.

Keppen, O. 1864. "Sel′skokhoziaistvennoe polozhenie Tavricheskoi gubernii v 1863 godu." *ZhMGI* 86, no. 8: 476–98.

Khizhniakov, V. V. 1899a. *Prishlye sel′sko-khoziaistvennye rabochie v Khersonskoi gubernii.* Kherson.

———. 1899b. *Polozhenie rabochikh v sel′skom khoziaistve v sanitarnom otnoshenii.* Kherson.

———. 1900. "Sel′skie rabochie na rynkakh Khersonskoi gubernii." *Zhizn′* (January): 128–41; (February): 159–74.

Khliudzinskii, V. 1880. "Organizatsiia naemnogo truda v iuzhnoi Rossii." *ZIOS* (pt. 3, August–September): 505–18.

Khmirov, I. 1899. *Ekaterinoslavskaia guberniia.* 2nd ed. Katerynoslav.

"Khod zemskogo khoziaistva Khersonskoi gubernii za 1871 god." 1872. *SKhZ* (June): 1–61.

Khodskii, L. V. 1891. *Zemlia i zemledelets.* 2 vols. St. Petersburg.

Khristoforov. 1865. "Dannyia dlia otdachi zemli v naem, priniatiia skota na vypas i platy rabochim v Novorossiiskom krae." *ZIOS*: 161–98.

Khromov, P.A. 1963. *Ekonomika Rossii perioda promyshlennogo kapitalizma.* Moscow.

Kingston-Mann, Esther. 1991. "Peasant Communes and Economic Innovation: A Preliminary Inquiry." In Kingston-Mann and Mixter 1991, 23–51.

Kingston-Mann, Esther, and Timothy Mixter, eds. 1991. *Peasant Economy, Culture and Politics of European Russia, 1800–1921.* Princeton.

Kiriakov, M. 1837. "Sostoiane khlebov i trav v Khersonskoi gubernii." *Listki*: 116–20.

Klaus, Aleksandr A. 1869. *Nashi Kolonii. Opyty i materialy po istorii i statistiki inostrannoi kolonizatsii v Rossii.* St. Petersburg. Reprint: Cambridge, 1972.

Klibanov, A. I. 1965. *Istoriia religioznogo sektanstva v Rossii (60-e gody XIX v. - 1917 g.).* Moscow.

Kogon, E. 1928. "Krest′ianskoe dvizhenie v Ekaterinoslavskom uezde v 1905 g." *Letopis Revoliutsii* (no. 6): 169–229.

Kohl, J. G. 1842. *Russia: St. Petersburg, Moscow, Kharkoff, Riga, Odessa, the German Provinces on the Baltic, the Steppes, the Crimea, and the Interior of the Empire.* London: Chapman and Hall. Reprint: New York, 1970.

Kolchin, Peter. 1987. *Unfree Labor: American Slavery and Russian Serfdom.* Cambridge, Mass.

Kolesnik, N. 1904. "Ocherk sostoianiia sel′skogo khoziaistva Slavianoserbskogo uezda." *VEZ* (nos. 41–42): 1227–30.

Korelin, A. P. 1979. *Dvorianstvo v poreformennoi Rossii, 1861–1904 gg.* Moscow.

Korolenko, S. A. 1889. "Zemledelie v Novorossiiskom krae." *TIVEO* (no. 3): 10–21.

Kotelnikov, V. V. "Zhivotnovodstvo," in Timiriazev 1883–, vol. 1, 1–70.

Kotsievskii, A. S. 1962. "Krest′ianskoe dvizhenie v iuzhnoi Ukraine v kontse XVIII–pervoi chetverti XIX v." In *MISKh*, 224–57.

———. 1964a. "Svobodnye arendatory po pomeshchich′ikh zemliakh iuzhnoi Ukrainy (konets XVIII - pervaia polovina XIX v.)." *EAIVE*: 360–67.

———. 1964b. "Evoliutsiia form zemlepol′zovaniia i gosudarstvennykh krest′ian iuzhnoi ukrainy v kontse XVIII–pervoi treti XIX v." *EAIVE*: 420–26.

"Kratkoe istoriko-statisticheskoe obozrenie Tavricheskoi gubernii." 1867. In *PKTG*, 144–247. Simferopol.

"Krest′ianskoe obshchestvo sel′skogo khoziaistva v sel′ Pokrovskom Aleksandriiaskogo uezda." 1903. *VEZ* (11 Dec. 1903): 19–20.

Krestling, I. 1845. "Opisanie zamechatel′nykh khoziaistv v Rossii." *ZhMGI* (no. 17): 107–19.

Kreits, Vitol′d. 1863a. "Rabota loshad′mi." *ZIOS*: 81.

Kreits, Vitol´d. 1863b. "Torgovlia i proizvoditel´nost´ khleba, Ekaterinoslavskoi gubernii, Aleksandrovskogo uezda." *ZIOS*: 416–38.

Krstvtsv, L. 1861. "Khoziaistvennyia vesti iz Pavlogradskogo uezda." *TIVEO* (no. 3): 1–20.

———. 1864. "Khoziaistvennyia vesti iz Pavlogradskogo uezda za 1863g." *TIVEO* (no. 2): 328–41.

Kroeker, N. J. 1981. *First Mennonite Villages in Russia, 1789–1943: Khortitsa-Rosental.* Vancouver.

Krutikov, V. V. 1971. "K voprosu o vlianii zheleznodorozhnogo stroitel´stva na razvitie tiazheloi industrii Ukrainy v 60–70 gg. XIX v." In *Nekotorye problemy sotsialno-ekonomicheskogo razvitiia Ukrainskoi SSR*, pt. 2: 97–107.

Kuleshov, P. N. 1949. *Izbrannye raboty.* Moscow.

Kuntshevich, F. P. 1964. "Razvitie tovarnogo zernogo khoziaistva v Tavricheskoi gubernii v kontse XIX–nachale XX v." *EAIVE*: 613–25.

Kuromiya, Hiroaki. 1998. *Freedom and Terror in the Donbas: A Ukrainian-Russian Borderland, 1870s–1990s.* Cambridge.

Kushakevich, A. 1865. "O saranche na iug Rossii." *SKhL* (August): 365–80.

Kutov, P. 1906. "Zemlevladenie Pavlogradskogo uezda." *VSKh* (5 February): 13–14; and (26 March): 8–10.

Kuzmin, [first name unknown]. 1863. "Sel´skokhoziaistvennoe polozhenie Ekaterinoslavskoi gubernii v 1862 godu." *ZhMGI* 84, no. 9: 42–70.

———. 1864. "Sel´sko-khoziaistvennoe polozhenie Ekaterinoslavskoi gubernii v 1863 godu." *ZhMGI* 85: 199–240.

Lavrentev, L. 1867. "Ocherki khoziaistva v Khersonskoi gubernii." *TIVEO* (no. 3): 112–20; 271–99.

Lavrentov, S. 1867. "Vesti iz Khersonskoi gubernii." *TIVEO* (January): 381–404.

———. 1870a. "Sel´skoe khoziaistvo i sel´skii byt´ Khersonskoi gubernii." *ZIOS* (February): 87–113.

———. 1870b. "Kriticheskii obzor slabykh storon sel´skogo khoziaistva Novorossii." *ZIOS* (August): 551–76.

LeDonne, John P. 1984. *Ruling Russia: Politics and Administration in the Age of Absolutism 1762–1796.* Princeton.

Lenin, Vladimir I. 1986. *Razvitie kapitalizma v Rossii.* Moscow.

Leshchenko, N. N. 1959a. *Krest´ianskoe dvizhenie na Ukraine v sviazi s provedeniem reformy 1861 goda.* Kyiv.

———. 1959b. "Izmeneniia v agrarnykh otnosheniiakh na Ukraine v rezul´tate provedeniia reformy 1861 g." *EAIVE*: 191–99.

———. 1970. "Rezul´taty provedeniia reformy 1861 g. v Ekaterinoslavskoi gubernii po ustavnym gramotam." *EAIVE*: 381–88.

———. 1971. "Reform 1861 goda v Khersonskoi gubernii po ustavnym gramotam." *EAIVE*: 424–34.

Liashchenko, P. I. 1927. *Russkoe zernovoe khoziaistvo v sisteme mirovogo khoziaistva*. Moscow.

Lincoln, W. Bruce. 1977. *Nikolai Miliutin, An Enlightened Russian Bureaucrat*. Newtonville, Mass.

———. 1990. *The Great Reforms: Autocracy, Bureaucracy, and the Politics of Change in Imperial Russia*. DeKalb, Ill.

Linkov, Ia. A. 1940. *Krest′ianskoe dvizhenie v Rossii, vo vremia Krymskoi voiny, 1853–1856 gg*. Moscow.

Litoshenko, L. N. 1910. "O poshlinakh na sel′sko-khoziaistvennyia orudia." In *TOSP* 3 (Katerynoslav): 775–90.

Livanov, F. V. 1872. *Raskol′niki i ostrozhniki. Ocherki i rasskazy*. 2 vols. 2nd ed. St. Petersburg.

Livshits, R. S. 1955. *Razmeshchenie promyshlennosti v dorevoliutsionnoi Rossii*. Moscow.

Lohrenz, Gerhard. 1947. *Sagradowka: Die Geschichte einer mennonitischen Ansiedlung im Sueden Russlands*. Rohstern.

———. 1976. *Storm Tossed: The Personal Story of a Canadian Mennonite from Russia*. Winnipeg.

———. 1977. *Heritage Remembered*. 2nd ed. Winnipeg.

Lonachevskii, S. I., ed. 1891. "Obshchiia zamechaniia khoziaiev, chastnykh vladeltsev, i krestian." *ZIOS* (April): 80–100.

Lorimer, Frank. 1946. *The Population of the Soviet Union: History and Prospects*. Geneva.

Löwe, Heinz Dietrich. 1987. *Die Lage der Bauern in Russland, 1880–1905*. St. Katharinen.

———. 1990. "Differentiation in Russian Peasant Society: Causes and Trends, 1880–1905." In Bartlett 1990, 165–95.

Lozinski, A. 1875. "O mnogozemel′nykh khoziaistv Ekaterinoslavskoi gubernii." *SKhL* 120 (December): 367–70.

Lutkovskii, [first name unknown]. 1862. "Khoziaistvo v m. Alekseevka." *ZIOS*: 81–110.

Lyall, Robert. 1825. *Travels in Russia, the Krimea, the Caucasus and Georgia*. London. Reprint: New York, 1970.

Madariaga, Isabel de. 1981. *Russia in the Age of Catherine the Great*. New Haven.

Magocsi, Paul Robert. 1996. *A History of Ukraine*. Toronto.

Maksimenko, M. 1957. *Krest′ianskoe dvizhenie v Tavricheskoi gubernii nakanune i posle otmeny krepostnogo prava*. Simferopol.

———. 1964. "Ustavnye gramoty Tavricheskoi gubernii." *EAIVE*: 458–59.

Manning, Roberta Thompson. 1982. *The Crisis of the Old Order in Russia*. Princeton.

Markevich, A. I. 1912. "Osvobozhdeniia krest'ian v Tavricheskoi gubernii (po arkhivnym materialam)." *ITUAK* 26, nos. 47–48: 1–65.

Markovskii, A. 1900. "Krest'ianskoe khoziaistvo iuzhnoi Rossii i mery k ego uluchsheniiu." *SKhL* (July): 1–22.

"Mariupol'skii uezd po otchetu uezdnoi zemskoi upravy za 1903 g." 1904. *VEZ* (nos. 14–15): 409–13.

Martin, Terry. 1992. "The Empire's New Frontiers: New Russia's Path from Frontier to *Okraina*, 1774–1920." *Russian History/Histoire Russe* 19:181–202.

Materialy dlia istorii krepostnago prava v Rossii: Izvelecheniia iz sekretnykh otchetov ministerstva vnytrennikh del za 1836–1856 gg. 1872. Berlin.

Materialy dlia otsenki zemel' Ekaterinoslavskoi gubernii. 1899. Vol. 1, *Ekaterinoslavskii uezd.* Pts. 1 and 2. Katerynoslav.

———. 1902. Vol. 2, *Aleksandrovskiii uezd.* Katerynoslav.

———. 1904a. Vol. 3, *Verkhnedneprovskii uezd.* Katerynoslav.

———. 1904b. Vol. 4, *Mariupolskii uezd.* Pts. 1 and 2. Katerynoslav

———. 1906. Vol. 5, *Slavianoserbskii uezd.* Pts. 1 and 2. Katerynoslav.

———. 1911. Vol. 6, *Novomoskovskii uezd.* Pt. 1. Katerynoslav.

Materialy dlia otsenki zemel' Khersonskoi gubernii. 1883. Vol. 1, *Odesskii uezd.* Kherson.

———. 1886. Vol. 2, *Elisavetgradskii uezd.* Kherson.

———. 1888. Vol. 3, *Aleksandriiskii uezd.* Kherson.

———. 1889a. Vol. 4, *Tiraspolskii uezd.* Kherson.

———. 1889b. Vol. 5, *Ananevskii uezd.* Kherson.

———. 1890. Vol. 6, *Khersonskii uezd.* Kherson.

Materialy po statistike dvizheniia zemlevladeniia v Rossii. 1902. Vol 13, *Pogubernskie itogo mobilizatsii zemel' i srednye tseny za 40 letie 1863–1902 gg.* St. Petersburg.

Materialy po voprosu o stoimosti obrabotki v Evropeiskoi Rossii. 1889. St. Petersburg.

Materialy po voprosu o zemskoi statistike v Khersonskoi gubernii. 1874. Kherson.

Materialy po zemskoi statistike Khersonskoi gubernii. 1875. Kherson.

Materialy vysochaishe uchrezhdennoi 16 noiabria 1901 g. Komissii po issledovaniiu voprosa o dvizhenii s 1861 g. po 1900 g. blagosostoianiia sel'skogo naseleniia srednezemledel'cheskikh gubernii, sravnitel'no s drugimi mestnostiami Evropeiskoi Rossii. 1903. Vol. 1. St. Petersburg.

McCaffray, Susan Purves. 1983. "The New Work and the Old Regime: Workers, Managers, and the State in the Coal and Steel Industry of Ekaterinoslav Province, 1905–1914." Ph.D. diss., Duke University.

———. 1996. *The Politics of Industrialization in Tsarist Russia: The Association of Southern Coal and Steel Producers, 1874–1914.* DeKalb, Ill.

McKay, John P. 1970. *Pioneers for Profit: Foreign Entrepreneurship and Russian Industrialization, 1885–1913.* Chicago.

Mechnikov, I. 1879. "O bolezniakh lichinok khlebnogo zhuka." *ZIOS* (January): 21–49.

Melton, Edgar. 1998. "The Russian Peasantries, 1450–1860." In Scott 1998, 227–68.

Menning, Bruce W. 1980. "The Emergence of a Military-Administrative Elite in the Don Cossack Land, 1708–1836." In Pinter and Rowney 1980, 130–61.

Mironov, B. N. 1972. "Sotsial′naia mobil′nost i sotsial′noe rassloenie v Russkoi derevne XIX–nachale XX vv." In *Problemy razvitiia feodalizma i kapitalizma v stranakh Baltiki* 1972, 156–83.

———, and Z. V. Stepanov. 1975. *Istorik i matematika.* Leningrad.

———. 1978. "Vlianie krepost′nogo prava na otnoshenie Russkogo krestian′stva k trudu." In *Sovetskaia istoriografiia agrarnoi istorii SSSR (do 1917 g.)* 1978, 119–26.

———. 1984a. *Istorik i sotsiologiia.* Leningrad.

———. 1985a *Khlebnye tseny v Rossii za dva stoletiia (XVIII–XIX vv.).* Leningrad.

———. 1985b. "The Russian Peasant Commune after the Reforms of the 1860s." *Slavic Review* 44:438–67.

———. 1996. "When and why was the Russian peasantry emancipated?" In Bush 1996, 323–47.

———. 1999. *Sotsial′naia istoriia Rossii perioda imperii (XVIII–nachalo XX v.).* 2 vols. St. Petersburg.

Mixter, Timothy. 1991. "The Hiring Market as Workers' Turf: Migrant Agricultural Laborers and the Mobilization of Collective Action in the Steppe Grainbelt of European Russia, 1853–1913." In Kingston-Mann and Mixter 1991, 294–340.

"Mnenie odnogo iz chlenov obshchestva na stat′i I. A. Petrova." 1864. *ZIOS*: 289–94.

"Mnenie deistvitel′nogo chlena I. A. Petrova o predotvrashchenii pasezhei rogatogo skota." 1864. *ZIOS*: 280–89.

"Mnenie inostrantsev ob 'Anisoplia autriaca.'" 1880. *ZIOS* (August–September): 566–67.

Moon, David. 1992. *Russian Peasants and Tsarist Legislation on the Eve of Reform.* Basingstoke.

Morachevskii, V. V. 1910a. "Promysly i zaniatie naseleniia." In STS, 228–417.

———. 1910b. "Odessa i raskhodiashchiiasia ot nego puti." In STS, 456–555.

Mordovskii, P. 1889. "O znachenii merinosovogo ovtsevodstva v mestnom khoziaistve." *SKhL* (15 February): 350–54.

Mulligan, Gerald A. 1976. *Common Weeds of Canada.* Toronto.

Musin-Pushkin, Iu. 1870. "Zapiski chitannia 1 iunia 1870 g. na sel′sko-khoziaistvennii s″ezd v g. Slavianoserbska." *ZIOS* (July): 611–13.

Naidenov, M. 1955. *Klassovaia bor′ba v poreformennoi derevne (1861–1863 gg.).* Moscow.

Nekotoriia danniia o khode i razvitii sel′skogo khoziaistva v Khersonskoi gubernii. 1896. Vol. 1. Kherson.

Neruchev, M. V. 1877. "Rabochii vopros v ego sovremennom vide." *ZIOS* (March): 135–42.

———. 1880. "Kultura v borbe s khlebnym zhukom." *ZIOS* (May): 257–84.

———. 1890. "Nash khlebnyi vopros." *ZIOS* (October): 81–105.

Nifontov, A.S. 1974. *Zernovoe proizvodstvo Rossii vo vtoroi polovine XIX veka.* Moscow.

Nikolai-on. 1893. *Ocherki nashogo poreformennogo obshchestvennogo khoziaistva.* St. Petersburg.

Novoselskii, S.A. 1914. *K voprosu o ponizhenii smertnosti i rozhdaemosti v Rossii.* St. Petersburg.

"Ob istreblennii vrednykh zhivotnykh i nasekomykh." 1871. *SKhZ* (February): 106–34.

"O posledstviiakh mer k istrebleniia saranchi v iuzhnom krae Rossii v 1859–1860 godakh." 1861. *ZhMGI* 78: 175–94.

"O zhelezno-dorozhnykh tarifakh." 1887. *ZIOS* (April): 131–44.

Odessa, 1794–1894. 1895. Odesa.

Oganovskii, N. P. 1922. *Ocherki po ekonomicheskoi geografii Rossii.* Vol. 1, *Sel′skoe khoziaistvo.* Moscow.

Okun, S. B., ed. 1962. *Krest′ianskoe dvizhenie v Rossii v 1850–1856 gg.: Sbornik dokumentov* Moscow.

———, and K. V. Sivkov. 1963. *Krest′ianskoe dvizhenie v Rossii v 1857–mae 1861 gg.: Sbornik dokumentov.* Moscow.

Okushko, A., ed. 1890. "Opyty, nabliudeniia i zametki po sel′skomu khoziaistvu iuga Rossii." *ZIOS* (August–September): 137–52.

Oleksenko, S. 1842. "Opisanie menonistkikh kolonii v Rossii." *ZhMGI* (pt. 4): 1–42.

———. 1889. "Berdianskii uezd v sel′sko-khoziaistvennom otnoshenii." *Izvestiia Petrovskoi sel′skokhoziaistvennoi akademii*: 21–88.

———. 1910. "O zavisimosti uspekha agronomicheskikh meropriatii ot urovnia obshchei kultury sel′skogo naselenie." *TOSP* 1:35–50.

Opyt statistiki dvizheniia naseleniia Khersonskoi gubernii. 1882. Vol. 1, *Khersonskii uezd.* Kherson.

———. 1883. Vol. 2, *Odesskii uezd.* Kherson.

Osadchii, T. I. 1894. "Krest′ianskiia zemel′nyia priobreteniia v Khersonskoi gubernii." *ZIOS* (July–August): 1–43.

Otchet Ekaterinoslavskoi gubernskoi zemskoi upravy po agronomicheskomu biuro za 1895–1896 ekonomicheskii god. 1897. Katerynoslav.

Otchet Ekaterinoslavskoi gubernskoi zemskoi upravy po agronomicheskomu biuro za 1897–1898 ekonomicheskii god. 1899. Katerynoslav.

Otchet Ekaterinoslavskoi gubernskoi zemskoi upravy po agronomicheskomu biuro za 1898–1899 ekonomicheskii god. 1900. Katerynoslav.

"Otchet o deistviiakh Imperatorskogo Obshchestva sel′skogo khoziaistva iuzhnoi Rossii v 1867 godu." 1868. *ZIOS*: 305–40.

"Otchet o deistviiakh Imperatorskogo Obshchestva sel′skogo khoziaistva iuzhnoi Rossii v 1870 godu." 1871. *ZIOS* (April): 237–97.

Otmena krepostnogo prava na Ukraine: Sbornik dokumentov i materialov. 1961. Kyiv.

Owram, Doug. 1980. *The Promise of Eden: The Canadian Expansionist Movement and the Idea of the West, 1856–1900.* Toronto.

P., L. 1888. "Obezzemelennye 'vol′nye matrosy' v d. Nikopole Khersonskoi gubernii." *Kievskaia starina* (no. 12) 124–29.

Pakhman, S. V. 1877–1879. *Obychnoe grazhdanskoe pravo v Rossii.* 2 vols. St. Petersburg.

Palimpsestrov, I., ed. 1855. "Zemleobrabotyvanie Razdvizhnoi raspashnik" *ZIOS*: 38–49.

———, ed. 1868. *Sbornik statei o sel′skom khoziaistve iuga Rossii.* Odesa.

Pallas, P. S. 1812. *Travels through the Southern Provinces of the Russian Empire in the Years 1793-1794.* 2 vols. 2nd ed. London. Reprint: New York, 1970.

Pallot, Judith, and Denis J. B. Shaw. 1990. *Landscape and Settlement in Romanov Russia, 1613-1917.* Oxford.

Pamiatnaia kniga Tavricheskoi gubernii. 1867. Simferopol.

Parker, William N., and Eric L. Jones, eds. 1975. *European Peasants and Their Markets: Essays in Agrarian Economic History.* Princeton.

Passek, V. 1839. "Svedeniia o Khar′kovskoi Troitskoi iarmarke za 1832, 1833, 1835, 1836, 1837, i 1838 gody." *Listki*: 177–87.

Pavlovich, V. 1862. *Ekaterinoslavskaia guberniia: Materialy dlia geografii i statistiki Rossii sobrannye ofitserami general′nogo shtaba.* St. Petersburg.

Pedunov, [first name unknown]. 1889. "Ocherk ovtsvodstva v Onufrievskom imenii (Khersonskoi gub., Aleksandriiskogo uezda) grafa M. M. Tolstogo i uchet dokhodnosti za 11 let c 1877 po 1888 god." *ZIOS* (May–June): 49–62.

Perepelkin, A. P. 1882a. "O sovremennom polozhenii ton′korunnago ovtsevodstva iuga Rossii." In *ISPT*, appendix, 39–60.

———. 1882b. "Sherstianye Moiki na iuge Rossii." In *ISPT*, 11–24.

Pervaia vseobshchaia perepis′ naseleniia Rossiiskoi Imperii 1897g. 1903. Vol. 13, *Ekaterinoslavskaia guberniia*; vol. 41, *Tavricheskaia guberniia*; vol. 47, *Khersonskaia guberniia.* St. Petersburg.

Pinkerton, Robert. 1833. *Russia; or, Miscellaneous Observations on the Past and Present State of that Country and its Inhabitants.* London. Reprint: New York, 1970.

Pinter, Walter McKenzie, and Don Karl Rowney, eds. 1980. *Russian Officialdom: The Bureaucratization of Russian Society from the Seventeenth to the Twentieth Century.* Chapel Hill.

Pisarevskii, Grigorii. 1909. *Zapiski Moskovskago arkheologicheskago instituta.* Vol. 5, *Iz istorii inostrannoi kolonizatsii v Rossii v XVIII v.* Moscow.

"Po voprosu o peresmotre norm, opredeliniushchikh pravo uchastiia v zemskikh izbiratel΄nykh sobraniiakh." 1905. *VEZ* (17 February): 130–32.

Pogibka, A. 1896. "Sadovodstvo v Tiraspol΄skom uezde, Khersonskoi gubernii i ego nuzhdy." *ZIOS* (March): 37–52.

Polnoe sobranie zakonov Rossiiskoi imperii. 1830–1916. St. Petersburg.

Polozhenie i nuzhdy sel΄skokhoziaistvennoi promyshlennosti na osnovanii vsepoddanneishikh otchetov general-gubernatorov, gubernatorov i nachal΄nikov oblastei za 1901 g. 1904. St. Petersburg.

Polozhenie i nuzhdy sel΄skokhoziaistvennoi promyshlennosti, na osnovanii vsepoddanneishikh otchetov general-gubernatorov, gubernatorov i nachal΄nikov oblastei za 1902 g. 1904. St. Petersburg.

Postnikov, V. E. 1891. *Iuzhno-Russkoe krest΄ianskoe khoziaistvo.* Moscow.

Predmetnyi ukazatel΄ materialov v zemsko-statisticheskikh trudakh s 1860-kh po 1917 g. 1926–1927. 2 vols. Moscow.

Price, Roger. 1983. *The Modernization of Rural France: Communications Networks and Agricultural Market Structures in Nineteenth-Century France.* London.

———. 1987. *A Social History of Nineteenth-Century France.* London.

"Prigovor Kalginskogo sel΄skogo shkola Ivanovskoi volosti, postanovlen noiabria 28 dnia 1905 goda." 1905. *VTZ* (December): 165–67.

"Prilozhenie k dokladu kommissii po voprosu o rabochikh." 1872. *ZIOS* (no. 2): 7–15.

Pritsak, Omeljan. Forthcoming. "The Turkic Etymology of the Word 'Qazaq' [Cossack]." *Harvard Ukrainian Studies* 28.

Problemy razvitiia feodalizma i kapitalizma v stranakh Baltiki. 1972. Tartu.

"Proekt sel΄skokhoziaistvennogo uchilishcha s. Bobrovskogo." 1869. *SKhZ* (February): appendix no. 1.

Prokopovich, S. N. 1912. *Agrarnyi krizis i meropriiatiia pravitel΄stva.* Moscow.

"Protokol zasedaniia sel΄sko-khoziaistvennogo Soveta Aleksandrovskogo Zemstva." 1905. *VEZ* (27 October): 1081–82.

Protokoly delegatskago soveshchaniia Vserossiiskago Krest΄ianskago Soiuza 6–10 Noiabria 1905 g., v Moskve. 1906. Moscow.

Pukhov, A. 1878. "Staroe i novoe khoziaistva." *ZIOS* (August): 364–96.

Quiring, Walter, and Helen Bartel. 1974. *In the Fullness of Time: 150 Years of Mennonite Sojourn in Russia.* 3rd ed. Kitchener, Ont.

Raevskii, Ia. 1894. "Iz Aleksandriiskogo uezda, Khersonskogo gubernii." *SKh* (7 January), 190–91.

Randall, Adrian. 1991. *Before the Luddites: Custom, Community and Machinery in the English Woolen Industry, 1776–1809.* Cambridge.

Rashin, A. G. 1956. *Naselenie Rossii za 100 let (1811–1913 gg.). Statisticheskie ocherki.* Moscow.

"Remesly i promysly Khersonskoi gubernii." 1905. *SKhZ* (February): 1–56.

Rempel, David G. n.d. "Mennonite Agriculture and Model Farming as Issues of Economic Study and Political Controversy, 1870–1917." Unpublished paper. Conrad Grebel University College Archive.

———. 1933. "The Mennonite Colonies in New Russia. A Study of Their Settlement and Economic Development from 1789 to 1914." Ph.D. diss., Stanford University.

———. 1973–1974. "The Mennonite Commonwealth in Russia: A Sketch of its Founding and endurance, 1789–1919." Reprint in *MQR* (October 1973) and (January 1974): 1–99.

Robinson, Geroid T. 1932. *Rural Russia under the Old Regime.* London. Reprint: Berkeley, 1961.

Romanov, A. A. 1901. "V Tavriiu za volei." *Istoricheskii vestnik istoriko-literaturnyi zhurnal* 84 (April): 264–73.

Rudnytsky, Ivan L., ed. 1981. *Rethinking Ukrainian History.* Edmonton.

"Rukovodstvo dlia istrebleniia saranchi." 1876. *ZIOS* (January–February), pt. 3: 44–56.

Rybkin, N. 1873. "Dorogovizna rabochikh ruk po iug." *TIVEO* 2, no. 3: 303–23; and 3 (no.1): 1–3.

Ryndziunskii, P.G. 1978. *Utverzhdenie kapitalizma v Rossii 1850–1880 gg.* Moscow.

Saburova, L. M. 1987. "Sel′skokhoziaistvennye orudiia i postroiki." In *Etnografiia vostochnykh Slavian: ocherki traditsionnoi kul′tury*, ed. K. V. Chistov, 187–203. Moscow.

Saunders, David. 1992. *Russia in the Age of Reaction and Reform, 1801–1881.* London.

Sazonov, G. P. 1896. *Obzor deiatel′nosti zemstv po sel′skomu khoziaistvu (1865-1895 gg.).* 3 vols. St. Petersburg.

Sbornik po osnovnoi statistike. 1903. Vol. 1, *Perekopskii uezd.* Pt. 1. Simferopol.

———. 1906. Vol. 2, *Simferopolskii uezd.* Pts. 1 and 2. Simferopol.

———. 1909. Vol. 3, *Berdianskii uezd.* Pts. 1 and 2. Simferopol.

Sbornik po tekushchei statistike. 1909. Vol. 1, *Za 1905 i 1906 gg.* Simferopol.

Sbornik po tekushchei statistike. 1910. Vol. 2, *Za 1907 i 1908 gg.* Simferopol.

Sbornik statisticheskikh svedenii po Ekaterinoslavskoi gubernii. 1886. Vol. 2, *Bakhmutskii uezd*; vol. 3, *Slavianoserbskii uezd*. Katerynoslav.

Sbornik statisticheskikh svedenii po Tavricheskoi gubernii. Statisticheskiia tablitsy o khoziaistvennom polozhenii selenii. 1885. Vol. 1, pt. 1, *Melitopolskii uezd*. Simferopol.

———. 1886a. Vol. 2, *Dneprovskii uezd*. Simferopol.

———. 1886b. Vol. 3, *Feodosiiskii uezd i Kerch-Enikalskii gradonachal′stvo*. Simferopol.

———. 1886c. Vol. 4, *Simferopolskii uezd*. Simferopol.

———. 1887a. Vol. 1, pt. 2, *Krest′ianskoe khoziaistvo v Melitopolskom uezde*. Moscow.

———. 1887b. Vol. 5, *Berdianskii uezd*. Simferopol.

———. 1887c. Vol. 6, *Perekopskii uezd*. Simferopol.

———. 1887d. Vol. 7, *Evpatorskii uezd*. Simferopol.

———. 1887e. Vol. 8, *Ialtinskii uezd*. Simferopol.

———. 1889. Vol. 9, *Pamiatnaia knizhka Tavricheskoi gubernii*. Simferopol.

Scott, Charles Henry. 1854. *The Baltic, the Black Sea, and the Crimea*. London.

Scott, James C. 1976. *The Moral Economy of the Peasant*. New Haven.

———. 1985. *Weapons of the Weak: Everyday Forms of Peasant Resistance*. New Haven.

Scott, Tom, ed. 1998. *The Peasantries of Europe: From the Fourteenth to the Eighteenth Centuries*. London.

Sekirinskii, S. A. 1963. "Iz istorii krest′ianskoi kolonizatsii Tavricheskoi gubernii v kontse XVIII–pervoi polovine XIX v." *EAIVE*: 356–62.

———. 1964. "Vidy povinnostei krepostnykh krest′ian Tavricheskoi gubernii nakanune reformy 1861 g. *EAIVE*: 351–59.

Sel′sko-khoziaistvennoe opisanie Aleksandriiskogo uezda. 1888. Kherson.

Sel′skokhoziaistvennyia i statisticheskiia svedeniia po materialam, poluchennym ot khoziaev. 1884–1905. 12 vols. St. Petersburg.

Sel′sko-khoziaistvennyi obzor Tavricheskoi gubernii za desiatiletie, 1899–1908 gg. 1911. Simferopol.

Sel′sko-khoziaistvennyi promysel v Rossii. 1914. Petrograd.

Semenov-Tian-Shanskii, V. P., ed. 1910. *Rossiia: Polnoe geograficheskoe opisanie nashego otechestva*. Vol. 14, *Novorossiia i Krym*. St. Petersburg.

Seregny, Scott J. 1989. *Russian Teachers and Peasant Revolution: The Politics of Education in 1905*. Bloomington.

———. 1991. "Peasants and Politics: Peasant Unions During the 1905 Revolution." In Kingston-Mann and Mixter 1991, 341–77.

Shanin, Teodor. 1986. *Russia, 1905–1907: Revolution as a Moment of Truth*. Vol. 2, *The Roots of Otherness: Russia's Turn of the Century*. New Haven.

Shaw, Stanford. 1976. *History of the Ottoman Empire and Modern Turkey*. Vol. 1, *Empire of the Gazis: The Rise and Decline of the Ottoman Empire, 1280–1808*. Cambridge.

Shchepkin, S. P. 1869. *Ovtsevodstvo v Rossii*. St. Petersburg.

Shcherbina, F. 1880. "Zemel′naia obshchina v Dneprovskom uezde." *RM* 4:38–63.

Shestakov, A. V. 1924. *Kapitalizatsiia sel′skogo khoziaistva Rossii (ot reformy 1861 g. do voiny 1914 g.)*. Moscow.

Shimkin, A. 1873. "Sel′skokhoziaistvennyi ocherk Novorossii." *SKhL* (August): 265–315.

Shmidt, A. 1860–1863. *Khersonskaia guberniia: Materialy dlia geografii i statistiki Rossii sobrannye ofitserami General′nogo shtaba*. 2 vols. St. Petersburg.

Siminova, M. S. 1987. *Krizis agrarnoi politiki tsarisma nakanune pervoi Rossiiskoi revoliutsii*. Moscow.

Skal′kovs′kyi [Skal′kovskii], A. O. 1836–1838. *Khronologicheskoe obozrenie istorii Novorossiiskogo kraia, 1730–1796*. 2 vols. Odesa.

———. 1846. *Istoriia Novoi Sechi ili posledniago kosha zaporozhskago*. 2 vols. Odesa.

———. 1848. *Bolgarskiia kolonii v Bessarabii i Novorossiiskom krae*. Odesa.

———. 1850–1853. *Opyt statisticheskogo opisaniia Novorossiiskogo kraia*. 2 vols. Odesa.

———. 1867a. "Zaniatie Kryma v 1783 godu." In *PKTG* 1867, 1–39.

———. 1867b. "O nogaiskikh koloniiakh Tavricheskoi gubernii." In *PKTG* 1867, 358–412.

———. 1873. "Pochva i rabochiia sily Novorossii." *ZIOS* (no. 3): 47–68.

———. 1885–1886. *Istoriia Novoi Sechi ili posledniago kosha zaporozhskago*. 3 vols. 3rd ed. Odesa.

———. 1887. "Russkie dissidenty v Novorossii." *Kievskaia starina*, no. 4: 771–82.

Skotovodstvo v Kherskoi gubernii v 1891 godu. 1892. Kherson.

Skuratov, D. 1863. "O raznykh sposobakh pol′zovaniia pomeshchich′imi zemliami." *ZIOS*: 189–201.

Slicher van Bath, B. H. 1963. *The Agrarian History of Western Europe A.D. 500–1850*. Trans. Olive Ordish. London.

Smirnov, Aleksei. 1904. "Iz Aleksandrovskoi volosti (Berdianskogo uezda)." *VTZ* (October): 62–64.

Sokolov, G. 1837. "Ob ovech′ei ospe." *Listki*: 73–80.

Sokalskii, P. P. 1869. "Vzgliad na sovremennye zadachi sel′skogo khoziaistva iuzhnoi Rossii." *ZIOS*: 15–29.

Solov′eva, A. M. 1955. *Razvitie ugol′noe promyshlennosti Donetskogo basseina*. Moscow.

Solov′eva, A. M. 1975. *Zheleznodorozhnyi transport Rossii vo vtoroi polovine XIX v.* Moscow.

"Sostoianie tonkorunnogo ovtsevodstva v Rossii." 1843. *ZhMGI* (no. 8): 23.

Sovetskaia istoriografiia agrarnoi istorii SSSR (do 1917). 1978. Kishenev.

Spisok naselennykh mest po svendeniiam 1864 gody. 1865. Vol. 41, *Tavricheskaia guberniia.* St. Petersburg.

Spisok sel′skikh obshchestv Aleksandriiskogo uezda. 1894. Aleksandriia.

Staples, John R. 2003. *Cross-Cultural Encounters on the Ukrainian Steppe: Settling the Molochna Basin, 1783–1861.* Toronto.

Starr, S. Frederick. 1982. "Local Initiative in Russia before the Zemstvo." In Vucinich 1982, 5–30.

"Statisticheskiia svedeniia ob inostrannykh poseleniiakh v Rossii." 1838. *ZhMGI*: 1–83.

Statisticheskie tablitsy Rossiiskoi imperii. 1863. St. Petersburg.

Statisticheskie tablitsy Rossiiskoi imperii za 1856 god. 1866. St. Petersburg.

Statisticheskii vremennik Rossiiskoi Imperii. 1866. St. Petersburg.

Statistika pozemel′noi sobstvennosti i naselennykh mest Evropeiskoi Rossii. Po dannym obsledovaniia, proizvedennogo statisticheskimi uchrezhdeniiami Ministerstva Vnutrennikh Del po porucheniia statisticheskogo soveta. 1885. Vol. 8, *Gubernii Novorossiiskoi gruppy.* St. Petersburg.

Statistika zemlevladeniia 1905 g. 1906. Vol. 14, *Ekaterinoslavskaia guberniia*; vol. 16, *Khersonskaia guberniia*; vol. 42, *Tavricheskaia guberniia.* St. Petersburg.

Statistiko-ekonomicheskii obzor Khersonskoi gubernii za 1905 g. 1908. Kherson.

Statistiko-ekonomicheskii obzor Khersonskoi gubernii za 1906 g. 1909. Kherson.

Statistiko-ekonomicheskiia tablitsy po Ekaterinoslavskoi gubernii. 1886. Vol. 1, *Slavianoserbskii uezd.* Katerynoslav.

———. 1887. Vol. 2, *Mariupolskii uezd.* Katerynoslav.

Stavrovskii, I. A. F. 1910. "Istoricheskie sud′by Novorossii i kul′turnye ee uspekhi." In STS, 126–71.

Stoimost′ proizvodstva glavneishikh khlebov. 1915. Petrograd.

Strukov, D. 1860. "Elisavetgradskii s″ezd zemlevladel′tsev." *Sel′skoe khoziaistvo* (July): 87–99.

Strukov, N. A. 1870. "O sokhranenie v Rossii sherst′ianoi promyshlennosti i ispanskogo ovtsevodstva." *ZIOS*: 219–25.

Stumpp, M. 1957. "Die Schwaben-Kolonien bei Berdjansk." *Heimatbuch der Deutschen aus Russland* 4: 39–46.

Subtelny, Orest. 1981. "Cossack Ukraine and the Turko-Islamic World." In Rudnytsky 1981, 120–34.

———. 1988. *Ukraine: A History.* Toronto.

Svavitskii, N.A. 1961. *Zemskie podvornye perepisi, 1880–1913: pouezdnye perepisi.* Moscow.

Svod dannykh po 50-ti guberniiam Evropeiskoi Rossii. 1907. St. Petersburg.

Svod statisticheskikh svedenii po sel´skomu khoziaistvu Rossii k kontsu XIX veka. 1902–1906. 3 vols. St. Petersburg.

Taranovski, Theodore. 1995. *Reform in Modern Russian History: Progress or Cycle?* Cambridge.

Tarasiuk, D. A. 1981. *Pozemel´naia sobstvennost´ poreformennoi Rossii: Istochnikovedcheskoe issledovanie po perepisi 1877–1878 gg.* Moscow.

Teetsman, Fr. 1838. "Skotovodstvo v Evpatoriiskom uezde." *Listki*: 80–91.

Teziakov, N. I. 1891. *Sel´sko-khoziaistvennye rabochie voobshche i prishlye v chastnosti v Khersonskoi gubernii v sanitarnom otnoshenii.* Kherson.

———. 1896. *Sel´sko-khoziaistvennye rabochie i organizatsiia na nimi sanitarnogo nadzora v Khersonskoi gubernii (po materialam lechebno-prodovol´stvennykh punktov v 1893–1895 gg.).* Kherson.

Theide, Roger L. 1970. "Town and Function in Tsarist Russia: A Geographical Analysis of Trade and Industry in the Towns of New Russia, 1860–1910." Ph.D. diss., University of Washington

Tiessen, Henry B. 1979. *The Molotschna Colony: A Heritage Remembered.* Kitchener, Ont.

Timiriazev, D. A., ed. 1883–. *Istoriko-statisticheskii obzor promyshlennosti Rossii.* St. Petersburg.

Toews, Gerhard. 1939. *Schoenfeld: Werde- und Opfergang einer deutschen Siedlung in der Ukraine.* Winnipeg.

Toews, Jakob C. 1954. "Das mennonitische Gutsbesitzertum in Russland." *Der Bote* 26 (30 June–24 November).

Toews John B., ed. and trans. 1981. "The Emergence of German Industry in the South Russian Colonies." *MQR* (October): 289–371.

Troinitskii, A. 1861. *Krepostnoe naselenie v Rossii, po 10-i narodnoi perepisi: statisticheskoe issledovanie.* St. Petersburg.

Trudy chetvertogo s"ezda Russkikh sel´skikh khoziaistv. 1874. Kharkiv.

"Trudy chetvertogo s"ezda Russkikh khoziaiev v Kharkove." 1875. *ZIOS* (March–April): 7–195.

Trudy kommissii po preobrazovaniiu volostnykh sudo. 1874. Vol. 5, *Ekaterinoslavskaia guberniia.* St. Petersburg.

Trudy mestnykh komitetov o nuzhdakh sel´sko-khoziaistvennoi promyshlennosti. 1903. 58 vols. Vol. 12, *Ekaterinoslavskaia guberniia*; vol. 40, *Tavricheskaia guberniia*; vol. 46, *Khersonskaia guberniia*, St. Petersburg.

Trudy piatogo s"ezda Russkikh sel´skikh khoziaistv v Odesse, v Dekabre 1878 goda. 1879. Odesa.

Trudy s"ezda deiatelei agronomicheskoi pomoshchi mestnomu khoziaistvu (10–19 fevralia 1901 g.). 1901. Moscow.

Tsentral'nyi gosudarstvennyi istoricheskii arkhiv SSSR v Leningrade. Putevoditel'. 1956. Leningrad.

Turner, Frederick Jackson. 1920. *The Frontier in American History.* New York.

"Über die Gründung und Entwicklung einiger Kolonien." 1958. *Heimatbuch der Deutschen aus Russland* 5: 65–67.

Ukrainian Dumy: Original Texts. 1979. Trans. by George Tarnawsky and Patricia Kilina. Toronto and Cambridge.

Ulissov, A. N. 1910. "Puti soobshcheniia." In STS, 418–55.

Umiss, Anton Ivanovich. 1874. "Sovremennoe polozhenie zemledelia na iug Rossii." *SKhZ* (July): 1–123.

Urry, James. 1989. *None but Saints: The Transformation of Mennonite Life in Russia 1789–1889.* Winnipeg.

"Usovershenstvovannyi malorossiiskii plug kolonista Bekhtol'da." 1868. In Palimpsestrov 1868, 208.

Vassal, V. 1870. "O sostoianii sel'skogo khoziaistva na iug Rossii." *ZIOS*: 479–96.

Vassel, E. 1855. "Ovtsevodstvo—o sparivanii merinosovykh baranov s voloshskimi i chundukskimi ovtsami." *ZIOS*: 89–92.

"Vedomost ob epizooticheskikh bolezniakh i obshchem kolichestve rovshago skota...." 1864–74. *DZhK*, vol. 1, appendix 5, 20–23.

"Verkhnedneprovskii uezd po otchetu uezdnoi zemskoi upravy za 1903 g." 1904. *VEZ* (no. 18): 554–61.

Veselovskii, B. B. 1909–1911. *Istoriia zemstva za sorok let.* 4 vols. St. Petersburg.

Veselovskii, K. 1846. "Tonkorunnoe ovtsevodstvo v Rossii." *ZhMGI* (no. 20): 105–54.

"Vidy na urozhai." 1878. *ZIOS*: 294–99.

Viola, Lynne. 1996. *Peasant Rebels Under Stalin.* New York.

Voenno-statisticheskoe obozrenie Rossiiskoi imperii. 1849–1850. Vol. 11, pt. 1, *Khersonskaia guberniia*; pt. 2, *Tavricheskaia guberniia*; pt. 4, *Ekaterinoslavskaia guberniia.* St. Petersburg.

"Volneniia krest'ian na Khersonshchine v 1905 g." 1935. *KA* 71:17–38.

"Vol'nonaemnye rabotniki v guberniiakh Volynskoi, Podol'skoi, Kievskoi i Khersonskoi." 1861. *ZhMGI* (no. 2): 114–38.

Von Pantser, V. 1861. "O preimushchestve vol'no naemnogo khoziaistva pred barshchinskim." *Sel'skoe Khoziaistvo* 3 (August): 17–46.

Voprosy istorii sel'skogo khoziaistva, krest'ianstva i revoliutsionnogo dvizheniia v Rossii. Sbornik statei k 75-letiiu akademika Nikolaia Mikhailovicha Druzhinina. 1961. Moscow.

Vucinich, Wayne S., ed. 1968. *The Peasant in Nineteenth-Century Russia.* Stanford.

Wallerstein, Immanuel. 1989. *The Modern World-System.* 3 vols. San Diego.

Weber, Eugen. 1976. *Peasants into Frenchmen: The Modernization of Rural France, 1870–1914.* Stanford.

Webster, James. 1830. *Travels Through The Crimea, Turkey and Egypt: Performed during the Years 1825–1828.* 2 vols. London.

Westwood, J. N. 1964. *A History of Russian Railways.* London.

Wilbur, Elvira M. 1991. "Peasant Poverty in Theory and Practice: A View from Russia's 'Impoverished Center' at the End of the Nineteenth Century." In Kingston-Mann and Mixter 1991, 101–27.

Wirtschafter, Elise Kimerling. 1997. *Social Identity in Imperial Russia.* DeKalb, Ill.

Wolf, Eric R. 1982. *Europe and the People without History.* Berkeley.

Worobec, Christine. 1991. "Victims or Actors? Russian Peasant Women and Patriarchy." In Kingston-Mann and Mixter 1991, 177–206.

Wynn, Charters. 1992. *Workers, Strikes, and Pogroms: The Donbas-Dnepr Bend in Late Imperial Russia, 1870–1905.* Princeton.

Yang, Anand A. 1987. "A Conversation of Rumours: The Language of Popular *Mentalités* in Late Nineteenth Century Colonial India." *Journal of Social History* (Spring): 485–505.

Zabarinskii, P. 1893. "Khlebnaia torgovlia Odessy." *ZIOS* (March–April): 82–94.

Zablotskii, A. 1841. "O nekotorykh guberniiakh iuzhnogo kraia Rossii." *ZhMGI* 1:12–55.

Zabudskii, A. 1870. "O zasukhakh na iug i o sredstvakh k sokhraneniiu i uvelicheniiu syrosti v nashikh stepiakh." *TIVEO* 1, no. 1: 8–23.

Zaionchkovskii, P. A. 1960. *Otmena krepostnogo prava v Rossii.* Moscow.

"Zapiski o soderzhanii ovets i ikh bolezniakh pomeshchika Bakhmutskogo uezda." 1860. *ZIOS*: appendix no. 1.

"Zapiski predprinimatelei proektiruemoi zheleznoi dorogi ot st. Dolinskoi Khar′kovo-Nikolaevskoi i Ekaterinoslavskoi zheleznykh dorog, cherez Voznesensk, v Odessy." 1889. *ZIOS* (March): 5–12.

"Zemledel′cheskii s″ezd v Elisavetgrade 20, 21, i 22 Aprelia 1860 goda." 1860. *ZhMGI* 75 (no. 1): 65–110.

Zemlevladenie nemtsev-byvshikh kolonistov v Khersonkoi gubernii. 1891. Kherson.

Zertsalov, S. 1891. "Stepnoe skotovodstvo v Novorossiiskom krae, ego proshloe i nostoiashchee." *ZIOS* (February): 11–76.

Zhigalev, E. 1892. "Zadolzhennost′ chastnogo zemlevladeniia v Rossii." *RM* (no. 11): 41–69.

Zhurba, N. 1891. "Dvizhenie zemel′noi sobstvennosti v Ekaterinoslavskoi gubernii za poslednii period vremeni." *Novorossiiskii kalendar na 1892 god.* Odesa: 31–42.

"Zhurnaly zasedanii Khersonskago gubernskago zemskago sobraniia." 1870. *SKhZ* (April): 257–59.

Zinov′ev, A. 1900. "Peremeny v organizatsii sel′skogo khoziaistva v Khersonskoi gubernii i voobshche v iuzhnoi Novorossii," *ZIOS* (nos. 5–6): 29–40; and (nos. 7–8): 11–20.

Zusman, A. 1880. "K voprosu ob uluchshenii polozheniia nashei sel′sko-khoziaistvennoi promyshlennosti." *ZIOS* (February): 13–26.

Index